Reflections on the Neches

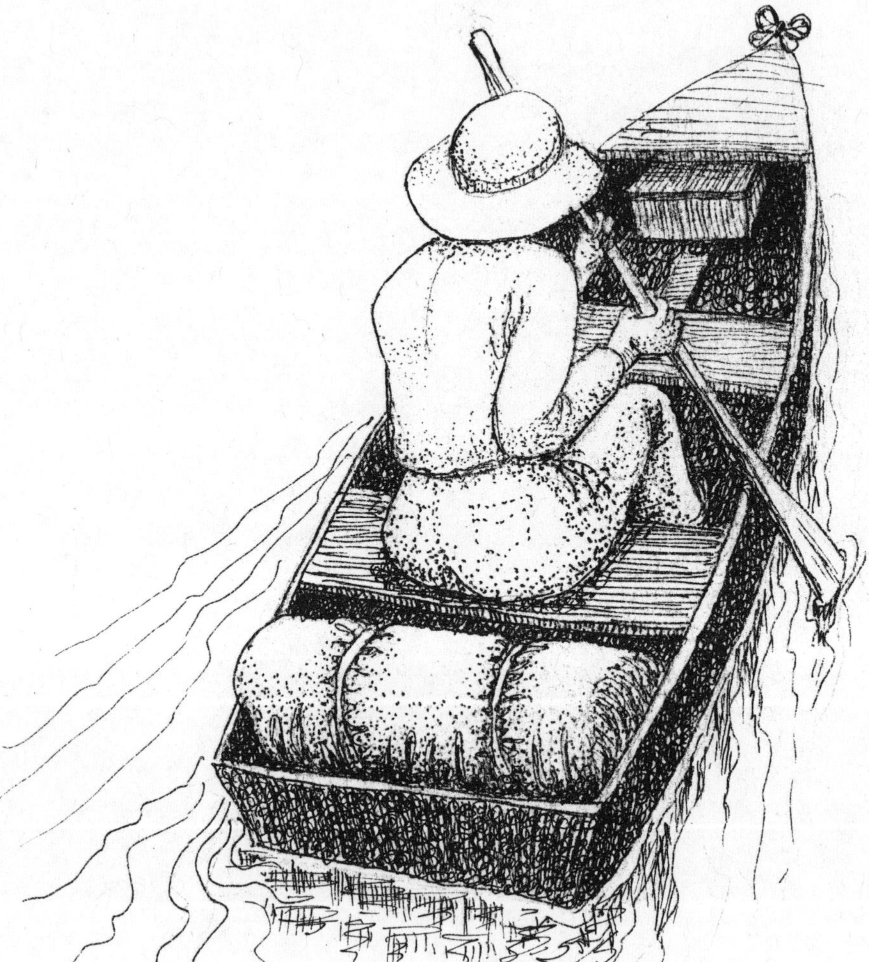

Reflections on the Neches:

A Naturalist's Odyssey along the Big Thicket's Snow River

Geraldine Ellis Watson

Number Three in the Temple Big Thicket Series

Big Thicket Association
University of North Texas Press
Denton, Texas

Printed in the United States of America.

10 9 8 7 6 5 4 3 2

Permissions:
University of North Texas Press
1155 Union Circle #311336
Denton, TX 76203-1336

The paper used in this book meets the minimum requirements of the American National Standard for Permanence of Paper for Printed Library Materials, z39.48.1984. Binding materials have been chosen for durability.

Library of Congress Cataloging-in-Publication Data

Watson, Geraldine Ellis, 1925-
Reflections on the Neches : a naturalist's odyssey along the Big Thicket's Snow River / Geraldine Ellis Watson.
p. cm. — (Temple Big Thicket series ; no. 3)
ISBN 978-1-57441-160-7 (cloth : alk. paper)
ISBN 978-1-57441-535-3 (paper : alk. paper)
ISBN 978-1-57441-428-8 (ebook)
1. Natural history—Texas—Neches River Valley. 2. Neches River Valley (Tex.)—Description and travel. I. Title. II. Series.
QH105.T4 W35 2003
508.764'15—dc21
2003001869

Design by Angela Schmitt

Reflections on the Neches is Number 3 in the Temple Big Thicket Series

This book was made possible by a generous grant from the T.L.L. Temple Foundation and the assistance of the Big Thicket Association.

The electronic edition of this book was made possible by the support of the Vick Family Foundation.

DEDICATION

My Father, Herbert Ellis

Dr. Saul Aronow

Dr. Richard Harrell

Maxine Johnston
Without whom this book would not have been published

Ernest Spell
Without whom there would be no Jack Gore/Neches River Unit

Arthur Temple, Jr.
Good and Faithful Steward of this land and its people

CONTENTS

List of Maps and Illustrations

Maps

Photos

Drawings

PREFACE

This book is written primarily for the layman, so I have given few scientific names of plants or animals; also, I have not given references. While I have done voluminous research in order to be factual as to people, places, and events, much of what I have written has come from my own experience, what I have read, and people with whom I have spoken over a period of many years.

This book is a series of essays about a river and its environment, and the kind of people such environs produce, which includes myself. I have expressed my personal opinions, often strongly, on many subjects, for I have put down the memories and thoughts that were evoked by what I saw and did while on the river. It is expected that some readers will differ and, regrettably, be offended, for we all have different backgrounds, knowledge, and experiences. A work designed to offend no one and to please everyone must inevitably be insipid and generic and in no way reveal the heart and soul of the writer, nor do service to historical accuracy. Anyway, there is enough diversity of topics that if the reader comes upon one which does not suit his fancy, he can just skip it and go on to another.

Since I have no time nor taste for all that goes with fame, nor desire the lifestyle money provides, it is difficult to justify the years, expense, and labor involved in compiling this book. Reading the reasons the great biographer/historian, Plutarch, gave for his monumental work on the lives of the great Greeks and Romans, I concluded that perhaps my motives were the same: "It was for the sake of others that I first commenced writing, but I find myself proceeding and attaching myself to it for my own. The virtues of these great men serving me as a sort of looking glass in which I may see how to adjust and adorn my own life; to study their stature and their qualities and select from their actions all that is noblest and worthiest to know. My method is by the study of their history to habituate my memory to receive and retain images of the best and worthiest characters." Yet, this conscientious historian presented his subjects realistically with all their faults and foolishness as well as their virtues so that we might view them as fellow human beings, emulate their virtues and avoid their foibles.

The Neches River and the people and events associated with it are worthy of remembrance, and I hope that I have presented them in a way that will do them honor and justice.

Introduction

The Neches River rises in Van Zandt County in Northeast Texas. It meanders 416 miles to Sabine Lake and then to the Gulf of Mexico, discharging six million acre-feet of water per year. It has its beginning in a small lake called Rhine Lake and is interrupted only twice by the dams of Lakes Palestine and Steinhagen (locally called Dam B).

The river was called Snow River by the many Indians who lived along it because the wide expanses of sandbars reminded them of the snows that covered the land on rare occasion. Later, it was named Neches by the Spaniard, Alonso de León, after one of the tribes that lived nearby. The old name was recognized in 1874 when the newly organized Masonic Organization named their chapter Snow River Lodge.

The French in Louisiana were finding trapping and trading with the Indians of Texas a lucrative business, so the Spanish in Mexico sent de León on five separate expeditions into Texas preparatory to establishing mission colonies and thereby preventing a takeover. On the fifth expedition, in 1690, he established a mission, San Francisco de los Tejas, named for the Tejas Indians, one of the Hasanai Confederacy of tribes. ("Tejas" means friendly.) Eventually, the state became known by that name, but it is spelled "Texas" today.

The river has always been important to these who live in its watershed, whether Indian, early settler, or modern man. It offered a fast, easy means of travel during days when the overland traveler would flounder in deep sand one moment and in deep mud the next, or fight his way through miles of dense thicket or swamp. The inhabitants of the Neches River watershed today are the descendents of the pioneers who felt the oppressive pressure of expanding population, increasing industrialization, and the regimentation of society in the East, and kept moving westward ahead of it. Now, there is no place left to escape to. Humanity has moved westward until it has gathered on the Pacific Ocean shores of California like the lemmings in the Arctic. When population levels reach numbers over and above what the environment can sustain, all lemmings make a massive, blind migratory rush to the sea where they plunge in and drown by the millions.

My father loved the woods and river and spent his boyhood there, but time and the necessity of supporting a family took him first to the sawmills of Southeast Texas and then to the petrochemical megalopolis on the Gulf Coast. Daddy always said that his greatest desire was to retire and become a river rat. In my younger days, I deplored Daddy's lack of ambition and appreciation of a "better" life, but as time has passed and I often grow weary and disillusioned with the world and everybody in it, I finally understand. Oh, the peace and rest! The glory of waking in the morning and seeing the sun rise over the water and watching the last, glittering speckles of fire through the branches as it sets behind the forest horizon! To be awakened by the singing birds and lulled to sleep by the calls of owls and the sound of the river swishing past snags! In short, to live the life of a river rat. Paradise regained! A preview of Heaven! In this day and age, it is almost impossible to find an acre of land that has not known the destructive, deforming, and defiling hand of man. The Neches River, by its floods and shifting, filling and cutting, his erased all evidence that it was once an important route of commerce and transportation, so one can still see there a bit of this world as God made it, and find refuge as Daddy did and as I have done.

Why am I doing this? Why would a woman over sixty decide to leave family, a comfortable home, television, automobile, rich food and all the other amenities of the good life and take off down a river alone where one could go for days without seeing or hearing anyone or anything except the sights and sounds of nature, or a few river rats with whom to pass the time of day and perhaps share a pot of coffee. It could even be at the risk of my own life.

When I try to justify this voyage down the Neches, or to explain why I am doing it, I'm not sure myself what drives me. Perhaps after a quarter of a century of political activism to try, if not to save the world, at least to make it a little better for my having been here, I need to spend my remaining days free from strife. I'm tired of trying to explain to people why they shouldn't blow up the world or why there needs to be a few acres of unspoiled nature. I'm tired of confrontation. I want to rest my body, my brain, and my emotions, but am finding it hard to find a stopping place. Perhaps there is no rest as long as one lives in this world and cares what happens to it and its inhabitants.

Sometimes, in saving something, it is necessary to call the attention of the world in general to how marvelous it is. Then the whole world will want to see and experience it, and the rush is on. We have "saved" the Neches River—at least that section between Steinhagen Lake and Beaumont—and I want to experience it one more time before it is bow-to-stern in canoes, and the mobs of boaters, picnickers, and campers descend. I know I shouldn't begrudge others their legal and moral rights to enjoy what belongs to us all, but to some of us, its greatest attraction is the silence and solitude. Let me take it to my heart just this one last time and then I'll say, "Here it is world. It's yours. Take care of it."

Another reason I wanted to make this trip was to duplicate a trip Daddy made when he was a boy. He and a cousin spent the summer floating the river from Town Bluff to Beaumont. The only provisions they took were flour, corn meal, salt and lard, fishing tackle, and their guns. They ate fried fish and squirrel stew (squirrel boiled in salted water with flour dumplings) and fried cornbread. All my life, I listened to Daddy tell about his experiences and observations on this trip, and about the steamboats, the log rafts, animals, and people along the Neches. And all my life I dreamed of repeating this adventure. For me, time is running out for the fulfilling of dreams, and I decided that this one was going to be realized before I die.

Still another reason for my trip was to show women of all ages that they can still have adventures. If they have someone compatible to share them, fine. If not, don't say, "I would love to go, but no one will take me." Just go! Some say: "Oh, I would be scared to death! What if someone should rob you?" My poor, dear 94-year-old mother missed many joys of life because of "what if." That was the refrain with which she sought to restrain me all my life. I respect the rights and territory of wild creatures and people. I walk the woods or city streets with a smile on my face and goodwill in my heart, and I receive the same in return. "As ye give, so shall ye receive." Fear and hatred beget fear and hatred; love and trust beget love and trust. What if someone knocks me on the head? What if I fall in the river and drown? Some day I am going to die—that is certain. How and when is not certain, but this much I do know: I'm not going to live a life of fear and deprivation of joy and adventure because of some bad thing that *might* happen.

I chose the time of year for my trip for a purpose, also. Mosquitoes are less active in late autumn, and the river is low and clear. The gorgeous weather of Indian summer is more pleasant and less likely to produce violent storms. My dog and I are in the autumn of our lives. Springtime on the river, with its burgeoning buds, leaves and flowers, the fast-rising, full-flowing water, and quickening life is for the young. I am old. What more defiant gesture to the approaching decrepitude of old age than to embark on an adventure that most young people would not dare, and to do it in the autumn. I, my dog, the trees, the river, the animals—we know that winter is coming; but we're going to go out in a blaze of glory.

GEOMORPHOLOGY

I seem to have been born with a sense of "why," for I always felt a need to know the reasons for everything I see in this natural world. Around 40 years of age, when I began to wonder why the river changed its course, why the vegetation changed on different parts of the floodplain, why there were high, rocky banks and boulders in parts of the river and not in others, I suspected it all had something to do with geology. I sought out the answers in university classrooms and in any published literature I could get my hands on, as well as talking with any and everybody who thought they had answers.

Since that time, I have become absolutely certain about only one thing—that nobody agrees about anything concerning the geological history of the Neches watershed. There is very little published, and the only people who have extensively delved into and studied the substrata of the area are the oil companies who jealously guard their secrets. After they have spent large amounts of money on seismographic explorations to determine where oil is likely to be, why should they share the information with the world, which includes both scholar and competitor?

My comments on the geomorphology of the lower Neches watershed are based on observation, knowledge of the behavior of streams, climate and sea level changes, and, hopefully, logical conclusions—in other words, educated guesses. The late Dr. Saul Aronow, geomorphologist at Lamar University and a well-known authority on the Pleistocene geologic epoch during which most of our land in the Neches valley was being formed, was a valued friend and advisor. Unfortunately, he could not approve all my hypotheses as there is no published scientific documentation to confirm or deny some of them. If one wishes to go more deeply into river geomorphology, the following books will be helpful: *Water in Environmental Planning* by Dunne and Leopold; *Indians of the Gulf Coast* by Aten; and *Geomorphology* by A. L. Bloom. Since I did my research, other studies have certainly been done on the geology of the Neches watershed.

The Neches River formed as a drainage pattern over alluvial deltas which were laid into the Gulf of Mexico during the 500,000 to 2,000,000 years (plus or minus) of Pleistocene geologic time. There were at least four major glacial advances during the Pleistocene Epoch. The glaciers did not reach this far south, but the changing climates and fluctuating sea levels that they caused directly influenced and created the streams and landforms of Southeast Texas. As the great ice masses formed, they took up so much of the earth's water that sea level fell, and the coast receded hundreds of miles out from its present location. Rainfall was heavy, and the streams, trying to reach the lowered sea level, cut wide, deep valleys.

As the climate warmed and the ice melted, the sea level rose and the streams began to fill the valleys with sediments and the alluvium spread into the Gulf. It appears that the last incursion into the Neches valley formed an embayment which reached up somewhere around river mile 75 or 80 below the Highway 1013 crossing. This silt-filled depression was exposed much later than the terraces above, and the surface is therefore younger. The upland adjacent to the floodplain terraces above Highway 1013 is older and has both acidic and calcareous soils, which were carried by erosion onto the stream terraces. This could explain why the vegetation and drainage patterns are so different on these surfaces. This line of demarcation has been considered by some a geological nick point dividing the Pliocene and Pliestocene Formations.

This process of incursion and recession of the sea, and the erosion and deposition by streams was repeated with each glaciation. The deltas, or alluvial plains, created by deposition into the Gulf lie atop one another with their northern ends exposed in narrow east/west bands across the Texas coastal plain. The weight of the later deposits pressed down on the earlier, tilting the ends and forming the ridge of hills of Polk, Tyler, Jasper, and Newton Counties. Highway 190 follows this ridge, which is the end surface of the Willis and Fleming Formations. The present river cuts through this uplift between Steinhagen Lake and Sheffield's Ferry crossing, exposing deeply buried rock, and causing high, colorful bluffs and rocky shoals. This is a geological nick point or fault line. The bluff line of the ancient floodplain is also high and steep at this point and the erosional gullies dissecting it form the proposed Canyonlands Unit of the Big Thicket National Preserve.

Some of the deeper of these erosional gullies cut into a stratum of fine white sandstone once called the Lagarto Formation, but which Dr. Aronow believed to be either Catahoula or Whitsett. Ten thousand or so years ago, there was a tectonic period in West Texas and Northern Mexico when forces inside the earth upheaved level plains, exposing deeply buried metamorphic rocks. Volcanoes built up mountains of lava and other debris and spewed forth fine volcanic ash into the stratosphere. Wind currents carried this debris throughout the world, and it fell like rain upon the earth. The fine sandstone exposed in these gullies is composed of these deposits, called "volcanic glass."

On rivers that have been subjected to valley cutting and filling, floodplains have more than one level called terraces. In seeking sea level, streams meander about over the surface, cutting and washing away soil. As the river moves in one direction, the soil over which it has just moved is eroded and carried away downstream, so that that side is lower than the side into which it is cutting. As the river meanders back and forth over the floodplain, it creates a ridge and swale topography with sand hummocks where large pointbar sand deposits lie. While there are many minor terraces in the Neches floodplain, there are two major terraces. The higher, inactive terrace is called the Deweyville Formation, while the lower levels are referred to as Alluvium, or the active floodplain. Locals simply call them the upper bottom, or hummock land, and the lower bottom. These different levels are the result of climate changes thousands of years ago.

About 18,000 to 20,000 years before the present, the stream cut a deep valley. With a climate change and rising sea level, the valley filled with alluvium, burying the forests that had developed on each stratum. About 2,500 to 4,000 years before the present, when the stream valley had almost filled, the climate became more arid, rainfall decreased, and the stream became smaller and the floodplain narrower. The old floodplain, with its ridge and swale topography and abandoned-channel lakes, was no longer flooded by the stream, so the ridges developed a less water-tolerant community dominated by beech, magnolia, loblolly pine, and white oak trees. The oxbows and abandoned channels began to fill with organic debris, and those abandoned earlier were filled, becoming shallow, acid swamps called baygalls. The stream then began cutting another system of lower terraces which flood frequently, and the ridges developed forests of water-tolerant oaks and gums. The abandoned channels on these lower terraces, called sloughs, are flushed with fresh, oxygenated river water each time the river rises. Stream terraces are numbered according to age and elevation. The best way to determine the different terrace levels is to simply mark the frequency with which areas are flooded.

The streamward edges of the upper terraces often have areas of deep sand with xeric (desert-type) vegetation. These are ancient pointbar or stream levee deposits. When the stream floods over its banks, the water movement slows and the heavier particles are dropped near the bank, forming a berm or levee. The silt-size sediment remains suspended until the water moves into the forest, where vegetation slows it enough that the silt settles in the swales.

There are three conditions of streams which are readily apparent on the Neches and give it an unusual diversity and character: cutting, at grade, and depositing. When the stream is above sea level, it is in the cutting stage during which it erodes and carries away large quantities of sand, clay and gravel. Depending on the age of the stream, the channel and floodplain are narrow, the banks are high and the water swift. At sea level, it deposits the alluvium brought down from the cutting site. The banks are low and marshy, and many channels are formed as the stream fills one bed quickly and moves to a route of less resistance. During dry cycles, cypress, tupelo gum, and water ash become established and form canopied forests in the shallow water. The open, shallow areas acquire emergent aquatic vegetation typical of the coastal marshes. This area of deposition is called a delta.

Between the cutting and the depositing segments, the river is said to be at grade; that is, the same amount of suspended alluvium leaves the section as enters it. One might say that it is "wallowing about in its own alluvium." The stream has medium-sized banks with wide meanders and expansive sandbars. With each flood, sand is moved from one sandbar to the next, and they remain the same in size. They do not remain in the same location, however, for the stream meanders about its floodplain in this section as well. Sometimes, a sandbar disappears, and the deep, cutbank curve of the river is filled and becomes dry land. As I have watched the river change over the years, I have seen it do some surprising things, some of which are quite contrary to textbook behavior.

On the Neches River, the section between Dam B and Sheffield's Ferry is cutting. From there to just below Evadale, it is at grade; and, near its confluence with Village Creek where it reaches sea level, it is depositing. However, there is a section between John's Lake and Evadale where the stream has cut a new course and the channel is narrow and the water swift. There are always exceptions to the rule.

FLOODS

Floods come in predictable cycles. There are annual floods of normal height and coverage. The 10-year flood level is higher than the annual floods, 25-year flood still higher, but the 100-year flood is talked about for generations. Terrace levels that are not inundated any other time are under water then. There are probably 500, 1,000, and even 5,000-year flood cycles of which there are no records. The flood of Noah's day could have been a 5,000-year flood. All cultures have tribal memories and legends of such a flood so there must be some truth in it.

The normal and natural flood cycles in America, however, have been greatly influenced by the activities of European man. Beavers once dammed every streamlet, holding back runoff in thousands of small reservoirs. The prairies were covered with dense grasses where deep mats of roots held the soil in place and formed a cushion against beating rains and acted as a sponge to hold water. Forests with their deep roots and thick mulch also prevented erosion and sudden runoff of rainwater. After the vegetation used what moisture it needed for growth, the excess was gradually released as springs on downhill slopes.

With the coming of Europeans, the beavers were trapped out by the fur industry, prairie turf was plowed under, and forests were cleared for agriculture and lumber. As a result, disastrous floods occurred throughout the country, carrying billions of tons of rich, virgin topsoil to the sea and dissecting farmland with erosional gullies. In addition, large areas began to be paved or covered with buildings, assuring total runoff of rainwater. Not until President Franklin D. Roosevelt's Civilian Conservation Corps put emphasis on soil and water conservation was this devastating condition checked. Roosevelt's leadership during World War II might have saved our political system, but his Civilian Conservation Corps saved America!

In past times, flooding was accepted as natural disasters or "Acts of God," but attitudes have changed today. When the streams are within banks, floodplains are very attractive, and they have become popular with real estate developers who hope to build and sell before the next "big one" comes. Then the homeowner, up to his eaves in water, cries out for flood control. Some mind-boggling schemes, from both an engineering and financial feasibility standpoint, have been proposed to control flooding in this area. We often have hurricanes when the watershed might receive twelve to fourteen inches of rainfall in a day, while at the same time the winds are pushing tide water up into estuarine areas, forming a bottleneck. The floodwaters then have nowhere to go but over the land.

Floods are necessary to maintain a healthy biological balance in the floodplains. Holding back or manipulating floodwaters causes serious alterations of the sandbars. Sandbars support unique, though small and seemingly insignificant, communities of plants that appear late in summer when the water is low. Normally, plants position themselves in relation to water in this order: hydric plants are those nearest water, xeric on high, dry surfaces, and mesic needing not too much or too little moisture in the middle. On sandbars, the xeric community takes the middle position while mesic plants are found at the top of the slope at the wood's edge.

Moisture in the sand near the water is constantly replenished, so in late summer during low water, the lower sandbars are covered with ephemerals that come up, bloom, and set seeds before the winter floods. Further upslope, the sun heats the sand and perhaps the top two or three inches are dry, but there is moisture beneath the surface, so there are deep-rooted semi-hydric species growing with shallow-rooted xerics. Still further upslope, the sand might be dry and hot a foot or more deep and only xeric species can live. The change to a mesic stage comes abruptly at the wood's edge as shade from the pioneer trees, sycamore, persimmon, river birch, and others, cools the sand. Fallen leaves and plant debris create humus, so grasses, shrubs, vines, and young pioneer trees become established. The winter floods scour everything off the sandbars and carry the seeds to the next sandbar where the cycle repeats itself.

Unseasonal flooding can prevent the annual plants from setting seeds or even from coming up at all, and these species, so specific in their requirements, can be lost completely. With no flooding at all, these species increase, and more are added each season until the sandbar is covered with a dense tangle of weeds, vines, and brush. I watched this happen to a large sandbar near my parents' home at Deweyville on the Sabine River, in three short years after Toledo Bend Dam went in and water was held back to fill the large reservoir. Local residents who had been crying for the dam to control the flooding of their homes, which they were foolish enough to build flat on the ground in a floodplain, are crying now about the loss of their sandbars. To this day, they haven't "got" the connection.

Another result of dams is the interruption of the migration of sand from the original point of erosion, from bar to bar and on to coastal beaches. I have watched the sandbars on the Neches below Dam B recede until only mud and gravel remain. The first sandbar below the dam is now at Barlow Lake Estates where input from Walnut Run and Big Creek replenish sand lost by migration. This is happening all over the United States. As an example, California is experiencing a severe loss of beach sand because all their streams are dammed for irrigation and to supply water to its exploding population. Winter downshore currents are carrying away the sand already on the beaches and none is being brought down to replace it. Long breakwaters are being built out into the water to hold the sand in place.

Floodplain sloughs are nursery grounds for river life. While the water is high, fish go into the sloughs and lay their eggs, knowing that the river will recede, and their young will have their own private pool to grow up in without fear of large predators. When the young are large enough to survive in the river, the next year's flood carries them out. These reservoirs also keep the water table at a level necessary for the types of trees that grow here. Since Dam B and Rayburn Dam have been installed, I have seen thickets of pine, not normally found in lower floodplains, growing on the edge of sandbars.

Even if there were not sound biological reasons for opposing the damming of rivers, I would oppose it from an aesthetic view. I would hate to lose those acres of white sand, or see the sloughs with their magnificent stands of cypress become stagnant mudholes and then disappear altogether. The huge oaks which form closed canopies over the parklike forest and provide acorns for wildlife would also disappear, and the open woods would become choked with brush. All things change on this earth—that is inevitable—but with nature, the change is gradual and life can adapt. With human interference, change can be sudden with catastrophic harm to plant and animal life—and to man.

Some floods in this country have been unusual enough to enter into legend. Oldtimers along the Neches remember their grandparents' tales about the flood of 1884. The Ramers lived on a high sand hummock called Ramer Island below Sheffield's Ferry where they built a house and raised a crop of corn, sugar cane, and garden vegetables. They had no warning. There was no rain and not a cloud in the sky when the river began to rise. Within 24 hours, it had covered their 125-acre hummock except several acres on the north end where Bill Ramer had his house. All exits from the hummock were under water, so the Ramers tore the house apart and made rafts on which to float to safety. The flood spared a 10-acre field of corn, sugar cane, and peas, but the rail fence was washed away and the few cattle that survived ate everything. They lost most of their cattle, all hogs but two, and all their chickens. Later, they returned in boats and dove for the turnips, onions, and other root crops that could be salvaged. While I have not learned how they survived, they probably got some help from more fortunate neighbors, but it was no doubt a desperate time.

Another flood still talked about was the flood of 1928. As the water rose, some cattle congregated on a hummock that eventually went under a foot of water. The cattle's feet and legs rotted until there was nothing left but bone, and since there was nothing for them to eat, they died of starvation. To this day, that hummock is called the boneyard because of the piles of cattle bones on it. Son Gordon told me how he had hauled hay by rowboat to cattle stranded on hummocks during the flood of 1957.

People also became stranded in the bottoms during high water. Not having access to weather information, they had no idea what was going on in the upper watershed until the river began to rise. I. C. Eason, as a boy, once stayed at their place on the river a little too long. As the water covered the high levee bank on which the cabin was built, he began to try to make his way to high ground by wading and swimming from tree to tree. The weather was cold, and when he finally got out, as he put it in his inimitable way with great expression and emphasis, "I wuz ez blue ez a guinea egg!"

When Daddy was a boy, he and his family went to the river for a week of camping and fishing on the Jasper County side in the Boat Lake area in what is now the Neches Bottom Unit of Big Thicket National Preserve. As was usual, women, children, and old folks rode in a wagon while the men rode horseback. While they were there, the river rose and cut off their access to the upland. As it became apparent that the bluff where they camped would soon be under no telling how many feet of water, they began to float the wagons with the weaker ones riding in the wagons and the rest riding horses or wading and swimming. They made it to upland, but it was a dangerous situation that Daddy never forgot.

The floods of 1884 must have been nationwide, as I have read references to record floods in many parts of the country during that time. The famous

Johnstown, Pennsylvania, flood, in which 2,200 lives were lost, occurred in 1889. Perhaps these floods were the combined results of the near extermination of the beaver, the conversion of the prairies and bottomlands to plowed fields, and the stripping of the virgin forests. In 1984, we again experienced a 100-year flood in Southeast Texas. Perhaps it also could be attributed to the clearcutting and bulldozing of the regrown forests for pine plantations, extensive drainage projects for agriculture and real estate developments, and large areas being covered with pavement and roof tops. The attitude of the public in general seems to be like that of the woman who bought a large, expensive home in the Pine Island Bayou watershed, knowing it had already been flooded. When the muddy waters of the bayou reached her eaves during one of our frequent hurricanes, she screamed bloody murder. Her comment was: "As an American, I have the right to live anywhere I choose, and, as a tax-paying citizen, I have the right to expect my government to protect me where ever I live." Because she had political clout, the government spent hundreds of thousands of dollars on a study of flood control on Pine Island Bayou which included a proposal to reactivate the Rockland Dam Project on the upper Neches River and a mind-boggling system of channels and levees on both Village Creek and the Neches, only to arrive at the same conclusion others had reached long ago: the only way to prevent lower Pine Island Bayou from flooding is to stop the tides and control rainfall in the entire Neches River watershed. All so one woman can live in a floodplain basin and expect not to be flooded! Insane!

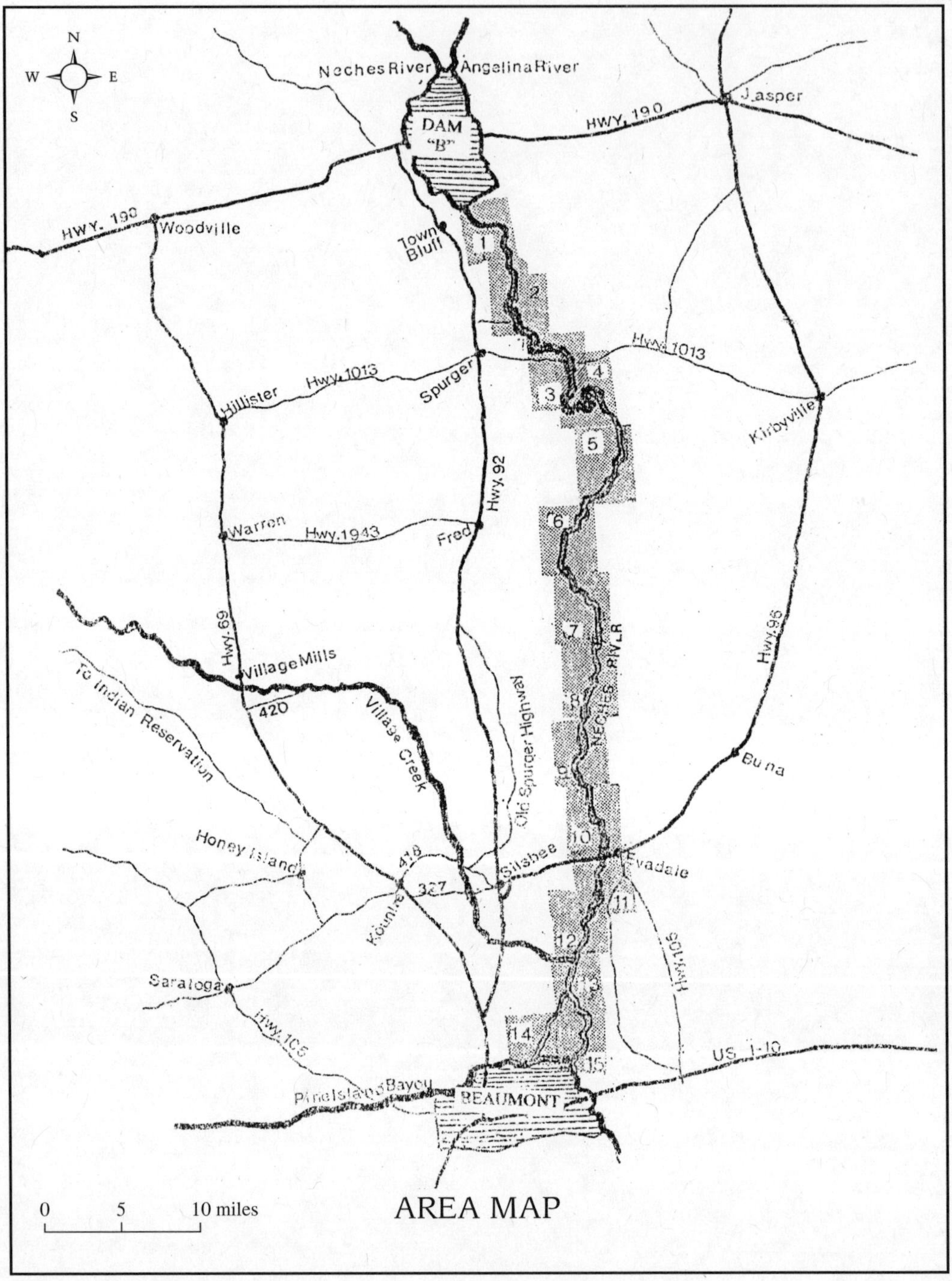
N
S
E
W
Neches River
Angelina River
DAM "B"
HWY. 190
Jasper
Woodville
Town Bluff
Hwy. 1013
Spurger
Hillister
Kirbyville
Hwy. 92
Warren
Hwy. 1943
Fred
Hwy. 69
Village Mills
420
To Indian Reservation
Village Creek
Old Spurger Highway
NECHES RIVER
Hwy. 96
Buna
Honey Island
418
327
Silsbee
Evadale
Kountze
Hwy. 105
Saratoga
US. I-10
Pine Island Bayou
BEAUMONT
1
2
3
4
5
6
7
8
10
11
12
13
14
15
0
5
10 miles

AREA MAP

PART ONE

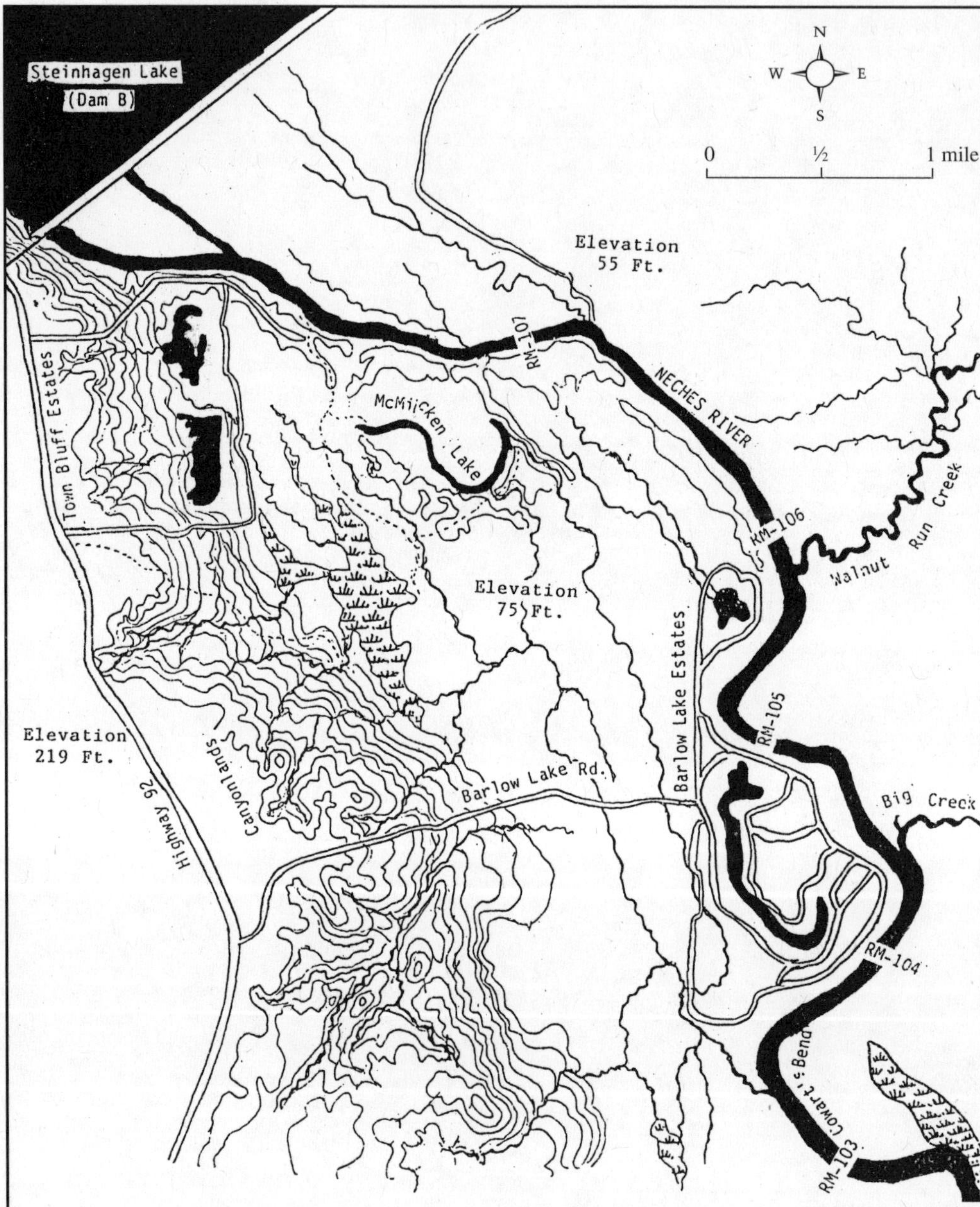
Steinhagen Lake
(Dam B)
N
W
E
S
0
½
1 mile
Elevation
55 Ft.
RM-107
NECHES RIVER
McMillcken Lake
Town Bluff Estates
RM-106
Walnut Run Creek
Elevation
75 Ft.
Barlow Lake Estates
RM-105
Elevation
219 Ft.
Canyonlands
Barlow Lake Rd.
Big Creek
Highway 92
RM-104
Cowart's Bend
RM-103
RM=River Mile

MAP No. 1

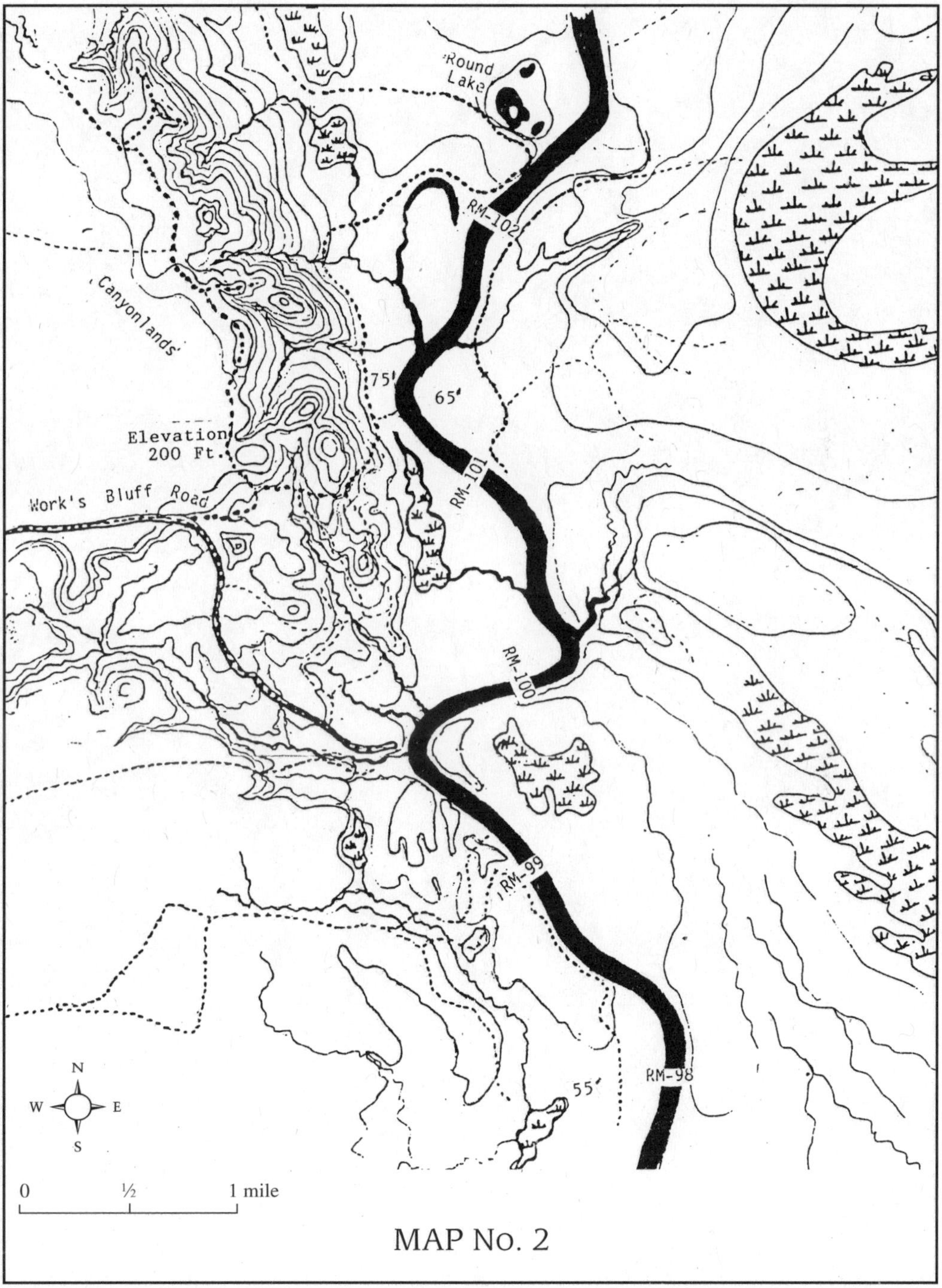
Round Lake
Canyonlands
Elevation 200 Ft.
Work's Bluff Road
RM-102
75'
65'
RM-101
RM-100
RM-99
55'
RM-98
N
W
E
S
0
½
1 mile

MAP No. 2

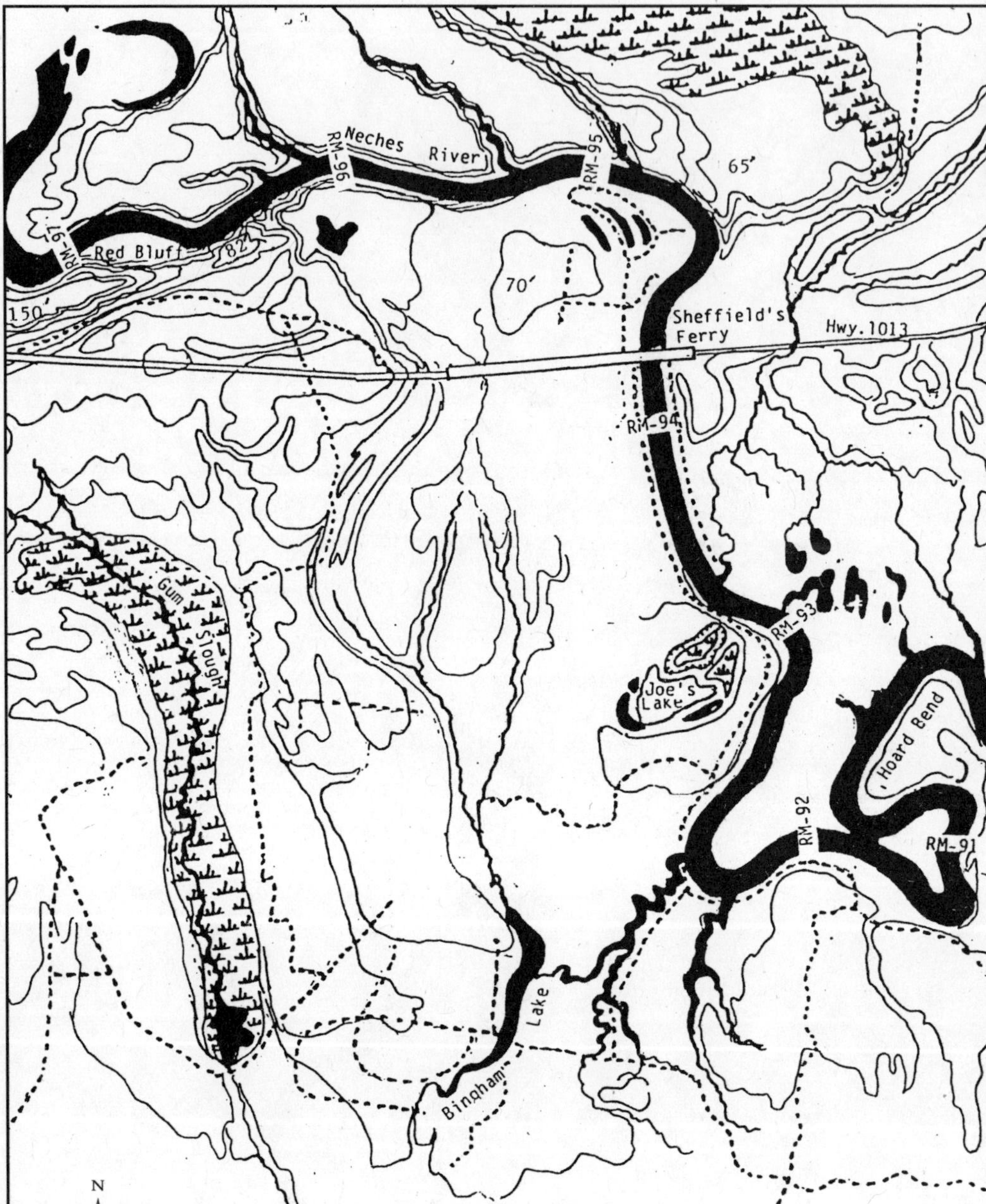
Neches River
RM-97
RM-96
RM-95
Red Bluff
82'
150'
70'
65'
Sheffield's Ferry
Hwy.1013
RM-94
Gum Slough
RM-93
Joe's Lake
Hoard Bend
RM-92
RM-91
Bingham Lake
N
W
E
S
0
½
1 mile

MAP No. 3

Launch off at Town Bluff

Part One

Day 1

LAUNCH OFF

River Mile 108   12:00 Noon

It was a glorious autumn day, the river was just right, my boat was packed with simple necessities, I was ready. My 15-year-old blind samoyed dog, Ulysses, Jr., was also ready, and David, my son, was ready to launch us off. We were putting in at Town Bluff and I had left my VW van at Sheffield's Ferry (Highway 1013), the takeout point. Junior and I climbed aboard my 14-foot flat-bottom riverboat, and David pushed us off into the current to begin our odyssey. Ulysses, Jr., posed proudly like a figurehead in the prow, his ears erect to catch the sounds of all the things his poor blind eyes were missing. How joyously he had leaped into the boat when I said, "Yes, Darling, you can go!"

At this point, I should have sailed grandly and majestically off onto the river and into my great adventure, but, alas, the Corps of Engineers, who regulate the release of water at Dam B, just a few hundred yards upstream, had decided to hold the water for awhile, so there was no current. A strong wind came up and pushed my light craft backward, so there I sat, paddling furiously and going nowhere. David stayed long enough to have a good laugh and left me to the mercy of the wind and river. Finally, the wind slacked, and I made enough headway to get downstream into some current. I continued to wield the paddle with vigor, however, in order to get away from the developed areas below the dam before night fell. My heart was set on camping the first night on the big sandbar at Cowart's Bend. Another reason was that my muscles, unused to sustained paddling, were reaching the limits of endurance.

Once out of sight and sound of civilization, I was overwhelmed by a sense of peace and well-being. I began to feel a lifting of weight from my shoulders—a lightening of spirit and a clearing of the mind. It took a mile or two before I overcame the urge to fight the paddle. Hurry, hurry, hurry! "I have to do this or do that! So-and-so is depending on me, etc., etc.!" Finally the point of no return was reached (I simply couldn't paddle upstream) and I was irrevocably bound to stay on the river until the current and my paddle carried me to my destination. There was absolutely nothing I could do about family problems, the world situation, and the myriad of routine chores that are a necessary part of living in a "civilized" technological society.

As I was borne along by the gentle undulations of the current, caressed by the sun and the soft, cool breeze, with the wind in the streamside trees and the songs of birds in their branches the only sounds, the words of Job expressing his desire for a place of refuge came to my mind:

There the wicked cease from troubling;
and there the weary be at rest.
There the prisoners rest together;
They hear not the voice of the oppressor.
The small and the great are there;
And the slave is free from his master.

Gradually, my paddle strokes, my heartbeat, breathing, and pulse developed a rhythm that was in harmony with the flow of the water, the drift of clouds, the flight of birds, and I became one with them all—one with the river.

TOWN BLUFF

River Mile 107.5 12:45 P. M.

The first point of interest we encountered about three quarters of an hour after launching was the site of Town Bluff Ferry. The ferry site was below the actual bluff, which is probably the highest point on the lower Neches. On the bluff, where the old road between Woodville and Jasper crosses the river, was a pioneer village called, appropriately, Town Bluff. A thriving river port and center of commerce, it was referred to as "Natchez on the Neches." Town Bluff was the county seat of Menard County, until 1842 when the county was divided into Hardin and Tyler Counties, and the Tyler County seat was located at Woodville by popular election. The coming of the railroads around the turn of the century put an end to riverboat transportation and to ports like Town Bluff.

There was a ferry here in the early 1800s operated by Wyatt Hanks, a member of another pioneer family. Hanks, Argulus Parker, and John R. Bevil became involved in a feud over land frauds, and a number were killed on both sides. Hanks left the area and settled on Wolf Creek farther to the north. After that, the ferry was operated by Austin Ogden until 1928 when Thomas (Babe) Barlow acquired it and operated it from 1928 to 1945 when the dam was constructed at the site.

The ferry site was changed from time to time, but the last ferry, run by Babe Barlow, was about a quarter of a mile below the dam site. The Barlows were an early family and are still represented in the area. A few years ago, I visited with his son, Joe Barlow, and his wife, who still lived at Town Bluff.

At first, Mr. Barlow was reluctant to waste time talking with me about local history, but he gradually warmed up enough to invite me into their home. What a lovely home! And what gracious hospitality they showed me. Coffee was made, and it was served with fresh, sweet, clotted cream and a delicious cake. Many a year had passed since I had cream fresh from the cow in my coffee. The home was furnished with solid, golden oak furniture, no doubt brought over from the East with the first Barlows into Texas. The Barlow farm is an excellent example of how a small family farm should be run. In the well-kept green pastures, fat red-and-white cattle grazed. There were rows of fruit trees and forage crops as well as vegetable gardens. The outbuildings were neat and well cared for. I'm sure taking care of such a place kept the Barlows busy, but what better way to spend one's time than working about your own place in the fresh air. Sure beats some stinking refinery or smoking factory. Then there's always the children and grandchildren to entertain when they visit. Who knows, one of them might want to continue the tradition.

Along with the Barlows, another family well remembered in relation to Town Bluff was the Collier family. Zacharia Cowart Collier was an early settler whose entrepreneurial talents gave Town Bluff its importance. He, with other members of his family and neighbors, came to Town Bluff before the Civil War. These were people who had a tradition of strong moral and religious values and personal freedom—at least for themselves, for they owned slaves. Z. C. Collier was a man of many talents and ample means. Although he was educated as a physician, he performed many other duties including those of storekeeper, banker, postmaster, pharmacist, and cotton gin and sawmill operator. All of the trade of the area went through Collier's store. In addition, he operated the Town Bluff Ferry for many years. Collier's store was sold to the Barlows who donated it to be moved to Clyde Gray's Heritage Village near Woodville where it was restored and supplied with goods and furnishings of that era.

One might think Z. C. Collier was something of an exploiter profiting off slave labor and virgin natural resources for his own enrichment, but one action that came to light in my research proves his worth as a brave and noble human being. A yellow fever epidemic was devastating Sabine Pass and Galveston. It was near the end of the Civil War, and famine abetted disease. People were fleeing the area, but Z. C. Collier went into the scene of death and pestilence to use his medical skills to help the stricken.

The Collier family is still represented in Southeast Texas. I spent an afternoon with Virginia Collier at her lovely home in Beaumont, where she generously gave time and information about her Town Bluff forebears. She served tea in the manner of those gentlefolk who, pioneers though they might be, still maintained the gracious, aristocratic lifestyle of the Old South.

The Pedigo family was also prominent here. Atop the hill at Town Bluff, just as you drop off into old bottomland cotton fields, is a house which was the home of Judge Henry Clay Pedigo. It once had a row of small cottages to the side which were slave quarters before the war. The family lived closer to the river in times past in a two-story log house, but moved the house up to the top of the hill in 1884, I suspect in response to the great flood of '83, when many families who had once felt secure living close to the river moved onto high terraces or bluffs. The Pedigo house was pulled up the steep hill on rollers by mules. They had to first clear a path, then knock off the chimneys and some of the top. What a tremendous labor that must have been! As I viewed the hill where they raised that house, I was stunned! What daring! I never cease to be amazed at what these people dared to do in those days with nothing but the strength of their arms and backs, primitive tools, and mules and oxen.

The Pedigo plantation was only a short distance from Town Bluff, but had its own post office between 1902 and 1938. The bottomland Pedigo fields were surrounded by slopes of Fleming Clay, which is rich in lime, essential to most crops, so the Pedigo fields were especially productive. Sometime in the 1940s, I remember passing by and seeing the "colored folk" scattered about the fields picking cotton. The remains of the log shacks where the cotton was weighed and stored are still there.

But, back to the ferry. . . One of my earliest childhood memories was crossing the river on the ferry in 1932. We were making what was then a long journey from Doucette to Bessmay. Leaving at about 4:00 A.M., we four children were placed in the back seat of Daddy's Model T Ford and bundled up in quilts, for it was winter. Eisenglass curtains were buttoned onto the sides of the automobile to keep out the rain. Highway 69 and the Town Bluff road were not paved then, the red clay hills were slick as glass when wet, and it took a really skillful driver to go either up or down them. If the hill were steep, Daddy would turn around and back up it. There was something about the gravity flow fuel feeder that wouldn't operate at a certain angle. With the rear end higher than the front, the fuel flowed freely. On the small creeks there were no bridges. A large tall tree was felled across the streams and split in half with the flat side up. It must have taken iron nerve to aim those skinny Model T wheels at those narrow planks and charge across.

When we reached Town Bluff, Daddy went into Collier's Store and bought cheese, boiled ham, crackers, and red soda pop, which we ate in the car. It was still raining. The river was in flood, and the steep clay bank down to the landing was slick. Mother got us children out of the car and we walked down the embankment while Daddy drove onto the small ferry. It was a fearful moment, and my daddy never appeared more heroic to me as when he was wrestling the wheel of that Model T down that slick clay and onto that small raft of lumber in the boiling water. The muddy bottomland on the other side of the river was horrendous, what with the rain. I remember him replenishing the water in the boiling radiator from roadside bar ditches and repairing a flat tire.

We got into Bessmay after midnight. The trip, an hour's drive today, took over twenty hours. It was an epic journey, but crossing the river on Town Bluff Ferry was the most memorable part.

MC QUEEN'S LANDING

River Mile 106.9 1:10 P.M.

After leaving the Town Bluff area, I saw an interesting-looking little streamlet entering the river on the east side, so I decided it might be a good time for a belated lunch and an exploratory stop. A short distance up the streamlet, I was surprised to find an outcropping of rock and a charming little waterfall.

Further, the streamlet wound through a grove of cypress trees, presenting a most lovely picture. This was my first intimation on this trip that, to see the real Neches, one must climb the banks and discover what the river has done and is doing to the land and forests through which it courses.

Beside the little waterfall is a bluff known as McQueen's Landing. A road leads from the river into the woods and ultimately winds up at Highway 190. There is a rocky shelf here and two men had brought lawn chairs and thermoses of coffee and had settled down for a fine day of pole fishing. I stopped and chatted a while before re-embarking. I have never yet found an unfriendly fisherman. Perhaps after a few hours of clutching a pole and staring at the water, they are glad to break the monotony.

The steamboat *Dixie Queen* was wrecked on the shoals here at McQueen's Landing and was abandoned. Fortunately, the accident happened by the warehouse on the river, so planks were placed from the sinking ship to the warehouse wharf, and the deckhands were pressed into service saving the cargo, which consisted of hundreds of sides of bacon. There was a door in the front of the warehouse and also a door in the rear facing the woods, so the deckhands ran into the front door with the bacon, right through the warehouse, out the back door, and into the woods where they stashed the meat for future collection. They were found out, however, and made to bring the bacon back into the building. They say the remains of the *Dixie Queen* can still be seen in low water.

RIVER RESIDENTS

Birds

After I had mastered the paddle and current enough to avoid disaster, I began to give some attention to my surroundings. Many of the nonhuman residents were out to enjoy what could be the last pleasant weather of the year. The first resident to note and announce to the river world my invasion into their watery realm was the belted kingfisher. Zooming from a high snag on the cutbank, he skimmed just inches over the water like a strafing fighter plane—"ak, ak, ak, ak, ak!!" This is a territorial display, for the kingfisher is extremely territorial, guarding his stretch of river with authority and vigor. When fishing, he flies high over the water, and spotting a small fish just below the surface, slants his wings and descends like a meteor, emerging later with the fish impaled on his beak.

A mating pair of kingfishers dig a tunnel, sometimes as much as ten feet long, into a steep cutbank inaccessible to all but them. The predator they can do little about is the water snake. I once heard an account of a great battle between a large water snake and a pair of kingfishers. Aiming their attack at eyes and head, the birds were successful in driving the monster from their tunnel entrance and sent it flailing and twisting into the deep water below.

Along with the sound and action, kingfishers attract one's attention because of their large size and handsome blue-and-white coloring with black markings. They are so much a part of the stream scene, one can be sure to thrill and delight at their antics at any time on the river.

Whether on land or water, one should be certain to take along binoculars and bird identification book such as the Golden field guide, *Birds of North America.* It is not recommended to ornithology students, but it suffices for the ordinary bird lover like me.

Managers of commercial upland forests do not allow aged, decaying trees to take up space where profitable young pine trees could grow, so the floodplains are the last bastion of many birds, and animals as well, which require hollow trees in which to nest. Since there are many old, dead, or dying trees in our floodplain forests, there are naturally many woodpeckers to take advantage of them for food and nesting sites. Red-headed and red-bellied woodpeckers, the small downy and hairy, and the spectacular pileated woodpeckers are to be seen in the floodplains. If you get a one-in-a-million treat, you might catch a glimpse of the ivory-billed woodpecker. Most ornithologists believe the ivorybill to be extinct, but it was sighted several years ago by ornithologist John Dennis and Dr. Armand Yramategue along this stretch of the Neches River. Bald eagles have been sighted also by National Park rangers along the river just below Dam B Lake.

One of my favorite streamside birds is the prothonotary warbler, locally called the wild canary because it is largely a golden yellow. They like to streak across the waterway from bank to bank. Along with the resident blue jay, cardinal, scarlet and summer tanagers, yellow-billed cuckoo, and a myriad of sparrows and warblers, there are also many transients migrating through here during the autumn.

Our floodplain forests also have the dubious distinction of serving as roosting sites for the millions of blackbirds and grackles which feed in the rice and soybean fields in Jefferson County. They are the noisiest gang I've ever come across. You actually can't hear another person speaking for the great commotion. Late in the evening, they come in flocks which cover the sky from horizon to horizon and one wonders, "Will they never stop coming?" Then they settle down and, apparently discuss the day's doings for awhile before total darkness puts them to sleep.

As I rounded bends in the river, great blue herons rose and floated low over the water before me until, finally, they climbed, banked, and turned back upstream to their fishing in the shallows.

Clouds of small birds, mostly warblers, kinglets, and sparrows, stirred bankside bushes for insects and seeds. Every sandbar had its sandpipers, dipping heads and bobbing tails as they fed on small crustaceans buried in the sand. They flitted away like wind-scattered leaves at my approach. Can it be possible those tiny wings have just brought them from the white frozen Arctic and they only pause here before continuing to the summertime of the Antarctic at the southernmost end of the world?

Flocks of large birds high in the sky proved through binoculars to be anhingas—known variously as water turkeys and snake birds. Diving deep with only long neck and head emerging, they resemble a snake in the water, and their tail is long and turkey-like, thus the common names. Anhingas frequent the deep cutoff lakes of the forests and do their fishing under water. Unlike the waterproof covering of ducks and geese, their plumage becomes water soaked, so they climb out of the water onto a snag or low branch, spreading and turning their wings and tail before the sun to dry.

One can also expect to see ducks, mallards mostly, which will swim a few yards ahead of your boat, and wood ducks in the cutoff lakes and backwater. Unlike a noisy motorboat, a paddle boat gives no advance warning of its approach and one comes upon birds and wildlife at their natural behavior. Notes taken along my route frequently mention ducks in the water ahead, doe and fawn on sandbar, armadillos at water's edge, etc., etc.

Turtles

The river residents most in evidence on my first day were the turtles. Taking advantage of the sunshine, they covered every inch of bare space on logs and snags, even climbing onto overhanging limbs many feet above water. Being cold-blooded reptiles, turtles' body heat and, therefore, activity, varies with the temperature of their environment. Active when the weather is warm, they are dormant when it becomes cold, burrowing into mud at the bottom of the stream or pond to hibernate. In this state, they don't require much oxygen, but obtain sufficient to maintain life by absorbing it through the thin skin of their underparts, or by pulsing water in and out of their mouth and rectum where fine capillaries in the epithelium extract the oxygen from the water.

Some "sportsmen" like to roar down the river in their motorboats with guns blazing, blasting turtles off logs. While I don't like shooting any form of life for any reason, the turtle massacres didn't particularly bother me until I researched this item and developed a personal interest and appreciation for turtles. I found them to be a varied and fascinating group.

There are four categories of turtles in our area: bottom walkers, baskers, softshells, and box turtles. The bottom walkers, such as alligator snappers, are poor swimmers and spend most of their time walking on the bottom of streams and ponds. Many acquire a thick growth of algae on their shells as they grow old, which results in one of their nicknames, "Old Mossback." Since they are nocturnal (active at night), they are rarely seen unless you lift a trotline and find one in the place of a hoped-for catfish. Another exception is in the spring when the amorous snapping turtle, or loggerhead, might go a-roaming across the forest in search of a female of his species.

The most sedentary of the bottom walkers, as well as the largest of North America's turtles (over 30 inches broad and 250 pounds), are the alligator snappers. They are much like snapping turtles, with the exception of having three ridges down the back shell (carapace) which are absent on the snapper. Since the alligator snapper isn't such a great swimmer, it has learned to "angle" for its dinner. It lurks on the bottom of the stream with its huge mouth agape. On the floor of its mouth is a small fleshy object which, when engorged with blood, resembles a pink worm. He waves this bait back and forth, luring unwary fish into reach where they can be snapped up and eaten. When Archie Carr, the famous "turtleologist" described the turtle as having a "philosophy of meditative and passive resistance," he certainly had forgotten the snapper, which can and will without provocation take off an assortment of fingers or toes cleanly and quickly. Their extremely long neck, normally withdrawn into the shell, can lash out with the speed of a rattlesnake.

The turtles with which we are most familiar are the baskers. On sunny days, you might see turtles of every size covering every thing protruding from the water. If space is limited, they will even stack up three or four turtles deep. Most fall off quickly into the water when approached, so one should use binoculars to identify the various species. Common basking turtles are: map turtles, named for the intricate pattern on their shells; the chicken turtle, a desirable eating turtle which tastes like chicken and is usually found in sloughs or ponds; and mud or musk turtles, also called stinkpots because they exude a musky secretion when disturbed. The stinkpot climbs the highest to bask, usually several feet, sometimes into the limbs of overhanging trees. The slider is so named because he is the first to slide off the log when alarmed. Sliders comprise eight out of ten in the turtle population. The cooter (the African word for turtle), was named by the early slaves, who were fed large amounts of them on Southern plantations.

The softshell turtle's claim to fame is its speed. With its streamlined shape and broad, webbed feet, it can out swim a fish, or more necessarily, an alligator. Daddy sometimes caught softshells on his trotline and would bring them home. Mother would not cook or eat anything which looked strange, (especially frog legs which would literally jump out of a frying pan) so Daddy would cook the turtle meat and he and I would eat the dish, which was tasty. Old timers say that a softshell turtle has meat resembling chicken, fish, pork, beef, and bear meat. I never researched the matter, but have found there is always more than a grain of truth in anything the oldtimers claim.

Box turtles are terrestrial and can completely withdraw into their shell and close it up. We call them terrapins in East Texas. My little granddaughter from Los Angeles caught one when visiting here and kept it for a pet. After we returned to L.A., we took it to a local pet shop to determine its sex and perhaps buy a mate, but found they were selling for $45 each! All forms of turtles are popular pets in big cities where apartment managers don't allow dogs or cats. When I look at a turtle close up, they are pretty repulsive-looking creatures—though I am told there are some herpetologists who think they are beautiful. Turtles are incapable of emotion—joy, grief, anger, fear—unlike, for instance, a dog, so it's pretty difficult to establish any kind of relationship with them. They just plod along or hunch up in a corner somewhere. Personally, I would just as soon have a slug as a companion. The snapping turtle's vicious disposition at least sets him apart as a creature with spirit. Good for him!

While turtles seem to be unemotional creatures, they appear to be capable of romantic feelings toward each other during the courting season, which is usually early summer. Male and female aquatic turtles swim together in unison. Facing one another, they move their heads in a rhythmic sideways motion, gaze intently into one another's eyes, gently stroke and pat the other's face, then finally clasp in the nuptial embrace. I once sat on a bluff overlooking the Neches and watched a group of turtles in an orgy of mating. Very interesting!

When egg-laying time comes, the female comes out of the water onto the sandbar. During this season, numerous trails can be seen coming from the water and ending in a bit of disturbed sand. The female digs a hole in the loose sand and deposits six to twelve eggs, buries them, and goes back into the water, leaving them for the warm sunshine to hatch, or, more likely, to provide meals for raccoons, 'possums, or skunks. During late summer or early autumn, any eggs left will hatch and the young turtles scramble to the water for dear life. If they escape the predators on land, they have to face gars, alligators, larger turtles, and catfish when they enter the water. Surviving the first couple of years, they have a chance of living a good, long life and becoming one of the eating rather than the eaten.

Turtle eggs have been relished not only by wildlife, but also by humans, and snapping turtle flesh has become such a popular delicacy in restaurants in the South that they are being considered for endangered species status. Along with predation by animals and humans, turtles are susceptible to pollution, so it is amazing that they not only are surviving but doing quite well. They have been around since dinosaur days and will probably, like the cockroach, be here long after we are gone.

The small woods box turtles that we call terrapins, seem so sweet and inoffensive that my granddaughter named her turtle Tinkerbell. This is all a front, believe me. As anyone who gardens can attest, they voraciously attack tomatoes, cucumbers, strawberries, and everything else they can reach. My experience with them has proven that they are anything but vegetarians, however. Let me tell you about "the terrible terrapin."

I once bought seven fine white leghorn pullet chicks and put them in a cage two feet by eight feet in size with two-inch chicken wire all around, over and under, and one-inch wire around the lower half. Since the arrangement was temporary, I laid a cardboard box on its side at one end and put some plywood over the cage top. After they were a few weeks old, I began to find a dead chick in the cage every morning with its head gone. One had a wing missing. What on earth was happening!! Nothing could get into that cage! Finally, with only two chicks remaining, the mystery was solved. I came out early and found a chick wedged into a three-inch space between the box and the wire. It had jumped on top of the box and tried to get out through the two-inch wire at the top but missed its footing and fell into the narrow space.

Nothing could protrude through the one-inch wire except the head, and a terrapin was calmly munching on it! Apparently the chicks, in their death throes, extricated themselves to finish dying on the cage floor, so we were previously unable to establish the site of attack. When I carried the terrapin into the house to show my daughter and relate the amazing tale, he lashed back to the fullest extent of his neck trying to bite me. I then threw him across the road as far as I could. Cruel? Perhaps! But think of those poor chicks—trapped, helpless—and that turtle chomping away on the eyeballs, the tongue, the brain—aghhh!

While the omnivorous turtle is eating away on all forms of life, both living and dead, other forms of life are eating away on him. I have seen leeches attached to the necks of turtles, and a parasitic turtle fleshfly deposits its eggs on the turtle's soft parts. The eggs hatch into grubs which bore into the flesh and eat away until mature when they emerge, leaving holes in the body, drop, and burrow into the earth where they pupate and eventually dig out and fly away, as adult fleshflies. Chiggers also feast on turtle blood, and young turtles are preyed on by mink, otters, and raccoons, and both young and adults are relished by gars and alligators. Nature is gruesome! At least by human standards of civilized behavior.

Probably one reason for humans' interest in turtles is the turtle's longevity. Outliving all other vertebrates, some have been known to live over one hundred-fifty years. It is also a most ancient group as turtle fossils from the Mesozoic Era (60,000,000 years ago) have been found, and our modern species goes back to the Cretaceous Period which is almost as old.

For some incomprehensible reason, the turtle has a prominent place in legend and religion. There are people living today, the Buddhists, for instance, who believe the world rests on the back of four elephants which, in turn, rest on the back of a turtle. What the turtle stands on is anyone's guess. Our resident biologist at the Park Service, supported, no doubt, by the soundest scientific principles, suggested that it stands on a mountain of elephant manure. Actually, I think they say something about it swimming about in a primordial sea. If a storm hits that sea or the elephants get restless, perfectly natural for something trying to balance on the back of a floating turtle while holding up a whole world, that world gets shook up a bit and we have earthquakes. And I'll bet you all thought it had something to do with shifting plates in the earth's crust.

Aquatic Insects

The turtles, though numerous, are only a small part of the varied population of creatures living in the water. The water surface itself serves as a habitat for certain species. Where water meets the air, the molecules crowd together and cling tightly as if to say: "Just hang on tight and that old sun won't draw you up into the sky!" This condition creates what is called surface tension. It is not stable enough to hold up any weight to speak of, but just enough for creatures like water spiders and the water strider to skate along. The wide-spreading legs of the water spider evenly distribute its weight while hairs on its feet form air pockets which help suspend the body over the water. Others, mosquito larvae, for instance, hang from the surface film with just the tip of an air tube protruding. While the lower part consumes microscopic water life, the upper part is consuming oxygen from the air. Any disturbance of water surface sends them wiggling and scuttling downward to hide under the bottom detritus. We children called them wiggletails.

Many insects spend a phase of life in an aquatic stage, and their forms and behavior are simply too bizarre to describe. Take a cup of backwater and a hand lens and enter the science fiction world of aquatic biology. The characters in children's television programs and comic books are pretty weird, but are as normal as peanut butter compared to the offspring of insects and amphibians. And if you really want to blow your mind, get a microscope and take a look at the microscopic water life. The mathematical precision of the intricate designs of these forms is truly astounding.

Apparently, there are no limits to the diversity nor the smallness and vastness of living things: from the one-celled animals to the visible, complex organisms, to the ecosystems, solar system, universe, galaxies, and the even vaster system of which the galaxies are no doubt a part. The electron microscope and other sensitive devices have revealed even smaller nonliving forms than ever before known, and, I suppose as more powerful devices are invented, they will show an even smaller world; and powerful telescopes together with space exploration will reveal galaxies beyond any now known. "World without end, Amen and Amen!" The infinite is incomprehensible to our finite minds. We can only look in awe and be amazed. I wonder if, as we now understand lightning and solar eclipses and comets which our ancestors looked upon with superstitious awe, generations to come will understand these matters which now boggle our minds.

Fish

The river people are concerned with more prosaic aquatic life—things like food fish. The fish of the Neches also take many forms, sizes, and shapes. There are a number of species of minnows, along with the young of larger fish, only inches long, which inhabit the shallows and riffles out of reach of predators, where they feed on algae and microscopic water life. Also among the small fish is the spotted pike, or pickerel, which grow large in northern waters but remain small down South.

The toothed gars and grinnels (also called bowfins) are among the most primitive forms of animal life left on earth and, since they are air breathers and can survive in water too stagnant for other species, are found mostly in still sloughs and backwaters. They are not preferred for eating, but the French in Louisiana and Southeast Texas made a fish dish called coupion from them. I tried some once and must have done something wrong—it was like chewing a wad of cotton. Grinnels are the last surviving members of an ancient group of fish. Their skin feels smooth and leathery, but is actually covered with small, smooth, hard scales.

We have three kinds of gar fish: the spotted gar, the alligator gar, and the long-nose gar. Gars are not classed as reptiles though they resemble the alligator and many are almost as large. Alligator gars up to twenty feet long and three hundred pounds have been reported. James and Leslie Eason caught one in a gill net that was almost eight feet long. They sold the meat, which was considerable since gars have no bones—only a skull and backbone. They gave the head to me, and it is the most vicious-looking object I've ever seen to come out of the river. The two rows of needle-sharp teeth are three-quarters of an inch long. Daddy always said that a big gar was more to be feared than 'gators. Their razor-sharp teeth have been known to strip the flesh from hands and feet dragging in the water from boats. Gars are voracious, eating everything, even their own young. Sportsmen don't like them because they clean out a water body of more desirable fish. If you should want to catch one, either for coupion or the thrill of the fight, use a tuft of nylon netting on the end of your line instead of a hook. The gar's teeth get entangled in the netting and it can be landed—if it doesn't break the line.

Gars are the last fish left in sloughs that dry up in the summer. They eat the other fish, then the turtles, then one another, until only the big ones are left. Then the buzzards eat them. That's what is called the "survival of the fittest," I suppose. Once in the Neches Bottom Unit, I came upon a slough which had only a few gars, three to five feet long, some dead, some still thrashing about in the muck. A flock of buzzards were feasting on the dead and dying and it was a gruesome sight.

An interesting thing about gars is this: they lay their eggs indiscriminately and go off and leave them to fate; but nature, to make allowances for mother gar's lack of maternal instinct, has caused her eggs to be extremely toxic to anything eating them—and the rest of the water world knows it!

Gasper gou, or drum, and buffalo are river fish which are eaten but are not highly valued because they have so many small bones. Prime eating fish are bass, catfish, and sunfish, which we often call perch. Here, a "perch" is anything smaller than a bass. Sunfish are also called pole fish because people fish for them with a cane pole, hook and line, and a worm for bait. I've seen people, especially old ladies, sit on the bank all day with pole in hand, a can of worms by their side, and a bucket of perch that they caught. Personally, I have never had the patience for pole fishing. While in Southeast Texas we call all sunfish perch, there are many varieties. They are also called bream (pronounced "brim"), and white perch are called crappie (pronounced "croppie"). Each variety prefers a particular habitat. The goggle-eye (also called sunfish or rock bass) prefers weed beds or tangles of snags and logs. The most colorful, the long-ear perch, is found in creeks and small streams. Other colorful perches are bluegill, green, yellow-belly, and red ear. Most fishermen throw small sunfish back, or use them to bait trotlines to catch catfish, but some are large enough to eat from the bones. The Negro people and backwoods whites fry them in deep fat so crisp that they can be crunched whole—bones, tails, fins, and all.

Bass (called "trout" by most oldtimers) found here are black bass and spotted bass and are found mostly in creeks, backwater, and active sloughs. Bass are a fighting fish and put up quite a struggle to gain freedom from the hook and line. A rod and reel are bass tackle, and they are seldom caught on trotlines.

The favorite eating fish in this area is the catfish, and our varieties are blue cat, yellow cat, mud cat, and channel cat. Catfish are usually caught on set hooks, limb lines, or trotlines. Set hooks are baited lines tied to stout poles which are pushed firmly into the ground on the bank. These can be tended without a boat. Limb lines and trotlines must be run by boat. Limb lines are hung from tree limbs overhanging deep water, and a trotline is stretched across a wide expanse with drop lines attached every few feet. (Don't ask me why they are called trotlines. I don't know.) In the afternoon, trotline hooks are baited. Every fisherman has his own favorite bait which might be smaller fish, chicken guts, yellow laundry soap, cornmeal balls, congealed blood mixed with something else equally nasty and smelly, and once, birds were shot for the purpose.

Fishermen have been known to take an old-fashioned, crank-type telephone and stick the wire into the water and crank away. This sets up an electrical current in the water, which stuns the fish and causes them to float to the top of the water where the desirable ones are collected. The practice of "telephoning" was much frowned on by right-thinking fishermen, and it was soon outlawed. It wouldn't take long with such a device to rid the river of all fish.

After baiting the trotlines, the fishermen return to camp, eat and drink, and run the lines every few hours all night to, hopefully, take fish off and rebait the hooks. In between running the lines, the fishermen sit around the campfire, playing cards, telling lies about the number and size of fish they had caught, and drinking quantities of black coffee and/or whiskey. Alcohol doesn't mix very well with trotlining, for the instability of the boat, the darkness, and swift water current, together with the brain- and reflex- numbing effects of the alcohol make a sometimes fatal combination.

There are two rare varieties of fish in the Neches River: the paddle fish and, perhaps, the walking catfish. The paddle fish has a long, paddle-shaped snout which is half as long as the body. The underside of the snout has sensory pits to locate plankton and other small prey, so it swims about with its mouth agape to catch whatever comes along. Paddle fish are boneless and their backbones are made of cartilage. They are on the list of rare and endangered species. I'm told that Texas Parks and Wildlife biologists restocked the paddle fish into the Neches, but many years ago, a woman called me and described this "weird" fish she had caught and was keeping it alive in a tub in her home. She described the paddle fish perfectly, so they have been around, though rare, for some time. Another P. & W. biologist told me that a walking catfish had been found in Village Creek close to the mouth of the Neches, but Dr. Richard Harrel, biology professor at Lamar University, questions the identification. It is native to Southeast Asia, but sometimes tropical fish escape aquaria and become adjusted to local waters.

My daddy had quite a store of fish stories—all of which no doubt were true but embellished and enlarged upon by time and each telling. To Daddy, there were few satisfactions in life to match that of pulling up your line and coming face to face with the broad, whiskered visage of a giant catfish. Once, on successive days, he caught two that weighed 105 and 78 pounds respectively, from the same deep bend. The whole neighborhood ate fish for a week, and Daddy was supplied with yet another addition to his store of fish tales.

I once observed an amusing incident involving a catfish while visiting a friend who had a fish pond in her pasture where she raised catfish, some of which were her breeding stock and were quite large. We were walking along the banks with her large tomcat when the cat stopped by the water's edge to peer into the water. A big catfish stuck its whiskered head out of the water and spit right in the cat's face, startling it out of its wits. The story has a tragic ending. I was lucky enough to have my camera focused on the spot and snapped the scene—an award-winning photo, I was certain. Due to some malfunction on either my part or the camera's, the entire role of film was ruined, and you only have my word that it ever happened. And, since I am no fisherman, you can believe it.

One of the strangest fish to inhabit the river, and one with the most unbelievable life history, is the eel. Born in the Sargasso Sea, a vast mass of floating seaweed in the deepest part of the Atlantic Ocean, the immature eels, scarcely an inch long and called elvers, make their way to the coast and up the rivers and small creeks to the very spot where their parents came from. Several years later, when they reach maturity, they stop eating, change from black to a silvery color and begin the long journey back to the Sargasso Sea where they mate, lay their eggs, and die. Pulitzer Prize-winning author, Edwin Waye Teale, related that migrating eels, if cut off from their course by dried-up sections of their stream, will, on dewy nights, slither across a mile or more of wet meadow to reach water and continue their pilgrimage.

I never knew of any of this when Daddy used to bring eels caught on trotlines home to fry, but recently, when I found about a dozen elvers milling about in a small depression on the sandy bottom of a small spring branch, I knelt over the little voyagers in awe and spent nearly an hour in contemplation of the mind-boggling wonder of it all.

Once, I knew nothing of the world beneath the surface of the river, but now, enlightened, I look out over the placid film and see it as a division between worlds, as is the ionosphere that divides earth's atmosphere and outer space. To mere mortals, to cross either barrier is death if one does not have some special life-support system to protect oneself. I wonder—is death itself only a barrier between worlds? One, the familiar, known world we can see and touch, the other—what? Will humans some day develop some life-support system that will allow us to travel back and forth? The spiritualists claim to be able to leave the body during their trances, and there are those who claim to get a glimpse of that other world while clinically dead; otherwise, I know of none who have entered that other world and returned. They are still held by the surface tension of the barrier.

This much I have learned in my 70-plus years: just because I am not aware of nor understand something, does not mean it is not true or does not exist. The apostle Paul, said: "Now we see as through a glass, darkly; but then, face to face. Now I know in part; but then shall I know even as also I am known" (I Cor.13:12). He also said, "Eye has not seen, nor ear heard, nor can the mind of mortal man even conceive of the things which God has prepared for those who love him" (I.Cor.2:9). If that other world beyond death is more wonderful than our earth, water, and sky, it almost makes one want to jump off a cliff in an ecstasy of anticipation. But I do think I'll wait. There are still thrills of discovery to be experienced on the Neches.

GEORGE SMYTHE

River Mile 105.8 2:55 P.M.

Just before arriving at the populated area at Barlow Lake, I passed the mouth of Walnut Run, a nice, clear, spring-fed creek. On the south of the creek mouth was the steamboat landing and wharves for the farm of George Smythe.

George Smythe was quite a celebrity in his day. He came from Alabama in 1803 to join Stephen F. Austin's colony on the Brazos, but stopped off in Nacogdoches where fate tied him for life to the Jasper County side of the Neches River opposite Town Bluff. He was appointed surveyor by the Mexican Land Commissioner. In 1836, when Texas declared independence from Mexico, he became the Texas Land Commissioner. Other positions he served were judge for the municipality of Bevil, state congressman, and, after annexation, U. S. Congressman for the Jasper District. He engaged in politics, read the classics in Greek and Latin, and, like his fellow Texan, Mirabeau Lamar, wrote bad poetry and engaged in flowery oratory. His capable wife, the former Frances Grigsby, daughter of the prominent merchant, Joseph Grigsby, of Grigsby's Bluff (now Port Neches), with the help of a few slaves, took care of the farm. It was ever thus in pioneer times. The man was usually running around chasing Indians, fighting Mexicans, hunting, or fishing while the woman stayed at home and she and the children did all the work.

Smythe's life had two major contradictions: while he was one of the signers of the Texas Declaration of Independence, he joined the panic-stricken thousands of Texans who made a rush for the Louisiana border in what has been called the "run away scrape," leaving Sam Houston and his pitifully small and ill-equipped army to face the juggernaut of Santa Anna's hordes. Also, he and Sam Houston bitterly opposed Texas' secession from the Union prior to the Civil War, only to give sad and reluctant consents to their eldest sons to enter the Confederate Army.

While George Smythe was well-known in his day, his fame has been eclipsed by his brother, Andrew, the riverboat captain, due to William Seale's book, *Texas Riverman*. I'm glad Andrew Smythe received his share of glory. Texas was built, not by the flamboyant orators and public figures to whom the statues are erected (excepting Houston and Austin, of course), but by ambitious hard-working men and women who had an unimpeachable sense of honor and integrity and devotion to duty, and wanted to make Texas a place for decent people to live.

Back in the woods here is a marker placed by the Texas Historical Commission in 1936 at the site of George Smythe's farm, commemorating his service to his state and country. As I paused and looked over the bluff, there was, of course, no indication that it was once busy and active. The farm itself has become overgrown in forest and nothing is left of the family home or the people who made it a lively, happy place.

Somewhere along this stretch of the river, a large landowner came into disagreement with President Sam Houston, so the squire (I've never learned his real name), together with several of his neighbors, declared independence from the Republic of Texas and formed their own country. Sam Houston came and discussed the matter with the squire, and they agreed to settle the dispute with a round of poker. They played, Houston won, and the new republic was disbanded. It sounds like something George Smythe would do, but his life has been well documented, and no mention was ever made of it.

FAMILY FARM

George Smythe's farm was typical of the farms of that day. They were completely independent, manufacturing everything needed until steamboats began to bring trade goods from the East. It was my good fortune to spend two years in the early1940s on the Jim Martindale farm in the Beech Grove Community in Jasper County near what is now Dam B. The Martindales were a large family who had settled the area after the Civil War, so the surrounding farm families were all kin and shared the usual activities involved in growing crops, hog butchering, cane grinding and syrup making, and running cattle in what was then open range. Jim Martindale also did some contract work on roads, etc., with his mules and workmen. At the time I was involved with the family, no cash crops like cotton and corn were grown but only what was needed by the family and emphasis was placed on the animals. The hogs ran wild in the woods eating mast until winter when they were penned and hardened on corn. Neighboring families and Negros who lived on the place came to help and take home a share of fresh pork. Hams, shoulders, sides, and tongues were salted down and placed in the smokehouse while the rest of the meat was trimmed from the bones, ground, and stuffed in sausage casings (cleaned intestines), which were also hung in the smokehouse. Jim Martindale was famous for his sausage, which people came to buy. The fat was trimmed from the carcass and rendered into lard. Fannie Martindale made her own soap from this fat which she mixed with lye from wood ashes. Fried fresh pork was served at every meal during this time as there was no refrigeration to store what was not smoked. Pork was the principal meat of that day for the same reason, but sometimes a beef was killed and "corned": packed in salt.

Another annual chore was the making of syrup. Mr. Martindale had the only cane mill in the vicinity and as with his sausage, he was famous for the quality of his syrup. The cane was cut and brought from the field in wagons and fed between two large stone wheels, which were turned by a donkey pushing a pole around in a circle. The juice ran into containers which were emptied into the great metal pan over a clay oven where a fire was kept going. Baffles in the pan kept the juice flowing gradually until it came out the other end into jugs as syrup. At the end, some syrup was cooked longer than normal so that it crystallized when it cooled. These crystals were washed and hung in flour sacks to drain and dry, then beaten into a coarse but delicious sugar.

An important event was the rounding up of cattle in the spring and the fall to brand, vaccinate, and castrate those that needed attention. Families and neighbors joined in. Men, boys, and the older girls, of whom I was one, rode horseback through the woods rounding up the cattle into a large bend in the river called Smith's Point. The forest was open and parklike in those days due to cattle grazing, periodic burning, and shading canopy and one could drive through it and see herds of deer far off. The women and old folks would come through the woods in wagons bringing food, and a steer and goats were barbecued. Young men would dash about on their horses and wrestle the steers trying to impress the girls and old men would sit on the fence telling all about how it was in their day.

After crops were laid by in the summer it was time for rest and recreation. An arbor of brush was built and a protracted meeting was held. People came in wagons, camped out, brought food, and dinner on the ground was served. Preaching, singing, visiting, and courtin' carried on for a week or two. Then, everyone—men, women, old folks, boys and girls, children, and babies—all went to the river for a week of camping and fishing.

These activities weren't labor but were festivals in which everyone participated. There boys and girls met neighbors' boys and girls and married those of the same culture and religion, perpetuating the sense of kin and community. World War II changed everything. The boys went away to war, met and married girls from different backgrounds, and nobody wanted to go back to the primitive life of the farm. They all disappeared into the Beaumont-Orange-Port Arthur petrochemical megalopolis. Very sad!

Hey! Just a minute! I just realized I have been rhapsodizing over the idyllic life of a pioneer *man*! Let me tell you about a woman's life back then. And, as one who lived it, I can safely call myself an authority. It is no coincidence that every man's grave in the old cemeteries has three or four wives' graves alongside. Many died in childbirth but most were just worked to death. Let's start with Monday morning—before daylight. First, make a fire in the cookstove and cook breakfast from scratch. Wash dishes. Go out to the milking shed and feed and milk the cow. (In rainy weather, wear boots, for the cow lot is ankle deep in gooey, stinking stuff.) Take care of the milk; let it down in the well to keep cool. Draw water from the well to fill three washtubs; build fire under iron washtub. Make beds, sweep floor, gather clothes to be washed. Put white clothes into boiling pot with lots of homemade soap. At this point, go to the garden and gather vegetables for dinner, to the smokehouse for meat, and begin dinner. Pour hot water from boiling pot into washtub, put in colored clothes and scrub over a corrugated rub board. (Hard on the knuckles.) Wring, put into tub of clear water to rinse, wring again. Take white clothes from boiling pot, lay over the battling block and beat them with the battling stick. Wring and rinse. Finish dinner, serve, wash dishes. Saturate most clothes with starch, wring again, and hang all on a line. In the winter, they might freeze stiff as you hang them out. By this time, there is no skin on your knuckles or the insides of your thumb and forefinger. Washing all done, take the hot, soapy water and scrub the floors. Gather the clothes when dry, sprinkle with water and roll up to damp evenly for ironing next day. Prepare and serve supper, clean up kitchen, and sit down to mend or sew clothes by hand by the light of a kerosene lamp.

Next day, usual chores, keep fire going in the cookstove to heat the irons, iron all day—even though the temperature in the kitchen might reach 100-plus degrees in the summer time. In between chores, skim the cream from the bowls of soured milk and churn. Feed the clabber (skimmed milk, now called yogurt) to the hogs and put away the buttermilk (churned milk) and the butter. The rest of the week, hitch up the horse and plow the garden, prepare food for preservation, make clothes for husband and children, and help the husband with work in the field at planting and harvesting times. Even though in the summer time there are diversions like brush arbor meetings and fishing trips, the regular chores go on. In the middle of the summer, vegetables and fruit ripen and the time is taken up with preparing and preserving them in jars, sterilized and sealed in large vats of boiling water over the cookstove. A farm wife is seldom away from the cookstove. With the nausea of pregnancy, there is nothing like bending over a pot of boiling, rendering hog fat, or ironing over a hot stove. And, would you believe it? I was happy then! But let me say this unequivocally: I will NEVER again swelter over a hot cookstove in the summer time to iron a suit of khakis for my husband to wear in the field! But if a wife didn't do it, she was branded as lazy and neglectful. With all this, Fannie Martindale planted petunias and zinnias in her yard and played her old-fashioned organ. When they speak now of the women who juggle an office job and household chores as "super moms," I remember Fannie Martindale—a true super woman. As for me, I left it all and went to Port Arthur College to become a secretary.

(The foregoing is dedicated to Fannie Pickle Martindale who taught me how to make hot water cornbread and play the foot-pump organ.)

LAKES

River Mile 104 to 105 3:00 P.M.

In midafternoon, I reached the big sandbar at Barlow Lake Estates and was paddling serenely by when there was a loud "Pow" and something whistled over my head. On the woods edge of the bar I saw a young man with a gun apparently target shooting at the opposite cutbank. "Hey!" I yelled. "Don't shoot!" "Zing!" I couldn't believe he was not seeing or hearing me, but was just having fun scaring me, so I lay in the bottom of the boat and let the current carry me past the danger zone. The city folk who come to these weekend cabins are not the same kind as those downstream whose lives and ways are the river. River bottom people have a reputation for being wild outlaws, but they would have never have treated me so.

Barlow Lake Estates was developed on stream levee deposits around one of the midterrace lakes between Town Bluff and Works Bluff. McMicken Lake (RM107), Barlow Lake, and Brush Lake were apparently cut off from the river during the great flood of 1884, at least Joe Barlow said that Barlow Lake was cut off at that time and the ages of the cypress trees in and around the lakes seem to verify this.

Brushy Lake is part of the development, but McMicken Lake and Round Lake (RM103) are surrounded by forest. These incredibly beautiful bodies of water—deep, clear, blue-black with tannic acid—are ringed by groves of cypress trees both in and out of the water. These lakes are seldom flooded by the river, but are fed by seepage springs at the base of the uplands. McMicken Lake has a different quality from the other three. It is not as acidic since it is fed by milky-tinted branches issuing from the calcareous clays of the Fleming Formation on the bluff.

McMicken Lake was included in the half of the proposed Canyonlands Unit which was above Barlow Lake Estates Road. The floodplain terrace between this lake and Barlow Lake Road was bordered on the west by the slopes and canyons, and on the east by the river. Southward, between McMicken Lake and Barlow Lake Road was a parklike forest with giant oaks, gums, and loblolly pines on the ridges and monster cypress trees in the swales. It was the closest to the virgin forests of my childhood that I've seen in many years. One cypress tree was so large it took nine of us to reach around it. Awesome! This forest had been left alone by the timber company that owned it, probably because of difficulty of access. A north/south pattern of wet swales and streamlets divided the entire forest into linear ridges. Unfortunately, this upper half of the proposed Unit was excluded from the plan in order to ensure the inclusion of the Big Sandy portion of the Village Creek Corridor. This corridor had already been so thoroughly devastated that it would be 25 to 50 years before it would recover enough to be of any value recreationally, aesthetically, or ecologically, and would be utterly impossible for the Park Service to manage or patrol except by helicopter. It was interrupted by private holdings which neither the public nor the Park Service could cross. There was nothing further that could have been done to threaten the Big Sandy Corridor, but this pristine forest was at dire risk and should have had priority. Assuming that everyone could see what I saw and come to the same logical conclusion, I did not fight for this area, and it was lost.

As soon as the boundaries were delineated in the bill before congress, the loggers with chainsaw, trucks, and skidders were tearing away at the forest. The canyons above Barlow Lake Road with their rare ferns, orchids, tiger lilies, etc., were reduced to utter ruin by the skidders. The oak trees were so large and heavy that they shattered where they fell. The devastation was sickeningly complete. This couldn't have been a profitable operation, as only one short log could be taken from the few good trees. It was done for spite or to ensure that no other "preservationist" would ever again look on this forest and want to save it.

I don't know that I could say that this broke my heart, but I do know that it broke my spirit. Since that time, I've had no desire to participate in environmental activities. I don't go out much anymore, for if I see something that is especially beautiful, I weep over it, for I am overwhelmed by a feeling of certainty that it is doomed. I can be certain that my little preserve at Hyatt will be managed properly and its rare plants saved at least during my and my son's lifetimes. Beyond that, I can't be sure of anything.

Joe Barlow expressed regret to me that he had ever sold Barlow Lake for development after he saw how ugly its surroundings had been made with shacks and camphouses. Hopefully, the terrain around McMicken Lake is not suitable enough for building houses and will be spared.

There is a launch site on the river at Barlow Lake Estates which is indicated on Detail Map No. 1.

COWART'S BEND

River Mile 103.5 4:35 P.M. First Night

By the time Cowart's Bend was reached, I was dead tired. Turning the prow of my boat toward the head of the sandbar, I got out and pulled it out of the water several feet up on the sand, not taking any chances that an unexpected rise of the river might sweep it off and leave me marooned.

Cowart's Bend sandbar is several acres in extent and is divided by a narrow band of willows about halfway to the tree line. My tent was pitched against a thicket of loblolly pines that have colonized the upper edge of the sandbar and where a thick mat of bermuda grass made a good pad. Wanting to watch the sunset turn to dusk without groping about necessary chores in the dark, I hurriedly pitched the tent and lit a small fire in a grass-free depression to cook my simple supper.

Sitting on a knoll with a cup of hot coffee in hand and Junior by my side, I gazed over the sweeping panorama of willows, sandbar, river, and the tall, dark forest on the opposite cutbank side. The willow leaves were just turning a golden yellow-green and the setting sun outlined them with a shining aura against the dark blue-green-brown background. I watched until the sun dropped behind the tall trees—a time of power according to Carlos Castenada's Don Juan—an auspicious, magical moment. Just as the last rays dimmed, two skeins of geese crossed the sky. The last glitter died out in the spaces between the leafy branches, and the mellow afterglow, which had turned the green pine needles and the scarlet, yellow, and orange autumn leaves to jewels on the still sunlit side of the river, began to fade, leaving just plain, dull shades of color. The sky darkened to a metallic prussian blue, and a perfect half moon rose in the east. After the last tint of suffused gold faded in the west, the sky changed through shades of blue, darkening to pure indigo with the evening star sparkling alone like a diamond solitaire. The river had mirrored all these changes, doubling the intense pleasure I was experiencing.

It began to get cold, so Junior and I crawled into the tent, I into my sleeping bag, and he snuggled against me. We shared each other's warmth, and prepared to sleep.

Then the motorboats began. This section of the river was so serene, so lovely with no sign of civilization to disturb the wildness of the scene that one could believe one were in the middle of a vast wilderness. Apparently, all the residents of the upstream developments set out trotlines and ran them all night. I heard one stop near where my boat was tied up and thought I had best check to see if it were still there. It was, and, ashamed of my distrust in my fellowman, I resolved to go back to bed and forget the boat, but was so struck by the beauty of the night that I got my heavy coat, and Junior and I returned to our knoll to star gaze. In spite of the brilliance of the half moon, the sky was spangled with stars. I lay on my back in the grass and with binoculars picked out some of the few constellations I remembered from the days when my oldest son, Bobby Lee, went through his astronomy phase. Orion had not yet risen, but Venus, the evening star, was still hanging just over the horizon. There was the red planet, Mars; Polaris, the North or Pole star; and the dippers I could recognize; Syrius, the dog star; the northern cross or Cygnus the Swan; and, just above it, the twins, Castor and Pollux. How long it was since I took the time to sit and watch stars.

It was surprising to see so many satellites pass across the sky. With what incredible speed they move from horizon to horizon! Surely they are going to collide if we keep sending up so many! With a shudder, I thought how horrible it would be if each of these heavenly bodies should be carrying laser beams or death rays that could incinerate whole cities. What is even more unthinkable is that so many people want such a system and are even working toward it. Such madness! But I am here on the river to forget for awhile that the world has gone mad, that America has abandoned reality, logic, morality, and legality in order to have its way in the world! That's all on that subject!

And so to bed! The motorboats finally stopped. Again, Junior and I snuggled in our tent, and then the howling began. For an hour or more, it seemed that every coon in the forest must have a hound hot on its trail, baying every step. A few shotgun blasts hinted that a night hunter was also on the prowl. But, finally, blessed silence!

With the silence of man and dog, other sounds, more subtle, became audible. The sandbar was coming to life! Soft footfalls and gentle rustlings. What a lazy thing I am! Snuggled in that warm cocoon when I could be hiding in that fringe of willows ready to spotlight their doings with my light. Oh well! I felt I could always trace their activities in the sand next morning.

About 2:00 A.M., it got warm and a gentle rain began to pepper the tent. Soft showers fell intermittently the rest of the night. I expected as much, for the sunset had not been red. The old saying: "red morning, sailors' warning; red night, sailors' delight" can be relied upon better than the weatherman.

At daybreak, a heavy fog hid the river, and I barely had time to make a fire from stashed, dry twigs and prepare my hot oatmeal breakfast before rumbling thunder brought a heavier shower. Still no wind—thank heaven. Rain is no problem, but my fragile tent would sail away with the first puff.

Daddy had a simple arrangement for shelter: a rope tied between two trees, a tarpaulin thrown across and its four corners tied to trees or bushes. A mosquito bar made of cheesecloth completed his shelter. If the weather were really cold, he built a large, hot fire, waited for it to die down, then moved it over against a log while he occupied the warm ground where the fire had been. I was reminded of Daddy every bend I rounded and everything I experienced. This is the first time I had ever gone to the river just for pure pleasure, as he did. Always, there have been people to try to influence, to persuade, to sell. What a wonderful feeling of freedom not to have to interpret everything seen or done!

Part One

Day 2

BURIED FOREST

River Mile 103.5 10:30 A.M.

It was a misty, magical morning. The gentle rain lasted a short time; a dense fog lay over the water, but it was dispersing, so I packed and stowed my gear and pushed off over the glassy water into the mist.

About ll:00 A.M. just below Cowart's Bend, I came upon a high, colorful bluff. It was once a steamboat landing, and was the terminus of a branch of the Magnolia Springs road. The cutting action of the river here reveals about 25 feet of floodplain history covering possibly 5,000 years. At normal water level, there is at the bluff base a shelf of the rock-like gray clay found at various shoal sites between Dam B and Sheffield's Ferry. It appears to be of Fleming Formation age as it tests high on the pH scale. (I carry a small bottle of 10 percent hydrochloric acid to test materials suspected to be calcareous.)

Above this rocklike clay are several strata of different materials. There is a layer of ocher-colored silt above the clay, then a layer of compressed snow-white, fine-grained sand, over that a layer of red iron oxide sandy clay, all topped by a dark topsoil. The erosion of these materials has created many strange and beautiful shapes and colors. They are transient in nature as the heavy rains, water seepage, and floods erase them and make blank walls for new creations. One white wall had an abstract design of brilliant red oxide painted onto the surface by water seepage from above. Buff-colored walls had white figures, and the red was decorated with black streaks from topsoil containing charcoal residue from past forest fires.

The wash-out of a large tree on the bluff side left a shallow cavity in the red clay where seepage created stalactites and stalagmites of white sand. It reminded me of the sand castles we children built at the beach when wet sand was poured onto castle walls to create fanciful minarets.

These walls were sculpted and painted by alternating rain, erosion, and seepage deposition into patterns, colors, and forms that would require a Michelangelo if humans were to attempt to duplicate it. I spent at least an hour perusing and enjoying nature's masterworks of art on this bluff.

An even more remarkable facet of the bluff was the revelation about 25 feet below the present forest surface, of a prehistoric forest, buried perhaps thousands of years ago by some great postglacial flood. The typical ridge-and-swale topography of a floodplain forest was revealed. Some giants on the ridges lay prone, apparently felled by the swift floodwaters and buried beneath the silt deposited as the flood abated. In the swales, the stumps of cypress trees and their knees appeared. The cypress trees seem to have been broken off or rotted away at the top of the silt level. Apparently, what had been covered by the silt was protected from deterioration by the exclusion of oxygen, while anything protruding from or fallen upon the surface of this silt layer rotted away and was lost. Dr. Saul Aronow hazarded a guess that this forest was in existence about 5,000 years ago. Mind you, I said, "hazarded a guess." Dr. Aronow was very wary about making statements not backed up by published fact. What a priceless opportunity for some student of paleobotany to learn something about our prehistoric environment! The only problem is that the studies must be done at low water level and these don't always coincide with university schedules.

Dr. Aronow, Dave McHugh, river ranger for the Big Thicket National Preserve, and I made a canoe trip down this section of the river once when the water level was at an all-time low. At this bluff, the river flow was confined to channels and pools cut in the colorful clays and siltstone bedrock of the streambed, and at one point, the water rushed through a narrow channel and over a four- to five-foot drop. I am unaccustomed to boating in swift current or rapids, and Saul was terrified of any water not confined in a bathtub. Dave had a good laugh as we went over the small waterfall, my scream echoing from the bluff and Saul sitting soundless, white knuckles clutching the gunwales of the canoe.

This river has so many interesting facets, and it is never the same. No matter how many times you see it, there is something different about it each time. People accustomed to a thrill-a-minute, whitewater stream are bored to death with it, but they are usually the type who get into a canoe, bow their heads, bend their elbows, and fight the paddle until they get to the other end. Those setting out just to enjoy the day and whatever it might present, bring along a pair of binoculars, a couple of field guides for birds, reptiles, amphibians, animal tracks, etc., and really don't care how many miles they can cover in X number of hours. They just relax and go with the flow and the Neches doesn't disappoint them.

SYCAMORES

The banks of the river are lined with my favorite stream-side tree at this time of the year—the sycamore. In the autumn, its large, saucer-shaped leaves turn ocher yellow and then burnt sienna. The leaves and the stark white upper trunk and branches sparkle against the cobalt blue of the autumn sky. While the sycamore's natural habitat is newly-laid floodplain land, it survives and flourishes almost anywhere. This adaptability made it a favored tree to plant around farm homesteads. The broad leaves provide cooling shade in summer, yet fall early and let the sun through during the cold months.

I never gave the name of the tree much thought until I read that the poet, Rosanne Coggeshall, stated that "sycamore" is the most intrinsically beautiful word in the English language. Mouthing "sycamore" over and over, I began to appreciate the different sounds and intonations required to say it. Interesting, yes, but most beautiful? I don't know about that.

The word sycamore comes from the French "sycamour" which, in turn, is derived from the Greek "sykomoros" which is a modification of a Semite word akin to Hebrew: "shigmah." Our sycamore of Eastern and central North America is *Platanus occidentalis*, while the sycamore of scripture and of Egypt and Asia Minor is a completely different species, *Fiscus sycamorus*, a member of the fig family. There is another tree called a sycamore, a beautiful European shade tree, actually a maple, *Acer pseudo* (false) *platanus* (sycamore).

It is surprising how often the sycamore tree, in its varieties, is mentioned in literature. From Zacheus, the short man who climbed into one to better see Christ, to Xerxes, the Persian king, people have appreciated the sycamore. History tells us that Xerxes, on a long, desperate march with his army of thousands, came upon a sycamore tree of such beauty that he halted the entire expedition for days so that he might contemplate it to his satisfaction. The ancient Romans so revered the sycamore that they watered its roots with wine. Since I carried no wine for a libation, I recorded the sycamores against the sky on film with my camera so that I could show them to others, and we could contemplate them to our hearts' content in the comfort of our homes.

Round Lake

ROUND LAKE AND BUZZARDS

River Mile 102.3 11:45 A.M.

After leaving the colorful bluff, I continued downriver and around the bend. From the river surface, there is little variety in vegetation. Most pointbar or cutbank forests look the same, so one begins to look for subtle indications that there might be something interesting behind the screen of foliage. The topographic map showed some fair-sized lakes in the next large bend. I chose a narrow cleft in the high stream-bank berm where a small streamlet trickled into the river, and, using vines and roots, pulled myself over the top. Standing up, I gazed upon a scene so incredibly beautiful that I was stunned. The small

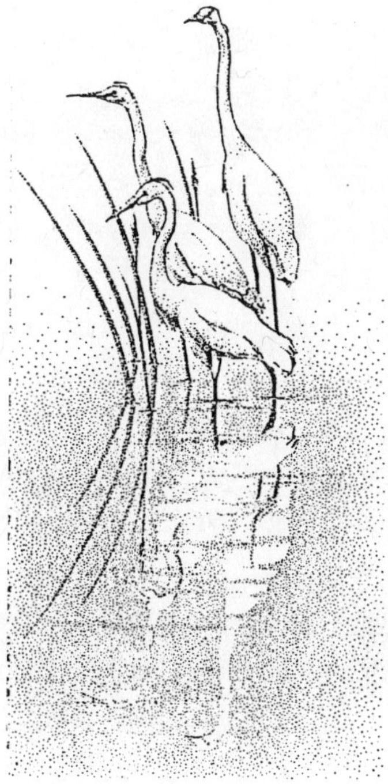

Herons
Drawings by Regina Watson

streamlet wound through a magnificent grove of towering cypress trees in an ocean of lush ferns and jewel flower. Through the trees a small mirror lake could be seen and, beyond that, a larger lake. When capable of movement, I walked among the mighty trees toward the small lake and was so overwhelmed by the beauty and grandeur around me that I could only weep.

I climbed a bank which seemed to halfway encircle the larger lake and walked around the south side. There was an island in the center, comprising about an acre in size, covered with cypress trees. The water was a clear blue-black and its mirror surface was broken by hundreds of water birds—anhingas, ducks, egrets, geese, etc.—which were splashing and cavorting joyfully about and raising a veritable cacophony with their calls and cries.

As I sat on the high bank to watch, Junior trotted up and joined me. How he, blind as he was, had left the boat, climbed that high, steep bank and found me, only he and God know. We sat silently for a long while, until I noticed on the back side of the lake a gathering of large, black birds and decided to go around and investigate.

The tree limbs hung heavy with the birds. It was impossible to tell from the distance whether they were anhingas or cormorants—there were both in the lake. I raised my binoculars and saw they were black vultures ("buzzards" in the vernacular). Black vultures have black heads and white patches on the underside of wingtips while turkey vultures have red, turkey-like heads and are a brownish color.

I walked slowly around the lake, giving them a wide-enough berth not to cause alarm, but as I came nearer, they moved tree-to-tree ahead of me. This was obviously a roost, for the ground beneath the trees was covered with foul-smelling excrement.

Some birds fight with buzzards that get too close to their territory. Shortly after leaving Cowart's Bend, I watched a dogfight between two crows and a buzzard. The buzzard was clearly on the defensive and seemed to be more intent on gaining altitude and escaping than fighting. I saw a similar battle once between a crow and a buzzard. When the crow had soundly trounced the enemy, he returned to the nest tree and sat on a limb shaking himself and preening his feathers with an "I guess I showed him!" attitude. The smaller female lit beside him, cuddled up as if to say "My hero!" and kissed him on the beak. I saw it through my binoculars.

Buzzards frequently share rookeries with herons and egrets, not to enjoy the camaraderie, but to prey on the eggs and young in the waterbirds' nests. I often wondered what buzzards do for a living when there is a dearth of road-killed armadillos, coons, and 'possums on the highways. I found they also eat over-ripe fruit and anything else that has a foul odor.

Just as buzzards prey on the young of other birds, their young are preyed upon. Mama buzzard makes predation easy for she is no nest builder. She just finds a convenient spot behind an old log, in a rotted stump, or in a clump of brush, and there deposits her eggs. Daddy once told me about finding a nest of fuzzy white chicks behind a log on a river island. The fact that a buzzard was frantically trying to drive him away, led him to conclude that it was a buzzard's nest, and my recent research confirms it.

Buzzards are rapidly declining—especially the black vulture—due largely to a decrease in food sources. Their staple food is carrion, and strong, soaring wings allow them to fly high and afar in search of it. At one time, large numbers of cattle and deer succumbed to diseases, especially screwworms. Most of these diseases have been controlled, and the screwworm fly has been virtually eradicated. Dead domestic animals are burned or buried to prevent spread of disease and to discourage predators. Black vultures are at a particular disadvantage because they rely on the turkey vulture's keen sense of smell to lead them to carrion. The gas emitted by decomposing animal matter is wafted into the upper air and the high-soaring birds home in on it. Nowadays, buzzards depend largely on nightly road kills.

The scavengers are an important link in the balance of nature. When we get so sanitary-minded that we keep every unpleasant thing out of sight and smell, we will take the vulture's place and he will become rare—like the California Condor, which you might call a great big buzzard. The last of the condors have been trapped and taken to a place where they are caged, protected, and released. We need them—if for no other purpose than an excuse to quote the childhood buzzard-counting poem that predicted our future:

> One for sorrow, two for joy;
> Three for a letter, four for a boy;
> Five for silver, six for gold;
> Seven for fortunes never been told.
> Eight for a date
> (nine and ten I don't remember);
> Eleven for Heaven and twelve for Hell.

Before we left Round Lake, I had to know one thing—did the boundaries of the Big Thicket National Preserve include this enchanted forest? I walked to the west until the familiar yellow paint on a straight line of trees told me that some farseeing, or lucky, planner had included the entire bend. It was then that I raised my eyes and said, "Thank you, Almighty God, for this beautiful example of your creative genius. Please, God, may it never be desecrated."

Later, at Park Service headquarters, I found that Tom Lubbert, Big Thicket National Preserve Manager, had cut off the large bend as an "uneconomic remnant" and included it in the preserve, having no idea of what was there. Call it luck, serendipity, or the providence of God—whatever—it survives! And the reason? Because it was deemed worthless by the owners.

BEAVERS

River Mile 101.4 2:00 P.M.

After Round Lake, the river makes a fairly straight course for a few miles with high ground on the east side. On the west side, a drainage enters the river from a slough, a cypress swamp, and a series of spring branches. I was attracted to the site by the many freshly gnawed stumps of willows on the

Beavers

upper sandbar, and found a series of classic beaver dams across the drainage, creating several small reservoirs.

The beaver, *Castor canadensis*, is North America's largest rodent and has been here a long time. In fact, during the Oligocene Epoch some millions of years ago, it was much larger than it is at present. In exploring the fossil beds in the eroded banks of the high bluff just below the dam at Town Bluff, I once found a tooth that was identified as having belonged to the Texas giant beaver.

Beaver-gnawed sticks are common sights on sandbars or sometimes floating down the stream. Each individual tooth mark is five millimeters wide. They eat the soft cambium layer and leave the wood white and bare. Unlike the omnivorous otter, they eat only plant food, preferring birch, willow, and cottonwood. They also practice "copraphagy," the eating of their own soft, green excrement. It seems it must go through their digestive system twice before the nutrients are absorbed.

Beavers spend a great deal of time under water, sometimes fifteen minutes per dive. Their over-sized liver provides extra storage space for oxygenated blood, and nostrils and ears have valves that close automatically when the animal submerges. They also have extra eyelids which close under water but through which they can still see, and lips that close behind front teeth allowing them to chew under water without drowning. The tail is large and flat and acts as a heat-regulating organ as well as a warning device. If a person or animal enters its territory, which is marked by scented mounds, the beaver hisses and slaps his tail on the water. It makes a rather loud splash which is alarming when heard at dusk or night time. Its voice consists of low to high-pitched whines, whimpers, and whistles. Ranger Ken Tiege told me of reading a book about a man who raised a baby beaver and found that it had a definite language, using different pitches, tones, and sounds to indicate whatever message it wanted to convey, and they learned to communicate with each other.

The beaver is monogamous, that is, one female and one male live together for life and raise a litter of three or four kits per year. Breeding takes place in water or in underground dens. Normally, three generations stay together as a family with a maximum of twelve to the colony. The yearlings begin to wander and the two-year-olds disperse and establish new colonies. They are not forced out—there is no aggression—rather, they enjoy one another's company, dancing, and wrestling and playing like children.

Most activity is nocturnal, though I have watched them play around in the daytime at my place on Lake Hyatt where I watched one chase a duck round and round in a circle. They build and repair their dams at night and will dig canals to ponds so they can float building materials from a distance. The term "busy as a beaver" was come by honestly. The beaver was born to gnaw. In fact if he does not, his teeth grow until he can't close his mouth and he starves. They're pretty ambitious, too, for I have seen trees thirty inches in diameter gnawed almost through.

Beavers have been both benefactor and malefactor in their relations with humans. Their role in protecting the environment and in the conservation of soil and water is legend. Their dams on small streams and tributaries hold back rainwater in small reservoirs where it seeps into the soil, elevating the water table. The water trickles gradually through the loose material of the dam rather than rushing downstream to join that from other streams and flood lowlands. Loose soil is held behind the dams instead of being washed away by floodwaters.

In the 1700s and 1800s, beaver fur was the most widely and intensively sought natural resource in America and was almost completely depleted by the 1900s. In order to help control flooding, the U. S. Soil Conservation Service began restocking beavers in the 1920s to 1950s. There were beavers here in times past, as records of a fur company which headquartered at Tevis Bluff show that they bought beaver pelts from the Indians and French trappers, but I don't know whether these here in Big Thicket country now are descendents of the original population or migrated from restocked areas. They were practically extinct when I was young. There is a tale told that the U. S. Soil Conservation Service people were transporting some beavers in wooden cages through Tyler County in the 1930s when they stopped in Woodville for lunch. Returning to their truck, they found that some beavers had chewed their way to freedom and escaped down nearby Turkey Creek and that this is how they returned to our area.

Beavers are not appreciated here in Southeast Texas as their pelts in the South are not valued for fur and their dam building is deplored by the large land owners. Many acres of pasture and timber land are inundated by their activities. The late former Governor Bill Daniel, who owned the famous Plantation Ranch near Rye, got apoplectic when beavers were mentioned. A dam on a small drainage through his ranch flooded over two hundred acres of improved pasture. The dam was bulldozed away but the beavers then moved it downstream to a fence and incorporated the fence into the new structure. It too, was bulldozed and the water deepened enough to discourage further dam building. Not to be discouraged, the little engineers then moved into the center of a large culvert which carried the little stream under a road and stopped it up. The only way it could have been removed was to blow the whole thing up with dynamite, so Daniel retreated and left the field to the beavers.

A tale is told of a bulldozer that was lost to the beavers. A lumber company bulldozed a dam, which was flooding a good portion of timber-producing woods. It was rebuilt, so they bulldozed it again. The third time, the soil was so thoroughly worked up that the bulldozer got hopelessly mired, and the second dozer brought in to pull it out almost got stuck also, so it was abandoned. Chalk another one up for the beavers.

I have been peeved at the little critters myself as I have watched our small streams like Turkey, Hickory, and Theuvenin (pronounced Toodleum) Creeks littered with trees that had been undermined on the cutbank and toppled across the creek. While they will build the traditional dams and lodges, they prefer to dig their homes into the cutbank of streams with an entrance just below water level. A few years ago, there must have been a population explosion of beavers on Turkey Creek as there wasn't a bend which didn't have all the big trees on the cutbank sides lying across the stream, which made canoeing impossible.

Apparently, there has also been an increase in predator population for there is much less evidence of beaver activity in recent years. Recently, I have seen more otters, which with wolves, bobcats, and minks, prey on beaver, than ever before. Eventually, a balance will be achieved and maintained.

Beavers posed quite a mystery for me on my trip down the Neches. In the mornings, I found tracks with broad, wavy lines alongside which I could not, for the life of me, identify. On the last lap of my trip, I pulled my boat up on the head of a sandbar late in the evening and walked down to the other end. I heard a loud slap on the water and, after approaching the area, found a freshly gnawed willow branch. Another freshly cut branch had been dragged down to the water's edge, making the wavy lines which had so mystified me, and beaver tracks! The mystery had been solved! Also, the loud splash in the water which had so alarmed me my first night on the river, was identified. Ah well! Life would be dull if we didn't find at least a few things to wonder about.

CANYONLANDS

River Mile 101.3 2:30 P.M.

If you have planned a leisurely voyage down the river, not wanting to miss any feature, you will surely want to devote an entire day to exploring the canyonlands of the Big Thicket. The best place to leave the river is at River Mile 101.3. Someone has cleared a landing here, and there is a rough roadway up the short bluff to the terrace above the river. This opening soon intersects an old road that follows the lower slope of the ancient bluff line of the Neches River between the uplands and the swamps and sloughs of the floodplains. Since the uplands here are over 100 feet above the floodplain, the bluff line is dissected by deep erosional gullies that I call canyons. Following the road, you cross many small spring branches, each of which comes from a canyon, and you will want to explore each to its head. Don't count on seeing them all, though, for it would take several days to explore the whole area.

There are no more beautiful forests anywhere than can be seen here. While the uplands have been clearcut and bulldozed, the slopes of the canyon walls are canopied over with beech, magnolia, white oak, and loblolly pines, as are the crests between canyons. Most of these crests have been butchered. It is the utmost incompetent forest management to bulldoze bare a steep, sandy slope, yet it has been done here. It immediately erodes. There is one section just north of the access point I mentioned which belongs to Temple Inland and which has been only selectively harvested over long intervals. There, one can see what the rest of the area would look like if properly managed. Perhaps the enlightened environmental policies of Temple-Eastex (now Temple Inland) can be attributed to the fact that Arthur Temple, Jr., a third generation Southeast Texan, dictated those policies and not some computer in Chicago or New York. It makes a difference when it is the land you and your forefathers trod that is being "managed."

The canyons have abrupt, steep headward erosion into the uplands, perennial springs bubble up at the base and flow downward over small waterfalls, sometimes through steep, narrow walls, or over broad, flat beds of white sand. The water is ice cold at all times of the year and pure—at least I have not experienced any unpleasantness after drinking it.

Each canyon is different due to the fact that one portion of the bluff might be an exposure of gray, limey Fleming Clay while another, of acidic white sands and red clays of the Willis Formation. Streams coming from the Fleming exposure will have a milky tint while those from the Willis will be crystal clear. Plants have a decided preference for soils of a particular pH. The high pH of the Fleming supports plants not found anywhere else in the Big Thicket area. In fact, some of them, such as the chalk maple, are not found elsewhere in Texas.

Another factor in botanical diversity is when forests have not been disturbed for a long time and a deep, rich mulch has accumulated. Plants that have become rare such as mayapple, Indian pink, bloodroot, cranefly orchid, etc., cover the forest floor here.

One of the most exciting botanical experiences of my life was when I found the yellow lady's slipper orchid in one of the canyons. I was working on a floodplain study with a young man from the U. S. Fish and Wildlife Service, David Tilson, and we were looking for a route down the steep slope into the floodplain around Round Lake when our vehicle became stuck in the slick clay. While David was looking the situation over to arrive at a plan of action, I began to explore the nearby forest. Suddenly, the ground seemed to drop beneath my feet and I was looking straight down 20 feet or so. I began to descend, sliding on a mat of leaves, and reached a shelf where I again peered downward perhaps another 15 feet or so into a pool of blue water surrounded by ferns and jack-in-the-pulpits. Descending and circling the pool, I saw, rising tall amid the lush ferns and mosses, the unmistakable stalk and seedpod of the yellow lady's slipper orchid and was simply transported to regions of ecstasy. David came scrambling down at my whoops and hollers and I grabbed him and danced around him several times before I could tell him what I had found. It just takes a fellow botanist to understand the feeling.

This orchid has all but disappeared in Texas due to collecting and loss of habitat, and it is unheard of that it be found so far south. Later, in the spring, I returned here and found three plants in bloom and several immature ones. Since then, I have scoured these canyons for other locations, but it appears that this is the sole site in Southeast Texas, though a few survive further north in one of the National Forest Wilderness areas. That is sometimes the way with this orchid—one or two plants might be found and no others within a hundred miles.

In exploring the various canyons, I have found that each seems to have a dominant botanical feature, so I have named them accordingly: there is the Lady's Slipper Canyon, Tiger Lily Canyon, Jack-in-the-Pulpit Canyon, Fern Canyon, Azalea Canyon, Bloodroot Canyon, etc.

At the present time, the canyonlands are still owned by timber companies and are not open to the public. Hopefully, the bill now in Congress creating a Canyonlands Unit of the Big Thicket National Preserve will make this beautiful area available for all of us to enjoy. In the meantime, if you do have reason to go there, let me give a word of warning. The forest edge here is a favorite place for the timber rattler. It lives in the cool, shady forest and forages out into the cutover areas for rats, rabbits, and ground nesting birds. I have seen several here and they are huge! About as frightening a sight as one can imagine. I have read that a number of these monsters hole up together in sheltered places. When I think of how I have scrambled around the slopes of these canyons possibly coming within biting distance of many of them, I shudder even today.

A very short distance below the canyonlands exit I saw a small waterfall on the western bluff side of the river and, naturally, wanted to see where it originated. Usually, they signify something interesting back in the forest and this didn't prove a disappointment.

Following the small stream, I came upon a beautiful cypress swamp and, walking around it, I discovered that the old bluff line of the ancient Neches was almost in sight of the river here. The topography rises sharply and has many fern-fringed springs. These springs feed the cypress swamp. It is an area well worth exploring, especially if one does not have the time to take in the canyonlands.

"NIGGER" BEND

River Mile 100.1

Downstream from the canyonlands access at the next bend on the low side, a small stream enters the river, The area has been grazed by cattle and is open and parklike—a very pleasant place to camp. This bend was once known as Sycamore Bend but was later called "Nigger" Bend. My inquiries as to the origin of this name brought several different responses. One said that two fishermen found the body of a Negro man caught on their trotline and, since they could not find out who he was, the body was buried nearby. Another said that the Jones boys had hung him for some reason and thrown his body into the river. (That is not their real name. Some of the Jones boys are still around and are not the kind of folks I would want to be upset with me.) Another said, "Oh, he just couldn't swim the river with that chain he stole." A macabre joking way of saying the chain was wrapped around him and he was thrown into the river to drown.

Unfortunately, it was common in this area, since the Civil War, that white men would take matters in their own hands and kill a black man for a real or imagined offense, or just to make sure they would "keep their place," and the lawmen would just look the other way. A sad but true commentary on our history.

My mother would not permit us children to use the word "nigger," but to use the correct term "Negro" which is an ancient and honorable designation. I don't like the term "Black" because it is inaccurate, for most of the people so-called are not black at all, but different shades of brown. Ah well! There will always be something real or imaginary to divide humans for somebody's advantage or profit.

WORK'S BLUFF

River Mile 99.8 4:00 P.M.

It's easy to know where you are when Work's Bluff rises high on the east bank of the river. There are a few camphouses there and always some boats tied up at the base. When I was exploring and mapping out the canyonlands, this was an important spot, for there is an artesian well gushing ice-cold water into a large concrete vat right beside the road. On a summer day of fast walking in 100-degree heat, this oasis practically saved my life more than once. I'm told it has been here for many years.

The Work's Bluff Road crossed the Neches and continued to join the north/south Weiss Bluff/Bevilport Road. There was a ferry that operated until the late 1920s. The last operator was Tom Bower.

Work's Bluff was named either for Philip A. Work or his father, Dr. John Work, who came to Texas from Kentucky in 1838. He and W. B. Hay acquired six tracts of land in the Pemberton League along the Neches. While Philip Work was better known, the bluff was probably named for his father who had a plantation here and a steamboat landing with warehouses on the bluff. Philip Work was associated with the Neches also, however, for he owned the steamboat *Tom Parker*.

Philip Work had an illustrious career in the military and in the law. Admitted to the bar at age 21, he practiced law in Woodville until the Civil War. He was a delegate to the state secession convention in 1861, where he strongly supported Texas' secession from the Union and went home to organize a company of Texas militia called the Woodville Rifles. It was mustered into the Confederate Army at New Orleans and became Co. F. of the First Texas Infantry Regiment, Hood's Texas Brigade. He became regimental commander during the battle of Gaines Mill and led the Texas Infantry in eight major battles where they suffered 82.3 % casualties—the worst sustained by any regiment of the war, either Union or Confederate. The Mann family of Woodville lost five sons in this regiment to the war—a grievous loss! In speaking with the Mann patriarch in Woodville, I was much moved at the fervor still evinced by the family. It was just as though it happened yesterday! I could understand, for I was brought up on stories of our family's involvement in the war, the trunks full of worthless Confederate money, and the ominous "Northerners." (My family did not call them "Yankees.")

Dr. John Work was a surgeon for the Texas Infantry during the war and served during the most terrible battles. Philip Work became ill during the battle of Gettysburg and was returned to Texas where, after he regained his health, he raised and commanded a company that joined Col. Terry's Texas Cavalry Regiment from 1864 to the end of the war. After the war, Work resumed his law practice in Woodville, spent nine years in New Orleans in the law and steamboat business, but returned to live out his life in Hardin County where he specialized in land law until his death in 1911. He and his wife, Adeline Lea, had four children.

I had tried unsuccessfully to find information on the Work family and was winding up my manuscript when Cecil Tebbs, a land lawyer I had known when he worked with the Corps of Engineers land acquisition team when the Big Thicket Preserve was acquired, telephoned me. It seems that Cecil is a great-grandson of Philip Work and a conversation with Bill Jewel, his former supervisor at Big Thicket National Preserve, reminded him to contact me. He promised to send me some family history. What a thrill when I received that packet of information in the mail! I still didn't find the answer to one matter about which I have wondered: where was the plantation house of Dr. Work? Was it on the bluff, which would have certainly been a beautiful site, or on the adjacent upland? Perhaps it had been on the bluff and had been, like the Pedigo house, moved upland after the flood of 1884. There are two lovely sites on midslope between the bluff and the uplands, which are no doubt old homesites for there are liveoak trees growing there. Liveoaks do not grow this far inland but were planted by the settlers as shade trees.

Work's Bluff is cut in half by a spring branch that, in trying to reach the water level of the river, has created a series of small, noisy waterfalls in the sandstone. I followed this little stream to its source in a brake in the uplands. Unfortunately, its watershed had been clearcut a few years ago and the stream and its environments were choked with brush. Someday perhaps, with enlightened management, it will recover. How sad that every time the hand of man touches something beautiful, it is made ugly!

Just below the bluff, the cutting action of the river has created a sheer face, which exhibits at least three strata of varying soil types. Over a base of sandstone, in midbluff, there is a stratum of rocklike gray clay overlain by a porous sandy silt. Where these strata join, water from the porous strata seeps out and drops into the river below, giving the impression that the bluff is continually weeping. Ferns and mosses growing in the moist soil of the junctures and the sound of the falling water create a very pleasing effect.

NIGHT SOUNDS

River Mile 98 4:30 P.M.

My campsite the second night of my voyage was behind a fringe of willows on a short sandbar and under a thicket of sycamore trees at the woods' edge. It got dark early, as the sky was cloudy, so I hurried my few chores and spent the early part of the night writing by flashlight. It wasn't long before a gentle wind came up and raindrops began to patter on the tent roof. I love to sleep where I can hear rain on the roof and the wind in the trees overhead, but the sound of wind in the dry sycamore leaves is not as pleasant as in pine boughs.

The windsong of deciduous forests is a harsh rustle and clatter, which alarms rather than soothes as the pinesong does. It gives a premonition of a storm approaching, of restless spirits rushing endlessly from one place to another seeking rest. The darkness beneath the heavy canopy of leaves is oppressive and you want to put something between you and that darkness, so you snuggle into your sleeping bag and peer out at the luminescent fungi which glow on dead, rotted logs.

It takes a summer night to appreciate sleeping under the canopy of a hardwood forest. There is no feeling of airy openness. It can be an interesting experience, especially if you are an entomology aficionado, in other words, a bug nut. You must stop all conversation, lie very still, and concentrate on listening to the night sounds. Suddenly, you realize all space is filled with deafening noises—shrieks, squeaks, squawks, trills, and cadenzas—each insect and frog in mad competition to be heard by something to which its sound has some vital, urgent message. The night sounds range from the highest note discernable to the ear, all the way down the scale to the basso profundo of the bullfrog, until a crescendo of sound is reached. Then, as if the hand of some unseen maestro draws an abrupt close to the rhapsody, there is dead silence. Soon, some impatient musician tootles a cautious note and off they all go again into the same never-to-be-finished—only interrupted—symphony.

If one takes advantage of those periods of silence to listen even more closely, one hears a very subtle pattering sound. Something is showering like tiny raindrops from the overhead canopy of leaves. Some evening when you are in a hardwood forest overnight, stretch a bedsheet over the ground and next morning you can see what this "rain" was. Each tree overhead is a banquet table to the larvae of a myriad of insects. Moths and butterflies lay their eggs on the type of tree that their offspring eat. They do nothing in this caterpillar stage but gobble and grow and pass pellets of chewed vegetation from which their digestive systems have extracted the nutrients. The amount and different sizes and shapes of pellets on your sheet give an indication of the number and variety of caterpillars eating away over your head the night before.

One of our park rangers came in once with a strange tale and a sample of some material taken from a forest floor. He said that the entire forest floor was covered with what looked like frost, but, of course, was not.

Examining his sample, I saw that it was a caterpillar pellet invaded by a fungus which in fruit produced a pale-gray furry covering for the pellet. Since the entire forest floor was covered with the pellets, the impression was eerie to say the least.

OWLS

Another reward of sleeping in hardwood forests in the summer is that they are the habitat of owls, and you can get caught up in a hooting match. It is impossible to resist joining in when all around you they are calling and answering: "Hoo Hoo Hoo!" And sometimes, on clear nights in the winter and spring, they will give a loud, frightening scream. The horned owl can navigate in forests, but prefers open land or water courses. It is called "the tiger of the air" and can even catch bats in midair. I've known of them taking puppies and even dogs from the yard.

The barred owl lives in woods and swamps, but at night it moves into open country to hunt. It is not as fast or as powerful as the horned owl, but depends on its stealthy, quiet approach. It is the noisiest of owls, however, in its calling, with a variety of chuckles, grunts, and laughs, sometimes sounding like a barking dog. It gives eight accented hoots in two groups of four hoots: "Hoohoo-hoohoo-hoohoo-hooaw!" It is said that the owl is saying: "I cook for my wife and who cooks for you all!" It can be heard throughout the year, but especially in the winter and spring.

The screech owl lives in forests but is also frequent in cities. It does not screech nor hoot but has a tremulous wail, a mournful whinny, or it gives out a soft tremolo running down the scale or sometimes on a single pitch—something to make your hair stand on end on a dark night. It is most vocal in the fall, winter, and early spring.

Frequently, if you are near a grassy opening or sandbar, the rush of great wings can be heard as some owl swoops down and nips up a foraging mouse. Sandbars are safe foraging grounds for owls, but, unfortunately, so are grassy roadsides where mice and rabbits feed in the evenings, so their mortality rate is high on highways where they often swoop into speeding cars. I once picked up what I thought was an owl carcass, thinking to skin and mount it, when it came alive. I immobilized it by wrapping its broken wing and leg and took it home where it survived. I fed it on chicken gizzards and such, but it would not eat except from my hand. When it recovered, I decided it should be in the barn where it might capture some of its natural prey, but the resident crows and blue jays resented its presence, and the last I saw of it, it was winging its way through my woods escorted by a flock of smaller birds.

One of the worst things that can happen to a camper in the forest is to have a chuck-wills-widow roost within a half mile of your camp. All night long without cease they scream in a piercing, raucous voice: "Chuck WILLS-widow! Chuck WILLS widow!" Over and over and. Don't plan to get any sleep.

When daylight comes, each little singer (or screamer) crawls back into his rotted log, under the forest floor litter, or just disappears as green-on-green or brown-on-brown. You look all around and just can't believe that there is not a shred of visible evidence of all that noise. The sun bursts through the dawn mist and the other group of singers, the birds, take over. In a paean of praise to the earth, the swells of music rise with the sun. After having been awake all night, high on starlight and drunk on dew (or cursing a chuck-wills-widow), this shining climax so surrounds and fills you with its brilliance that you feel as though you have just emerged from a dark womb, the first human to rise on its feet on the newly created earth and face the first dawn.

Before finally going to sleep that night under the sycamore trees, I opened the flap of my tent and stuck my head out to see what the weather was doing. A pale moon appeared and disappeared behind thin clouds, and I realized that it hadn't been raining at all. The wind was causing the dead sycamore leaves to turn loose and fall, and the sound of their dropping on my tent roof was exactly the same as raindrops.

WILD GEESE

The wild geese had flown over all that second day and into the night. The long V skeins against the cobalt blue skies of the dying Indian summer, and their faint, nasal gabble hinted that not far behind them were gray, cold masses of clouds and fading vegetation. Since geese are vegetarians, they find little to eat after frost kills the tender greenery, and submerged aquatic plants are locked under sheets of ice. So they move southward ahead of the killing freezes in the same ways as countless generations of their ancestors, until some genetic voice says, "You can stop. This is the place."

White-front and snow geese nest in the Arctic while Canada geese choose the wetlands of western Canada and Hudson Bay. In early October, they begin a gathering of flocks. This is called mobbing. These groups leave together and return together and each skein is an extended family group. Geese have

Wild Geese

strong family ties and are among the rare animals that mate for life. Led by the family patriarch, they fly the 1,200 to 2,000 miles at an average 61 to 63 miles per hour and arrive at the coastal plains of Texas and Louisiana within 35 to 50 hours. While flying over mountains, clouds, or at night, they go as high as 8,000 feet. They fly higher over land than at sea and higher at night than day. Over water, they fly only two or three feet above the surface of the water to avoid adverse winds.

Routes and stopovers are long established and known by the leaders. At one time, many ducks and geese stopped over at Steinhagen Lake (Dam B), but herbicides were used to destroy the aquatic vegetation because it interfered with boating and fishing, so the flocks sought another feeding and resting area. Very few have returned. Once a migration pattern is broken, it is almost impossible to reinstate it.

Mortality is heavy on these migrations. Many collide with tall lighted structures or TV towers, and sometimes bad weather catches up with them. Heavy snowfall once forced large numbers to drop into Lake Huron and drown, and over 5,000 dead geese were counted in one mile of shoreline on that occasion.

The geese that are seen along the Neches River during migration are usually there because some mishap or a storm has separated them from their group, and they have come down to get reoriented or to recuperate. I saw a moving example of this once while floating the river with some birdwatchers.

A pair of white-front geese were swimming just ahead of our boat. Occasionally, the male would rise and fly a short distance ahead but would come back and alight between our boat and his mate. He kept between us for a considerable distance and, finally, they went to shore on a secluded sandbar. It was evident from her limping gait that the female was injured and unable to fly and her mate just wouldn't leave her, even putting his own life between her and danger.

Thousands of geese spend the winter on the coastal marshes and rice fields of Jefferson County just south of us. The Anahuac Wildlife Refuge is a good place to see them. Snow geese, Canada geese, white-front, and blue geese are very common there. These are the geese we see and hear flying overhead.

The cry of the wild goose has always stirred the heart of man. In seventh century China, the poet, Po Chu-I, wrote:

Against the lamp I sit by the South window
Listening to the sleet and the wind in the dark;
Desolation deepens the night among the villages.
Through the snow I hear the lost wild goose calling.

A recent comment on the subject by that raconteur of yesteryore, Don Streeter, is not so romantic, but is certainly realistic: "There's no denying that the sight of a V of geese high and ghostly against the moon gives you a sort of 'Hey, wait for me' feeling. But, I beg of you! Don't go! And don't be lured by that old song 'I must go where the wild goose goes,' or you'll end up in a marsh full of mud and squirmy things, or out in a prairie where a cow may step on you. Believe me, you're better off where you are."

To me, there is no feeling quite so cozy as lying in bed under warm quilts on a cold wintry night, listening to sleet hitting the window panes and the faint call of wild geese passing overhead. It stirs a feeling in us so primitive that we can't quite give a name to it: a vague restlessness, an urge that we, too, must be moving on, to somewhere. It's going to get colder. Gather up the tents, cooking pots, sleeping furs, and trail food. Shoulder the packs and move on with the animals ahead of the ice. No matter how secure we feel today with Social Security and insulated houses with central heat, all it takes is the cry of the wild goose to remind us that all things are transient, and so are we.

As I lay in the darkness listening to the omens of approaching bad weather, these lines from William Cullen Bryant's poem, "To a Waterfowl," came to mind:

> There is a Power whose care
> Teaches thy way along that pathless coast—
> The desert and the illimitable air—
> Lone, wandering, but not lost.
>
> He who, from zone to zone,
> Guides through the night thy certain flight,
> In the long way which I must tread alone,
> Will lead my steps aright.

Part One

Day 3

BOB PARVIN

River Mile 97.8

Just after launching off on my third morning, I discovered that I had stopped too soon the previous evening, for just around the bend was a perfect camping site. There were two open-water lakes in a broad, short-grass pasture with a ridge between the lakes and the river. The ridge was populated with young pine trees which provided a cozy shelter. Apparently, grazing cattle kept the area as clean of weeds and brush as a mowed lawn. Several shore birds were wading the shallow edges of the lakes. They were common egrets, little green herons, and what appeared to be willets. I took my binoculars and walked over the berm, around the lakes and behind a grove of vegetation in the center of the large opening. Behind the vegetation was a beautiful oxbow lake, a remnant of what had once been a large bend in the river. Judging from the tracks, many animals come from out of the woods to graze on the grass, so it is a good site for animal watching as well as birdwatching.

On a recent foray downriver with photojournalist Bob Parvin, we chose the site for a night's camp. Bob Parvin is one of my favorite people. Handsome and charming, he is the Hollywood image of the globe-trotting photojournalist, has had worldwide experience and success in his field and, unlike many professionals I've encountered, is most generous with his knowledge and his work. That evening, we set up our shelters: mine a simple one-man tent and his a Viet Nam-style hammock that he hung rather high between two pine trees. I laughed and told him he would have quite a jolt if he fell out during the night. We built a campfire and sat there on the ridge overlooking the river and ate cheese and snacks and drank a bottle of wine he had brought, and talked.

Presently, a motorboat came upstream with a spotlight and stopped at the mouth of the inlet near us. A voice called up and apologized for disturbing us and said they were just going to set a net and would then leave. Bob answered: "No problem. You're not disturbing us at all." Then, suspecting what they were doing was against rules and regulations, and thinking to have a little fun, I called out: "You boys ought to be careful. I happen to be a park ranger," which was true. Suddenly, the spotlight flashed in my face and the voice laughed and said: "Aw, we know you. Y'all come on down and have a beer." Bob said: "We have plenty. Come up and have a beer with us." So they came up and we talked about how it used to be, and the sins of the Park Service in trying to regulate their life on the river. I carefully led the conversation around to the advantages of the Preserve—what was happening to the woods and river, and that the Park Service had taken it from the lumber industry, not from the people, and was trying to protect and save it for them the best they could. They knew I was right, but you don't turn loose from generations-old habits overnight. After awhile, they announced they had to go and set the rest of their nets and invited us to go along. Bob eagerly assented, not having had the experience, but I declined. Later, I told Bob that if law enforcement rangers had caught them, he would have been hauled into jail with the rest, charged, and fined. Actually, that was an exaggeration. They would have probably only issued tickets and confiscated the net if it were indeed illegal.

In the middle of the night, I heard a thump and a grunt and, looking out my tent, saw that Bob had indeed fallen through his hammock (it had split) and hit the dirt. Apparently, it had picked up a bad case of jungle rot in Southeast Asia and was ready to disintegrate. He spent the rest of the night on the ground.

Someday, the Park service will develop the Neches for a canoe trail with designated campsites. My vote is for this site and Round Lake as the two best sites on this section of river to spend a night.

RED BLUFF

River Mile 97.3 9:00 A.M.

Next morning, after leaving the land-locked lakes, I began to round a bend with a big sandbar, but, looking up on the west side of the river, I saw a high bluff covered with beeches, magnolias, and white oaks, and had a sudden desire to climb it. Cutting across the current, I pulled in where a small streamlet came into the river, climbed out and made my ascent. There were rock outcroppings with small springs trickling out here and there and clumps of Christmas fern all about. Upon reaching the top, I sat and surveyed the scene before me. Below and to my left was a beautiful clear-water cypress swamp, a low berm, the river, and the wide sweep of white sandbar on the opposite side, all framed by the trunks and overhanging branches of dark-green magnolia and green-gold beeches. What a view! Inspection showed that the Park Service boundary came very near the edge of the bluff, but at least that much was preserved!

River Mile 97 10:00 A.M.

Returning to my boat, I continued to paddle around the bend where the river, turned aside by a stratum of resistant rock and clay, makes a sharp turn to the east. The bluff, which loomed high above me, is called Red Bluff because of the rich red-brown color. It rises at least a hundred feet, and the river cutting into it has exposed a stratum of rock which has broken into large boulders at the base. Such a sight is rare on the Neches, so it is somewhat of a shock to come upon it unaware.

There was a riverboat landing at the lower end of Red Bluff and I should have made a greater effort to dig into its history but was running out of time. Important pioneer families here were Thompson, Jeffcoat, Jenkins, Ramer, Sheffield, Jordan, Mayo, Bingham, and others.

According to local residents, there is an old cemetery called Thompson cemetery somewhere on this bluff, so I thought I'd pull in and investigate. Finding an erosional gully which provided an easy ramp up the steep bluff, I climbed up and found the usual people evidence: the ruts of an old road parallel to the river with branches leading away into the forest. These roads no doubt connected the riverboat landing and warehouses with the farms that used the riverboats to ship produce and receive goods. Pioneer plant species have densely populated what evidently were open areas with buildings and gardens and a few scattered mounds, which turned out to be trash piles. The age of a community can be determined by the contents of trash dumps. The earlier residents did not have tin cans or glass bottles and most utensils were made of wood which rotted when broken and thrown away.

After a few years' covering of leaf fall and blown and washed silt, these trash piles are only nondescript mounds until the digging of armadillos and other small burrowing animals exposes the rusty tin and shards of glass and crockery. The old trash dumps in this area are choice habitats for the delicate little ebony spleenwort fern. These mounds on Red Bluff had a velvet covering of mosses and clumps of ebony spleenwort fern the beauty of which took the breath when viewed unexpectedly. Nature seems to have a habit of trying to hide the ugliness that we humans strew liberally everywhere we roam over the planet.

THOMPSON CEMETERY

All that could be found of the Thompson Cemetery were two aluminum markers, such as funeral homes place on new graves, in a thicket of young pine saplings at the edge of an abandoned field called the red field. Imprinted in the soft metal were: Ephraim Thompson, Born 1794 in Kentucky, Died 1836; and Susan Grigsby Thompson, Born 1799 in Kentucky, Died 1849.

According to my maps, we were on the Ephraim Thompson survey, so Mr. Thompson, was, therefore, an important member of the small group of Anglo-American pioneers who settled a "league and a labor" of land in the Neches River valley. He was not mentioned in the *Handbook of Texas*, so I retrieved Mrs. Vivian Jordan's thorough and informative "History of the Spurger Area" from Park Service files and found that Ephraim had been among a group of local men who met with Sam Houston when old Sam was trying to drum up support for the inclusion of Texas in the Union. Here, I ran into a snag. If Ephraim had indeed died in 1836, he couldn't have been around to greet Sam Houston in 1840. Either the inscription on the marker is inaccurate or it was Ephraim, Jr., who met with Houston.

While I could get little information on Ephraim, his wife's maiden name, Grigsby, gave a clue to her identity. Joseph Grigsby arrived in Texas in 1827 with eleven of his thirteen children and settled on the east side of the river adjacent to George Smythe's holdings. Smythe married Grigsby's daughter, Frances. Since Joseph's mother was named Susannah, it is likely that Susan Thompson was also his daughter. Apparently, the life of a merchant suited

Joseph Grigsby better than the unremitting toil of pioneer farm life, for just after the war of independence, he moved to a site downriver which is now Port Neches, but was then called Grigsby's Bluff, where he operated a mercantile store, steamboat wharves, and warehouse.

Ephraim and Susan probably married in Kentucky for she was 28 years of age when they came to Texas, far past marrying age in those days. Did he really die at age 42? Did they have children? Why are there no Thompson descendants in the area? So many questions arise as I try to conjure up flesh and blood human beings from the molecules of minerals now mingled with the clay of Red Bluff and a few fragments of written information. One thing is certain: There is no lack of mystery in Big Thicket country. At least Ephraim and Susan have not been completely forgotten. The Raymer family saw to it that their last resting place was marked with their names.

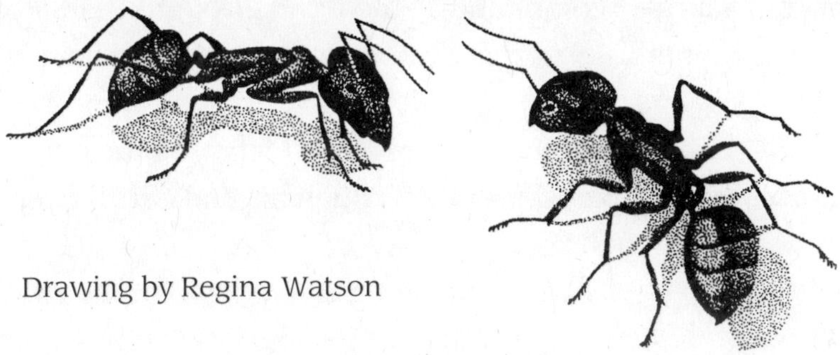

Drawing by Regina Watson

TOWN ANTS

In my search for Thompson Cemetery, I found an open area, sparsely vegetated, probably because of the deep sand. Well-drained, sandy sites are preferred habitat of town ants, sometimes called farmer ants because they plant and cultivate their own food; or umbrella ants because they run about carrying a circular piece of leaf over their heads. *Formes*, as they are formally known, are the most interesting of the many native species of ants in Southeast Texas. An average colony measures about ten paces in diameter. On the surface, it is a collection of sandy mounds with an entrance passage in each, but five to ten feet below is another world with a civilization that matches our own in complexity and far surpasses ours in efficiency. Every ant citizen is born and bred to fill specific needs of the community. The city consists of many chambers called formicaries, some of which contain gardens, and some are nurseries where the young are kept and cared for.

The lowest cavity is empty for it serves to drain rainwater which might enter the main entrance.

The town ant society is a matriarchy: ruled by a queen. She is fertile throughout her lifetime as she receives a supply of sperm at her one and only mating, so there is no need to support a nonproductive consort. The queen apparently knows the needs of the colony and regulates the numbers and types of workers by feeding the larvae chemicals called pheromones which her body produces. Since there is no need for males for procreation, all workers are female, even the "police persons."

The ants constantly communicate with one another by touching antennae. Pheromones are used in this process. Different combinations and concentrations of pheromones are left along a trail to relay certain messages: "This way to the food!" or "Here is the trail!" "Danger! Some sisters got smashed here!" The pheromones are used to permit individual and caste recognition, but ants also communicate by sound through stridulatory organs, much like grasshoppers. Sensory receptors are located in various parts of the body: thorax, legs, and antennae. One wishing to send a message scrapes her legs against her body, producing sounds which are barely audible to the human ear and which send vibrations through air and earth. Their language consists of different tones and pitches of stridulation. The message is transmitted through the soil and can be received down in the city. I've often wondered how an entire colony could know so quickly that something was happening on the surface. Smash a few ants and the entire population comes boiling out before you jump out of the way. Not ESP, just sonar.

It would be of academic interest to understand the language of the ants—much like learning to communicate with extraterrestrials whose language might even consist of wiggling the nose or batting the eyes. Who knows? It is hardly likely any such study will ever be done. There's no way in the world any money can be made from talking to ants, and economic feasibility is the name of the game in research. I do remember, however, how invaluable the Navajo language proved to be during World War II as an unbreakable code. Why not ant language? Anyway, it's a thought.

It is difficult to assign an order of importance to the different jobs the ants do. Every activity is pursued to ensure the perpetuation of the species through reproduction and food supply. There is no place for pleasure or leisure. Some castes are engineers, cutters and carriers, cleaners, chewers, farmers, nursemaids, and police.

The engineers are important because the design and construction of the colony is critical. If the entrance shafts are not planned properly, the city will flood and the colony drown. The gardens require an exact amount of light—either too much or too little and the crops will die. Highways about two inches wide are routed and cleared to facilitate the gathering and transport of leaves. I once followed an ant highway over a torturous route down a high, sandy bluff to a slough, over the slough on a fallen tree onto a hummock and up to the top of a tall water tupelo tree. Why they chose the tupelo leaves over the plentiful yaupon which was also being harvested on the bluff right in the midst of the colony, only God and the Queen know.

The cutters' jaws are equipped with special tools for cutting a small circle of leaf. The ground at the base of trees and shrubs being harvested is littered with these green bits, whether accidentally or intentionally dropped, I do not know unless the cutters and carriers are separate castes. It would certainly save time if the cutter should spend the entire day cutting and not waste time and effort climbing up and down with every bit.

I have sat for long moments over these highways watching the trail of leaf bits moving like the current in a stream, over, under and around obstacles, and wondering such things as whether the engineer had road crews clear and prepare the roadways before leaf harvesting began, or if each ant, as she came across an obstacle, removed it until the sheer numbers of travelers cleared the road as they worked. I have watched small ants staggering along with loads that outweighed them by tens, and sometimes several ants cooperate in moving something too large for one ant.

Apparently some ants decide they have bitten off more than they can carry, for there were leaf bits scattered along the trail where they had been abandoned. They could have been dropped, however, when the time for work stopped. Above-ground work is carried on largely in mild, sunny weather. Ants do not work when it is dark and cloudy, or at the heat of noonday, nor in hot, dry weather because the heat dries out the bits of leaf before they reach the gardens. So they plug up the entrances to the city to prevent moisture loss and stay inside and probably do repair work. They certainly don't sit down and rest.

Some ants are construction workers, clearing passageways and digging and enlarging rooms. Others, born with large pinchers and bigger than the rest, are the police and will rush out to attack anything threatening the nest. These large ants are called maxima, the medium-sized are called media, and the smaller are called minima ants.

When an ant carries a leaf bit into the city, she is met by a smaller ant who cleans her body meticulously. They are very fastidious, probably to prevent spores of "weed" species of fungi from invading the gardens.

The leaf bit is turned over to the chewers who carefully cut the bit into a precise piece, moisten it with saliva and work it into a soft wad, which is then placed on the garden. The saliva contains an antibiotic that inhibits the growth of all fungus except the one they cultivate, which is the genus *Bromatia*. The saliva also fertilizes the fungus along with the ants' own excrement. Additional fertilizer is provided by pellets of caterpillar castings that are brought into the gardens. The threadlike mycelium permeates and feeds upon the leaf pulp and sends up fruiting bodies which are pruned to produce buds much like brussels sprouts. The buds are the staple diet of the ant. Great care is taken to remove any foreign species of fungus which might take over the gardens. When the growing medium has lost its fertility, it is removed and taken out of the city to a refuse heap.

While these workers are dedicated to the perpetuation of the colony through providing a stable, year-round food supply, others are concerned with reproduction. The queen lays eggs that are taken by nursemaids and stacked in nursery caverns. When the eggs develop into larvae, the nursemaids feed them constantly. They are stacked with their heads facing the hallway so the nurse ants go down the rows poking food into open mouths. They know which have not yet been fed, because the hungry babies cry with a mewing sound, opening wide their little mouths.

At a certain time of the year, the queen lays eggs that produce future queens and male consorts. When they mature, there is great excitement in the city. The nursemaids bring a starting (spores and mycelium) of the food fungus and place it in a receptacle called a buccal pocket on the heads of the young queens so they can begin their own gardens in the new colonies that they will establish. Males and females fly into the air. They are the only ones provided with wings. Mating takes place and the male falls to the earth and dies—his only reason for existence having been fulfilled—and the female finds a suitable place to settle her new city, alights, and begins to lay eggs. Her wings drop off, as they will never be needed again, and she lives off energy stored in her wing muscles and perhaps eats a few eggs until workers are mature enough to plant and tend the gardens and produce food. And thus the cycle continues. Her colony may reach upward of 500,000 individuals.

There are many other species of ants in our area, with many interesting and diverse cultures. Harvester ants gather all manner of seeds, especially in the autumn when most grass, legume, and forb seeds are maturing. The gatherers bring the seeds into the caverns where a special caste of chewers, born with enormous jaws, spend their entire life grinding grain and storing it in warehouses. When seed-gathering time is past and winter comes, the hapless gatherers and grinders are put to death, their bodies eaten, and the hard, inedible heads taken outside the burrow and stacked in neat piles. After all, more grinders can be raised in the coming year so there is no need to waste precious food on unproductive members of the colony. I must protest that this is efficiency carried somewhat to the extreme. Surely, after the busy harvest time, these industrious laborers should be allowed to loll around, eat a little gruel, and relax a bit.

Honey ants gather nectar from flowers and store it in the huge, swollen abdomens of ants called repletes, which spend their entire lives hanging from the ceilings of the caverns head downward. They receive nectar and dispense the honey they produce to hungry members of the colony.

My interest in ants began when my children were small and fire ants had invaded our yard. My usual philosophy of laissez-faire didn't extend to poisonous snakes or ants that invaded our home territory and attacked my little ones, so I took measures to exterminate them. The poison bait provided by the U.S. Department of Agriculture gave me more concern than the ants, so I followed a friend's advice: I poured kerosene on the mound, stirred it, and set it afire. An hour or so later, I returned to check out the situation and saw that some ants were moving about. I squatted over the remains and watched. The courageous survivors were rescuing the babies, the trapped and injured, and trying to restore the city. A few larvae had been placed in piles and the injured and dead were being collected in different places. Occasionally, the pile of dead was inspected and any ant showing movement was removed and placed with the injured. As I watched, I became taken up by the immense catastrophe which had overwhelmed this "city" and its "people." I felt like God looking down on Sodom and Gomorrah after that holocaust and wondered if he, as I, felt sorrow over what had been wrought.

We all have a tendency toward anthropomorphism, what scientists call ascribing human motivations and emotions to animal behavior. In order to test an ant's ability to solve problems according to reason and not prepatterned behavior, I captured a colony of fire ants and set them up in a glass-sided container two by two feet by ten inches wide in my livingroom. I lost the first two colonies trying to feed them what the U.S.D.A. said they ate, and finally discovered they would eat only fresh, raw meat or raw egg. Apparently, in the wild, they kill and eat insects and worms. As the first colony died out, I sat over them for hours with a large hand lens, fascinated as I watched them cope with the situation. Only one ant at a time left the nest, apparently scouting for a food source. As ants began to die, they were carried to a special area on the surface and tenderly cared for. An ant would stay beside it, stroking its head and antennae. This was also done with ants which I intentionally crippled to watch reactions and responses. Sometimes it would take two or three ants to carry the injured party to the "infirmary." Once dead, they were taken to the "cemetery" outside the city. In this case, taken to the edge and dropped over the side.

After establishing a successful colony, I put them through exercises to test their intelligence. Some say that the difference between humans and the lower life forms is the human's ability to reason—that animals do not have emotions but only respond to genetically programmed reproduction and food urges. Apparently, these people haven't been closely associated with many animals, let alone those with intelligence and a means of communication alien to our own, like ants. My dog is capable of love, fear, hatred, jealousy, and sadness, and shows these emotions in every way that a human does. He remembers. He watches me get things together that I use for camping and gets very excited, eager to jump into the van. He observes, weighs the evidence, and arrives at a conclusion. I've seen ants cope with problem-solving in the same way. If this isn't deductive reasoning, then there just ain't no such thing.

Once, I thumped the glass adjacent to a nursery chamber. The ceiling collapsed. There was chaos. Ants were running around waving their "hands" in the air and clutching their brows (so to speak). Presently, the queen, ponderous but dignified, appeared at the opening of an inner passageway. The distraught, confused ants rushed to her, touching antennae. Immediately, order was restored. Debris was removed, the room tidied and the "babies" neatly stacked. When all was done, the queen turned and moved her swollen body back to her inner sanctum. My experience with ants has led me to believe that the queen is more than egg-laying machine, that she leads and directs her queendom with intelligence and logic.

Another experiment was to put food in a certain place and construct an impassable gulch between it and the ants. It was remarkable how quickly they studied the situation and tried alternative solutions, until, finally, they built a bridge of their own bodies and reached the food. As far as I am concerned, they think and reason, even as I do.

I've often wondered what ants do to amuse themselves when enough food is gathered and the living area repaired and neat, that is, those who are deemed worthy to carry on to the next season. Perhaps, when time hangs heavy, they decide, like those of old: "This is the time when Kings go forth to war" (2 Samuel ll:1). Who makes the decision? Why? Who goes out to fight? Does population pressure trigger some urge to mass an attack on a neighboring city and take over its living quarters and food supplies? Or perhaps it is nature's method of population control when ant numbers outweigh the capabilities of the environment to sustain the colony. Do the pressures of overwork or hunger stimulate one tribe to mount slave raids on their neighbors? Does the queen declare all-out war to rid the territory of competing colonies?

I once sat for three days on the reclining trunk of an old willow tree on a Village Creek sandbar where my children and I camped. I spent the entire three days watching a battle between two groups of large, black carpenter ants. How did they distinguish between friend and foe (they were identical). Perhaps by odor or chemical sensors? At the end, there were few survivors, and they were in various conditions of fatigue, amputation of legs, antennae, etc., moving about in slow motion, shoving, hanging on to various portions of each others' bodies. One staggered around with a severed head on its antenna, the jaws locked in a death grip. The field was strewn with heads and bits of bodies. When we left, annihilation was either complete or the few survivors dragged themselves to their respective homes. Were they received as heroes? Were their wounds tended and cared for, or were they thrown out on the ash heap as detriments and unproductive?

I saw another conflict between two ant colonies. One group of ants swarmed around and into the burrow of an ant hill. The resident ants rushed out, and the battle commenced. After a half hour or so of heated conflict, hostilities ceased abruptly and the victors began carrying away the surviving inhabitants for slaves. One ant, half the size of his fellows, was valiantly staggering along carrying on his back a big ant, helplessly waving its legs in air. Who decided to give up and why? Was the queen killed? Did the "general" of the conquering army meet with the resident queen and a compromise arrived at: "You may take as many slaves as you can carry, but leave me enough workers that my kingdom will not perish"? What caused the big ant to allow the little ant to pick him up and carry him away? Perhaps he really didn't care. After all, he is going to work his life away, no matter in which burrow or for whom.

On the order of slaves, but concerning another species of insect, some ants also keep "milk cows" (plant-sucking aphids), which they herd out each morning, up the stalks of plants to "graze," then herd them back in the evening to "milk" them of the sweet nectar. Other ants keep certain small bugs which serve no apparent purpose other than pets. There are a number of other lesser creatures that live in some sort of relationship with ant colonies. The term for these hangers on is myrmicophyle, which is Greek for "ant lover." The ant world is indeed diverse and intriguing. The more we know about them, the more we have to wonder about.

Aside from their own species, ants have few enemies. Those that nest above ground, such as the imported fire ant, have armadillos, skunks, raccoons, etc., to destroy nests and eat the larvae. There is one little predator that probably doesn't capture enough ants to be important in their population control, but is nevertheless interesting. It is an insect variously called ant lion, doodlebug, etc. It digs a hole in loose sand and hides just under the surface at the bottom. Loose sand falls to the center forming an inverted cone with unstable sides. The unwary ant scurrying about its own business, falls into the pit. Loose sand prevents its crawling back out, so the bug jumps out, yells "surprise!" and gloms onto him. As children, we stuck straws into the center of the hole, chanting "Doodlebug, doodlebug, fly away home. Your house is on fire, your children alone." There's more, but I've forgotten it. Any way, the doodlebug, thinking he must have a whopper of an ant in his trap, leaps up, grabs the straw and gets jerked out—an outcome he, no doubt, did not anticipate.

Another predator, more gruesome than the doodlebug, is a type of fly that lays an egg on the back of the leafcutter's neck. When the larva hatches, it eats out the ant's brain. Ugh!

There are many similarities between ants and people and it is ominously foreboding that, though they have had millions of years to perfect their social structures, they still rely on slavery and warfare to solve their problems. It is also depressing to think that we, with the advantages of a superior, reasoning brain, the ability to record, read, and evaluate history and manipulate our social structure, have not risen above the lowly ant when it comes to problem solving. Just when population increases to the point that joblessness becomes a problem and competition for necessities causes prices to rise, we pick a fight with another nation and get rid of our surplus young men and put the women to work manufacturing armaments. A sad commentary on the human race—masters of the universe! (I can just hear an ant queen chuckle with amusement if she could hear that accolade.) At least we have risen above cutting off the heads of unwanted and undesirables: we just give them a lethal injection.

King Solomon was apparently an ant watcher, for he observed: "The ants are a small people, but they lay up store for the winter." And when he said: "Go to the ant, thou sluggard, and learn her ways," he not only exhibited a knowledge of the unisexual nature of ant colonies, but gave some darned good advice, which, after all, was his forte. Perhaps I have told you more about ants than you would ever want to know, but I'll bet you no longer pass by an ant hill without stopping and meditating over the wonder of it all.

After an hour or so contemplating the ant city, I prepared to descend the bluff—an accomplishment more rapid than its ascent since it had rained the night before and the clay of the erosional slope was slick. I slid most of the way down. Junior jumped into the boat ahead of me and I blithely stepped from the hard clay of the bluff shelf onto the boat. My foot on the ground skidded east, the boat shot out into the stream to the west, and I did a neat backflip into the very cold, very wet water between boat and bluff. Fortunately, it was only deep enough to saturate my heavy clothing but not to drown me. Since it was cold that morning, I had put on everything I had brought with me except a three-quarter-length coat.

Retrieving my boat, I paddled around the bend to a sandbar where there was room to do something about the situation. I built a fire and arrayed a pair of jeans, shirt, and socks where they might dry enough to wear, ate the last bread and cheese and drank coffee made over the fire, and decided not to wait for the clothes to dry. Spreading them over the boat in the wind and sun, I put the hip-length coat over my naked body, buttoned it up and proceeded to paddle downstream, hoping that all the fishermen would have better sense than to get out on the river on a day like that. At least it would have given them something to tell their buddies about—meeting this crazy old woman paddling down the river with nothing on but a short coat. The last sandbar and bend before Sheffield's Ferry, I pulled in and put on my cold, wet garments in order to make a socially acceptable appearance in public.

SHEFFIELD'S FERRY

River Mile 94.4

The site of Sheffield's Ferry is one of scenic beauty. After flowing directly eastward about a mile and a half, the river again makes an abrupt turn, this time to the south. In the bend is a spacious sandbar, and, spanning the entire channel, are shoals of rocklike gray clay. This material must be extremely hard for it has resisted the force of many floods for untold years. When the water level is low, pools and narrow channels appear in the river which, with the sandy beach, make a great recreation area.

The ferry crossed below the shoals where the river is broad and deep and the ramps on both sides of the river can still be seen. I don't know when the first ferry was at this site, but Jeff Sheffield ran one here where the road between Spurger and Jasper crossed the river in the 1860s. He also operated the riverboat landing at the lower end of Red Bluff at the "red field." There was another field a little lower down called the white field, because the soil was largely white sand while the soil of the upper field was red clay.

In 1881, the Tyler County Commissioners' Court officially authorized the ferry at this crossing and set the rates to be the same as those at Town Bluff.

The rate for a wagon and pair of horses was 25 cents, 40 cents for a wagon and two pairs of horses, 25 cents for one or two horses and a buggy. A man and a horse was 15 cents, and a man afoot was only five cents. This was called short ferriage rates, for when the river was high the rates were doubled. There was a creek a short distance from the river which was also impassable when the water was high, so another ferry was kept there. If both ferries had to be used, the fare was doubled.

After the Sheffields sold the ferry, it was owned at different times by a Dr. Ogden of Spurger, a Hardy Sirmons, Henderson & Pool of Jasper, and finally, the Jenkins family in 1917. They ran it until the bridge was built in 1959. The Jenkins family didn't operate the second ferry over the creek, and if the water was too high to cross it, people just had to wait until the water went down.

The ferry looked like a bobbing chip of wood on the raging flood, and it took steel nerves to get on it. If the driver of a wagon was too nervous, the Jenkins boys would drive it on for them. It must have been fairly safe, for I have heard of few accidents, though some did occur. A truck carrying a cage of chickens went on the ferry and off into the river because the driver panicked and hit the gas pedal instead of the brakes. The driver survived, but the caged chickens drowned. On another occasion, a driver, while descending the ramp, failed to lock the wheels of his loaded wagon and the mules couldn't hold it. Mules, wagon, and all went into the river and the ferry, attached to its cable, shot to the other side all by itself. The Jenkins boys retrieved everything except one mule that drowned. High or low, swift or slow, the river was all the same to these people. Like the water rat in *Wind in the Willows*, they lived by it, in it, with it, on it, and loved it. Fannie Jenkins, the family matriarch, when interviewed for a book on Tyler County history, told of her happy life there. She lived in the ferry house twenty years after the ferry was gone until failing health forced her to go live with family.

The ferry house still stood on its high stilts overlooking the river until the 1990s. I wanted that house. I would have restored it and kept it as a historical treasure, but when I tried to buy it, the person who bought it from the Jenkins family said he was going to "fix it up." When I went back later, it had been demolished and a junky camphouse built in its place. It signaled the end of an era, but then I guess all eras must end sooner or later.

Another prominent pioneer family in the Sheffield Ferry area was the Mayo family. Richard C. Mayo came to Texas in 1843 and farmed the red field. He put in a steam sawmill, cotton gin, grist mill, and blacksmith shop and must have been fairly well-to-do to have the capital for such enterprises. In order to provide an education for his own children and to entice good families to settle in the area, Mayo set aside land and built a schoolhouse. He also gave land to new residents and helped them build their houses. Such work was a community effort in those days. When a house was to be built, a log rolling was held. All the men and boys cut and peeled the logs and hoisted them in place while the women cooked and served food for the lot. This activity led to one of the many idioms in our language. When my mother had prepared too much food, she would say, "My goodness! There's enough food here for a log rolling!"

Such community spirit led to the founding in 1874 of one of the first Masonic organizations in Texas. I am told that it was originally founded at Town Bluff as the Tyler County Lodge, but it was reported to their authorities that drinking had been going on there, its charter was revoked, and it was moved to Spurger and renamed the Snow River Lodge. (The Masons are extremely adverse to alcohol.) It is still located there in a nice brick building and is very active in the community.

SHEFFIELD'S FERRY BRIDGE

River Mile 94.3

As I neared the Highway 1013 bridge, I remembered the times when the children were small and we would come here, just across on the Jasper County side where Mill Creek crosses the highway, and look for Indian artifacts. Mill Creek is at the base of the floodplain bluff line, which was a favorite site for Indians to live. They were out of reach of floods, had fresh water from the small creek, and the Neches River nearby for fish, alligators, turtles, and clams, and for transportation. After heavy rains, arrowheads and other stone and pottery shards could be easily seen, and the children had an exciting time. The area is fenced and posted now, so don't bother to go look for it.

While these three days had been all and more than I had hoped they would be, I must admit that, cold and wet as I was, I was overwhelmed with relief to see the span of bridge over the river. It isn't an attractive bridge, just a utilitarian structure of steel and concrete. It does have a feature which gives it special interest, though.

During spring and summer, barn swallows construct mud nest condominiums on the beams beneath the bridge. Both mates work together building the nest, spending up to fourteen hours each of eight or more days. Actually, they prefer to repair old nests as it takes much less time. These nests are in the shape of an inverted half cone and are built painstakingly of small blobs of mud reinforced with grass or straw. Strange that these birds could have learned even earlier than humans that mud must be mixed with straw to be suitable for building purposes. Perhaps humans learned this from watching swallows build nests.

The barn swallow is a beautiful bird with a long, forked tail, burnt orange underside, and a black topside that flashes with iridescent shades of blue and purple in the sunlight. Their graceful, intricate flight is a delight to watch but there were no swallows to watch during my trip as it was late in the season and these insectivorous birds were wintering in the tropics where flying insects were plentiful. Due to the frenetic activity involved with pursuing and capturing insects on the wing, they must consume a large part of their body weight in flying insects each day.

River bridges make ideal nesting sites for swallows. Predators can't climb up the concrete pillars standing in the water, so they are safe. Many types of insects spend their larval stage in the water and emerge in great numbers, and the broad expanse of water and highway make easy flight paths for the birds. I once watched a large flock of swallows, which had just returned in the spring, conduct their mating exhibition flights at a bridge over the Neches River at Dam B. They flew over and under the bridge in frenzied orbits, many of them hitting the tall structure over the bridge and being crushed by automobiles crossing the bridge. The next day, the surface of the bridge was littered with little corpses.

Within sight of the bridge, I pulled my boat into what at one time was a boat landing at the old ferry slip but is now eroded so badly, I could see no way to pull my boat up it. However, since this was where my van was parked, I unloaded everything, lugged it up the steep, rugged incline and then began to try to pull the boat up to the top of the bluff. Just then, a bank fisherman rushed up to help me. He was drunk as a lord but courteous to a fault. Together, we got the boat up and into the back of my van. I didn't know then that Clyde Scott had put in a great boat ramp at his camp just on the other side of the bridge, but then my gallant, if inebriated, friend would not have had the opportunity of extending his assistance to me. So ended the first lap of my voyage.

PART TWO

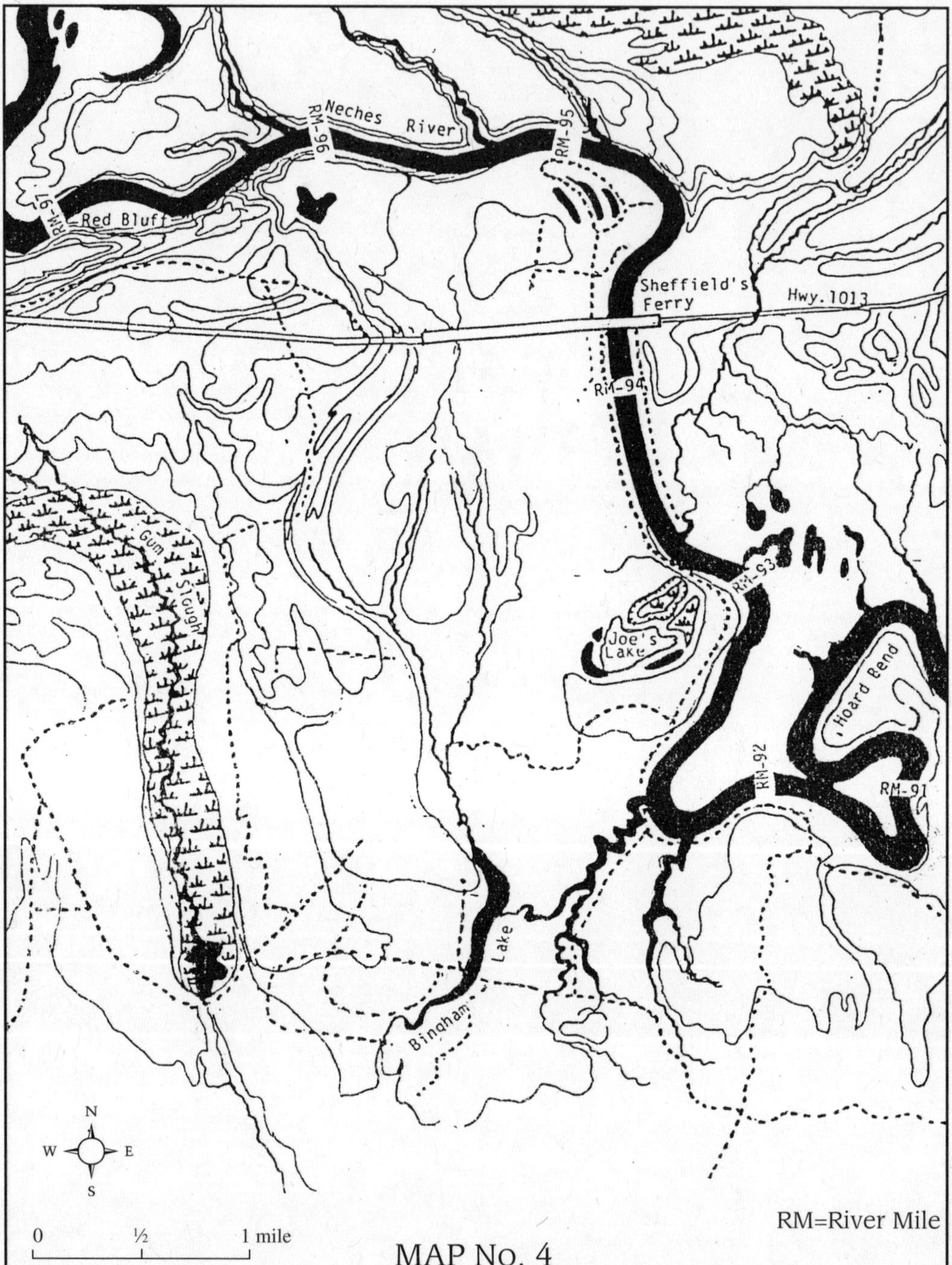

Neches River
RM-97
RM-96
RM-95
RM-94
RM-93
RM-92
RM-91
Red Bluff
Sheffield's Ferry
Hwy.1013
Gum Slough
Joe's Lake
Hoard Bend
Bingham Lake
N
S
E
W
0
½
1 mile
RM=River Mile

MAP No. 4

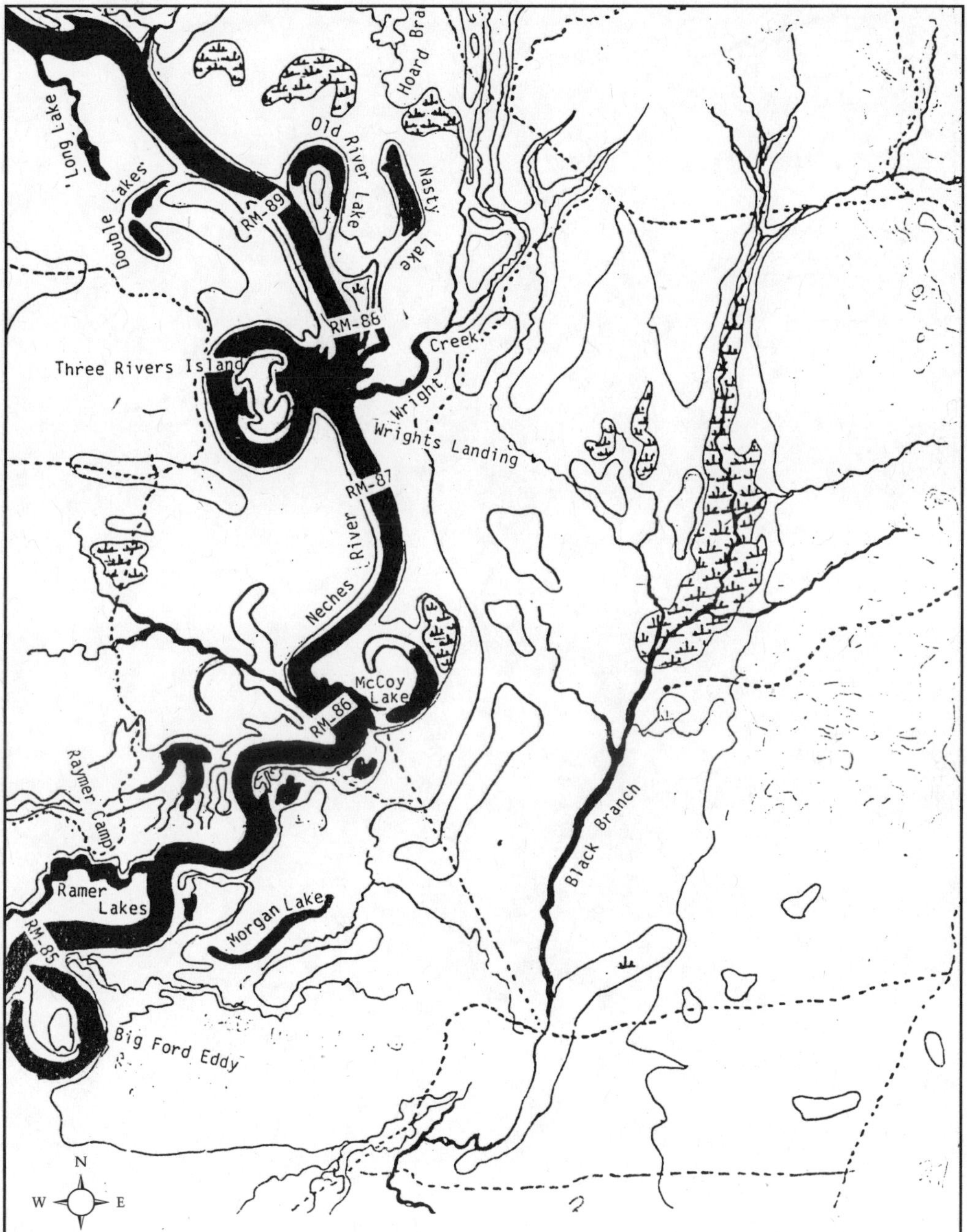

Long Lake
Double Lakes
Hoard Bra
Old River Lake
Nasty Lake
RM-89
RM-88
Three Rivers Island
Wright Creek
Wrights Landing
RM-87
Neches River
McCoy Lake
RM-86
Raymer Camp
Ramer Lakes
Morgan Lake
RM-85
Big Ford Eddy
Black Branch
N
W
E
S
0
½
1 mile

MAP No. 5

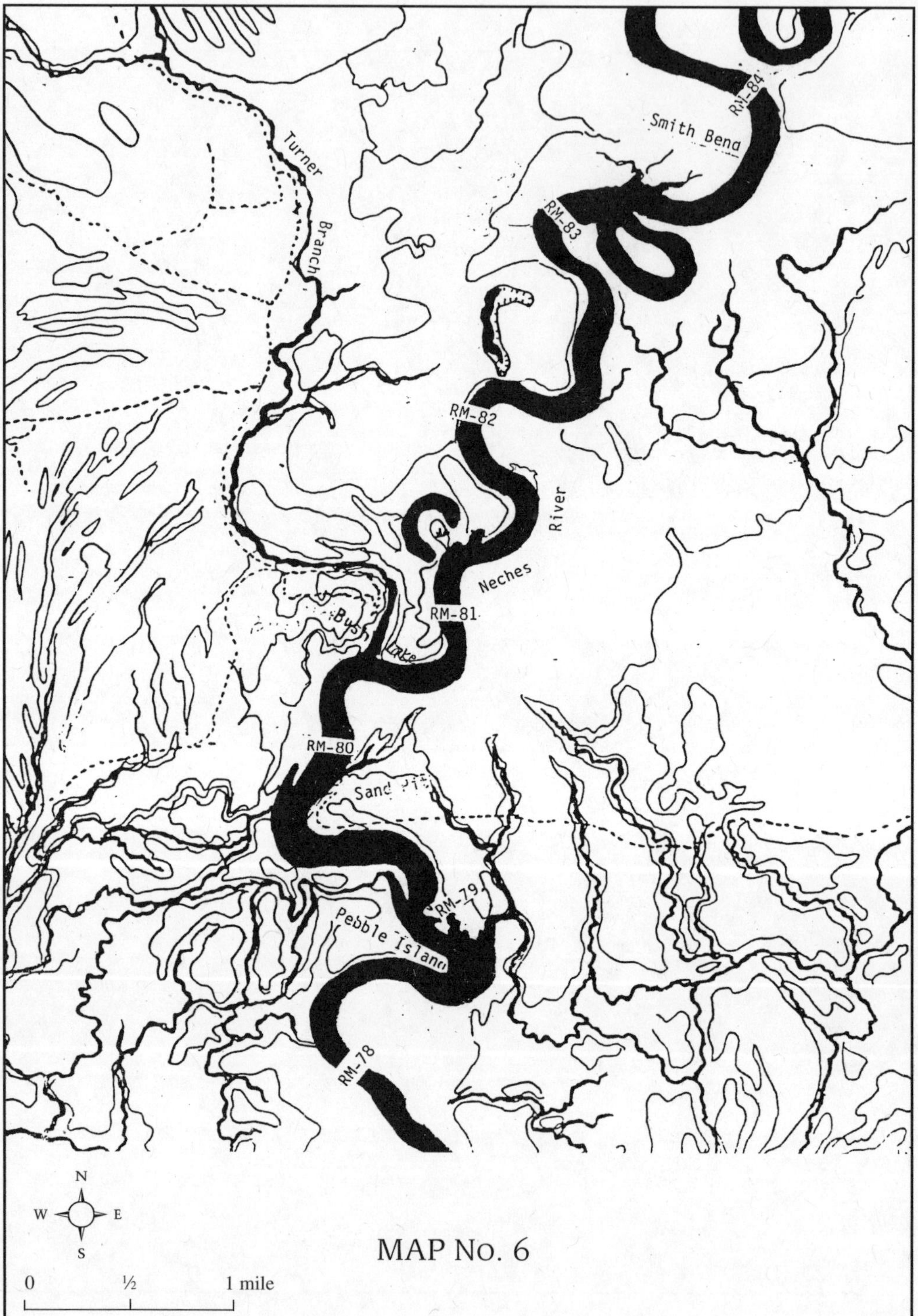

Smith Bend
Turner
Branch
Neches
River
Bush Lake
Sand Pit
Pebble Island
RM-82
RM-83
RM-81
RM-80
RM-79
RM-78
N
W
E
S
0
½
1 mile

MAP No. 6

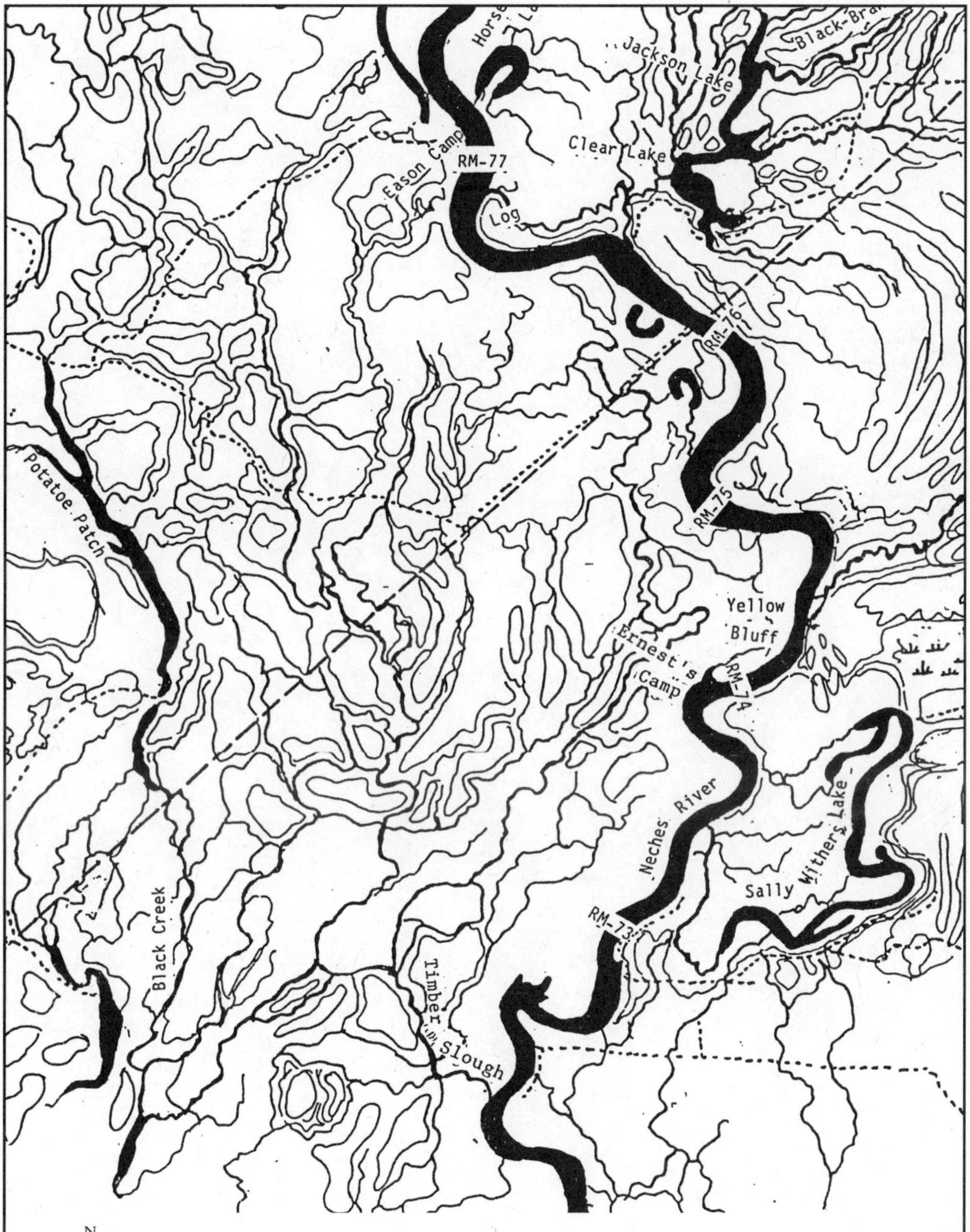
Jackson Lake
Clear Lake
Eason Camp
RM-77
Log
RM-76
RM-75
Potatoe Patch
Yellow
Bluff
Ernest's
Camp
RM-74
Neches River
Withers Lake
Sally
RM-73
Black Creek
Timber
Slough
N
W
E
S
0
½
1 mile

MAP No. 7

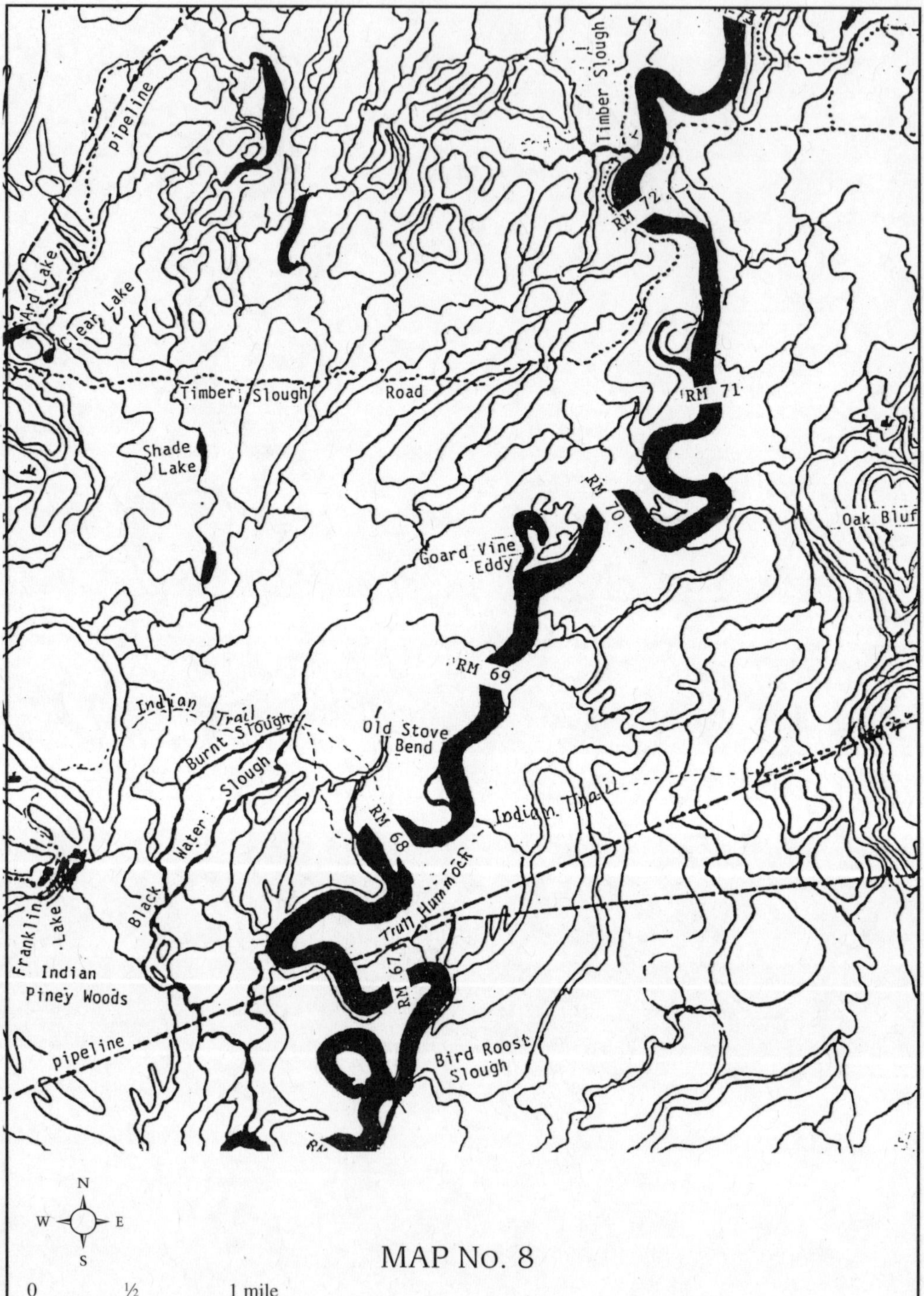

pipeline
Timber Slough
RM 72
Ard Lake
Clear Lake
Timber Slough Road
RM 71
Shade Lake
RM 70
Oak Bluf
Goard Vine Eddy
RM 69
Indian Trail
Burnt Slough
Old Stove Bend
Black Water Slough
RM 68
Indian Trail
Truit Hummock
Franklin Lake
Indian Piney Woods
RM 67
Bird Roost Slough
pipeline
N
W
E
S
0
½
1 mile

MAP No. 8

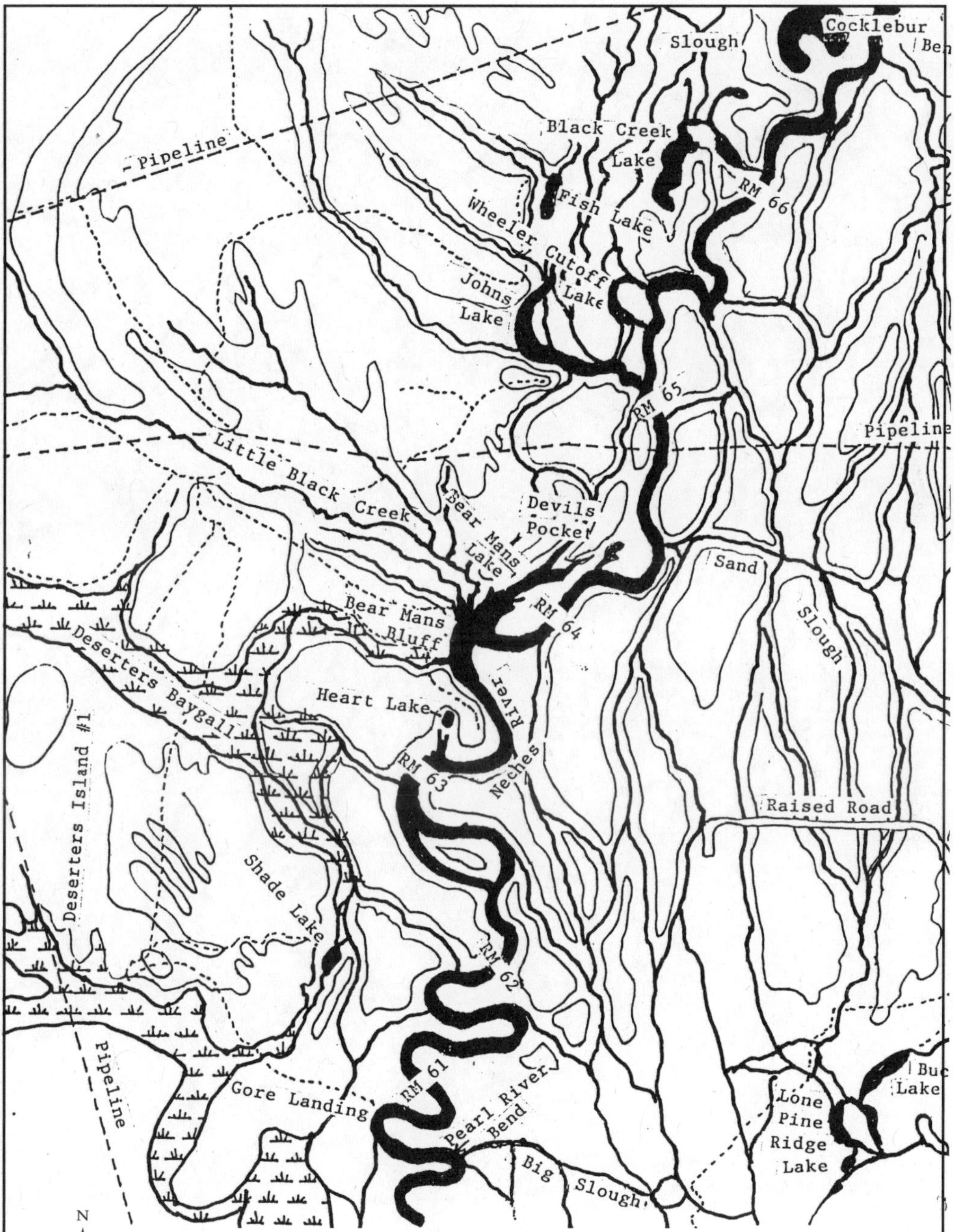

Cocklebur
Slough
Pipeline
Black Creek
Lake
RM 66
Fish Lake
Wheeler Cutoff
Lake
Johns
Lake
RM 65
Pipeline
Little Black Creek
Bear Mans
Lake
Devils
Pocket
Sand
Slough
RM 64
Bear Mans
Bluff
Deserters Baygall
Heart Lake
River
Neches
RM 63
Deserters Island #1
Raised Road
Shade Lake
RM 62
Pipeline
Gore Landing
RM 61
Pearl River
Bend
Big Slough
Lone
Pine
Ridge
Lake
N
W
E
S
0
½
1 mile

MAP No. 9

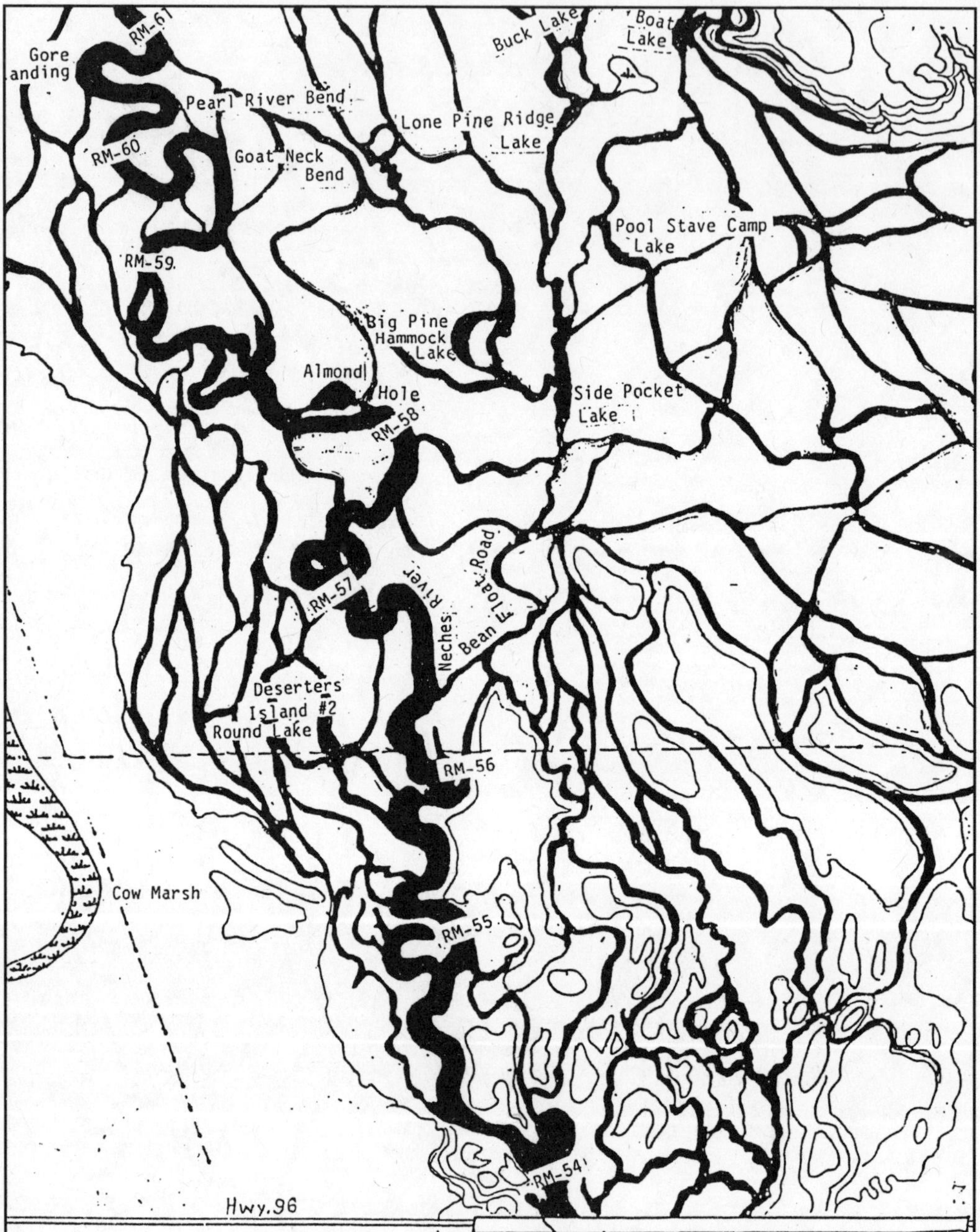
RM-61
Gore
anding
Pearl River Bend
RM-60
Goat Neck
Bend
Lone Pine Ridge
Lake
Buck Lake
Boat
Lake
Pool Stave Camp
Lake
RM-59
Big Pine
Hammock
Lake
Almond
Hole
RM-58
Side Pocket
Lake
RM-57
Neches River
Bean Float Road
Deserters
Island #2
Round Lake
RM-56
Cow Marsh
RM-55
RM-54
Hwy.96
N
W
E
S
0
½
1 mile

MAP No. 10

Part Two

Day 1

SCOTT'S LANDING

River Mile 94 3:30 P.M.

A year passed before I continued my journey. It was autumn again. The weather couldn't have been more perfect: cobalt blue skies, brilliant, sunshiny days and cool, crisp nights. And I had just been given my annual no-pay furlough from the Park Service, so it seemed a most auspicious time to begin the second part of my Neches River voyage. I had just finished building my little backwater boat and tried it out on Massey Lake near my home and it didn't sink, so I packed the bare necessities for survival, and my daughter, Regina, drove me to Sheffield's Ferry (Highway 1013 crossing) to launch me off.

I hadn't intended to build a boat for this trip. I had thought for years that I would return to Deweyville where the old boat maker lived from whom Daddy had bought his backwater boat many years ago and try to find him, but kept putting it off. I didn't even know his name. Then one night I had a dream. Daddy came to me and said, "Sister, if you want a backwater boat, go to that Gulf Station in Deweyville and they will tell you where to find the fellow who builds them." Mother had wanted to visit some old friends in Deweyville where they had made their retirement home before Daddy became ill, so we went.

The Gulf Station was abandoned and, questioning neighbors, we found that the owner had died. (So much for dreams.) Anyway, since we were there, we decided to visit with one of Daddy's cousins, Lyman Scott, who still lived there. When I told him why we had come to Deweyville, he didn't laugh, as some people take dreams and other premonitions seriously, and told us that the boat maker had died but that his brother, a Mr. Smith, had two or three backwater boats and might sell one to me since he was getting too old to go out. The old couple had been good friends of Mother and Daddy and she was delighted to have a chance to see them again. Mr. Smith didn't want to sell his boats but took me to look at them and gave me much valuable advice. I went home and went to work.

Since this was to be an experiment, I didn't want to spend too much money on it. Where Daddy's boat was 12 feet long, mine was only eight feet. I used one eight foot by four foot by quarter-inch sheet of Luaan plywood (around four dollars) and about five dollars worth of treated one-inch lumber, which I ripped to desired sizes on my little table saw. A heavy chunk of oak served as the prow, since I wanted to compensate for my weight in the rear of the boat. Brass boat nails and a caulking adhesive put it together. The two seats were cushioned with foam covered with a pretty blue and white checked vinyl fabric. The paint cost more than the whole boat. In spite of the fact that all my material was exterior grade, I saturated it with a water-repellant preservative and painted it first with a sealant and then several coats of an oil-based enamel—bright cherry red! Oh! It was such a little jewel and presented such a pretty picture floating in the green and blue reflections on the water! And it was so easy to build. If I can find the time, and the reason, I would like to build a 12-foot model.

I suppose I should include in the cost the price of a dental accident. Every project I take on has its own special stupid accident—like the time I was building a camper to go on the back of my pickup and stuck my hand into an active table saw. I had surgery about 10:00 that night, where they managed to save all my fingers except about half of one, came out of the anesthetic and the recovery room at 9:00 A.M., went home and finished my camper. I'm convinced that the most debilitating effects of surgery are due to the enforced inactivity and hospital food. Anyway, while building the boat, the nail I had poked into the end of the caulking tube was stuck, so, being in a hurry as always, I grasped it with my front teeth and pulled. "Pop" went my two beautiful front teeth, just reconstructed at great expense. Some people just seem to go through life making stupid mistakes and paying for them.

At first, the boat paddled like a wash tub—round and round—and I remembered how Daddy had put a little rudder on the rear of his boat, so I constructed one that would stabilize the forward motion and raise up and slide over underwater obstacles, and I would not have to compensate so much for paddling on one side only. It worked very well.

As I said, the boat was a jewel. We took it to Clyde Scott's boat ramp on the south side of the river bridge and prepared to launch off. But first, there was a ritual to observe. I never put in there without first having coffee and chitchat with Clyde. Usually, there was more than coffee. He was the world's best East Texas-style country cook, and always had lots of food on the stove and you just had to eat with him. He smoked his own pork sausage and it spoiled you forever against the store-bought, packing-house variety.

Clyde and I were somewhat related—possibly third or fourth cousins. His father was Law Scott and my father had an uncle in the area named Lee Scott and I think they were cousins. Anyway, most everybody around here can scrape up kin if they dig deep enough. But I called him Cousin Clyde.

Clyde was around 70 years of age and had led a checkered life. Born to a respected, well-to-do pioneer family, he left the area to roam the world. He was many things—one of them a spangled rodeo star—but had come home to finish his life where it had begun, on the banks of the Neches River.

There was a laissez-faire atmosphere at Clyde's camp. Under a large, tin-covered roof on the bluff were domino tables, hammocks, soft-drink machines, a television set, and radio. There was always an assortment of people: nobody just put his boat in the water, brought it out, and left. They enjoyed the camaraderie of their own kind, and many a family reunion and celebration of some sort was held there.

I attended a gala party there once honoring the patriarch Walter Cole, a member of another pioneer family and father of Jasper County's popular sheriff, Aubrey Cole. It was his 93rd birthday party, and there were so many cars and people you couldn't stir them with a stick!

I had come in with a group of Park Service people after a day on the river and noticed a big party going on at the camp next to Clyde's. The Park Service people, stiff necks that they are, minded their own business and went back to the office in Beaumont, but I, being in my own vehicle, decided to go see what was going on. People miss a lot of good things in life by always minding their own business, I always say. Fortunately, there happened to be a few friends of mine in the crowd who invited me to stay and join the celebration and share the food. There were long tables of everything from fried catfish to barbecued steer and I fell to. A great band called the County Line was playing and a plywood platform had been laid. The band struck up a lively tune, Snookie Van Pelt grabbed me, dragged me to the dance floor and we did the backwoods stomp—me in full Park Ranger regalia—Smokey Bear hat and all.

I photographed the event so that everyone could see how people on the Neches River enjoy themselves, and the pictures are in the National Park archives.

As I type this, a year after my voyage, I have just returned from Clyde Scott's funeral. I expected him to go sooner, really, for you never saw him without a fifth of whiskey in one hand and an unfiltered Camel cigarette in the other, and he had a terrible cough. By my standard of values, he wasted his health and his life and it was sad to me, but he loved me and was kind, though brusque and rough-spoken, to everyone. He will be missed and things won't be the same at Sheffield's Ferry for a long time.

But Clyde was there to admire my boat and see me off. Regina helped me carry the boat down to the water—I didn't want to scar the bottom on the rough concrete ramp. I got in, she shoved me off into the swift-moving current a 3:30 P.M., a few strokes of the paddle and I was well on my way.

Not quite out of sight of the landing, I looked back and saw Regina waving and hollering something about the radio, and I realized that I had left behind the two-way radio. (The Park Service thought it judicious that I carry one and keep in touch along the way, their not having the same trust and confidence in the river people that I had.) Realizing it was hopeless to fight the current back upstream, I pulled to shore, got out on a bank and fought my way through brush and briers back to Clyde's camp, hoping Regina hadn't given up and left. She hadn't, so retrieving the radio, I made my way back to the boat and was off again, hoping that this was not an omen of things to come.

I don't know why I can't seem to get off to a dignified start on these trips. There is always some hiatus which turns my bon voyage into a comedy, but back on the river with a brisk north wind at my back, in fifteen minutes I was past the first bend and out of sight of the bridge.

A few minutes downstream, the mouth of Mill Creek was the first feature on the landscape to come into view, though it is hard to tell it from the many sloughs coming into the river in this area. The next bend of the river on the right offered a view of sandbar, trees, and water so pleasing that I spent a half-hour photographing. The river water had a Nile-green tinge to it, apparently from an almost microscopic algae which forms in late summer

Trip launch-off

when the water is low and the flow not so swift, but it seems to enhance the color composition of the landscape.

Approaching what was last year a narrow strip of land where the river doubled back after making a wide bend, I found a broad passage cut and the full flow of the river passing through it. I wasn't surprised as, a year or so ago, someone dug a cave through this sandy bluff, planning that the river would do just what it did, cut through and form a sizeable island.

Some lawyer had told the locals that these river islands belonged to no one and could be homesteaded, so a family had moved onto this island, lock, stock, and barrel, and started a crop. Since the area had not yet been acquired by the Park Service and was owned by Temple-Eastex, it didn't take their security people long to evict the would-be settlers. Eventually, in less than a half-dozen years, the river would have cut through anyway, but we now have a stretch of river here which will become a backwater and, as sand is deposited along the banks of the new watercourse, both ends will be closed off and it will become an inland oxbow lake.

Lesley Eason
Hog Hunting

DOGS

The remainder of this voyage I will make alone. Ulysses, Jr., my old friend, died of complications following cancer surgery. His veterinarian warned me that he probably would not survive surgery at his advanced age and physical condition. Without it, he might live perhaps another month, but in terrible agony. I left him at the animal hospital that morning and went to my job. When I told him goodbye, I held him close and thanked him for the love and companionship of all those years and told him that we would be together again, and I cried as I had not cried for many years. He cried too, his head pressed against my shoulder. I didn't call that day to see how he was, because I didn't want to hear that he was dead. Finally, when the day's work ended, I went to the hospital to get his body and take him to our place on the hill overlooking the lake where he so loved to go, and bury him. The vet said, "Why, he's just fine. Want to see him?" Junior came to meet me with a big smile, just as bright and frisky as ever, and I took him home.

Two weeks later, he began to weaken and refused to eat. He had kidney and liver failure and, in spite of everything that could possibly be done, he died. I sat with him before leaving for work that last morning. He lay without moving but when I spoke, he indicated by a slight wave of his tail that he heard. I told him that I would be back and that he must wait for me. He knew what this meant because every time I prepared to go somewhere, he became excited and ran to the van. If I said, "You can't go. Stay here and wait for me. I will be back," he would be pretty depressed, but was always at the gate waiting for me when I returned. Whenever I talked to him seriously, he would put just the tip of his tongue between his teeth and smile to indicate that he understood. If I said: "Yes, you can go," he would go into ecstasies and leap into his seat in the van.

He was still alive when I came in that evening and I went straight to him, sat beside him, and stroked his smooth, silky head. Between his last throes, I talked with him, "You can go, darling. Go ahead, but wait for me when you get there. I will come." The tip of his tongue came out and I knew he heard me and understood. He died shortly after. Few humans have left me so bereft.

Dogs have meant a great many things to humans throughout history. As pack animals, herders of domestic live stock, guardians of man's possessions, even as food. I don't think they have ever been important as companions to people until recent years. At one time, old folks remained in the home as a part of the family, but now, they either live alone or in a retirement home. Loneliness and a sense of uselessness have become crippling diseases of the elderly. If you are fortunate enough to have a dog to care for, it gives you a reason to get up in the mornings. It needs you. In return for a little food and care, it gives total, unconditional love. My dog would have died for me. He didn't know or care that I was growing old and ugly. He would rather be with me, no matter where, when nobody else did, and would stay at my feet, no matter for how long.

I miss him. He would come to my bedside at night and put his paw on my arm. I would give him a goodnight hug; he would lay his head on my shoulder for a moment, then lie down to sleep. I miss it like the goodnight kiss of a loved, lost child.

He will be missed on this trip. I don't know. I might get another dog—a pup that would learn my ways and that could outlive me. Junior would understand. He wouldn't like it, but he would tolerate it and would fight the world to protect it because it was mine.

In Big Thicket country, the average dog owner values his dog somewhere between his livestock and his children. I remember Daddy holding his hog dog, Blackboy, in his arms and weeping as the dog died of distemper. I cried with him.

In Jasper County, somewhere around the 1930s or 1940s, I remember reading in the newspapers about the famous Garlington murder case. It was a family feud with casualties on both sides—all because somebody killed somebody's dog. Jasper County Sheriff Aubrey Cole, remembers it also. It seems Travis Ellis, his son, Richard Morris, and Roy Munich were deer hunting with dogs on land adjacent to the Garlington Ranch. The dogs ran the deer onto the ranch and were shot. Travis Ellis and Munich drove their pickup into the ranch to talk with Garlington about the dogs when the Garlingtons met them. It was never decided who fired the first shot, but Munich fell mortally wounded and Ellis was injured. Ellis' son and Morris, hearing the shots, hurried to the scene, and a free-for-all shootout took place. Either they ran out of bullets or felt that the injured needed immediate attention, but the hostilities ceased. Travis Ellis and Sherril Garlington were charged and tried. Ellis was tried in Jasper County where he was acquitted, but Garlington's trial was moved to Smithville where he also was acquitted. In trying to determine who fired the first shot and who shot whom, Munich's body was exhumed and examined to identify the bullets in his body. Joe Tonahill, a Jasper attorney, represented Ellis in the case. In this area people sort of settled their own differences, and, since everybody owned dogs and understood, they found no fault with the way the situation was handled.

The dog has always been important to us in the Big Thicket area. The Indians used dogs for hunting buffalo and bear, and, I'm told, ate them. The first pioneers depended largely on wild game for meat, but hunting was difficult because animals would run to the nearest thicket or baygall and hide out. The hunter could send his dog in to roust out the bear, deer, or whatever so he could see the animal, get a bead on it and bring it down.

Big Thicket hunters don't, as a rule, own bird dogs (setters or retrievers), which are sports dogs. They hunt to put meat on the table, and own and train squirrel, coon, deer, cattle, and hog dogs. These hunting dogs have been highly bred and have pedigrees just like fancier breeds. Since we no longer have open range in Texas, the cow dog is no longer needed and fewer people have need of hog dogs, but the breeds are kept up.

A squirrel dog is smaller and is usually a mixture of fiest and terrier, (a "bench-legged fiest" being preferable), and a well-trained one is valuable. The squirrel dog sniffs the ground until he comes across a fresh squirrel scent and follows it until the squirrel runs up a tree. The dog gives a certain bark when he finds a trail and another when he trees the squirrel. The hunter, following at a distance, says, "Well, Ol' Bob has treed," and goes in for the kill. The squirrel, no fool, hides on the opposite side of the tree from the hunter and Ol' Bob looks for a long vine, grabs it in his teeth and shakes heck out of the upper limbs to which it is attached. This sends the squirrel scampering away from the commotion to the other side of the tree where the hunter pops him in the eyeball. (You don't want squirrel shot in his body. The lead pellets will break your teeth when you eat it.)

A squirrel dog that takes off after a rabbit or armadillo is soundly chastised. If he continues to do so, he is not allowed to hunt anymore and is considered worthless. I once saw a hunter so angry when his squirrel dog chased a rabbit that he shot the poor thing with squirrel shot. Daddy was so furious at this display of cruelty and bad temper that he never went hunting with that man again.

While squirrel hunters use only one dog for a hunt, coon and cat, deer and hog hunters use packs of dogs. In a pack there will always be one whose personality and intelligence so stand out that he becomes a favorite and is even allowed in the house to lie before the fireplace at his master's feet. Ben Hooks, one of the last and most famous of the bear hunters in the Big Thicket, kept a pack of bear hounds, the favorite of which was a bluetick hound named Ramsey. Ramsey was famous as a bear dog without peer, and when he, with most of his pack, died of rabies, Hooks was so heartsick that he never owned dogs again. Like hog dogs, bear dogs had to be big, fast, and tough. It takes a pack of dogs to hold a bear at bay and subdue him, and the bear usually takes his toll of two or three dogs, disemboweling them with slashing claws, crushing them in its arms, and breaking their bones in its strong jaws.

Corralling wild hogs is almost as dangerous as bear hunting. It's a toss up which is the meanest: a cornered, wounded bear or a family of hogs. A two-year-old bar (boar hog) whose tushes (tusks) haven't curled backward but have reached two straight inches of razor sharpness, can really cut a dog up—or a man, either, if it can get to him. The last time I was at the Eason's, Leslie was worrying over his best hog dog, a Catahoula cur worth $500, which had sustained an injury in a hog hunt a few days previous. The hog had slashed the rear leg, severing a tendon, and the wound had become infected. I made a deal with Leslie to finance a trip to the veterinarian in exchange for a series of photographs of the hog hunt, and the last time I heard, the dog was doing fine but would be crippled the rest of his life.

Daddy had lots of bad hog stories, or should I say stories about bad hogs. He always said, "Don't worry about the bears and panthers. You just watch out for those hogs—especially a sow with little pigs." Rounding up and penning wild hogs was one of the things that kept life down on the farm from getting dull and uninteresting, and it couldn't have been done without some well-trained hog dogs.

Daddy told me once that he was hunting in the traditional Big Thicket around Saratoga when he heard a commotion ahead and saw a wave of hogs running toward him. He climbed the nearest tree and remained quiet and still while an ocean of hogs, followed by a pack of dogs, followed by men on horseback passed beneath him. It would have been life threatening to have been caught in that melee.

Feral hogs in our area are called razorbacks or pineywoods rooters. They were probably mean when DeSoto's Spaniards brought the first ones over from Europe, and fighting Big Thicket snakes, bears, and Indians just made them meaner. Bill Brett, cowboy raconteur of the Big Thicket, gets plumb lyrical when talking about pineywoods rooters. He claims the meat has a natural, nutty taste and that you can be sure it isn't pumped full of antibiotics, steroids, and water to make it weigh more. No doubt he's right.

Thinking Bill Brett was right, I acquired a small pig which a friend of my son, David, had found in the woods, and we proceeded to raise us a meat hog. That little booger was so mean he would try to chew the shoes off your feet when you entered his pen and he got meaner as he got older. Discussing the piglet's evil disposition with Ernest Spell one day, he asked if he had been castrated. He hadn't and, assuring me that the operation would calm him down, Ernest and Sonny Yawn came over and performed the surgery. I think it must have made him mad because he was meaner than ever afterwards. The pig never got very big but had such a prodigious appetite he would try to tear the sheet metal fence down if we didn't feed him constantly. When we finally did butcher him, he was 90 percent fat. There was practically no lean at all. Ernest said: "Why, that's a guinney hog—a grease hog!" It seems that in the past some hogs were bred for fat because hog lard was used exclusively for cooking, and we had got ourselves a grease hog.

Raccoon hunting has always been a popular sport in East Texas and a good coon dog is highly valued. Since coons are nocturnal feeders, coon hunting is done at night. Coon hunters use one or more dogs. The dog trails the coon, usually to a big hollow tree where he has hidden himself. The hunters build a smudge fire at the base of the hollow tree, driving the coon out the top where he can be shot. I've seen coon dogs so enthused they would climb ten or twelve feet up a tree before falling. Some get so excited that they just fall on the ground in a kicking fit and have to have cold water poured on them to bring them around. And—speaking of coon hunting—most people don't believe us when we talk about our coon hunting mules. Park Service people thought it was a joke when someone advertised a coon-hunting mule in the Woodville newspaper. It is a small mule which can follow the hounds through brush and trees easier than a horse can.

Some Southeast Texans of English descent still like to fox hunt and keep a pack of foxhounds for that purpose. I knew a Jasper County devotee of the sport who was sent into Jasper on Christmas Eve to buy fruit, candy, and toys for the four children of the house. Running into a few cronies, he shared a jug of white lightning with them. When he got home that night, he had 24 brand, spanking new collars for his foxhounds and nothing else. In those days, storekeepers would get up and open up for emergencies, and when his wife got through with him, it was an emergency. He rode horseback all the way back into town and returned with the goodies before the kids got up on Christmas morning.

From what I am told by the cognoscenti, the greatest pleasure in coon hunting comes from sitting on logs around a roaring camp fire with a compatible group of fellers passing around the coffee pot and the bottle and listening to the music of the hounds. Everyone knows his dog's voice and what it is telling him. Lots of tales are told around these fires: of past hunts and dogs they once owned, lots of jokes and "hoo rawing" one another. A city feller was once persuaded to go on one of these outings. It was misting rain and an icy wind was howling—perfect weather for a night hunt. As they huddled over the fire passing around the bottle, one would say, "Listen! That's ol' Bullet! He's treed." Another would say, "Listen! That's ol' Blue. He's on a trail!" Finally, the city feller said: "Listen!" They all cocked their ears and waited. "Listen! That's the north wind. I'm cold as hell, and I'm going home!"

There has been a great effort among so-called sportsmen to make hunting with dogs illegal. Most don't realize the difference in hunting in parts of Texas where visibility is virtually unlimited and a hunter can sit in his carpeted, heated deer blind (complete with bar) and wait until a deer walks to a water hole or to a spot where corn has been set out for bait during the year. In Southeast Texas, the hunter stands along an old road or a pipeline and sends his deer dogs into the thickets to fight the brush, briers, and swamps and drive the deer out past him where he can see it and get a shot at it. Another difference is that more often than not, the East Texas hunter depends on that deer to feed his family while the sportsman is killing for the fun of it and possibly a trophy so he can impress his friends with what a macho hunter he is.

According to Fray Juan Augustin Morfi, a Spanish missionary to the East Texas Indians in the early 1700s: "Along the banks of the streams and the outskirts of the woods, the droves of wild turkeys are so numerous that they disturb the traveler with their clucking." And John J. Audubon, when he visited East Texas in 1837, said: "I hardly supposed there were as many deer on the continent as I saw."

When Anglo-Americans came into East Texas, the woods were full of feral hogs and a man could fill his smokehouse with meat from them. They roamed the woods getting fat on mast (acorns and other nuts); then in winter, he would get his hog dogs and round up a few to butcher. He could go behind the house with his gun and little squirrel dog and get a mess of squirrels for supper, and deer and bear were also taken with the help of his dogs. Then, as markets became available, wildlife was a commercial commodity.

Venison and bear meat were served at all restaurants and even shipped out to other markets. Truett and Lay's *Land of Bears and Honey* had this to say: "Hunters killed thirty to forty deer in one day, and, near Silsbee, sports hunters killed as many as seventy deer in a day. In 1820, the mark of the white hunter upon the East Texas wilderness was faint. By 1900, he had skimmed the cream. Within three short decades after that, he had finished off all the bears and the panthers and most of the deer and the turkey. The great depression in 1929 administered the coup de grace."

Daddy always contended that it was the sports hunter who depleted the game. In the early 1900s, sportsmen from the cities would come to the Neches Bottom area around Boat Lake, to camp out, hunt, drink, and play cards. Daddy was at one of their camps once and they had filled a gully with squirrel bodies. They had made bets on who would kill the most and only took the tails to prove their claims.

I have ambivalent feelings about hunting. Man is a predator. He has always preyed on his fellow creatures for food. A clean death by bullet is preferable to a natural death from screwworms in the brain, eyes, and nose, or being torn to bits by another animal. Somehow, I don't worry as much about the victim as I do the hunter—the human who feels a need to kill and takes pleasure in inflicting pain and death on a fellow creature. I always went squirrel hunting with Daddy and my husband, Earl. Never carried a gun,just wanted to be in the woods. We were in the Neches Bottom once when my husband shot a squirrel in the top of a tall tree. It was only injured and as it fell it grabbed at every limb, twig, and clump of moss it passed in falling, but, each time, its grasp weakened and it would fall again. Finally, it hit the ground and the dog jumped on it. To see that little creature on its back, injured, facing that big dog and still fighting desperately for life, made me ill. To love life so! To cling to every hope on that long fall down to the ground and then be mauled to death by an animal ten times its size! We didn't need its body for food. Where is the sport, the triumph in mastery over such a small, helpless thing?

Many sports hunters graduate from guns to a camera. A camera shot of a beautiful wild creature gives something to keep and enjoy always and leaves something for the next person to see and enjoy.

Nowadays, most everybody is against hunting with dogs, and it has been made illegal in Texas Counties. It isn't dog hunting that has depleted the wildlife of East Texas, but greed, avarice, a man's need to project a macho image, and some people's sick idea of sport. Dogs aren't allowed in the Big Thicket National Preserve. When locals who live on the boundaries of the preserve are reproached about their dogs running in the preserve, they explain, "But Ol' Blue can't read no sign!" Two families I know who live about a quarter of a mile apart have two dogs that are good buddies. Every afternoon about 2:00, one trots down the sandy road to the other house where the second dog is already at the gate waiting. Together, they go off into the woods for an afternoon of rabbit hunting. Aside from a chunk of cornbread tossed to them occasionally, the only food most farm dogs get is whatever they can catch.

Dogs and dog hunting have been so much a part of our way of life in Big Thicket country that it is going to hurt deep when we have to chain them up. When I was young, we had freedom to roam the woods and streams. There was open range grazing for cows, horses, and hogs and a man could make a living from them. We have lost the freedoms that mattered most to us, that permitted us to live the way of life we had chosen. First, the land was taken by absentee corporations, then, open range was discontinued, the woods were fenced off, the access roads to the river were blocked, and the land leased to hunting clubs made up largely of city sportsmen who could afford the fee. Now, even the dogs aren't free anymore.

I know all the reasons why these things are so and that there's nothing that can be done about it. I'm not necessarily complaining—I'm just lamenting.

JOE'S LAKE PASTURE

River Mile 92.3 to 93.5

This large bend in the river is called Joe's Lake Pasture. Here, pasture means land on which cattle graze, and more often than not, it is heavily wooded. Joe's Lake is a deep cutoff or abandoned channel of the river and, since it is on and above normal flood levels, is a place for camps and cabins.

The land encircled by this bend was once proposed as the Joe's Lake Unit of Big Thicket National Preserve because of the magnificent floodplain forests. It was eliminated from the plan as it was especially valued by the owner, Southwest Timber Company. They had a clubhouse on the lake where they entertained visitors and held hunting parties. The area had been developed as a game preserve for company VIPs and guests. Also, they had some experimental tree farms there with which they did not want to part.

I stopped and strolled about the forest adjacent to the river and remembered special people with whom I had walked these woods. One of the proponents of the Joe's Lake Unit was Orrin Bonney, a Houston attorney, a great outdoorsman and organizer of the Texas Lone Star Chapter of the Sierra Club, and a strong voice, with his wife, Lorraine, for the Big Thicket cause. Orrin grew weak as he aged and died, as we all must, but I like to remember him strong and bold, walking in the forbidden forests of Joe's Lake to evaluate it for inclusion in the preserve. Lorraine is still climbing mountains and writing books.

Another Big Thicket champion whom Joe's Lake calls to mind is Ned Fritz, Dallas lawyer and environmentalist supreme, whose career is no less flamboyant than his red hair. The topography of the Joe's Lake area is undulating with giant hardwood trees forming a canopy over open, parklike forest floor. Ned Fritz and some others came here with me once. The forest floor was covered with jewel weed in bloom. Rays of sunlight through the high canopy sent sparkles flashing from the dewy flowers and, as we moved knee-deep through these members of the touch-me-not family, seed pods burst all about us, flinging their seeds about: pop-pop-pop! Ned was so enthralled, he named the forest Jewel Flower Cathedral, and promptly wrote a poem about it—as is his wont to do. Since Ned once had a court case the outcome of which depended on the meaning of the term "weed," he has worked assiduously to eliminate the word from botanical literature. He says the definition of "weed" as "an unwanted, useless plant" is in error, for no plant is useless, but has an important place in the balance of nature. He won the case, incidentally, but has ever since been paranoid about the word. Hence, it is no longer jewel weed, but jewel flower.

Wolves and Panthers

The Joe's Lake area is subject to flooding and has been left rather wild until recent years. I've heard more than one tell of seeing black bears and panthers here—which isn't too surprising. Both animals need wide roaming range and the floodplain forests of the Neches are ample enough to support a few. There are more of these predators, including bobcats, in this area than people realize and certainly more than biologists acknowledge. Wood rats, swamp rabbits, young birds, squirrels, and young armadillos are plentiful prey for bobcats and panthers.

Biologists say there are neither bears, panthers, nor wolves left in East Texas, but then biologists don't believe anything they haven't seen, heard, touched, and subjected to laboratory analysis and even then it has to be seen, heard, touched, and confirmed by other biologists so it can be proved they were not hallucinating or lying.

As for panthers, I've seen none myself, but my son, David, sitting on a bluff overlooking Village Creek near the Beech Creek confluence, watched a panther as it came out of the woods, crossed the creek on a log, and entered the woods on the other side. These big cats have a set route of fifty miles that takes about two weeks to travel. They don't shun human habitations, but might prowl about a homestead or camp at night. People frequently speak of hearing panthers during the night and they always say they "scream like a woman." I don't know about that—but then what do I know. I've never seen nor heard one. Now bobcats are something else. They are so plentiful that I see them frequently.

A hunter recently shot a panther on the east side of the river in Jasper County. There was much publicity about it that resulted in a real flurry of letters to the editor protesting the killing of such a rare and beautiful animal.

As usual in this area, the fellow thought he had done a great thing in ridding the countryside of a "dangerous varmint."

Biologists are unanimous in saying there are no true wolves in Texas, let alone Southeast Texas. The red wolf once roamed the coastal prairies and touched on our area, but they, it is said, have so interbred with coyotes and dogs that there are no true red wolves either. It is also said that there have never been any timber wolves in East Texas and what we have now is a mixture of red wolf, coyote, and dog. I have been in the western states and seen and listened to a lot of coyotes and I have recordings of coyotes, wolves, and dogs sounding off; and I do know the differences among their calls. In Southeast Texas, while camping out in remote areas, I have heard barks and howls of all three. In most of these counties, there are wolf, coon, and cat hunting clubs and some people trap them for the fur. Cattlemen set cyanide traps for wolves because, they claim, they prey on their calves. All of these knowledgeable people will tell you that they see coyotes, dog mixes and, very rarely, the old timber wolf, which was once plentiful in the forests of East Texas. I, myself, have seen them on very rare occasions. I have offered rewards for the pelt of what trappers are calling a timber wolf, but folks here are very wary of running afoul of game laws which are constantly changing and which exact a stiff fine when broken.

All the woods and river people say that wolves are increasing rapidly with the clearcutting of the forests for pine plantations. The grass, weeds, and brush of these vast clearcuts are ideal habitat for mice, rabbits, and ground-nesting birds, which are the prey of these canines. There has also been a population explosion of bobcats because of this increase in their food supply.

Rattlesnakes, also, are finding this a banquet of their favorite prey and are increasing, to me at least, alarmingly. They seem to prefer the boundaries between these clearcuts and slope forests, possibly because their prey is in the sunlit areas and snakes like the shade. At any rate, I have seen, stepped across, and levitated above some monstrous canebrake rattlers, and usually at the edge of clearcuts. I never fail to see at least one when I go into the canyonlands.

Little Critters

While the bears and panthers have all but disappeared in the Neches bottoms, smaller varmints such as 'possums, coons, and squirrels have thrived. Perhaps it is because they are omnivorous, which means they can and will

eat just about anything, and don't require a large foraging range, or that they are smaller and not as easily seen. Also it might be that the pioneers preferred to eat venison and bear steaks rather than coon and possum.

Their survival could be accredited to their ability to defend themselves. They both look like sweet little teddy bears but just try to grab hold of one when it is cornered! The possum has extremely sharp teeth and will fight until it is clear that he can't win; then he goes into a catatonic trance and falls over with his tongue hanging out and his eyes rolled back as if he were dead. Turn your back on him, though, and he is up and gone!

Coons also are formidable fighters and will fight man or dogs to the death. However, if one is captured while quite young, it will make an engaging pet. The Holifield boys gave my son, Marvin, a young coon once that they had been using to train coon dogs and it was understandably mean to the bone. Marvin named it Sugar. He won its trust but it loved my daughter, Regina, who had long, luxuriant hair. It would crawl up on her neck and snuggle underneath her hair, probably remembering its mother.

My own pet coon, which was sweet and lovable and had the intelligence and behavior of a three-year-old child, grew up and left, but after awhile returned with a mate. Taught to be trusting, they went to my daughter's home nearby to beg for food while I was gone and were both killed by her chow dog. I have raised many wild animals—rabbits, coons, possums, squirrels, and birds—and have had a loving relationship with all except the rabbit which had no personality, the possum, which was stupid, and a cowbird, which was an obnoxious, greedy little pig. Invariably, wild babies grow up and are no longer cute. When mature, they want to be with their own kind and can become serious problems, so they are not recommended for pets. Actually, I think it is illegal. Before taking one on, I recommend calling someone with the Texas Parks and Wildlife Department for information.

The most plentiful and visible of animals in the bottomlands are the squirrels. We have both fox and gray squirrels here, but fox squirrels prefer upland pine woods so the gray is the one most likely seen along the river. Squirrel populations wax and wane according to the mast crop. If there is not enough food, they simply do not breed. (A practice we humans would do well to emulate.) With plentiful food there is sometimes an explosion in the squirrel population and the excess migrate, as is true of many other species. Daddy saw one of these migrations on his trip down the river and marveled at it all his life. He noticed that all the trees on one side of the river were shaking and there was a noise like wind in the forest, though it was perfectly still. He then saw thousands of squirrels moving rapidly in one direction and the movement went on for some time before the forest was still again. I have often wondered what happens to these masses of creatures. They are probably reduced to normal numbers by predators such as hawks, owls, and wildcats. I also wonder what happens to them when their forests are clearcut.

Bingham Lake

Very near Joe's Lake is another, fairly large cutoff lake called Bingham Lake. Hugh Alexander Bingham, with his wife and four children, moved here about three miles below Sheffield's Ferry in 1845. He and his wife were buried on the banks of Bingham Lake where their graves can be seen to this day.

This series of waterbodies—Bingham Lake, Joe's Lake, Turner Branch, and Bush Lake—is all part of a route of the Neches River which was abandoned some centuries ago. During the hundred-year flood cycles, the river again courses through its old bed, marooning anyone caught on the hummock, as were the Ramers in 1884.

Hord's Bend

River Mile 92.3 4:30 P.M.

About three river miles from the highway bridge, the river starts to do some crazy things, looping up and doubling over. The second of the loops was a cutoff caused by tunneling through a narrow ridge, while the third and the largest is called Hord's Bend. I did some exploring of the land inside this bend and found some of the largest cypress trees I've ever seen, and in the most inaccessible spot imaginable, (probably the reason they were still standing). Hord's Bend was named for an early Jasper County settler, no doubt, as there is a Hord's Creek on the east side of the river. Johnny Swearingen, around the turn of the century, fenced the narrow neck of one of these bends to make a pen for cattle rounded up from the bottoms, and oxen which he used for his logging operation.

Before reaching Three Rivers, I noticed what appeared to be an open mature forest on the east cutbank. Tying my boat up, I climbed the sloping bank and entered the forest primeval. Scattered shafts of sunlight lit patches of woods fern which was the only forest floor vegetation. Close to the river, large vines snaked their way up into midair to share sunlight with the tree tops. No trace was left of the slender trees on which they had ascended. Only the spiral configuration of the vines was evidence that they had once embraced a small tree, held it close, and strangled it until it died, rotted, and fell away. These vines, and the dim, green light of the closed-canopy forest, created an eerie atmosphere. Across the undulating forest floor, through the widely scattered oak and gum trees, a herd of deer walked about, grazing on the acorns which covered the ground under the oaks. It was so reminiscent of the forests of my childhood, that for awhile I was transported back in time, wandering about idly as I did in those far-off days. I could almost hear Daddy's footsteps in the dry leaves behind me.

After an hour or so of wandering, I returned toward the river and saw two boats alongside mine. My heart sank. "Oh gosh! They're probably hunting club wardens who are going to give me hell for walking in 'their' woods." But quite the opposite was the case. I recognized the wide grin of I. C. Eason's sons, James and his "little" brother, Lesley, and two relatives, David and James Darrel Gore, who had been hunting up the river. They had recognized my boat and waited for me to appear. We laughed and talked for awhile and they gave me a couple of dressed squirrels for my supper. I told them that I would be passing the Eason camp sometime the next afternoon, so they insisted that I plan to spend the night there. When they assured me a big pot of squirrel dumplings would be waiting for me, my schedule for the next day was set. But for that day, I planned to visit with I. C.'s brother, Cat, Liege Lord of Three Rivers Island.

Friends, James Darrel Gore (left) and James Eason (right).

As I watched their boats circle and turn down river, the sunshine lighting sparkles on their wake, I was overwhelmed by a great sadness. It was as though I were watching them go off into oblivion. Their day is done. Their life as free rovers of the woods and water is near its end. Will they still find something to laugh over and be happy with in whatever limbo they are inexorably going toward? To be forced out of a bred-in-the-bone culture into a world where they can never find their own niche—never know self respect and fulfillment, to lose that on which they base their manhood. For some time now, they have played the role of Robin Hood and his merry men. While they rob no travelers, either rich or poor, they do roam their Sherwood Forest with boldness and take the King's deer as they have need. For the present, they are clinging desperately to the life of their forefathers. For how long, who knows!

FIRST NIGHT

River Mile 89.5 5:30 P.M.

My first camp was pitched on the first really large sandbar past Sheffield's Ferry. At one time, the sand was bare all the way to the forest edge, but apparently cattle were grazing the bottomlands then but have been removed, for all manner of vines, weeds, and brush are encroaching on the sand—cocklebur bushes being the most plentiful and the most obnoxious.

Cockleburs have hooked spines that grab and cling to everything that brushes against them. I remember once in Houston that Woolworth's variety store featured a novelty called porcupine eggs. It was a cocklebur placed on a bed of cotton in a little jewel box and sold for a dollar each! That's crazy, but not as crazy as the Pet Rock fad that had usually sensible people paying big money for a rock that had been given a name and a pedigree and instructions as to its feeding and care. People would talk to them as they would to a dog or cat! What was it P. T. Barnum said? "There's a sucker born every minute"? It's sad to think that people could be so lonely for companionship they would talk to a dumb rock, or so want to be doing the "in" thing they will make fools of themselves to fit in.

Regardless of the encroaching brush, this sandbar is quite impressive. The midbar slopes gently down to the shallow water's edge, but both ends are steep and the water deep. The lower end is the best place to tie up. You don't have to wade out into the shallows and drag the boat over the sand to water deep enough to float the boat with you in it.

As the late sun slanted behind the woods, the colors of everything came alive. As the last light hit the willows, their green turned gold against the dark green-purple-blue-shadowed background. At this time of day, the water becomes very still and mirrors forest, bank, and sky. When the sun finally went down, it still lit up the tall trees on the opposite bank in the most glorious afterglow. Cypress and sycamore trees, just beginning to get an autumn russet tinge, red maple already turning crimson, chains of golden muscadine vines, and the carnadine of blackgum leaves like drops of blood—all glittered in the light and threw their reflections on the water.

I couldn't stop snapping my camera. I couldn't bear to think that no one else would ever see this, and I knew that I could never adequately describe its incredible beauty in words.

No birds had been in evidence all day, but just before dark, jays and crows came out and fussed at me and continued a racket well into the night. They were announcing to the forest world that there were possibly dangerous invaders in the forest. A lone pileated woodpecker yak-yak-yaked across the river and was quiet. I had hoped to acquire a night light which would enable me to watch the wildlife on the bar without alarming them and making my presence known, but discovered the lights were too expensive. There is plenty of wildlife here. I've never seen such graphic evidence of nighttime wildlife activity. There are tracks of everything from deer to bobcats, otter, beaver, even alligator, and all the small animals.

After the birds quieted, I was serenaded by the creatures of the night—frogs and insects and a great splash down at the water accompanied by a deep grunt! How I miss my dog, Junior! Somehow, having him close, blind though he was, made me feel safe. I was not afraid or nervous—yet—but did decide to get inside my tent, zip it up, write awhile, and read my Bible before going to sleep. I later learned that the loud "splat" on the water was the alarm signal of a beaver as he discovered my presence and was warning his family to stay away.

Rustling sounds at the woods' edge announced the approach of animals that were too wary to cross the bar in the sight and smell of humans. A flashlight beam picks up glowing points of light which identify the animal behind them. Animals which are active primarily at night have a mirror-like layer behind the sensitive cells in the eye, which magnify the small amount of light received, thus enabling the animal to see better in the dark. Small sparkles low on the forest floor are the eye shine of spiders and higher up on limbs might be the bright yellow glow of raccoon eyes, or the vivid greenish eyeshine of a bobcat. At the water's edge, a bullfrog's eyes glow in opalescent green while alligator eyeshine is so brilliantly red that some backwoodsmen call them "old fire eyes." Before battery-powered spotlights came into use, hunters hunted deer at night with a fire pan containing burning pine, and they aimed their gun between the twin reflections, hitting the deer squarely between the eyes.

Shortly after turning off my lantern, I tried to go to sleep. It takes a couple of nights to adjust from a Sealey Posturepedic to the thin pad beneath my sleeping bag. And then something new was added to the sounds of the night: the distant howl of wolves. Not the yapping of coyotes or bellow of hunting dogs, but the long howls of a pack of wolves. They were evidently out hunting. The howls came closer, and presently I was startled out of my wits by something large crashing through the underbrush at the forest edge. Something was running toward my tent! Just as it reached me, I heard the loud whistling snort of a buck deer that was as startled to meet my tent as I was to have him there. After some brief stamping and snorting, he rushed toward the water, apparently planning to swim the river and thus throw the wolves off his scent.

At 10:00, another sound began—this time not a natural one. It sounded like an oil drilling rig in operation. It ended before daylight. Next day, I mentioned it to Kelton Wayne Eason and he said it WAS an oil operation going on a few hundred yards from the river, and in the middle of the night. Probably working illegal aliens and trying to hide it—a common practice nowadays. However, after a long day of unaccustomed paddling, I was too tired to let a little thing like noise keep me awake. I slept.

Explorer Scouts and Fog Flow

I scheduled this site for my first night camp not only because it is one of the largest and most beautiful sandbars on the river, but because I had camped here several years ago and witnessed a strange phenomenon: At dusk, a thick mist began to form in the forest on the opposite side of the river. There was an opening in the trees on the cutbank side that looked like it might have been an old pipeline and the mist was pouring into the opening and over the cutbank like a waterfall. It spread over the river until the water was covered. A large full moon rose and illuminated the mist like stardust. This is probably a common occurrence on the river, but I felt I had been privileged to a once-in-a-lifetime experience. Once in *my* lifetime at any rate.

It was on this sandbar that I learned to make a one-match fire. First, you gather an assortment of sizes of dry twigs, making a pyramid of the very smallest, then you build on this gradually with larger twigs as it grows, finally placing good-sized sections of dead branches on the top layer. As you build, you leave a space to put your hand into the center where you put a lighted match to the smallest twigs. The fine fuel ignites immediately, igniting those above until there is enough heat for the large chunks to burn and there you have a going campfire. It never fails.

My teacher was a young leader of a pack of Explorer Girl Scouts who had persuaded me to guide them on an expedition down the river from Steinhagen Lake to Evadale. They had their own canoes, had practiced handling them, and had long made plans for their great adventure, but were faced with an impasse when their parents wouldn't let them go alone and they couldn't find a responsible adult who would go with them. Somehow, the girls had heard of me and had the impression that I was familiar with the river and wouldn't mind leaving my husband, children, and home and giving three or four days to chaperoning them. I protested that I was having a bad bout of bursitis in my shoulders and couldn't possibly make the trip, but they begged so piteously, promising that I wouldn't have to pick up a paddle the entire trip.

Aside from learning to make a one-match fire, I got a first-class sunburn and my bursitis cured. The young girl with whom I was paired couldn't paddle well enough to keep up with the other canoes, so I did my duty. I thought I would die with pain the first day. The next day, something snapped and the pain left. Apparently, the calcium deposits freezing my shoulder joints broke loose and allowed free, painless movement for the first time in weeks. Then again, perhaps it was the willow bark I was chewing in lieu of aspirin. Aspirin is salicylic acid, named for the willow genus, *Salix*, and knowing that the Indians used the inner bark of willow as an analgesic, I peeled the bark from branches of streamside willows and gnawed them. Whatever—I survived.

When mealtime came, it seemed the person in charge of provisions had fallen down on the job. We were to have pancakes for breakfast, peanut butter sandwiches for lunch, and sandwiches of bread and canned meat paste for supper, but she had forgotten two essential items: bread and oil. Frying pancake batter in a dry, tin skillet produced a sort of scrambled mess which the addition of peanut butter at lunch and meat paste at supper did nothing to improve. After three days on that diet, we arrived at Bearman's Bluff, and I pulled in and went ashore to use the telephone at the camphouse there. When we reached Clark's Camp an hour later, hot and sweaty, David was there with ice cold cokes for everyone. Oh, with what rapture we fell upon those frosty bottles!

When we brought the canoes out of the water at Evadale, sunburned and about as scroungy looking as anybody can look, the girls' mothers came tripping down to the river (though not close enough to soil their designer shoes), all freshly made up and immaculately coiffeured and contoured. I said to myself: "Geraldine, you are some kind of a fool!" But then I thought: "I didn't do it for the parents, but for the girls, and they're worth it." These parents were obviously well-to-do, but I had given their daughters something they could not—or would not—give them. I'll bet those kids remember me. I especially remember the leader, though I'm ashamed to say I've forgotten her name. The last I heard of her, she was a graduate student at Rice University. Oh, and by the way, a father bought me a $2.98 straw hat to wear on the trip as I had none: their only contribution to the tour.

Anyway, I have had occasions since when the one-match trick came in handy. There's no suspense like being cold, hungry, and dying for a cup of hot coffee and having only one match and a high wind. And, of course, camping out just isn't any fun at all without a campfire. One of the minuses of having National Park Service protection for the Neches River is the prohibition of open campfires. There is some rationalization for this rule. Many pieces of driftwood are rare works of art fashioned by wind, sand, and the abrasion of swift water. They should be left for future voyagers to see and enjoy.

In the Western states, there is a paucity of wood to begin with and the low humidity and lack of rainfall means that unsightly campfire debris littering beaches and banks is forever. Here, in the Big Thicket, there is an unending supply of dead wood from trees fallen from cutbanks into the river when their roots are undermined by high water, and from debris washed from the forest floor during floods. I don't like mounds of charcoal dotting the pristine whiteness of the sandbars, though, and do wish people would go back to the woods' edge to build their campfires. But then during dry seasons, there would be a danger of wildfires. An alternative to total restriction of campfires and no restriction at all is to designate campsites along the river with a place for a campfire, carefully located and maintained where it won't be a fire hazard.

Everyone loves campfires, even in summertime. There must be something about them that takes us back to our caveman days. In the far-off past when humans had no weapons nor safe shelters from predators, the dark of night was a time of terror. A sick or injured straggler, failing to reach the safety of the cave, was pulled down and eaten by a night prowler. Or perhaps the cave sanctuary was invaded by a saber-tooth tiger and one of the clan is dragged out screaming and kicking to feed a litter of kits.

What a blessing it must have been when humans learned to control fire! Perhaps a slow-burning wood chunk lit by lightning was nurtured with mosses and punk (decayed wood) and fanned to a blaze whenever there was need to start a new fire. A night fire in the mouth of the cave, or out in the open plain, would keep away the most daring and ferocious animal, and no longer would the young and the weak have to freeze to death during the winter. Perhaps, too, they learned that cooked meat and vegetables were easier to eat with teeth worn down by grinding grains and fibrous plant material.

After domesticating wild plants, people learned that burning an area was an easy way to prepare a field for planting and fire became an important tool of primitive agriculture.

All that fire represents to humans—warmth, safety, useful tool— it has become such a part of man's psychological makeup that even in this age of technology when many homes have central heating, there is also a fireplace where one can sit and look into the flames. Why do we have this strange feeling of pleasure and well-being when we gaze into a wood fire? Is it the genes of our ancestors stirring in our cells? We still equate light with what is good, desirable, and positive, while darkness represents evil, fear, and ignorance. Why do so many of us fear the dark when reason tells us that there is nothing outside the door, under the bed, or in the closet that will hurt us? Our genes tell us "Beware! There is a thing with claws and long teeth there in the dark just waiting to grab you!" I do not fear man nor beast, yet why do I have this flashlight here beside me? Something tells me it's not just for the light.

Sandbar in morning

Part Two

Day 2

SECOND DAY

River Mile 89.5

That second morning simply could not have been surpassed for beauty. Where everything turns a rich, rosy gold at evening, the mornings are silver and pearl. Mist covers the river and the sun, rising into an opalescent sky, strikes the dew drops that cover every leaf, twig, and branch, and turns them to flashing diamonds. It is interesting to know that dew neither "falls" nor "rises." During the day, the sun heats the earth. At night, the air cools and the earth radiates heat back into the atmosphere, condensing water in the air one molecule at a time on objects that have a lower temperature than the air. There is no dew underneath objects, as even a leaf can prevent the radiant heat from rising.

There were no fresh animal tracks on the sandbar that morning. After the crows advertised my presence the evening before, all the forest knew that MAN was on the sandbar and avoided it. This is a good reason for barring camping on sandbars except in designated areas.

I did not stop to analyze nature's phenomena, however, but walked around like one intoxicated, taking roll after roll of film. Finally, I cooked oatmeal over a small fire and ate breakfast.

My campsite had evidently been used before, as there was a smooth area on the woods' edge with a pole nailed between two trees so a tarp shelter could be erected, and the remains of a campfire. It was unobtrusive and took nothing away from the natural beauty of the scene. I was careful not to leave any evidence of my having been there, so the next occupant could enjoy the same sense of undiscovered wilderness that I felt.

I pushed my boat onto the river at around 10:00. Ahhh! To float off soundlessly on glassy water into the silvery mist. A great blue heron lifted up and floated away. It was like a scene from the *Twilight Zone*. I plied the paddle vigorously as I wanted to visit with Cat Eason on Three Rivers Island sometime during the middle of the day.

ARMADILLOS

River Mile 89.5

I saw a few armadillos rummaging in the vegetation at the edge of the sandbar the second day after leaving Scott's Landing. Armadillos are sensitive to temperature extremes since they have no fur to cover their bodies, so normally they forage around at dusk in the cool of the evening, especially during the heat of summer; but it is not unusual to see them in daytime. In winter, they feed at midday when it is warmest. They suffer severely during long periods of freezing weather as they do not hibernate. Armadillos don't like the water. Because of their heavy armor, they need help when crossing a stream, so they swallow a lot of air until they can float. If the stream is narrow, they just wade in and walk across the bottom to the other side.

My brother once shot some armadillos and sliced them up to fry. The meat tasted a lot like pork. Some people make sausage out of them and say it's quite good. There were so many armadillos eaten during the Depression that they became known as Hoover hogs, for the unfortunate man who happened to be president at that time. I, myself, capitalized on this need as a child when, very much wanting to buy some oil paints and being poor, I chased armadillos down in the woods and carried them by the tails to the Negro quarters where I sold them for 25 cents each.

People don't eat much armadillo any more. They have welfare and food stamps. But the strange creatures that look like relics from the age of dinosaurs are being used for other, quite interesting purposes.

Armadillos always have identical quadruplet young—that is, all the young born at the same time develop from one egg. This makes them valuable for genetic and reproductive physiology research. They are also being used to develop a vaccine against the loathsome and dreaded disease, leprosy, since a form of the disease occurs in many armadillos in the wild. While I have never personally known it to occur, there are cases of humans contracting leprosy from handling armadillos, but it is not known which, man or beast, was the original transmitter. The relationship was first discovered near Carrsville, Louisiana, where there is a leper colony. Some suggest that the disease was spread by the habit of rural folk of blowing their nose between thumb and forefinger, slinging the mucus on the ground ,and wiping their fingers on their pants. Since leprosy germs survive for long periods in moist conditions, armadillos rooting about for insects and worms contract the disease. The rate of infected animals has been found to be as high as 25 percent in some populations, so one might give a second thought to close contact. It would be very interesting to conduct a study of the armadillos of the Big Thicket National Preserve to determine the presence of leprosy among them.

A giant form of armadillo (about nine feet from nose to tail) inhabited Texas around 11,500 years ago, but the present species is a recent immigrant to the United States, having crossed the Mexican border a little over a century ago. By the 1930s, armadillos had successfully populated East Texas and western Louisiana.

Around the turn of the century, a German immigrant named Charles Apelt saw commercial possibilities in the armadillo for the curio trade and founded the Apelt Armadillo Company and Farm near Comfort, Texas. The farm remained in operation until 1971. Baskets, lampshades, wall hangings, stuffed animals, and other ornaments were manufactured, but the most popular was the basket, said to have been invented by Apelt himself. The cleaned and dried shell was flexed until the end of the tail could be put into the mouth, thus forming the handle, and a colorful calico lining was sewn in. I haven't seen any of these baskets lately, but occasionally, a stuffed specimen turns up as a door stop in the offices of lawyers and others with similar dubious taste.

In the 1920s, farmers from Central and West Texas began to complain about armadillos, accusing them of digging up and damaging sprouting green crops as well as eating alfalfa and the eggs of quail, wild turkey, and other ground-nesting birds. The folks with the federal rodent control program requested permission to poison the offenders with strychnine, but were told to hold off as the animal was thought to consume insects and other life injurious to agriculture.

Research into the armadillo's eating habits showed that it was not interested in birds' nests in its territory and ignored eggs placed in its very path. Since armadillos are edentate (without teeth), they must be very selective in their food preferences. Ninety-three percent of their food was found to be animal material: 78 percent insects, 1.2 percent reptiles and amphibians, and the remainder spiders, millipedes, earthworms, slugs, etc. Skunks, ringtailed cats, crows, possums, roadrunners, and even cattle proved to be the chief destroyers of ground nests of birds.

Innocuous as the armadillo might appear, I do have a serious complaint against it. In rooting about for worms and insects in the organically rich soils of slope and terrace forests, they uproot the rare forest floor plants of these communities, especially during floods when the lowlands are under water and there are large concentrations of these animals on high ground. During drought, organisms in the soil go deep for moisture except on the slopes and terraces where seepage keeps the soil and humus moist. I have seen acres of forest floor look like a plowed field after one night of armadillo activity, with mayapple, trillium, bloodroot, etc., uprooted and dying. They don't eat the vegetation, but it is lost just the same.

Population control of the armadillo to protect endangered plant species can be justified since they have no natural predators to keep them in check. Their chief enemy seems to be the automobile, judging from the squashed carcasses on the highways. When very young, their shell is pink and tender and they are a treat for wild cats and canines, but the hard shell, along with the long, sharp claws of the adult, are pretty good protection. They are not all that swift, either, but rely on the safety of their holes, which they dig with their powerful claws and from which they seldom roam afar. When startled, the armadillo springs high in the air like a jack-in-the-box, then takes off, exhibiting great skill dodging and maneuvering among trees, shrubs, and brier patches. So—if a canoeist feels the need to stretch his legs and spots an armadillo in the woods, I don't think he will be doing the animal any harm by giving it a bit of a run.

When young, I had a pet armadillo and I could frequently be seen strolling down the sidewalk with my armadillo on a leash—very much to the chagrin of my beautiful, popular, and very proper sister who seemed to feel that the prestige and standing of the family in the community were being compromised by my eccentric behavior. She is still very proper, by the way, and I am still eccentric.

It has been many years since I chased armadillos for sport or profit. Guess one loses one's high spirits as one grows older and must have a logical reason for expending energy and effort. The SPCA will probably object to my suggesting armadillo chasing as a sport, but it is less cruel than shooting them with a gun and nobody protests that—probably because the NRA is stronger than the SPCA, and a lot meaner.

Before anyone decides to augment his income, supply his larder, or even protect rare plants by reducing the armadillo population, let it be known that they are under the same regulations as squirrels and rabbits and one must have a license to hunt them. Though I have never heard of a game warden giving anyone a ticket for shooting them, I. C. Eason was stopped by a park ranger once for bagging a few during legal hunting season. I think it was the ranger's uncertainty as to its classification as a game animal rather than mercy that decided him not to give I. C. a ticket and fine for killing non-game species in the preserve.

THREE RIVERS

River Mile 87.5 Noon

Three Rivers is a place in the river where a horseshoe bend was cut through by the current and one confronts not only the main channel, but both branches, so it appears to be three streams coming together. I came to this site once with I. C. Eason. We had come upriver from his camp to explore Joe's Lake Pasture. We didn't quite make it to Joe's Lake Pasture. As soon as we headed upriver, a storm came up. Dark clouds boiled out of the southwest and the bottom dropped out, dumping torrents of rain on us. We had reached Three Rivers and decided to take refuge under an overhang on the cutbank of the horseshoe where, squatting huddled in our narrow refuge, we watched as a small tornado formed on the far horizon. Lightning was getting rather close and I told him how you could count "a thousand and one, a thousand and two" between the flashes and the boom and determine how many miles away the lightning was striking. When we couldn't get past "one" before the sky split wide open with a deafening crash, I. C. decided that he wanted a man-made refuge and was determined to make a run for a cabin about a mile downriver at Wright's Landing. The idea of my being the tallest object out in open water with lightning striking all around didn't appeal to me, but I. C. was adamant. I sat in the floor of the boat with my eyes closed and head bowed, recalled and repented of my numerous sins, and commended my soul to God. I. C. gunned that 50-horsepower Mercury motor full throttle and the boat barely touched water, we were going so fast. The rain drops felt like bullets hitting my face. We made it to Wright's Landing, scrambled up the steep, red-clay bluff and squatted, wet and muddy, on the short porch. The camphouse was locked.

The dangerous thunderstorm passed away to the northeast, but the weather continued dark and threatening. My main purpose in making the trip had been to take photos, so we decided to return. We climbed down the bluff to the river and, as the rumbling thunder and the pounding of my heart abated, I. C. headed the prow of the boat downstream toward his camp.

Two friends of mine, the Van Pelt brothers, Ronnie and Donnie, when they were teenagers, decided to spend some time going down the river and live off the land enroute. They took gun and ammunition, fishing tackle, and a little food. By the second day, they had eaten all the food, game seemed to be nonexistent, the fish weren't biting, and they were getting hungry. A high wind came up and it started raining, so they pulled into the backwater of Three Rivers. As they looked into the far bend of the large cutoff, they saw a lone duck bobbing about on the water. Very quietly, they pulled to shore, got out and crawled to a good vantage point so that they could not miss, and blasted away. They shot the head off a beautiful, lifelike decoy someone had placed there to lure the real thing.

The boys decided to go back and, since paddling upstream in a river boat against a north wind was out of the question, they started walking overland. All night in the cold rain they struggled through sloughs both deep and shallow, through brush and briers and mud. After a lengthy, incredibly miserable journey, they staggered out on a highway where they hitched a ride back to their camphouse at Sheffield's Ferry.

Ronnie laughed a lot while telling about it, but, believe me, it wasn't the least bit funny when it was happening. I've been in similar situations a few times and know whereof he spoke. Sometimes, you have only two alternatives: pursue a difficult course or just give up and die. The extra adrenaline that comes from facing a desperate, life-threatening situation gives you the strength to survive and you make it.

EASON FAMILY

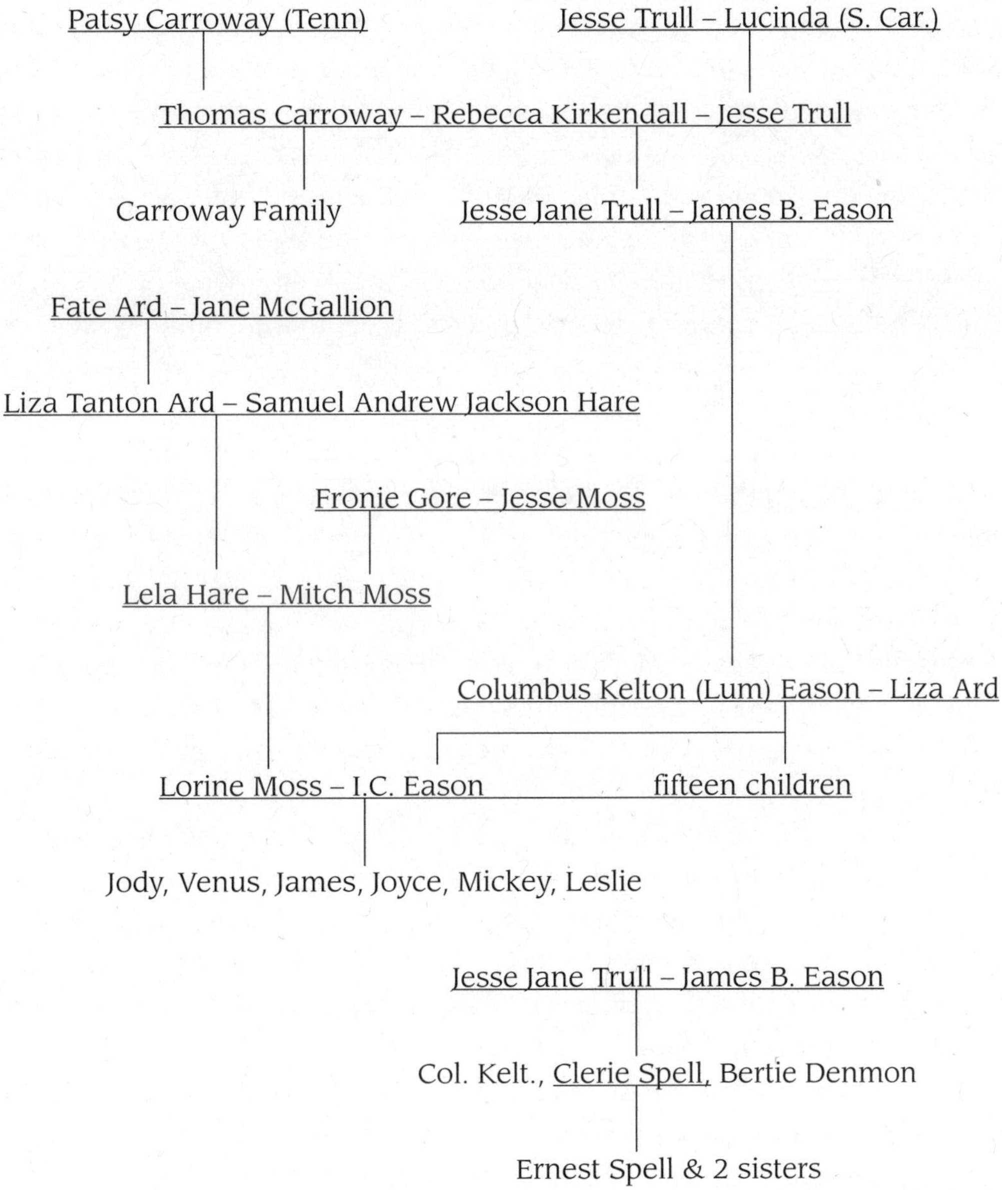

CAT EASON

This stretch of the river seems to have a special appeal to those who want to get away from it all. When word got out that the cutoff islands belonged to no one, Cat Eason and son, Kelton Wayne, were the first to stake a claim and they set up homestead on Three Rivers Island.

This island occupies about ten acres, has a lovely bit of woods on it, a sandbar and a deep channel on one side for a harbor. Cat and Kelton Wayne cleared enough land for a garden, put some tame ducks on the water, and brought in chickens, which just roamed about and scavenged for food. Catfish from the river, squirrels, coons, and feral hogs rounded out their grocery list.

I wanted to spend some time with Cat on the island but was somewhat intimidated by the sign at the entrance. Actually the sign is not translatable. Along with weathering, the fact that both Cat and Kelton Wayne can barely read or write, and, according to a reliable source, both were drunk when they were making the sign, it makes little sense other than a general raillery against the Park Service and trespassers.

Paddling noisily up to their boat landing, I helloed the camp before getting out of the boat. Presently, Kelton Wayne appeared and I identified myself. He invited me on up and put on a pot of coffee. Cat wasn't there at the time, as he had gone into Spurger, but his wife was. A shelter had been built of salvaged lumber and plastic tarps, and right out under the trees was a cookstove hand-made of sheet iron. There was a handpump water well and a gasoline generator for electric lights. Kelton Wayne has a house at Barlow Lake Estates but spends most of his time on the river. He lost part of his hand in a shotgun accident some years ago, so he is semi-retired.

It is a very pleasant place shaded by tall oak trees, a nice view of the river, chickens scratching around, and a pet deer browsing. We sat around awhile drinking coffee and talking politics. These backwoods people seem to blame everything that takes away what they consider their rights as "comminism," not realizing that their chief enemy all these years has been the lumber companies and their brand of capitalism. Kelton Wayne once ran for "high sheriff" of Tyler County and one of his campaign posters still hangs on a tree at the camp. He was a quiet, soft-spoken person—friendly and eager to get along, but the eyes above the smile were narrow and cool. You sensed that there was someone else behind that calm exterior--someone you would not want to catch doing something he did not want you to catch him doing. Just the same, if I were stranded and in trouble out on the river, I would have been extremely happy to see Kelton Wayne coming round the bend. Unfortunately, Kelton Wayne was shot by his wife, who apparently didn't agree that beating his wife was a man's perogative.

The Park Service had not yet acquired all the land in the Upper Neches Corridor Unit of which Three Rivers is a part. Temple-Eastex, the previous legal owner, had a hands-off policy and waited to bequeath the problem to the Park Service. When the Park Service did acquire the unit, I was afraid they would flex the muscles of the Federal Government and force Cat off the island. Cat swore they would have to take him off "feet first," and indeed, they were planning an all-out assault to evict him with federal marshals backing up law enforcement rangers. I told Bill Jewel, the Land Acquisition person, that Cat had had surgery for lung cancer, and was still smoking cigarettes and drinking whiskey, so he would probably die soon. Bill has a tender heart but is also pretty smart, so when he considered the unfavorable publicity and adverse effects on the already-shaky relations with the locals, he kept postponing the eviction event. When pressed by officials to take action against Cat, who was in the hospital at the time, Bill told them: "I'm not about to serve the papers on an old man flat on his back in the hospital!"

At least two years later, Cat was still among the living, could still leap from boat to boat going full speed down the river, and was trying to drink up all the liquor in three counties. I heard that he got into his boat at Scott's Landing, passed out, and fell into the bottom of the boat, which drifted all the way down to Evadale before he came to himself. Every time I saw Bill Jewel, one of the first things he'd say was, "How's Cat?" I think he had finally decided that Cat was going to live forever. The man did seem to be indestructible.

Cat shared his time between the island, the hospital, and a son's home when the weather got too cold. A young woman reporter from the Woodville newspaper met Cat while he was in the hospital and interviewed him. She portrayed Cat as the Thoreau of the Neches, living in harmony with nature. Thoreau, the gentle, vegetarian, pacifist, and Cat Eason? How I laughed! As a youngster, Cat and his brothers settled sibling rivalry by "Indian fighting": holding one another's left hand and slashing away with their knives. Once when the family was sojourning in Arkansas, a man molested one of Cat's beautiful twin daughters and Cat shot him—"I mean GRAVEYARD dead" so my informant assured me. His brother, I. C., was just as loud and threatening, but inside, he was a sensible man who would rather be your friend than fight you. Not Cat! He was mean and ornery to the bone and could out-fight, out-cuss, or out-drink any man in the bottom. Most people, when they see death and the Hereafter nearing, "get religion." Perhaps he did. I thought he would go out as he had lived but I heard he had quit drinking and he even looked pretty good when I saw him at his brother Cecil's funeral. Perhaps watching his brothers die one by one impressed upon him that it would soon be his own time to meet his Maker and he had better start getting ready for it. Cat had a lot of sins to repent. I could tell stories about him that would censor this book in short order. He finally died and his was the only Eason funeral I ever went to where nobody cried.

I didn't wait for Cat to come in, as I wanted to get on down the river. There were places I wanted to see and explore and still get to I. C.'s camp before dark.

WRIGHT'S LANDING

River Mile 87.1 3:15 P.M.

After leaving Three Rivers, I crossed over to the bluff side of the river, for I wanted to explore Wright's Landing. The old road coming to the bluff from the Bevilport/Weiss Bluff Road is still traveled, for there is a camphouse here; but there is no evidence of the activity that once kept this a lively place when the pioneer Wright family shipped and received goods by riverboats.

Two brothers, Alexander and Sherod Wright, left South Carolina in the early 1830s to come to Texas. The Mexican government was giving cheap land to anyone who would settle in East Texas, so the Wrights each homesteaded a league and a labor (about 4,430 acres) of land adjoining the other on the east side of the Neches.

Thanks to research done by Dan Lay and Joe Truett for their book *Land of Bears and Honey*, and the fact that Sherod's grandson, Solomon Wright, wrote an account of his family and of his life as a wanderer, we know quite a bit about the Wrights and their way of life. In 1906, Sol Wright lived at Ford's Bluff (now Evadale), on the Neches River in a houseboat that he built himself, and in 1915, made a trip down the river from Town Bluff to Beaumont. All he took was a shotgun and ammunition, bedding, axe, tent canvas, and coffee. He ate squirrel, turkey, duck, and catfish. That must have been a popular pastime in the early 1900s, as his trip paralleled my father's. Sol's wanderlust took him all the way to California where he died in 1931.

Sol's grandfather, Sherod, was a cattleman. He acquired four cows and calves in Carolina by substituting for a man who did not want to go to the Spanish-American War and had the money to pay his way out. Surviving the war, Sherod came with wife and cattle to Texas where his brother Alex was already established.

The Wrights soon discovered that they had chosen land that was the traditional hunting grounds of Indians who lived in a village approximately 40 miles to the west from them, but there was plenty of game for all so they amicably shared the land and its resources. There is no record to tell when or why the Indians no longer came. My guess is that the rapacious whites so decimated the wild animals for commercial purposes that it was no longer worth the trip to hunt there.

The longhorn cattle fattened on the rich virgin grasses of the longleaf pine uplands in the summer and the riverbottom canebrakes during the winter. The uplands were burned in the winter, so by spring, there would be a new crop of tender grass, fertilized by the potash and other minerals created by the fires, and the cattle would move up out of the bottoms. Sherod prospered so that in 1857, by the time he was 62, his property had increased from four cows to 1500 cattle, 75 horses, and 20 slaves.

The Wright and Richardson families worked their cattle together, rounding them up from the bottoms and uplands a couple times a year to brand calves, castrate the males, and gather the steers, 500 or so at a time, to drive them over the Old Beef Trail, across the Sabine at Hickman's Ferry, and on to Alexandria, Louisiana. After the railroad came into Orange in 1860, they drove to the railroad there.

While livestock had to be driven to markets, other products of the ranch—cypress shingles, cowhides, otter furs, barrels of bear fat, etc.—were taken to Wright's Landing on the river to be picked up by steamboats and sold at Sabine Pass.

The vast amount of land owned by the Wrights exhibited a diversity of topography, forest type, and natural resources: the superlative timber of the longleaf pinelands and cypress swamps, the productive virgin soils of the bottomland terraces, and plentiful game. Transportation provided by the living river gave a monetary value to all the foregoing which combined in a sure formula for increasing material prosperity, and depleting resources.

The oldtimers died off, and the increasing numbers of heirs resulted in a continual division of family holdings, with land being sold off as the town-dwelling owners had no use for it. There are still Wrights scattered about in Jasper County, and, in recent years, a great, great, great-granddaughter of Sherod Wright bought the site of the old home place and cemetery and built a modern home in the place of the log cabin her ancestors had built there so long ago.

After spending some time in observation and contemplation, I descended the bluff to my boat and pushed off into the current. It was getting late and I needed to select a campsite for the night.

WILLIS PAYNE CAMP

River Mile 84 4:00 P.M.

After the great loop of Three Rivers, the river takes a long, straight course where the bends are too subtle to show on the topographical maps. I was watching very carefully, for I especially wanted to visit the site of Willis Payne's camp and there would be no landmarks after the cabin at Wright's Landing.

After participating in the trench warfare of World War I in France, Willis Payne was so overwhelmed by the cruelty, savagery, and inhumanity he had witnessed, that, upon returning home, he went to the river to escape "civilization."

A high bluff, topped with tall oaks and pines, appeared on my left and, confident that this had to be the right place, I pulled in, climbed the bank and walked about among the tall trees. The area was open and parklike and a well-used road approached it, indicating it was still a favored spot for campers. In sight of the bluff and very near the river was a cutoff lake: a beautiful, clear black, cypress-fringed body of water.

Willis Payne was very close to me as I sat and viewed this peaceful scene, shaded by the great trees with the river and broad sandbar on my left and the mirror lake on my right. Man seems to be strapped to the wheel of endless cycles of war and its accompanying horrors and many of us, like the prophet Micah, have looked and longed for that day when:

> We shall walk in His paths and. . . they shall beat their swords into plowshares and their spears into pruning hooks; nation shall not lift up sword against nation, neither shall they learn war any more. But they shall sit every man under his vine and under his fig tree; and none shall make them afraid.

So Willis Payne found his peace under the vines and oak trees of this lovely place. Seeing and reading the world news today and knowing how easily the ignorant and the innocent are manipulated by the power and profit brokers to slay one another by the millions, I feel, as did the prophet:"Therefore, I will wail and howl; I will go stripped and naked; I will make a wailing like the dragons and mourning as the owls. . . ."

I have done my share of wailing and howling over my poor world, of marching in the streets, and organizing peace groups. At one time, I really believed that once people became educated and could read history and the teachings of the wise men of the ages, they would know the causes and consequences of war and will outlaw it for all time. I especially hoped that "Christians" would start taking the teachings of Jesus Christ seriously and live by them.

I learned at an early age that right does not triumph over wrong by force of arms. Once, my brother, sister, and I were playing with some neighbor children on a set of swings when the neighborhood bully pushed my brother off a swing and hurt him. Seeing my little brother crying outraged my sense of things as they should be, and I waded in to protect him. Of course, the bully, finishing with my brother, hit my sister in the stomach and beat the snot out of me and we all went home crying. My mother solved the problem by teaching us to stay away from the bully and to avoid situations that gave him the opportunity to abuse us. It would have helped if she could have gone to his mother and discussed the matter with her, but that poor woman was beaten and abused by her husband and could have done nothing with the son. So violence begets violence. By the way, the bully became an officer in World War II and came home a great hero. Killed lots of people and was decorated for it.

I've given up on the hope that I shall see the prophet's day of universal peace, but have consolation in the fact that it is possible that each individual can have that "peace that passeth understanding" in his own heart and life. Of course there will always be sadness and disappointments; they are a natural and inevitable part of living in this world, but when we don't have to deal with the guilt of knowing that they are a result of our own wrongdoing, we will have the strength to endure them.

And what does all this have to do with War and Peace? When we learn to control our own violent emotions and actions --when each of us makes a firm decision that civilized human beings do not resort to such behavior and that all violence against one another is totally inadmissable, then we have made a beginning.

I hope Willis Payne found peace. If ever peace of mind and spirit could be found, it could be found in this place. He didn't get to live out his life here, though. As he grew older and became ill, his relatives came and got him and took him to Burkeville where he died.

As much as I would have liked, I could not remain on this beautiful, peaceful spot, so after an hour or so of somber reflection, I returned to my boat, saddened to think that the world has not changed since Willis Payne came to the river.

Another bit of history is associated with this site. In the 1930s some desperados robbed the Kirbyville bank. They were chased to Willis Payne's camp where they attempted to escape by swimming the river where one of them drowned and thereby lost the money, or so the survivor claimed. If I were being hotly pursued and had to swim a river, I would hastily find some hollow tree or armadillo hole and stash the cash until it was safe to return and retrieve it. Knowing treasure hunters, this will probably inspire a rush on the river by wild-eyed gold nuts armed with metal detectors, shovels, and "waybills" (maps), thoughtfully provided by enterprising locals, and the whole bluff will soon look like a plowed field. So let me hasten to say that I am only saying what I would have done. But maybe with a posse on my heels, my thinking wouldn't be as cool and lucid as it is now sitting here at my typewriter.

Sheriff Aubrey Cole told me an amusing story about this bank robbery. It seems the local doctor was about the only person who had any money in the bank and when the cry went up that the bank had been robbed and the bandits were fleeing in a Model T Ford down the Law Scott road into the bottom, the doctor jumped into his own car and gave chase. A habitual hanger-on at the corner who happened to be hard of hearing said: "Boy! Somebody must be turrible sick! Jis lookit ol' Doc go!"

MARTIN RAMER

River Mile 85.4

The Martin Ramer family had a camphouse at this bend of the river. There was a fireplace in it and a water well. Here, after the first freezing weather, they rounded up their hogs and slaughtered them. The meat was taken out of the bottom by wagon to the farm where it was put in a smokehouse.

Martin and Lula Ramer

Martin Ramer came to Southeast Texas from Alabama with his mother, Celey Talor Ramer, one brother, and five sisters in 1877 at nine years of age after his father had been killed in an accident. They had come at the urging of Bill Ramer, an uncle, who lived on Ramer Island, a large sand hummock back from the river on a high terrace. Other members of the Ramer family had settled the area prior to that time. Bill Ramer painted a glowing picture of a land flowing with milk and honey where the forests were filled with game and "a line thrown from your porch would catch a catfish eight inches between the eyes." The new family moved to Ramer Island into a log cabin built earlier by Jim Ramer, where they lived until the disastrous flood of 1884 when they lost all they had. Martin and Ben Gore sat in a boat and dismantled the log house and floated it to higher ground on upper Ramer Island. Discouraged, they moved clear out of the area for two years but then returned to Tyler County and settled about three miles southeast of Spurger.

One of Bill Ramer's sons, Elias, returned to Alabama to live. While there, he received word that his mother was dying, so he started to Texas on his mule. Halfway there, the mule died, so Elias walked the rest of the way, which took a week. Arriving in Texas, he learned that his mother had already died and was buried at Turner Branch Cemetery. He visited his mother's grave, rested a few days, and walked back to Alabama. How's that for filial piety!

Around 1926, Martin Ramer built another house on a 34-acre tract of land three and a half miles southeast of Spurger. The house was spacious and constructed of virgin cypress and heart pine. The strength of bone, sinew, muscle, and determination to do the work required for such undertakings must have been prodigious. To cut the large, virgin cypress with axe and a crosscut saw, then saw or rive (split) it into planks, and move it from the swamps to the building site would have been labor enough, but then there was the task of raising the logs and other heavy materials into precise place and securing them with pegs. I have seen the tools which were available at that time (and even used some of them). Heavy loads were lifted by wooden pulleys made of dogwood and hardened by fire. Hand augers were used for boring holes for the pegs, special types of axes for cutting and smoothing the wood, and a froe for splitting cypress shingles for roofs. Mules and oxen were used for hauling, and then there were certain to be cousins and neighbors to lend a hand. The women were strong and worked right alongside the men.

Martin Ramer taught school at the Hare School, a one-room plank building across Black Creek on the Collins league. A schoolteacher's salary in those days was $25 a month plus eight dollars for room and board. If he had a college degree, he earned $70 a month plus $35 for room and board. In 1915, Martin decided to quit teaching and devote all his time to farming and stock raising. Since there was open range in those days, people could own large numbers of cows, goats, and hogs. At one time, he had about 2,000 hogs in the Neches bottom.

In addition to a large vegetable garden, Ramer grew cotton, corn, field peas, peanuts, sugar cane, and sweet potatoes. There was an orchard of pears, persimmons, peaches, figs, and citrus fruits. The family became expert at grafting citrus trees and had thousands of trees, both bearing and nursery stock. One year, they sold around 900 bushels of oranges from 100 trees. Lemon and grapefruit trees produced about 10 bushels of fruit each. In 1937, a severe freeze killed almost all their trees and took them out of the fruit-growing business.

At one time, there were so many citrus orchards in this area that Silsbee High School's annual yearbook was named *The Satsuma*.

Along with farming and stock raising, Martin Ramer rafted logs with Johnny Swearingen. Leaving the logs at Beaumont, they walked back home.

The Ramers lost much of the land that they had bought and settled when the land-grabbing robber baron, John Henry Kirby and his battery of smart lawyers, moved into East Texas like a plague of locusts, gobbling up woodland by hook or crook—mostly crook. There were probably several sets of owners of all this land: those who settled it on Spanish land grants, those who received grants for serving in the Texas Revolutionary War, and participants in the Texas Headright Program. And there were those who passed pieces of paper about in Houston, New York City, and New Orleans. Sometimes it was a matter of legal versus moral ownership. Nevertheless, some of those people had legal title to their lands and it was taken from them. Martin Ramer was a hero of those times.

The story was told me by a local attorney who was called by the Ramer family in the 1940s. Martin Ramer owned with legal title 165 acres of land, which was densely forested with fine virgin longleaf pine timber and Kirby Lumber Company coveted it. A Kirby lawyer came to Ramer and offered to give him 45 of the 165 acres if he would sign over title to them. Ramer's wife told the lawyer to leave the papers with them so they might read them over and to come back next day. The Ramers had two sons, Marvin (Puddin) and W. D. (Punkin). (These were terms of endearment often given to children and they happened to stick with the Ramer boys throughout their lives.) She and the boys took the paper to the attorney at Silsbee for his opinion. He immediately went to Spurger and told Mr. Ramer that the land belonged to him and he didn't have to sign the paper. Martin Ramer said, "No. I learned a long time ago that you can't fight Kirby and win, and I'm too old to try now." So he signed the papers. Two days after the settlement, Kirby began cutting and took over a thousand big trees off the tract.

Ramer was referring to an occasion when, during one of the bankruptcies that Kirby pulled from time to time in order to reorganize his affairs and legalize his holdings, Kirby claimed among his assets all the forestland in the Neches bottoms from Carthage to Beaumont. The presiding judge was one of Kirby's men. If a person owned land within the claimed area, he had to go to the hearings in Houston and present a clear title of ownership. Otherwise it would go on record as belonging to Kirby.

Going to Houston in those days was like going to China would be for us today. Few of the backwoodsmen could read or even sign their own names. Martin Ramer was an educated man and was trusted, so with documents in hand that proved his and his neighbors' legal title to their land, he made the long trip to Houston. He went by horseback to Yellow Bluff, caught a steamboat to Beaumont and from thence to Houston by train. The court hearings were simple and brief. When Kirby's lawyers saw that there were people present prepared to fight for their lands, one of Kirby's people suddenly became "ill" and the hearings were postponed for a month. When this happened the third time, Martin Ramer said, "I can see that I won't be given a chance to prove title to my land. I am going home and I'm not coming back, but I'm warning everyone to stay off my land."

When Ramer failed to show for the next hearing, he was declared in default and title to his land was given to Kirby. In time, a federal marshal came to take possession and serve Ramer with papers charging him with contempt of court and violating a court order. He was arrested and taken to jail in Houston where he was given nothing to eat but cornbread and blackstrap molasses. To obtain his release, an attorney would have to go to New Orleans to obtain a writ of habeas corpus, (whatever that is) but it was deemed impractical by the family. He was held in jail for several months without trial and, when finally released, the fight was all drained out of him. I'm told that he put it all behind him and even worked with Kirby as overseer of the land between Sheffield's Ferry and the county line.

One member of the Ramer family, Anna Ramer Swearingen, was a very strong influence on my life when I was a child. My schoolteacher, seeing that I had artistic talent, asked Ms. Anna to give me art lessons. It was in the Depression and we could not have afforded to hire a teacher. Each Tuesday afternoon after school, I went to Ms. Anna's house and she taught me to paint with oils and pastels, using her own materials. Not only that, she taught me to look for and see beauty in the world around me.

A women's libber ahead of her time, she talked bitterly of the days when her brothers would demand that she faultlessly iron their white shirts so they could mount their fine horses and go prancing off to have a good time on Saturday nights. When I married young and was shortly in the hospital having my first child, Ms. Anna visited me, bringing a pamphlet on birth control—the first I knew of such a thing.

Ms. Anna has been gone for some time, but I can just see her tall, thin, erect frame walking about Heaven, head lifted and sharp eyes surveying the scene, and commenting on the crystal stream, the flowers that never fade, and the tree of life and saying: "Yes! This is just how I knew it would be!" How I wish I could see her just one more time and tell her how very precious her memory is to me and how much she enriched my life. One should never miss an opportunity to express gratitude and affection where and when it is deserved. Flowers on a casket don't do it.

Fine people, the Ramers! A model of values for all time!

SECOND NIGHT

River Mile 86

At around 4:30, I came upon an expansive bar which at the downriver end had sand piled high, steeply encircling a small, deep harbor. Here, I moored my boat and set up camp. Just around this bend is a fishhook-shaped inland lake that was cut off from the river in 1939. On the cutbank side of this cutoff is the stump of a tremendous cypress tree which Sol Wright cut down in 1928. I viewed it as a monument to the man and his legendary prowess with an axe.

Part Two

Day 3

THIRD DAY

River Mile 86 8:30 A.M.

Next morning, after an uneventful night, I launched off and stopped at the next cutbank bend and climbed the bluff, planning to explore an inland lake called Morgan Lake. The once magnificent forests adjacent to the river here have been clearcut and the rough road, which led from the bluff toward the forests, fanned out in numerous branches into the clearcut. I was unable to locate the lake, but did find something else more interesting. Where the soil had eroded along the road leading from the bluff, I found flint chips, bits of charcoal, and pottery shards, which indicated that this bluff had been an Indian habitation site. All these bluffs where the river cut into higher terraces must have been inhabited by the aborigines. I would have liked to spend more time exploring here but planned to spend the night at the Eason camp and wasn't sure how long it would take me to get there, so I proceeded on my way.

SMITH'S BEND

River Mile 84

In the old days, this bend was known as the Bill Ramer Bend, for Bill Ramer had a camp there. I might be mistaken in my identification of the location of Martin Ramer's camp, as it could well be this site. On the Fourth of July, the

Ramer family would gather here to celebrate and on the opposite side of the river, the Walter Wright family would gather.

Walter Wright is still remembered as a man who loved to holler and it is said that he could be heard for ten miles. Hollering was a useful means of communication before the days of telephone and radio. When a man got up in the morning, he stood on his porch and hollered. If his neighbor a few miles away did not give an answering holler, then he went to see if all was well with him. My daddy always said he would give anything to hear just once more the old river holler. Log rafters coming down the river would holler so that people downstream would know to pull their boats ashore and let down the ferry cables. Different calls were used to call for help or locate lost people. If a person were lost in the woods, those looking for him would give an occasional holler. If he heard them, he would return the holler and they would continue until they could locate one another by the distance of the sound. Sometimes, it was just a form of entertainment or expression of exuberance. William Watts was another man remembered for his vocal abilities. Hog hunting along the river, he would holler when he had killed his limit and was ready to come home and butcher the hogs, and his family, all the way in the uplands, would hear and put the big scalding kettles on the fires. He also was one of the few white men who could do the "nigger holler." The Negroes in the area had a special holler all their own. Jack Jenkins' specialty was to holler like a freight train and you would swear that a train was right around the bend bearing down on you when he cut loose. Smoke signals were also used to convey messages, possibly a skill derived from their Indian forebears.

After the Ramers gave up their camp and no longer gathered here, the bend was called Smith's Bend, probably because Smitty the hermit lived here. I met Smitty when a photographer friend and I were on one of our many flower photography forays and were paddling down river in my flat-bottom riverboat when we saw him sitting in front of his abode—a species of shack made of old doors, pieces of plywood, chicken wire, roofing felt, and plastic. It was on a low cutbank bluff just about three or four feet above water line. He waved and we waved and I thought: "What the heck. He looks lonesome." So I pulled in and "howdeyed" him. "Come on up! Come on up! I just made a pot of coffee." So we sat awhile and chatted and drank some of the acid brew he poured into our cups. It was a tranquil scene. A couple of hounds were lying peacefully asleep after a brief fit of territorial display: barking and rushing about. A few mixed-breed chickens scratched around pecking at whatever looked edible. Wish I had had the sense then to draw him out and find out just why a relatively young man would seclude himself way out here on the banks of the river living on squirrel, catfish, beans, and cornbread, with only animals, tame and wild, for company; but I didn't.

I and the photographer friend met him again at the shindig the Dog People threw at Bush Lake to celebrate the opening of that road to the river, but then that's another story.

Smitty staggered into I. C. Eason's camp one night and threw himself across a bed. They thought he was drunk and would sleep it off, but when he didn't wake within a decent period of time, they discovered he was dead. He had been beaten and hit on the back of the head. Nobody knew when, why, or by whom, and apparently, nobody cared, so Smitty's death was as much a mystery as was his life.

The Ranch

In the 1870s, some investors (we called them carpet baggers) from Boston acquired around 3500 acres of land on the east side of the river here between the Collins and Cushing Leagues. It was cross fenced with five to twelve strands of four-barbed wire into sections called the East Ranch, West Ranch, Harris Ranch, and fields where corn, hay, and peanuts were grown to feed the livestock in winter. On the banks of the river were warehouses and a lodge where visitors and dignitaries were entertained and servants were retained to see that they were well fed and made comfortable. In the fall, three men named Leonard, Mayo, and Hunt, who were associated with the ranch, would come from Boston to hunt because game was so plentiful here. Martin Ramer was hired to hunt turkey and deer meat for the lodge table, as well as riding fence lines. Around the turn of the century, Tom Hennessy of Woodville superintended the ranch and, later, a man named Chapman was in charge.

Thousands of cattle roamed the bottomlands in groups. Each group was led by the oldest cow and a bell was hung about her neck so that the cattle could be located. If a storm were brewing or a norther coming, the cows came home. This was one of the signs that helped the locals predict the weather. Incidentally, there is a hierarchy, or pecking order, in cattle herds, with the oldest and strongest being boss cow. A neighbor, Hunter Macky, told me that in his herd, the lowest cow in the pecking order was old and decrepit and the other cows were always shoving her around, away from the feed trough, and hooking her with their horns. One day, he had them all tied in a row to give them their shots. The old cow was the first to receive her shots and loosed. She stood there a moment, looked the situation over and saw the other cows were still tied, so she went down the row, hooking and kicking each one in turn, then ran galloping away across the pasture to put lots of space between them and herself before they were loosed.

The ranch fences were constantly being washed away by the flooding river and, after sawmills came into the area and the fine timber of the terraces and bottomlands was being harvested, timber cutters ran roughshod over the fences, making it impossible to keep them up and contain the cattle. The absentee land owners decided that stock raising was no longer profitable and abandoned the ranch. Kirby eventually acquired the land and the ranch, like so many other of man's "important" activities along the river, exists only in the memories of the older people.

BUSH LAKE

River Mile 80.4

Bush Lake was named for the Bush family who built the first house beside it but moved away by 1900. The lake, where it enters the Neches, is broad and deep. It is part of a chain that includes Joe's Lake, Bingham Lake, and Turner Branch, which encircles Joe's Lake Pasture and, in my opinion, marks a former course of the Neches, possibly abandoned when the river cut its present bed during the 500-year flood which preceded that of 1884. There is a lot of fun in being an amateur. One can arrive at all sorts of hypotheses and conclusions without having to defend them before the scientific community or endangering one's professional reputation if proven wrong. In the topography, the river has left a record of its past as surely as if it had been written in books. To read it, one only has to have topographic maps, a little knowledge of hydrology, eyes in one's head, and reasonable intelligence.

It is impossible to miss Bush Lake, for its banks are lined with houseboats. Since the Park Service took over the river, those living in streamside cabins had to give them up. The cabins were built on sites leased from lumber company land and the companies chose not to renew leases behind the N.P.S. boundary. Of course it wasn't the companies that were anathematized, but the Park Service. If the Neches River is to be preserved in its natural state, these things must be. While I sympathize with the river people and understand the depth of their loss, it is so pleasant to go for miles on the river without seeing any evidence of man.

Anyway, the houseboats on Bush Lake are inhabited by these dispossessed denizens of the river. I don't know what, if any, regulations exist for the presence and maintenance of houseboats on public streams, and I'm sure the owners don't know either. No doubt their sewage goes right into the river.

I would be the last to insist that houseboats be ousted from the Neches, but I once had an experience which caused me to view them with a jaundiced eye. On one of our annual summer wanderings, my teenaged children and I planned to stop at a park on a beautiful lake near Austin to spend a couple of days. All the banks were lined with houseboats, some quite elaborate and expensive, and the water was filthy. When the children went in for a swim, they came out covered with oil and smelling of gasoline. The noise of motors didn't stop all night, so we packed up, got into the van, and left in the middle of the night. This scene always comes to my mind when anyone mentions houseboats on the Neches.

The bluff on the south side of Bush Lake was once the scene of a gala party the Dog People held to celebrate the legal opening of the Bush Lake Road to the river. My photographer friend and I were there, along with everybody and everything within miles of Caney Head. There was a barbecued steer, a country band, which was amplified by power from a gasoline generator, and, of course, a generous supply of that elixir which seems to liven up any get-together and makes everybody want to dance whether they know how to or not.

My attention was diverted from the revelers to a small group of people on the perimeter of the crowd. They were standing around two young men who were circling one another with drawn knives. I rushed to I. C. Eason, who was one of the spectators, and said: "Oh, I. C.! They have knives and are going to fight! Do something!" I. C., with a faint grin, said, "Yeaah." After a few passes at one another, a little blood was drawn, someone's honor apparently was satisfied, and they were separated by friends. It seems the disagreement was over who had a right to the affections of Venus, I. C.'s beautiful daughter, who lived up to her name.

PEBBLE ISLAND

River Mile 78.8 2:25 P.M.

In the middle of the afternoon, I came upon an extensive pointbar called locally Pebble Island because of the deposits of small gravel here. The small stones are mostly different types of quartz, sedimentary rock, and many fragments of petrified wood. The separate areas of gravel and sand form interesting mosaic patterns on this large bar. From river mile 78 to 85, sand and gravel deposits were sufficient to be mined commercially and trucked out a few years ago. I don't know why it was discontinued, for there is still plenty of it there. Just below Bush Lake, gravel was mined to build up the roadways when Joe's Lake oilfield was being developed. Pud Ramer told me an interesting story about this era. The field was being developed by the American Republic Oil Company in 1936. The Cullens from Houston and a fellow named George Ridden from Alabama were the owners. George Ridden came frequently to look over the situation and once found the road builders about to remove a huge oak tree from the route chosen. He immediately stopped the workers, saying that the tree had been there before any of them were born and would probably be there long after they died and it was going to stay there. Crossing a small bridge over Turner Branch, he noticed many small fish in the shallow water, so he had a crew enlarge the stream to make a shallow pool by the bridge. Every time he came to the oilfield, he had his driver stop and he would sit for a long time to watch the little fishes in the pool. Doesn't it make you feel good to know that even in those rapacious days, there were some who appreciated and protected the beauty of the land over which they exercised total control with no greater power to regulate them.

I have a theory as to the origin of the sand and gravel deposits at this point. It is my belief that they are the result of an embayment that reached up river to this point during the last incursion of the sea. Water rushing down the gradient can carry large particles, but when it reaches sea level, the water slows and the heavier pieces drop to the bottom. This deposition filled the upper bay and, with the lowering sea level of that time, created dry land.

I was surprised when reading about Jasper County in the *Texas Handbook*, to find Pebble Island listed as one of its topographical points of interest.

Sandbars are most extensive along this stretch of the river. The river side is either high bluff cutbank or pointbar sand beach, so all the wildlife come to water on the bars. If someone wants to know what types of animals inhabit a forest, let him come to a sandbar of a morning and read the footprints in the sand before the winds smooth it over. Raccoons come to the bar to catch crawfish in the shallow water. Often, one sees the delicate tracery of small rodent feet abruptly disappear where the huge footprints of an owl gouge into the sand, or the slithering trail of a snake encounters the mouse's path. Carnivorous predators come to the sandbar, not only to drink, but because they know the herbivorous mice, rabbits, and other small prey will be there. Deer, hotly pursued by wolves or dogs, cross the river from the sandbar to elude their enemies. One morning I came upon a set of footprints of a doe deer, a fawn, and canine tracks meeting in a flurry of sand. One could read the desperate struggle as the mother fought to protect her little one, but because of the extensive disturbance of the surface, I could only guess at the outcome.

Sand

> To see a world in a grain of sand
> And a Heaven in a wild flower,
> Hold infinity in the palm of your hand,
> And eternity in an hour.
> William Blake – "Auguries of Innocence"

Separate and apart from the life forms upon the sandbar, consider the sand itself. Many profound statements use sand as examples. When God promised the childless Abraham innumerable descendants, He described them "as the sands of the seashore." From the dawn of civilization, sand running from one container into another has measured time, so "the sands of time" denote the passage of the years into eternity. And to emphasize human limitations: "Can you count the sands of the seashore?" Instability is described, "As the shifting sands."

Sand seems to be always spoken of in a plural sense unless one wants to describe insignificance. One grain of sand, as one drop of water, is impotent, but enough drops of water can destroy a city and wear away a continent, and all together, sand has a subtle but very real power. Job, the suffering patriarch, lamented: "My calamity is heavier than the sands of the sea." And from Solomon's Proverbs: "A stone is heavy and the sand weighty, but a fool's wrath is heavier than them both."

An example of the strength of sand was the use made of it in sealing the sarcophagi, or coffins, of Egyptian pharaohs. The covering over the coffin was a carved stone weighing many tons held up by pottery containers of sand, each having a plug at the base. When the body was placed in the sarcophagus, the plugs were pulled and, as the sand poured from the containers, the cap stone slowly lowered into position, sealing and supposedly protecting the body forever.

Recently, having occasion to study some samples of sand from local sources, I learned to appreciate the wonder and uniqueness of individual grains of sand. When I placed them under the binocular microscope and looked, I was dazzled. It was as though I had fallen into Aladdin's cave where sparkling jewels covered floor and walls. Like snowflakes, no two grains of sand are exactly alike.

Along the creeks and rivers of Southeast Texas, most sand is white or clear, and composed of quartz eroded eons ago from disintegrating continental granite and brought seaward by the action of water. Most of the grains are clouded with structural flaws, but some have the purity and clarity of diamonds and literally shoot fire when the light hits their facets.

On California beaches, I was intrigued by gold and silver sparkles as the movement of the water shifted the sand in the shallows. These are mica, pyrites, and other minerals that are absent from the watersheds of our streams. Our sand contains fragments of varieties of chalcedony, a form of quartz. Mixed with the clear quartz grains, they show surprisingly brilliant colors: the coral of carnelian, apple green chrysophase, jet black onyx and obsidian, red jasper, etc.

One should never go out without a hand lens. It reveals a whole new world too small to be noticed by the naked eye, which is normally dominated by large, bulky objects. An insignificant item, such as a single grain of sand, can take on a marvelous beauty and wonder under the lens. It's too good to miss.

What a loss it will be when the last grain of sand is washed from the last bar on the Neches, leaving only mud and gravel! No one gives a thought to such things until it is too late to prevent it. Wouldn't it be wonderful if someone had realized that our land would be a much more pleasant place to live if some of the virgin forests and prairies, and habitat for ivory-billed woodpeckers and passenger pigeons should be preserved! Now that it is all gone, people stand around and say, "What a shame!" and proceed to obliterate the poor remnants in every way that will bring a dime of profit. And so it will be with the sand on the Neches.

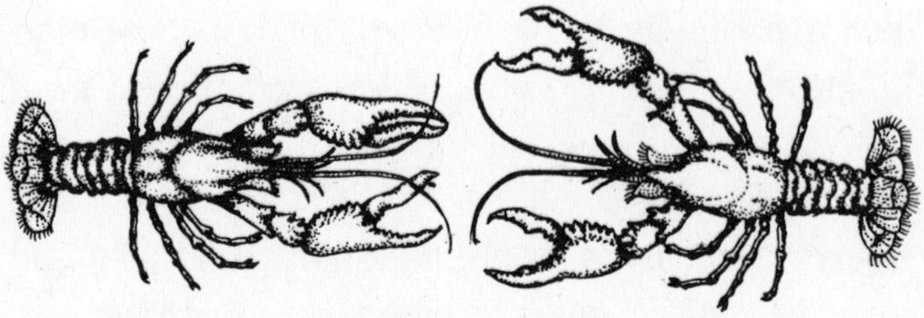

CRAWFISH

While lounging at the edge of the sandbar, I noticed the small river creatures, which were taking advantage of the shallow water where the large predators could not get to them, especially on the trailing edge of the point bar where mud and organic material had accumulated. There were tiny minnows and baby fish of all sorts, and lots of small, translucent crawfish.

Right off, I want to say that we in Southeast Texas say crAWfish, not the effete, affected crAYfish. "You get a line and I'll get a pole, and we'll go down to the crAWdad hole, baby"—not "the crAYdad hole"!

Crawfish evade predators by scooting backwards quickly. This explains a common term we use when someone has made a stupid remark or taken a stand he soon regrets and then attempts to justify or cover it. We say he is "crawfishing." In other words, backing up. "He can't crawfish out of that one," we frequently say about politicians and other public officials.

There are around thirty species of crawfish in Southeast Texas, each adapted to a particular habitat. Some burrow in wet mud, others live only in muddy ditches and ponds, and still others only in lakes or slow rivers. Some are restricted solely to stony, swift streams.

Crawfish that burrow in damp earth build interesting structures called chimneys. As they dig clumps of wet earth, they bring them to the top and deposit them around the hole. The height of the chimney, sometimes up to two feet, is determined by the depth of the water table, for they dig until they reach water. Wet meadows or savannahs are dotted with these structures. I am of the opinion that the vegetative composition of the pine savannah wetlands is influenced greatly by the action of crawfish, which dig their burrows so close together that the low chimneys touch, thus only those species of grasses and herbaceous plants that can withstand frequent covering of mud can survive. This also might serve as a covering and protection of sensitive growth buds from the frequent fires that sweep the savannahs. Ah, how everything in nature is knit together in a most intricate web which we are only beginning to recognize, let alone fully understand!

When you examine a crawfish closely—or any other living thing, for that matter—it is amazing how everything about its body and behavior serves a purpose. Among the three pairs of antennae, a short pair are organs of balance. If a leg is lost in battle, no problem; he has others and another soon grows in the place of the lost limb. But, if an adversary cuts off an antenna, the poor creature flops about helplessly and is totally defeated. C'est la guerre!

Males fight among themselves, especially during mating season. Mating occurs in early spring and autumn, usually in response to lunar and solar cycles. Some authorities say pheromones are involved in attracting mates, others say it is purely a matter of chance. The male, in the grip of passion, grabs every crawfish he encounters, flips it over and attempts copulation. If it is another male, he has a fight on his hands. If it is a female and she is in the right mood, romance results.

After mating in autumn, the males migrate overland by the thousands and when they become exhausted, soon die. One night on the river, Daddy saw a crawfish migration. He heard a strange clicking sound and rustling in the grass and leaves. Light from the campfire revealed hordes of crawfish moving in the same direction and clacking their claws. It was a mystery that he always wondered about.

The fertilized eggs, from ten to one hundred of them, are attached in a cluster to the female's abdomen and she is said to be in berry. After hatching, the miniature crawfish stay close to Mama until able to survive on their own.

Crawfish are omnivorous scavengers. While the bulk of their diet is succulent aquatic vegetation, grass roots, etc., I wouldn't want to be in the place of an earthworm that accidentally made its way into a crawfish burrow. They do relish a bit of fresh meat when available. As children, our favorite crawfish bait was a piece of bacon rind tied to a string. This would bring any crawdad out of his hole or ditch.

On the other end of the "eat and be eaten" spectrum, crawfish are the main diet of raccoons and are relished by many species of fish, animals and water birds. It is fortunate that they are such prolific reproducers.

In the role of predator on the crawfish, I must add man. A series of reverses in the economy of Southeast Texas and Southwesten Louisiana have combined to make crawfish farming a large industry and put crawfish etouffée, crawfish pie, boiled crawfish, etc., on the menu of many restaurants in the South. The economy of Southeast Texas is based on oil, timber, and rice. The sudden decline of the oil industry and changing world markets left many Southeast Texans out of work and they were ready to try anything to make a living. A glut on the rice market left large, flat fields, already designed for flooding and draining, abandoned. These made ideal crawfish ponds. So, voilà! A new industry emerged and former rice farmers became crawfish farmers.

While we might think of crawfish as being mindless, aimless creatures whose main purpose in life is as fish bait or ruining our lawns and clogging our lawnmowers, they apparently have established a sort of social order in their little realms. Dominant and subordinate relationships exist based on size and learned recognition of individuals. All crawfish might look alike to us, but to another crawfish, one might be the king, or a pariah, or Mama, or just one of the boys. Anyway, they are another of the seemingly simple things in this wonderful world that give us food for thought and belly.

I. C. EASON

River Mile 77 3:05 P.M.

I paddled onto the sandbar in front of the Eason cabin in late afternoon and pulled my boat up on the bar, and was soon sitting in the cabin with a hot cup of coffee in hand and talking about my adventures.

There is a swale between the wooded upper bar and the ridge where the cabin sits, but one still has a great view of the river. The cabin is a simple, large, one-room building that was once a houseboat anchored in the backwater by the Highway 96 bridge. The Eason boys attached two outboard motors to the houseboat and proceeded upriver with it. The women fired up the wood cookstove and cooked a meal while en route. Arriving at the campsite, it was winched up and over the bar, into place and levered up onto upright sections of cypress logs. Cypress is always used for house blocks as it is resistant to rot and insects. Many improvements have been made to the cabin. Electric lights, powered by a generator, a cookstove which uses bottled propane, and a hand pump water well outside. Even with four beds, a table and chairs, it is roomy and comfortable.

I. C. and his wife Lorine, James and his little wife Billie, Lesley and his wife Susan, and a cousin, James Darrel Gore, were present. The girls had children in school and weren't there. But Clyde was there. Clyde was a big, ferocious-looking pit bull dog who behaved like a sweet pussycat. He would roll his eyes up and look at you with such love as if to say, "Don't believe all those bad things they say about us." James Darrel called Clyde his "diller dog" because he loved to kill and eat armadillos. Clyde would grab the armadillo with his front legs and paws and, knowing he couldn't penetrate its hard shell, fall over on his back, flip the armadillo over, and rip out its insides with one big gollup of his powerful jaws. I believed Clyde's gastronomic capacity when I. C. and James came in with a mess of squirrels, skinned and gutted them, and threw the offal into a big dishpan. Clyde swooped down on that dishpan and with a few swipes of his head, the pan was empty.

Lesley and James Darrel decided to go get some fresh meat for supper, and got their guns and started for the boat. When they got there, Clyde was curled up in a tight ball in a corner, lying very still and thinking he was well hidden. When he knew he was discovered, he rolled his eyes around piteously begging to be taken along, and, being told he could go, leaped up joyously.

Sure enough, there was a big pot of squirrel dumplings for supper, and, when Lesley got back, some tender, fried deer meat.

That night, we sat around the wood heater, as it was getting rather nippy, drinking coffee and talking. Lorine got to telling about an old mule her mother had that followed her around and pulled at her apron strings when it wanted to be fed. One day, the mule got into some dried peas, ate a lot of them, and got foundered. It was so swollen that they thought sure it was going to die, but her mother told one of the boys to get on that mule and run it across the field. At first, the mule balked and wouldn't move, but finally, after a little high-life had been applied to its rear end, it took off at a fast, stiff-legged trot.

Every time a hoof hit the ground, the mule gave a bray and a loud fart, and there they went across the field, the boy bouncing up and down and the mule braying and farting. Thus relieved of the gas and pressure, the mule survived. Lorine, who had been sitting on the floor, got to laughing so hard over the memory that she just fell on her back and kicked her legs up in the air.

Some people seem to think you can't have a good time without beer or whiskey, but I never had such fun in my life, nor have I laughed so much. I. C. didn't drink alcoholic beverages nor allow them around his camp or home. He drank heavily in his youth, had a bad car wreck as a result, and almost died. He promised God that if He would let him live that he would never take another drink, and he kept his word.

There are a lot of things I could say about I. C. He was a backwoodsman extraordinaire. A faithful husband and loving father, a conservationist, and a valued personal friend. He was a king in his own realm.

The ancestors of I. C. were cultured, educated people when they moved to this primeval wilderness during the past two centuries, but as time passed and family fortunes either were spent or converted to worthless Confederate paper during the Civil War, the hard labor of survival left no time for contemplation of the classics; and a knowledge of producing food from farm, woods, and river was necessarily more valuable than a knowledge of Greek and Latin.

They grew corn, peas, greens, and sweet potatoes and hunted hogs, bears, turkeys, squirrel, deer, and other game from the woods and set trotlines to catch the big catfish in the river. The backwoodsmen became crafty and canny in the ways of the wild creatures, which was an advantage later in their dealings with the outsiders who came into their territory.

There was an unwritten and unspoken understanding of each family's hunting and fishing grounds and they acquired an intimate knowledge of their territory. To outwit the deer he hoped to shoot, the backwoodsman had to know their habits: where their trails to water were, what time they fed, and what time of the year their attention to herd dominance and mating caused them to become careless. How deep did the catfish lie and what did they like to eat? He was a master over the wild things of nature, over big, powerful horses and mules and they knew it. He was expert with the tools he used whether gun, fishline, axe and saw, primitive farming equipment and, later, the gasoline- and electricity-powered machines that made life a little easier.

In this culture, the man is lord and master of the home, and I. C. was typical of other men of his time and place. The children looked up to him as teacher, protector, and keeper of the traditions they were trying so hard to hold on to. The love and respect they gave him was awe-inspiring.

Lorine, his wife, still handsome with the black eyes and hair of her Indian heritage, looked at him with pride and good-humored affection. In an environment reminiscent of Erskine Caldwell's *Tobacco Road*, the marriage between I. C. and Lorine was a 50-year-old love affair. She bore him six children: Jody and Venus, Joyce and Mickey, and the boys, James and Lesley. The girls are extremely talented musically, especially Mickey, and, given a bit of influence and backing, could have made it big in Nashville or anywhere.

The boys are as different as night and day. How a rip-snorting, fire-breathing terror like I. C. could have raised a sweet, gentle son like James is another of life's mysteries. He does not drink alcoholic drinks, and his speech is free from the blue-streaked profanity so common to his family and peers. The first time I saw James (he must have been about twelve years old), I had stopped by I. C.'s house on Highway 92 to see him about taking some conservationists into the river bottom and, while I was waiting for I. C., James stuck his head out of the door and, with a broad grin said: "Mis Watson, you want some good ol' Caney Head coffee? Come on in!" While James is quiet and noncommittal, his wife, Billie, is quite articulate. She is tiny in size, but intelligent and capable in managing the home and raising the two children.

Lesley, on the other hand, is I. C. incarnate. He, of all the family, will continue the traditions that made I. C. a folklore legend in his own time. I remember once when Lesley was about four years old, his behavior was getting rather irksome so his daddy, after several admonitions, turned around and backhanded him one. Not hard enough to be brutal, but hard enough to impress him and to cause a cud of chewing tobacco to fly out of his mouth. He was the baby of the family and Mickey's special pet, so she rushed to comfort him, crying out: "Daddy! You done knocked his cud out!"

Lesley is no longer a baby but a self-confident young man, sure of his ability to survive on his skills and his wits, even in the face of events which are totally changing his world. He will probably wind up in jail for fighting for freedoms and rights which in case of war, would guarantee him hero status with medals pinned all over him. Ah well! Today's traitor is tomorrow's patriot—depending on who wins the battle.

One person who understands and appreciates Lesley's good points is his wife, Susan. A privileged only child, and good-looking enough to be a fashion model, Susan is the best educated in the family. I saw a touching reminder of her devotion when I was examining some photographs of Lesley hog hunting. She had made an attractive album of them, entitled, "Lesley's Hog Hunting Book," and in it were scenes of him in action on horseback, surrounded by his hog dogs, amidst a herd of wild hogs. On the inside cover was a heart inscribed, "Susan loves Lesley." Most of the marriages with which I am familiar today are a sorry mess with wives dissatisfied with what their husbands can give them. Susan seems to be satisfied to just love and be loved by a real man.

At home, the family gathers in the kitchen around the large table: a four by six sheet of plywood, corners resting on four large cypress knees and an eight-foot tall cypress knee reaching from the floor through the center of the table to the ceiling. To the side of this central column is an elaborate "crystal" chandelier that sheds its light over the loud and rambunctious cacophony of laughing, talking, arguing people gathered about the table drinking Seaport dark-roast coffee and smoking roll-your-own Bull Durham cigarettes. I was sitting at this table one day, eating fried squirrel legs, and the next day, sitting in a penthouse club in a Dallas skyscraper between a millionaire oil man and the crown prince of Belgium eating something real dainty—I've forgotten just what—but I can tell you this: I had a much better time at I. C. and Lorine's dinner table.

In the years we were trying to get support for the creation of a Big Thicket National Preserve, it was imperative that we take influential visitors in to see the bottomland forests and the river. None of us had boats or vehicles that could traverse the rough, muddy roads into the bottom, but all I had to do was put in a telephone call to Ernest Spell. He would contact I. C., and whatever we needed was made available when we needed it, with I. C.'s brother Deacon thrown in. Deacon, whose real name is I. V., got his nickname when his father, who was a preacher with a message to preach but no church to preach it in, got a pickup truck and, installing a loudspeaker on the top, had Deacon drive him around the countryside so he could preach to anybody within hearing, which was considerable becaue it was a pretty powerful loudspeaker. Even more valuable than their equipment was their good-humored whooping and hollering and prancing around. City people, accustomed to cool, carefully controlled behavior at all times, loved it. One day, we had a congressman and others of that ilk on the river bank about to be ferried across to the Neches Bottom Unit when I. C. complained of a severe toothache. "Well, blankety-blank, I tried to get you to let me pull it, but, oh no, you wouldn't do it!" "Well, if you've still a mind to pull it, have at it!" So Deacon got a piece of fishing line and tied it to I. C.'s tooth. I. C. got down on the ground, Deacon put his foot on his head, and yanked away. With a bellow from I. C. and a spray of blood and spit, the tooth flew into the air. Everybody looked on with their mouths hanging open and their eyes bugging out. I. C. got up, cussed awhile, and shortly they were going about the business of getting the boats into the water and starting their motors just as though pulling teeth was a part of their everyday routine.

Another story with which Ned Fritz loved to regale Dallas cocktail parties concerned another group that Ned brought into the Thicket hoping to get support money for our cause from them. The group consisted of Maxilla Evans, wife of the chaplain of Southern Methodist University, Dorothy Volk, of the Volk Department Store chain, a prominent attorney, and Mrs. Lucy Ball Ousley, widow of a former ambassador and heiress to the Ball jar fortune, a dowager-Queen-Mary type, and Gene Barrington, local attorney. We all piled into the bed of I. C.'s hoopie, Huldy, the erstwhile evangelical vehicle. Mrs. Ousley, being frail, was placed in the cab between I. C. and Deacon. We took off on what proved to be the wildest ride any of us had ever experienced, through muddy sloughs, over hummocks and sudden dips and swales. We finally stopped trying to keep from being thrown about and simply clung together, bouncing up and down in unison. When we finally arrived at the river and stopped, I jumped out, opened the cab door and cried, "Mrs. Ousley! Are you all right?" She tumbled out and gasped: "I've just had the time of my life!" En route, Deacon, trying to be gentlemanly, opened conversation with, "Ma'am, whatcher ol' man do?" When she realized Deacon was asking about Mr. Owsley's occupation, she said: "Well, Mr. Owsley is deceased, but when he was alive, he was the ambassador to Rumania, among other things. He also organized the American Legion. Are you boys Legionnaires, by any chance?" Deacon, who did not know what an ambassador was, nor ever heard of Rumania or the American Legion, thought on it awhile and answered: "Well, no, ma'am. You see, we are just too busy. You see if we ain't a-huntin, we're a-fishin." The Dallasites, who equated hunting and fishing with sports and recreation, thought the remark hilarious and it was repeated as a joke many times. In truth, fishing and hunting were serious business, as that was how they made their living.

Just as the sophisticated Dallasites went back to the city and talked about the wild ways of the river people, they were the butt of fun and jokes after they left. Ned Fritz was a favorite topic. The Dog People had a big gathering on the river once that Ned attended dressed in, of all things, a pair of very short red pants. I remonstrated with him, telling him that the locals had some rather strict moral codes about appropriate attire and were probably offended at his clothes, or lack of such. In Southeast Texas, the men DO NOT wear shorts, let alone short-shorts, not to even mention red ones. Afterwards, everybody was laughing and joking about Ned's knobby knees, hairy legs, and those red shorts.

I was present once at a confrontation between the Eason boys and a local game warden. We were at the Clark's Camp sandbar to take some important people, among whom was a congressman and a state game warden, across the river into the proposed Neches Bottom Unit. I had enlisted the aid of I. C. and Deacon who had brought two or three boats to the scene. As we were loading the V.I.P.s into the boats, the local game warden observed loudly: "Hey! This boat isn't registered and the sticker on that one is out of date." Deacon was half drunk and there was bad blood between the Easons and this game warden anyway. The warden's superior, noticing Deacon's lowered head, narrowed eyes, and his hand on his knife, hissed, "Shut up, you fool!" So we went our way across the river. It's hard for those whose lives have been with, on, and in the river for generations to submit to regimentation.

The land on which I. C.'s cabin sat was part of a section (640 acres) of the most beautiful floodplain hardwood forest you ever saw. About 25 years ago, Houston Thompson and Gene Barrington, Silsbee attorneys, made an attempt to help the Eason boys regain this land, which their grandparents had lived on and farmed. It was necessary that the land be fenced with a fence which would, according to the legal language, "turn a cow of reasonable disposition." I remember how Gene and I laughed about that definition while we were walking along those strands of barbed wire strung from tree to tree. I saw the aged crepe myrtle trees where his grandparents' cabin had been. Crepe myrtle and chinaberry trees were always planted around pioneer homes.

After Gene's death, Houston continued the case, which went on for years, and was finally settled a few years before I. C.'s death. The decision was made in favor of Temple Eastex Forest Industries and against I. C.'s claim, due to the fact that all the witnesses to the date the fence was in place were relatives of the claimant. No one remembered that I had been there in the beginning and could have testified to the fact. Another factor was that the judge must have been prejudiced as he owned a large amount of land in the general area and probably thought if what they termed "squatters" on Temple Eastex land could reclaim it, then his land also would be in jeopardy. I really never did hold much hope that I. C. would win. Temple-Eastex was just too powerful and had too much money and too much influence in East Texas, but the case served as a holding action that prevented the land's being clearcut and bulldozed until N.P.S. acquisition.

To say that I. C. was extremely wroth at the decision of the Special Master appointed by the judge to hear and rule on I. C.'s title claim, is putting it mildly indeed. He romped and stomped and raved: "I'll kill the somabitch!" Houston Thompson and I had discussed the ongoing case and its conclusion and I had kept Bill Jewel, the Park Service land acquisition person, apprised of the proceedings since the Park Service would have to acquire preserve land from whomever was found to be the legal owner, so I told him of I. C.'s reaction to the verdict. At that time, there had been a rash of killings of federal judges (usually in drug-related cases), and it was a hot issue. Bill Jewel got to thinking that if I. C. actually did kill the special master and Bill had prior knowledge, he would have been extremely derelict in his duty, if not in danger of prosecution himself by remaining silent, so he called the federal attorney and told him of I. C.'s threats so the judge could be advised to be on his guard.

I was horrified when I learned he had done so. I assured Bill Jewel that I. C. was all thunder and no lightning—that no way would he kill anyone—that I. C. was always "gonna kill" somebody and never had. I remember once at Ernest Spell's barbershop the subject came up that I. C. was "going to kill somebody"—I don't remember who or why. Ernest laughed and asked the fellow, "Hey! Did you ever see the Eason graveyard?" The fellow said that he didn't think there was one and Ernest said, "That's right, cause everybody who I. C. ever said he was gonna kill is buried there."

Sure enough, the next day, two agents from the F.B.I. came to the Park Service Office and asked to speak with me. Fortunately, I had insisted that Ken Tiege, the Assistant Superintendent, sit in on the interrogation. They wanted me to swear that on a certain date I had heard I. C. Eason threaten to kill the special master. I assured them I had no idea of dates and no way would my memory allow me to quote anybody verbatim; that I. C. was upset over the verdict and extremely vocal in his displeasure was true, but I couldn't say for sure what he said. Besides, much of it was hearsay, as I had heard most of it from his lawyer, Houston Thompson. They then said I could be charged with withholding information regarding a federal crime, and they would have to go to Houston Thompson and I. C. themselves. This really upset me. Houston had violated client confidentiality by discussing his client with me and I had repeated it and thus jeopardized his client. I had betrayed his trust. Then if I. C. were arrested and sent to prison for threatening the life of a federal official of the court, it would provoke overt warfare between the clan and the Park Service, and the lives of the rangers patrolling the Jack Gore Baygall Unit wouldn't be worth a plugged nickel. Also, I was an important liaison between the locals and the Park Service but would never be trusted again. Explaining all this to the F.B.I. men, I convinced them that I. C. would never harm the Special Master nor anyone else, that he was always "gonna kill somebody," but nobody was dead yet.

The agents were still insistent that I tell them things they wanted to know and Ken Tiege, seeing that I was on the verge of tears, told them: "That's enough! Mrs. Watson has told you everything she needs to tell you." Ken had an authoritative way about him, so the agents decided to drop the matter. They then asked if they could call on me if they ever needed to deal with the people in Caney Head. I replied that if I could help them understand the culture of the people and what to expect from them, yes, but I wouldn't be an informant. Afterwards, Ken gave me a stern lecture on how to conduct myself in an interrogation. Say nothing! Answer questions with a "yes" or "no" or the briefest of replies. Under stress I do tend to babble.

After I. C. died, the Park Service finally took possession of the land, including the cabin where the children had grown up and the family had had so many happy gatherings. Before the cabin was torn down and hauled away, they gathered there for the last time to more or less say goodbye. They said that you could hear them crying a mile down the river. They had lost everything that meant the most to them in life—father, homeland, livelihood—a terrible loss, indeed.

In consoling myself and assuaging my guilt for the part I had played in this tragedy, I remind myself of a statement I. C. made more than once. The lumber companies were laying bare the forests and exterminating the wildlife as far as the eye could see all around him and closing off what woods were left to all except hunting club members. When we proposed the Jack Gore Baygall area as a unit of the National Park system, I. C. devoted himself to the cause, stating that even if it meant that he would never walk in it or hunt in it again, he would rather see the Park Service have it and save it than to see the lumber companies clearcut it.

Of course, Park Service possession did not mean that the family could never walk in nor hunt those woods again, just that any citizen of the United States could do the same, under Park Service rules and regulations, of course. That is tantamount to a government agent throwing the front door of your home open and telling all the homeless "Come on in! Eat his food! Sleep in his bed! Its all yours!"

And so the Easons and the others of their kind were sacrificed for the ultimate good. When I see what has happened to the surrounding land, and compare it with this 640 acres of magnificent cathedral forests abounding with wildlife, I know it would not be so if I. C., Deacon, and their boys had not protected it with their guns and Houston Thompson forestalled its destruction in the courts of law. They will never go down in the history books as having fought for their country, but this book is to insure that those who really love our land and walk these beautiful woods will know that they do so at the cost of James Eason's grief, Lesley's rebellious anger and frustration, and the girls' sense of deprivation, as well as the thousands of hours, the money, and the legal expertise donated by Houston Thompson. In the fullest sense, they are heroes.

I. C. survived the loss of his longstanding court battle for his land, just as he had survived a hard and bitter life as a youth. In fact, as Blair Pittman stood over I. C.'s grave, he remarked: "Now THERE was a survivor!" He learned to survive in his early years when his father left the family to go seek work. The mother was sick, there was a house full of children to feed and nothing to eat but meal soup, a thin gruel made of corn meal and water. I. C., a boy of about twelve years, took his gun and two bullets to the river bottom, placed himself along an animal trail and waited. Presently, a big deer came along. He knew he had to kill this deer and he had to do it with his first shot, so he aimed carefully and cracked down on it. He was in the process of gutting the deer when he heard the clop, clop of horse hooves nearing, so he jumped behind a big tree nearby. Just as he feared, it was the game warden on his big gray horse, and it wasn't hunting season. As the warden came up to the dead deer, I. C. stuck his gun from behind the tree and said "Mr. Warden, you just keep on a-ridin'." When the warden hesitated, I. C. said, "I don't want to kill you, Mr. Warden, but I will if I have to." The warden said: "Son, I think you mean that." And I. C. replied: "Yessir. My mama's sick and hongry and my little brothers and sisters are hongry, and I'm gonna take this deer home." The warden turned his horse and rode away and I. C. shouldered the deer and carried it out of the bottom.

When the *National Geographic* magazine decided to do an article on the Big Thicket, they engaged Blair Pittman, a Houston photojournalist, to do the photography. Blair was my friend of longstanding so, for about two years, I was at his disposal as guide, advisor, and liaison between him and the locals. He was especially anxious to document the ways of the river people, so I took him to I. C., introduced him, and said: "Blair's O.K. You can trust him." This began a close friendship that lasted until I. C.'s death. I. C. nicknamed Blair "Arkie" when he learned that he had been born in Arkansas. Everybody in Caney Head has a nickname. Once seeking certain information, I was directed to a Poodle McKenzie, who owned a hardware store in Fred. It's a little awkward to say: "Pardon me, but are you Poodle McKenzie?" To a distinguished businessman, but that's what he has been called all his life. So Blair became Arkie.

After Blair's National Geographic article was published, as well as a book and various magazine articles on the area, I. C. told Blair: "O.K., Arkie, I've showed you my world. Now I want you to show me yours." So Blair took him to Houston as a guest in his house, which was rather sumptuous, and allowed him to accompany him on photo assignments, both by Blair's Landrover and by plane. (I. C. had never flown before.) Blair wrote a moving account of this unlikely relationship between an educated, sophisticated man of the world and an illiterate backwoodsman, published simply as *The Stories of I .C. Eason, King of the Dog People.*

It is amusing how so-called upper class Southeast Texans looked down their noses at I. C. and his way of life, while many people of importance the nation over respected and loved him. Cornell University had a number of professors and graduate students working in the Big Thicket at one time and they all got to know I. C. One of them, Dr. Peter Marks, had a special liking for him and really fell in love with little Mickey and her singing. Years later, he still asks about her when we talk. Once when Archer Fullingim, the celebrated editor of the *Kountze News* had a party, the Eason family was invited. Archer was famous for his mayhaw jelly so he had Lorine make a pan of hand rolled biscuits. That was not only the refreshment for the evening, but the entertainment also.

I think the reason so many people from such diverse backgrounds liked I. C. and his family is that they had the courage to be themselves. Today, you never know what people are really like —everybody puts up a carefully constructed front and you seldom get past it. And everybody is working on their image. Believe me, with the Easons, "What you see is what you get." They let you know what they really think about any subject at hand and in no uncertain terms. They feel no need to conform to society's standards or anybody else's idea of an acceptable lifestyle, but are secure in who and what they are and can look anybody square in the eye.

Each of I. C.'s thirteen siblings is different. While Cat, I. C., and Deacon are wild and uninhibited, Cecil is quiet and gentle and his family is practically "uptown Silsbee." Doc was somewhat of a celebrity in his own right, having been featured in Houston newspapers and magazine articles as "Barefoot Eason." Both he and his wife were well diggers in the days before mechanical drills and both had an aversion to footwear. Doc claimed the only time he ever wore shoes was on his wedding day. I knew three of their children: Elmo, who played the 12-string guitar and sang like an angel, Vivian, and Sugar Bowl (I never knew her real name).

Some of the Eason families who have moved up in the world (and that's certainly admirable) resent the TV, newspaper, and magazine articles that depict Easons as backwards and uncivilized outlaws. Writers do love to sensationalize and, as I personally have learned, if you aren't colorful enough, they will color you as brilliantly as they choose. The Easons have certainly been "colored." A daughter of a local Silsbee bank official wrote an article in the *Texas Observer* magazine, comparing the two worlds that exist side by side in Hardin County, specifically her country club, finishing school growing up and that of I. C.'s daughters—neither of them even aware of each other. She did not intend to be insulting, but it really had Caney Head in an uproar. Sitting in Ernest Spell's barbershop one Saturday, I listened to the article being cussed and discussed. (Mostly cussed) One of I. C.'s cousins, who had married an ambitious man who built up a fortune but still lived in Caney Head, held sway. Strutting back and forth, she announced: "I'm an Eason! I'm PROUD to be an Eason! I'm not pore and pitiful. I have the biggest house in Hardin County." (And she does! A Tara-style mansion replete with reflecting pool, gazebo, and statuary.) "And. . ." (posing) "I'm just as good looking as any woman in Hardin County!" (Which she is.) "And I have more diamonds than anybody in Hardin County!" (The proof of which was flashed before our eyes.) The rest of her tirade, directed at the journalist and the article, is best not recorded here. There's no doubt about it! The Easons are not boring people to be around.

Like many of the heavy-smoking people in Caney Head, I. C. succumbed to lung cancer. Lorine developed it also, and soon followed him. I stopped by one afternoon to see how he was getting along and most of his and Deacon's families were sitting out on the front porch. They helped I. C. out to sit with us and it was a shock to see his once strong, agile body so weak and frail. When I left, I knew I would never see him alive again.

I was at a Park Service party at the Turkey Creek Unit Clubhouse when one of the office personnel came over and told me that Ernest Spell had called and said I. C. was dead. Ken Tiege put his arm around me and said he had wanted to wait until after the party to tell me so I could enjoy myself. I left and went to the house where I. C.'s body was laid out. There were so many cars parked on both sides of the road in front of the house that I had to walk a half mile, and there were so many people there that the house, yard, and space on the roadside were filled and the floral offerings overflowed the house and onto the porch.

The gathering at the graveside funeral the next day emphasized his wide range of acquaintances. Blair Pittman was there, as were Bill Brett, cowboy author and raconteur, and Houston Thompson. There would have been others except for time and distance and not knowing about his death.

When someone remarked how nice I. C. looked in the casket, all dressed up and all, Ernest Spell, who always had something out of the ordinary to say for every occasion, said: "Yes. I can just hear him say: 'Blankety-blank! Ain't I purty!'" And he probably would have.

After the funeral, back at the house, I sat with the family and we talked about that other river, which is crystal clear and has never been polluted, where I. C. is sitting on the bank waiting for us all and what a great time that is going to be. And we all cried, for there was an empty chair at the table that is never going to be filled again.

Part Two

Day 4

LOG RAFTING

River Mile 76.8 8:30 A.M.

I hadn't left I. C.'s camp long when I came upon a bend where a big log raft once piled up. I. C.'s mother, Liza Ard Eason, was cook on the raft. The cook shack was usually a tent on the last crib. When the raft hit land in the bend of the river, she saw that it was beginning to break apart and pile up, so she dived into the water and swam clear. That must have been an awesome sight: those great logs piling up like match sticks. She always told I. C. that if the river ever got low enough to expose the logs, he should pull them out, for they were virgin longleaf pine logs and would be as good as new due to submersion in the water. The year Saul Aronow, Ranger David McHugh, and I canoed the upper Neches, it was lower than I had ever seen it and that was the year I. C. pulled out a good portion of the logs. The fence around his house on Highway 92 was made of hand-rived pales from these logs.

The river was the only way they could transport timber from the Neches watershed to the big lumber mills in Beaumont. Loggers would kill the trees by girdling them, wait a year for them to dry standing up, then cut them down with axes and two-man crosscut saws. Oxen and mules dragged the logs to the sloughs, then, when the winter floods came and water rose, the logs were floated. The main routes in the flooded bottomlands had the trees along them cut while the water was down, and they were called float roads. The logs were fastened with wooden pegs into cribs, or small rafts, and the cribs were connected by chains or ropes to make a long raft. The end of each log was struck with a sledge hammer that had a raised letter on it, thus branding the logs so the receiving mills would know to whom the logs should be credited. Perhaps the owner suspected some enterprising loggers might decide to sell a few logs on their own and pocket the proceeds.

The loggers waited until the foam on the river gathered down the center, for they knew then that the river water was falling. If the foam was dispersed out of banks, the water was still rising, the logs would be scattered in the flooded woods and be difficult to guide or retrieve.

Most of the early families rafted logs. According to Austin Withers, the Ellis family rafted logs from the Forks of the River (where the Neches and Angelina met); the Beans from near Kirbyville and below Sally Withers Lake; Ramers and Swearingens from near Spurger; Wrights, Withers, and Richardsons between Spurger and Evadale. The Beans had considerable property up and down the river and so hauled to different points. A large slough bisecting the Neches Bottom Unit around River Mile 56.5, is known as the Bean Float Road. Later, investors from the North, like the Fords, bought timber from family land to harvest it themselves and float to their sawmills downriver.

According to Bob Allen, now of Silsbee, he and his father, Ernest Allen, ran the last raft of logs, which had been hewn to square timbers, down the Neches in 1929. They floated all the way from near Diboll to Beaumont.

Loggers on the Neches must have been mighty men. I've cut down a few small trees with an axe and I can personally assure you it took a lot of muscle, time, and patience to fell the giants of those virgin forests. The strength, skill, and agility required to ride the individual logs through the swift currents of the flooded bottomlands to the watery roads to join the rafts, then direct the rafts down the raging river through snags, fallen trees, and around sharp bends, must have been prodigious. Men would stand on the lead rafts with long poles called peavey or jam poles to guide the rafts away from banks and snags. Even then, pileups were not uncommon.

When the log rafts hit a snag or anything that stopped the first cribs, the current continued moving the back cribs and piling them up until a log jam was created. Some were so big and so jumbled that dynamite was used to break the mass and disperse the logs. Usually, a rassle jack, also called a bull wheel, which was similar to a capstan on a ship, was used to pry the logs apart. Holes were drilled in a section of log and two cross poles of hardened hickory were placed in them for leverage. This was called the rassle jack. A rope was tied to a key log in the jam and the other to the pin which had been driven into the rassle jack. As the rassle jack log turned, the rope tightened and pulled the key log loose and the rest of the logs spread out over the water. A boom (a chain of logs connected by their ends) was placed across the river downstream to capture the freed logs and the loggers would leap from log to log with a long jam pole, pushing them close to shore where they could be reorganized into individual cribs.

The rafts were tied up at night at campsites on bluffs and these sites were used by all rafters year after year. They are still favored by fishermen and hunters who know the river.

As the rafts floated swiftly downriver the loggers would call out in a special holler so ferrymen would know to let their cables drop below the surface of the water and those who had boats tied up along the banks could pull them out. Daddy used to say that he would give anything to hear the old river holler just once more before he died. I found only one man who remembered it: Austin Withers. I was privileged to hear it, probably for the last time it was ever called, so I taped it for posterity.

When the rafts were sold in Beaumont, the loggers either bought a horse and rode it back home, or, more commonly, walked back. It is hard for us to imagine a man working for two years to cut and float logs, then walking fifty to a hundred miles back home to earn his pay, while we work an eight-hour day and are paid at the end of each week. The strength and determination of these pioneers could only have been exceeded by their patience.

WITHERS FAMILY

Matthew Keene Withers (d. 1850) - Sarah Speak (d. 1869)
Came to Shelby County from Virginia in 1790

Valentine James Withers (1818–1912) married:
Sarah McClelland (d. 1846)
Angeline Stott (d. 1855)
Margaret Louise Richardson (d. ?)
Josephine Bonapart Catherwood (d. 1879)
Amanda Williams (d. 1912)

Children by:
Sarah McClelland Died in childbirth. No children

Angeline Stott
1. Sarah Angeline (Sally) m. Dr. Benjamin Franklin Bean
2 . Clerie m. Dr. Benjamin Franklin Bean
3. William John m. Emma Gandy (Indian)
Matthew Keene m. Ida Malvina Westbrook
Children:
1. C. Austin
2. Matthew Keene
3. Emily Madelyn Haynes

Margaret Louise Richardson
1. William Amos (1850 – 1917) (built l00 Year-Old House)
2. Marlin
3. John Valentine (Uncle Tine)
4. Louis
5. James
6. Infant
7. Ina Angeline (Tarver)

8. Benjamin Terrell
9. Ola Delia (Stuart)

Josephine Bonapart Catherwood

1. Charlton King
2. Waller Barton
3. Clara Eugenie (Wright)
4. Laura
5. Josephine Euthemia
6. Robert Casey
7. Susan Rebecca (Wright)
8. Infant

Amanda Williams No children

Austin Withers

YELLOW BLUFF

River Mile 74.3 9:25 A.M.

At 9:25, I came upon the mouth of a small stream at the northern foot of a bluff and knew I was at Yellow Bluff. The river here had cut into upland where tall longleaf pines once grew and the soil was the yellow ocher color typical of long Indian habitation. This is near the vague line where Tyler and Hardin Counties meet and at one time the bluff was an important riverboat landing and ferry crossing. The eastern fork of the Old Wagon Road crossed the river at this site and went on to become the first road to connect the Neches and Sabine Rivers. According to Austin Withers, this route was once an Indian trail.

William John Withers had a ferry, warehouse, and steamboat landing at Yellow Bluff from 1875 until a few years after the disastrous flood of 1884. After the demise of the riverboats, the ferry sank near the bank and is still here because it was built of cypress and, being under water, is protected from the oxygen that causes wood to rot. Another of my impossible dreams is that the Park Service will someday raise the Yellow Bluff ferry and restore it to serve the hikers who will be walking the Old Wagon Road Trail.

I pulled into the backwater at the head of Yellow Bluff and climbed the gently sloping bank to the top of the bluff where I once sat with Austin Withers, grandson of William J. Withers, son of Matthew, and a member of a once numerous clan, and we talked of the past, the present, and the possible future. He had been a bachelor all his life and was a dear, sweet man strong in the Southern tradition of work and good moral values. At 93 years of age, his carriage was erect and his step firm and quick—in fact, not many men a third his age could keep up with him in the woods. His mind was alert and accurate as to the events and people of the river. He lived on the edge of the terrace on the eastern side of the river in the family home along with his sister, Mrs. Emily Withers Haynes.

Built of virgin lumber around 1908 by his father, the house was a comfortable dwelling with fireplaces, small rooms, high, beaded center-match ceilings and a couple of attic rooms reached by a narrow stair. A porch surrounded three sides of the house and the whole was shaded by huge magnolia trees. The spacious house was surrounded by a fence of hand-rived pales; there was a large garden space and an orchard of fruit and nut trees in a pasture where cattle once grazed. I visited Austin Withers often before he died and enjoyed sitting on the cool porch with him and talking of the past. What a pleasant place it was! I couldn't help but think what a wonderful place this would be to raise children. The house was a few hundred yards off the old Weiss Bluff / Bevilport road and at its intersection with the road from Yellow Bluff which connected the Neches with the Sabine River. Austin showed me one of the trees carved with Indian signs and Spanish writing that indicated its use by the early Indians. This tree overhung a big spring which, for some reason, was named Cairo Springs. A pioneer community by that name, now gone, was formed around it.

Near Austin Withers' place is a dogtrot house with a Texas Historical Society medallion. It was built in the 1870s by William Amos Withers and is owned by Inez Hughes, a granddaughter of William. I visited Mrs. Hughes there, and she very proudly showed the place to me along with the documents given by the Daughters of the Republic of Texas which qualified the house for a Texas Historical medallion.

The Withers family have all prospered, become educated, sold the vast timber and bottomlands, and left for other parts. Now that Austin and his sister are both dead, I don't know who, if anybody, lives in the old home place. What a waste!

Beartine Withers as a Young Man

Beartine Withers at age 90

It has been a matter of wonder to me why those who lived on the eastern side of the river differed so radically from those who lived on the western side. They all came from educated, fairly well-to-do people from the East and, from their own admission, both had Indian blood. A friend, (sorry, I can't remember who), suggested to me that it resulted from topography. The eastern side has a higher terrace, grew better crops, and had fewer swamps. The swamps bred mosquitoes that carried malaria. Most of the bottom dwellers had malaria off and on throughout their lives and it no doubt sapped much of their strength and energy. Or it could have been the simple fact that those who stayed were happy in the woods and river and satisfied with their lives. Even today, many of us born to the slow, quiet life of the backwoods are so overwhelmed by the noise, confusion, and milling masses of humanity in the cities that we feel an urgent need to return to the peace and security of that environment to which we were born and bred and to which we belong.

Another interesting point is that the people on the east side of the river almost never married with those on the west side, probably because they worked, worshipped, and recreated together with those whose land adjoined their own, and this would naturally throw the young marriage-age children together.

At any rate, most of the Withers family have scattered, but they were one of the important pioneer families of Southeast Texas. Matthew Keene Withers, his wife, Sarah Speak Withers and son, Valentine James, came to Shelby County from Virginia in 1790. Valentine, (called Beartine because he loved to hunt and eat bears), fought the Cherokees in East Texas in 1838 and was involved on the Regulators' side in the Regulator-Moderator War, which was more of a large feud than a real war. That was probably why he moved on down to the unsettled Neches River country. He was also in Johnson's Mounted Volunteers and was a commissioned officer during the Civil War.

Beartine had long scars on his back due to an encounter with a wounded bear that had him in a bear hug and was about to make a lunch off his shoulder. He yelled at his son, Charlton, to shoot the bear, but the action was so frantic that Charlton couldn't be sure that it would be the bear he shot, so he attacked the animal with a hunting knife and killed him. Beartine Withers was a mighty man in his time. Austin supplied me with pictures of him. One was of him in his youth dressed in full frontier regalia: buckskin shirt, bowie knife in a holster, and a rifle over his shoulder. Another showed him in his old age sitting on his favorite riding mule with gun in hand and his dog trotting alongside and he still presented an attitude of strength and vigor. Austin said that before Beartine died, he was making plans to move to Mexico where bears were still plentiful.

It was said that Beartine Withers was rather domineering over his household, even in small things like how his cornbread was fried. For breakfast, lunch, and dinner, he wanted cornbread. It had to be formed into three pones, placed in a round skillet of deep bear fat and pressed flat with the back of the hand. There had to be THREE FINGER IMPRINTS on the top of each pone! It is interesting that the old-time farmhouse wives I have known used the same method of making cornbread, even to the three pones and the three finger imprints on top.

In those days, the man of the house was lord and master to be revered, feared, and obeyed. A woman's life in the wilderness was hard. The men fished, hunted, chased Indians, and had whatever excitement they could stir up, while the women had the responsibility of keeping the farm and livestock, bearing and raising the children, and feeding the family. They grew cotton and wool, carding, spinning, and weaving it into cloth and sewing it by hand into clothing. Beartine Withers "wore out" four wives in his lifetime from 1818 to 1912. His first wife, Sarah McClelland, died the first year of marriage in childbirth. He had three children by his second wife, Angeline Stott: William John, Sarah Angeline (Sally), and Clerie; nine children by his third wife, Margaret Louise Richardson, and eight by his fourth wife, Josephine Bonapart Catherwood. A fifth wife, Amanda Williams, had no children and outlived him. The girls married into the Wright, Richardson, and Bean families. Clerie, having married Dr. Benjamin Franklin Bean, died, and Sarah (Sally) became his wife. Since the only people who would be offended by my mentioning this are dead, it won't hurt to say that Clerie Bean died from drug addiction. I knew of several wives of doctors who became addicts because their husbands kept such medications as laudanum (an opium derivative), paregoric, and morphine on the premises. Sally, already past the age when most women married in those days, married the doctor in order to raise her sister's children, whom she loved dearly. It is interesting that girls named Sarah were always called Sally even back in the old countries from which they came.

This foregoing information comes from a written family history as well as talking with family members. The Bean family history gives a different account: The sisters' names were Clerie and Sarah Sally and the two children were of the second wife, with a daughter named Maud. Inaccurate, I believe.

The Withers family owned slaves prior to the Civil War. One of them, David Crockett, about whom I will tell more later, was a close friend of Beartine and so valued by the family that he was nicknamed Old Jewel. Slaves were traded around between the pioneer families as they married with those of other families. Slaves of the Withers, Bean, and Wright families were closely related.

There is a lot of pride of heritage in the Withers family. In their book of family history, they have this to say about Beartine: "We, his children, feel proud of the impression he made on us from infancy to be brave, honest, upright, just, and to do right, regardless of circumstances." From all the Withers I have known, his descendents lived up to this creed.

Beartine Withers built a house on the edge of the bottom for his daughter Sally. The house, still standing to this day, was known locally as the Maud Bean House. Unfortunately, the house and land were sold to a local entrepreneur named Marvin Whitehead who had no knowledge nor appreciation of its historical and cultural value so he gave it to a relative who proceeded to "modernize" and "improve" it out of all recognition! It should have been included in the Sally Withers Lake section of Big Thicket National Preserve and maintained as a historical shrine. Ah well!

The abandoned channel lake between the house and the river is named Sally Withers Lake for Sally, as Beartine had given the land in its vicinity to her. When Daddy was a small boy, he would visit his "Aunt Sally" at this same house. I have not been able to find out if she was really blood kin or, if, as the custom was, she was called Aunt by younger people because of her advanced age. He told once of being there and playing a trick on Aunt Sally. He took some vinegar and went to the hen house, took a large, brown hen's egg and wrote on it with the vinegar. The letters were white. It said: "Sally, prepare to meet God." When she gathered the eggs, this mysterious message so frightened her that she almost had a nervous breakdown and Daddy was too scared by her response to admit to the hoax. I suppose, as time went by and she didn't die immediately, she decided the number of her days was going to be extended.

My grandfather Jim (James Calhoun) Ellis clerked at a store at the juncture of what is now Highway 96 and the road that went past the Antioch Church, crossed the Weiss Bluff/Bevilport Road, and went on to Yellow Bluff. Many of my people are buried in the Antioch Cemetery. Daddy and his young uncle, Lyman Scott, had a donkey and a sled that they used to carry their boat to the river when they wanted to go fishing and camping, and they would travel this same road, now much improved of course. When people didn't have a wagon, they would construct a simple platform on two runners, hitch an animal to it and it would slide along on the sandy roads as easily as a wheeled vehicle.

But, back to Yellow Bluff—after examining the old ferry cable still attached to the large tree at the base of the bluff, I sat and meditated a few minutes, remembering the times I had sat here with Austin Withers. I tried to visualize the scene as it would have been at the turn of the century, and as my father had seen it. There is nothing there now to even hint of its busy past. One of the pictures Austin gave me was a photograph of a painting of Yellow Bluff with its warehouse, and the ferry carrying a horse and wagon across the river. There was no resemblance whatever to the present scene. Things do change.

Sally Withers Lake

SALLY WITHERS LAKE

River Mile 73.5 10:00 A.M.

I continued to Sally Withers Lake, arriving at 10:00 at the mouth of the slough which empties it into the river. When the river is high, one can take a motorboat right up it into the lake, but, it was dry so I walked it to the lake. It was easier than making my way through the woods. Sally Withers Lake is another of the deep, clear, black-water, abandoned-channel lakes which occupy intermediate terraces of the floodplain and are only occasionally flooded by the river. The tall trees surrounding it form a wind barrier so the water surface is unbroken, creating a perfect mirror for the cypress trees which, at this time of the year, ring the water with golden russet color.

When the lake was part of the river, it had cut into a higher terrace, so the eastern bank is usually above flood level and has a canopied, open forest of beech, magnolia, oak, and loblolly pine trees. Before it became part of the Big Thicket National Preserve, a developer divided the land surrounding the lake into lots and a few weekend cabins were built there and roads put in. After government acquisition, the cabins were removed and the roads became overgrown. Even at their best, the roads were seldom passable. Ranger David McHugh and I once made our way to the lake overland and were up to the headlights in water much of the time. Dave McHugh shared many of my more venturesome experiences when I was with the Park Service. Since I was old enough to be his mother and had boys his age, I guess he felt a responsibility to go along and see that no harm befell me.

After walking about Sally Withers Lake, I decided to return by the old road which led to the river instead of following the winding slough—a big mistake. The road was overgrown with briers and brush, so I finally left it and cut across the woods back to the river. This side trip to the lake took an hour and a half: thirty minutes there and an hour back.

Alligators

The upper end of Sally Withers Lake is shallow and populated with scattered buttonbush and cypress trees. Austin Withers once took me there to see an alligator nest. The eggs had already hatched and the mother gator had wallowed out a small pool near the water so her young would have a place to spend their babyhood safe from the predatory garfish in the lake. There must have been over 25 of the little gators in that pool. They were about fourteen inches long and were a spotted black and yellow. As we approached, they raised their heads and tail ends out of the water and hissed at us, submerged a moment, then rose and hissed again. The mother was circling around in the lake, slapping her tail on the surface, so we got close enough to take a few pictures and retreated.

Female alligators are very protective of their nests and their young. Alligators mate in mid-June to early July after hibernation, and during the breeding season, the adults call to one another in a throaty, bellowing roar. The female gathers rotted wood, leaves, and mud into a mound five to seven feet in diameter and up to three feet high, usually on a bank close to water. She

Drawing by Regina Watson

lays a clutch of 25 to 60 hard-shelled eggs about three inches long in a cavity in the center of the nest. She covers them with the debris, and heat from the decaying organic matter incubates the eggs. The mother remains near the nest to protect it from predators and is extremely hostile during this period. After nine weeks, the young begin to hatch and call to the mother—"Ye-onk, ye-onk"—and she digs them out. The young hatchlings, nine to ten inches long, head for the nearest water with the mother and they remain together for one to three years. The mother gator grunts like a pig to call her young and the young respond with hisses.

Alligators eat almost anything: fish, small mammals, birds, turtles, snakes, and frogs. And, on the other end of the food chain, their tails have become a popular item on menus in restaurants in the South since they were taken off the Endangered Species list. Alligators are important, ecologically, for they dig deep holes during drought that provide water for the wildlife community.

At one time, alligators were very numerous in the Neches River bottom. Daddy said when the children swam in the river, a man stood on each end of the sandbar with a gun to protect them from the alligators. Actually, I never heard of an alligator eating anybody in this area, though a man named Bill Gordon showed Daddy two rows of scars across his middle that he said were made by a gator. He had started to wade across Tater Patch Lake and the gator grabbed him and took him underwater. A gator will dive with large prey to the bottom and roll over with it to break the bones and drown it, then wedge it on the bottom under logs and mud until it's right to eat. Gordon said he grabbed the front leg of the gator and twisted it and the gator let loose of him long enough for him to escape. Later, I was told that the fellow was a terrible liar, so one can use his own judgment as to whether or not to believe him. Sometimes, I have found that the river bottom people will tell the most outrageous tales just to see how gullible you are.

Travis Gore told me that hide hunters swept through the Neches bottom in 1936 and literally cleaned it out of alligators. He said that over 40 gators were taken from Tater Patch Lake in three days. Others have verified this account.

You hear all sorts of stories about alligators. Daddy was once fishing in a mill pond, wading in waist-deep water and casting for bass, when a large alligator appeared between him and the shore. He took refuge on a tall stump in the middle of the mill pond and, while the gator circled the stump, he yelled for help. An old man and two teenaged sons lived in a shack near the mill pond and they heard his cries for help. One of the boys laughed, dived into the water, and swam straight toward the alligator. Just before he got to the gator, he dived under water toward the gator and it turned and went in the opposite direction. He kept it up until, the last Daddy saw of the alligator, the boy had chased it to the far end of the pond and Daddy quickly made for the shore. They claimed that the only vulnerable part of a gator's body is its stomach and it won't allow anything to go underneath it.

A strange gator story was told me by Cecil Eason, one of the more urbane and serious-minded of his clan and less prone to exaggeration, so I believed him. Assuring me that he knew the difference between alligators and crocodiles, he nevertheless swore that he had caught a 14-foot one-eyed crocodile on a trotline and it had gone after him, even getting into the boat with him. Some alligator gars resemble crocs somewhat but surely an Eason would recognize a gar. He also told me of a big gator who had a hole in Maple Slough in the 1940s and preyed on hogs and calves that came there to drink.

Apparently the men of the river bottoms had little fear of gators as I have heard that they sometimes amused themselves by wrestling them. The Ramer boys, Puddin and Punkin, once caught one over 16 feet long. Isn't it an amusing contradiction that boys with such nicknames would wrestle alligators?

THE CLAN MACBAEAN

In my wanderings and readings, I often came upon mention of the Bean family of the east side of the Neches. I recalled that during land acquisition proceedings, the Park Service had correspondence with a Dr. Bean who owned land around Sally Withers Lake, but I could find none of the family who could give any information about its history. I found myself thinking a lot about a good friend of times past, Opal Bean Baxter, who had been a member of the Jasper County Beans before marriage, but I had long since lost touch with her. Since she was a retired schoolteacher and librarian, I knew she would have knowledge of her family history. Then one day, the phone rang and I was overwhelmed to hear that it was Opal Baxter. She had met my son, David, at church in Beaumont, asked if his mother's name might be Geraldine Watson, and so got my telephone number. It wasn't long before we met and were hashing over old times, times in between, and what we are both doing in the present. Not only did she know a lot about the activities of the family, but had just completed a genealogy of the Southeast Texas branch of the Clan MacBaean, the name by which they were known in Scotland. She also possessed several volumes of listings of the thousands of members of the American clan who were descendants of Alexander MacBaean, the first immigrant of that family to America.

Alexander MacBaean was born in Aberdeen, Scotland, in 1752 during the political and religious upheavals occasioned by the attempt to bring the Young Pretender, Charles Edward Stuart, to the thrones of England and Scotland. A lot of romantic nonsense has arisen about Bonnie Prince Charlie. He was idolized by the Scots, but, according to modern biographers, he was vain and arrogant, totally egocentric and self-indulgent, and thought his subjects existed only to gratify his every desire. The attempt to return the Stuarts to power failed, largely because of Charles' stupidity, his belief that he had a God-mandated gift to command, (and thus dictated military tactics to the disaster of all) and, finally, his betrayal of the clan chieftains. Defeated, he fled to France. King George's retaliation against the Scots was merciless. The Clan chieftains were tortured and executed.

Many of us of Scottish ancestry, of whom I am one, are descended from the remnants of Bonnie Prince Charlie's supporters, as well as the common folk who had to leave Scotland for economic reasons when the ruling classes started enclosing common lands.

In America, MacBaean was changed to Bean. Alexander apparently was neither a political refugee nor a debtor deportee, for he was 23 years of age when he emigrated to America with his 18-year-old bride, Christiana Matson, in 1775, on the sailing ship, *Georgia*, and he had enough money to buy 500 acres of land in Edgefield County near Charleston, South Carolina. Of course, one needed little money to buy land in those days. I have known of men who traded a hundred acres for a single yoke of oxen. Many people had more land than they could farm and the trees on it were considered a liability rather than an asset. Arriving in America at the outbreak of the Revolutionary War, according to records, Bean enlisted and fought in Washington's army. Perhaps he was motivated by the hereditary hatred the Scots bore for the English and did not wish to see their dominance continue in the New World.

Alexander and Christiana had eight children. They lived out their days in South Carolina, but their children moved westward—some into Georgia when the Cherokee lands were opened for settlement, some into Alabama, Louisiana, and Texas. As with most westward-bound families, brothers and cousins with their families and in-laws would travel together in long wagon trains. One such train with California as its destination included hundreds of the Bean clan. As they traveled, parts of the groups would drop off at some state where friends or relatives had formerly gone, or that appealed to them, and, sometimes, the entire group would stop for a year or two and raise a crop of corn, peas, potatoes, and other provisions.

Alexander, Jr., stopped off in Alabama and his son, Marshall Jacob, continued to Texas. M. J.'s son, John Egbert, with wife Jane also continued to Texas where they settled at Magnolia Springs in Jasper County near the Neches River. There they raised eight children and lived out the rest of their days. John Egbert was a well-known and much-loved minister of the Gospel and was referred to as Elder Bean. One of their sons, James, was the father of Dr. Benjamin Franklin Bean who married Sally Withers and her sister, Clerie, (separately, of course). Another of John Egbert's nine children was Jesse Mercer, whose son, Ector Estel with his wife, Nettie Hooks of Spurger, was the father of my friend, Opal Bean Baxter.

The Beans were active in the life of the Neches River, harvesting and floating logs and engaging in the steamboat business, but their main interests were academic and their contributions to the physical, cultural, and moral welfare of the community were enormous and continue to this day.

ERNEST WESTBROOK
Grandson of slave
David Crockett

DAVID CROCKETT

When I visited the Withers cemetery, I noticed that it was divided into two sections with separate gates. As I walked about and read the inscriptions on the stones, a picture on a tombstone of a dignified Negro man revealed that one of the sections was a Negro cemetery. The oldest persons buried here were David Crockett, born 1844 and died 1942, and Charlie Westbrook, born 1821 and died 1911. There was also a Jim Bowie and a few other "Texas heroes" names on the stones.

I couldn't get David Crockett off my mind. An old map showed a road through the river bottom called the David Crockett trail, so he must have been someone of some importance. Finally, I called Matthew Withers at his insurance agency in Buna who knew of Uncle Dave and gave me the name of one J. B. Westbrook who might provide some information. Mr. Westbrook lived in the Buna-Bessmay area and I planned to participate in the spring Bessmay Cemetery working on Saturday, so after "dinner on the ground" I went in search of him. Driving on down the road past the Withers cemetery, I overtook a Negro man driving a tractor with five hounds frisking around it. Hailing him over, I asked if he knew where I might find J. B. Westbrook and, with a friendly smile, he said, "That's me." I explained my purpose, asking if he would mind talking with me, and he said he would be glad to as soon as he finished delivering something to a nearby farm. Following his directions, I came to the mobile home on the old Weiss Bluff / Bevilport road and waited. He proved to be quite articulate and very knowledgeable about the history of area families, both whites and Negroes.

The mystery of the "heroes" graves was solved when he explained that they had been slaves of Mr. William Wright who had named them for Texas heroes. Mr. Wright had bought David Crockett and his two sisters in Georgia and raised them with his own family. David was a tall brown man with high cheekbones and straight hair. His sisters were also tall with long, curly hair. They were really Indians.

David was a skilled hunter and supplied the Wright household with venison, turkey, and other wild game. After the Civil War, Mr. Wright gave him a hundred acres of land and a yoke of oxen to begin his own farm. Ambitious and industrious, he was a skillful worker and did many odd jobs to earn money. One of his specialties was splitting pales (boards) for fences, barns, and shingles, all with a broad axe. J. B. recently found Dave's axe while working around his yard and he cleaned it and made a handle for it. The old Richardson house and its fences on the Weiss Bluff/Bevilport Road still have some examples of Dave Crockett's work. While his children worked the farm, he would cut trees, float them down the river to Beaumont and sell them. J. B. said he would return with his pocket full of money.

Dave Crockett married Mary Bean, a half-white slave of the white Bean family and, together, they had seventeen children. Dave was J. B.'s grandfather on his mother's side. His grandfather on the side of his father, Cornelius Westbrook, was Charlie Westbrook, slave of the white Westbrook family of Erin. Cornelius had fair skin and blue eyes. Charlie married Betty Withers who was a slave of Matthew Withers and half white. J. B. married an Adams who was the granddaughter of Nat Adams, the slave son of a prominent white Jasper County lawyer family. J. B.'s mother was Nicey Crockett Westbrook, a daughter of David and Mary Crockett.

In the past, many masters had a Negro family as well as a legal white family. They saw to it that their illegitimate children had an education and were taken care of. J. B. said that in the old days, white families acknowledged their relations with colored family members.

Apparently, the image of the fettered slave subdued by chains and whips and bloodhounds did not fit the situation in Southeast Texas, but all worked together for the common good and continued to work together after the Civil War gave the slaves legal freedom. J. B. said there was only one man in the community who showed any prejudice at all and that was Walter Withers. He had such an unreasoning hatred for the Negroes that they "just dreaded to see him coming." His children apparently atoned for their father's misdeeds, as they "went out of their way" to be kind and helpful. His son, Frank, organized a basketball team for Negro boys and since none of them had automobiles, he transported them to games at Kirbyville and Jasper. Walter's youngest son, Elmo, became a Baptist preacher and was well loved by everyone. The Bean family took a special interest in Dave Crockett's family and as long as Dr. Bean (Sally Wither's husband) lived, he was a protector and friend. J. B. said that Dr. Bean would come, "eat dinner with them and lay down to take a nap."

There must have been a good relationship between slaves and owners, for that era produced some fine people of both colors. J. B. told me how his father and grandfather emphasized the importance of keeping one's word and a good name: "If a man's word is no good, he ain't either." Relationships between the races must not have been as agreeable on the west side of the river, for no Negroes remained there and do not live there to this day. It would be very interesting to know the history behind this situation.

David Crockett and Charlie Westbrook saw to it that their children were taught to worship God and keep His commandments and to read and write. Near the intersection of the cemetery road and the Weiss Bluff/Bevilport Road still stands the building they constructed which served as both church and school. Two teachers J. B. could recall were Professor Marshall and Professor Glover. The school was called Fairview which was the name of their community. J. B.'s mobile home sits on the site of David Crockett's cabin and he said in the old days when the woods burned regularly and there was no brush, you could see through the tall pines all the way to the cemetery and it was indeed a fair view.

It seems I can't escape David Crockett. Recently, while in a local store, a young woman entered wearing a T-shirt advertising a reunion of the Crockett-Westbrook families. Of course I approached her, found the Crockett was "my" David Crockett and wangled an invitation to the reunion that was to be held in Buna. There were hundreds of descendents there along with long tables of food and drink, and I was introduced to Ernest Westbrook, a grandson of David Crockett. Later I visited with him and his wife, a retired, very intelligent, career woman, in their nice home in Beaumont. Ernest Westbrook was

93 years old, tall and erect with facial features showing his Indian heritage. One would guess his age at possibly 65 yrs. His wife said he mowed the lawns of all his neighbors. He had spent much time with his grandfather David Crockett and had much to tell me about him. His recollections of their life in Jasper County along the Neches would make a book in itself.

I'm so glad I got to "know" David Crockett and Charlie Westbrook and some of their descendents. History has been written in the past by the white man, and seldom has credit been given to the industry, hard work, and forbearance of the Negro man who stood by his side, nor the women who cooked their food, cleaned their houses, and raised their children. Together, they conquered and civilized the wilderness. Without his slaves, and later, fellow workers, it could not have been done.

HARDIN-TYLER COUNTY LINE

River Mile 74.3 9:30 A.M.

Between Yellow Bluff and Sally Withers Lake, on the west side of the river is the Hardin-Tyler County line. Hardin County was named for five Hardin brothers: Augustus, Benjamin, Milton, Franklin, and William. They came to this area in 1825 from Georgia a step ahead of the law. The Hardins were ministers of the gospel, lawyers, law officers, and cold-blooded killers, often all at the same time. One of the family, John Wesley Hardin, killed more than thirty men in his short lifetime and excused it all by saying that he never killed a man who didn't need killing. Anyway, some of the Hardins must have done something right—they named the county after them.

Hardin County was in the Lorenzo de Zavala colony and land grants were issued until 1835. Under the Republic of Texas, Hardin County was included in the counties of Jefferson and Liberty, but in 1858, it was established as a new county with Hardin as the county seat. After the railroad bypassed Hardin and the town declined, the county seat was moved to Kountze in 1887. There are tales that the Hooks, a powerful family in the Kountze area, wanted the county seat moved to Kountze, so one of the Hooks boys who was famous as a fast runner (and always ran barefoot) set the courthouse on fire, then ran to his home in Kountze and went to bed. When his accusers found him at home, asleep, they concluded that it would have been impossible for him to have been in Hardin burning down the courthouse that night. The town of Silsbee eclipsed Koutze in size and importance due to the large Kirby Mill there and the fact that it was a terminal for the Santa Fe Railroad.

Most of Hardin County is low and wet and humidity is high. The soil is wet, sour, and sterile and is said to be good for nothing except grazing and pine trees. It is also said to be a land of mud, moccasins, mosquitoes, and pot-boiling politics. The people of Hardin County are always mad about something or other and aren't happy unless they have something to raise hell about. After a 45-year residence here, I can personally attest to the verity of every claim! Perhaps it's that way everywhere and my range of experience is so limited that I'm not a reliable witness. Anyway, I've moved back to my native Tyler County to my private nature preserve. Tyler County has decided to base its economy on "eco-tourism" and is doing everything it can to restore and preserve what is rare and beautiful in that area. Hallelujah!

IVORY-BILLED WOODPECKER

River Mile 73.9

There used to be a nice camphouse on this bluff, the first on the west side after Yellow Bluff. Various people owned it, among them Ernest Spell. I first visited the camphouse when a fellow named Bill Lott was staying there. As a matter of fact, at the time, I was lost in the maze of roads and jeep trails in the river bottom between the Spurger highway and the river when I met Bill Lott.

When my children were all in school, I would drive the backroads in my little red Volvo in search of material for my weekly newspaper column: "The Big Thicket—Past, Present, and Future." I was wandering in this section of river bottom, running low on gas, and beginning to get uneasy when along came this pickup. I stopped it and rather shamefacedly asked where I was and how could I get back to the highway. We introduced ourselves; he was very nice and we chatted a bit. When I expressed my admiration for the huge trees in that bit of forest, he said, "Why, these are nothing. You should see the ones up at my camp!" That was enough to make me forget all about my nearly empty gas tank, so I followed him up the river road to this camphouse on the bluff where he was staying. Sure enough, there were some mighty forest giants there and I photographed him standing with them. We went back to the camphouse and he insisted I stay and eat some pinto beans and cornbread with him, and I did. (Incidentally, that forest was the one that the

Ivory-billed Woodpeckers

Easons and Houston Thompson saved until it could be acquired as part of the Jack Gore Baygall Unit.)

Bill Lott told me his health had failed and he was about ready to die when he came to the river. The quiet life, running a trotline for fish, shooting a squirrel now and then, and a plain diet had saved his life. He did look hale and hearty. Visiting him again later, I found he had not been to town for some time. A wild canary (prothonotary warbler) had built a nest in the inset where he put gasoline in his vehicle and he wouldn't move it until the young hatched and went their way. Later, when I was planning my river float trips, Bill Lott, Daddy, and I made an exploratory trip so I could check out the time it would take and the type of woods nearby, etc. Bill moved away from the river for some reason and I lost touch, but I haven't forgotten him—a gentle, kind, soft-spoken man.

Another memory that camphouse brings to mind is the days when ivory-billed woodpecker mania swept the birdwatching world. In the 1960s, there were reports by usually trustworthy people that the ivory-billed woodpecker, long thought to be extinct, had been sighted in the Neches River bottom. Dr. Armand Yramategue, of the Houston Museum of Natural Science, an ardent naturalist and birdwatcher, and John Dennis, an ornithologist from Leesburg, Virginia, proceeded to check out the reports.

Armand and John were in the forks of the river country (where the Neches and Angelina meet just above Town Bluff), when they sighted the bird. John Dennis wrote an article reporting the sighting, but Armand, scientist that he was and a stickler for exactness, took exception to the wording. In his opinion, the wording might mislead some to think that he and John had viewed the bird simultaneously when actually one had seen it and then the other had seen it separately—same place and the same time. The difference is important to some who might suspect birdwatchers of fabricating sightings. No one would doubt it if Armand had said, "Yes! Both of us saw it at exactly the same moment."

It seems to me that if they were capable of lying, they could just as easily say they saw it together as separately. Ah Well! It was then that I learned that scientists can be as petty and as murderously competitive as anybody, or even more so. Everyone who ever worked with John Dennis was furious that John had not mentioned their name in the article, and the storm broke.

John made another sighting in the Neches bottom near Boat Lake on the east side of the river. These reports pinpointed the Neches as the last bastion of the large and beautiful bird once so plentiful in our Southern floodplain forests but now thought extinct due to loss of habitat and unscrupulous collectors.

I, myself, had a couple of sightings. One was in the Sternenberg Preserve, a small remnant of virgin forest along Village Creek, now a part of the Turkey Creek Unit of the Big Thicket National Preserve. The outstanding feature of this area is a high bluff separated from the creek by a cypress slough and a small grove of tall cypress trees. The bluff itself was solidly hung with the evergreen Christmas fern and, on its upland were very tall pine trees. I was in the woods at the sloping end of the bluff with a couple of botanists from Houston when I heard the clear, distinct call of ivory-billed woodpeckers. "What was that?" the botanists asked. Scarcely believing it myself, I said,

"That sounded like an ivory-billed woodpecker, and it came from the top of the big cypress down in the slough. I'm going to get closer and try to see it." "Go ahead," they said. "We wouldn't know an ivorybill from a crane." So I proceeded to walk cautiously up the slope. When I reached halfway to the top, the calls ceased. Proceeding, I saw the outline of the bird against the sky, flying from the cypress tree to the tall pines on the bluff.

Arriving home, I immediately called John Dennis. As it was already dark and misting rain, he and his assistant, Peter Islieb, a cinematographer, waited until just before daybreak next morning and went into the preserve. They spent the morning there taping the clear calling of what sounded like more than one bird, but could get no pictures because of the dense foliage of the canopy. Since they had definitely located the bird, they determined to go back, set up blinds and get photographs later. Arriving back at their cabin, they called me and I rushed out to hear the tapes. You could hear the rustling of their footprints in the leaves and their whisperings as they walked into the preserve. Then the sound of the birds could be heard, first faintly, then louder as they neared the site.

Though Peter Islieb haunted the preserve for months, the birds did not return, and they were unable to verify the sighting with photographs. This is typical of ivorybill behavior as they are a vagrant species and only settle down to one location during nesting season. We did find typical ivorybill workings there. A large beech tree on the bluff slope, apparently in good health, had several square feet of bark chiseled off. It is thought that only ivory-billed woodpeckers are capable of such work.

And so the rush was on. I was a hot item in those days. As I knew the woods, river, and backroads and got along with the natives, I was in great demand as a guide. Those were interesting times. Birdwatchers from all over the world wanted to come to the Big Thicket. Thee is no fanatic like a bird lister. Your standing in such organizations as the American Ornithological Society and the Audubon Society depends on how many birds are on your "life list." There is an exclusive club called the Six Hundred made up of people who have seen six hundred different species of birds during their lifetime. They will travel all over the world to see a single bird and check it on their list. The sighting must be verified, however, by another person who sees the bird at the same time.

Most of my clients expected me to drive them into the Big Thicket and say, "And on your left you will see that rare and magnificent bird, the ivory-billed woodpecker!" They could look, from the car, check it on their list, and go back to their motel.

Life magazine decided to do an article on the ivory-billed woodpecker in the Big Thicket area and so sent Don Moser to do the research and write the article. We had great times as he was a good-natured fellow with a sense of humor. Meanwhile, the *National Geographic* magazine had contracted with John Dennis to get pictures and information for a forthcoming article in that publication. A free-for-all battle was being waged at that time to set aside portions of the Big Thicket in a national preserve and we saw these prestigious publications as a means of international propagandizing. If the Big Thicket could be proven as the last territory of the world's rarest bird, the bill in Congress would sail through.

Neal Wright, a hairdresser by vocation and naturalist by avocation, had reported seeing the ivorybill in the depths of the traditional Big Thicket in the Saratoga Triangle, an area of swamps, palmetto thickets, and baygalls. He even had a photograph he had taken of the bird, but experts were extremely dubious of its authenticity.

Among those drawn to the area by the ivorybill was a prominent birdwatcher and clubwoman from Austin and her husband who was a freelance sports writer. I arranged for Neal to take them into the Thicket in his specially equipped jeep, and Neal, good fellow that he was, took a day off from work to accommodate them. According to the three of them, they observed an ivorybill for eighteen minutes and the writer took innumerable photographs of the bird.

Within hours of the sighting, they were on their way back to Austin and the birdwatching world was electrified by their news. The article that the sportswriter would write, accompanied by the photographs, would command a fabulous fee, but after Neal had brought them out of the Thicket, the writer flipped a couple of one-dollar bills to Neal and said, "Here's something for your trouble." To begin with, Neal expected nothing—he had helped them because it was for "the cause." But the writer had placed his value on Neal's contribution by the "payment," and Neal was incensed. He had been insulted and swore that he would never even talk to another birdwatcher, let alone take one out.

The National Geographic Society, hearing the news, wanted to send the renowned bird photographer, Frederick Kent Truslow, to the Big Thicket to photograph the bird in the Saratoga Triangle, and called John Dennis to arrange to take them into the Thicket where the couple had seen and photographed the bird. Neal would have none of it, so the Geographic asked if I would persuade him to give the Society exclusive use of his services. "An article in the *Geographic*," they reminded me, "would assure the passage of the Big Thicket National Preserve bill." So I went to work on Neal and it was this argument that finally persuaded Neal to take Dennis and Truslow to the site. As is the way with the nomadic ivorybill, it was long gone to other realms when they got there and days of stalking and waiting failed to produce the bird.

Meanwhile, back in Austin, the sportswriter had his pictures processed and found to his dismay that none of them were acceptable. His excitement, (and possibly his heavy drinking), had produced hand tremors that made the photographs a blurred mess. He rushed back to Silsbee and telephoned Neal from the Pinewood Inn, casually stating, "I want you to take us back into the Thicket tomorrow to get more photographs." Neal informed him that he had agreed to give National Geographic and John Dennis exclusive rights to his services, and the writer exploded. One could hear his cursing John Dennis for blocks. I was present, but didn't have the guts to say, "It was my fault. I talked him into it." He swore to get even with John and they left for Austin.

Within hours of his departure, I began to get calls from concerned environmentalists: "Is it true that Armand Yramategue said that John Dennis was lying about having seen an ivorybill?" Or: "Is it true that Lance Rosier said John Dennis lied about having found evidence of ivorybill workings in the Big Thicket?" And so on! The sportswriter and his wife, having considerable influence, so slandered John Dennis that his credibility was seriously damaged and his career almost ruined.

The *Life* magazine article finished John off properly. Since the publication was owned by Time, Inc., the largest land holder in the Big Thicket area with lumber, plywood, and paper mills throughout, and the bitterest foe of Big Thicket preservation, the article was slanted, to put it kindly. It pictured John Dennis, as well as the rest of us who claimed to have seen the bird, as irrational, irresponsible fanatics with political motives who would stoop at nothing to insure the passage of the bill in congress. It also suggested that the tapes made in the Sternenberg preserve were spurious and that the same sound could be made by rolling hexagonally-shaped pencils on a desk and speeding up the sound! (I have a letter from the Bureau of Endangered Species stating that the tapes had been authenticated by the Cornell University Laboratory of Ornithology.)

Blair Pittman spent three years photographing for the National Geographic's proposed Big Thicket article, amassing over seven thousand photographs of people, places and things, and I was at his service at any and all times, day or night, at no remuneration—all for the "cause." After all the hullabaloo, the Geographic held off on publication of the Big Thicket article until after the bill was signed and it was no longer a "controversial issue." The ivory-billed woodpecker was scarcely mentioned. Not having photographs of the bird, they decided to focus their article on the folk culture of the Big Thicket. So about all it accomplished was to establish the Eason family as quintessential backwoodsmen.

The redeeming feature of the *Life* article was its watercolor paintings. Having given up on obtaining photos of the bird, they had a well-known watercolorist, John Groth, come to the Thicket for background research. Again, I was guide and hostess and enlisted the aid of Ernest Spell who arranged for I. C. and Deacon Eason to meet us at Ernest's camphouse where Bill Lott had once lived. Ernest was going to have some local musicians there to give the outsiders a taste of our kind of music. The weather had been wet, the Timber Slough road was barely passable, and we got stuck in the mud on the river road and had to walk the rest of the way to the cabin. There was good food and camaraderie as is always the case when the Eason clan gathered. There was I. C. and Deacon, their wives, and all their kids there. We waited hours and Ernest never did show up with the musicians, so we decided to leave. The Easons went with us to extricate our vehicle from the mire and we rode in the back of Huldy, the modified pickup truck.

During Huldy's days as an evangelical vehicle, a loudspeaker was rigged atop the cab. The pickup was used for other purposes also, the present one being to haul a couple of used automobile motors which had emptied their supply of motor oil into the bed of the truck. The condition of the pickup bed was not conducive to our snuggling down, so we all stood, holding on to each other as the pickup careened, plunged, and reared, skidded and roared through and around vast mudholes, trees, and stumps, all to the tempo of the loudspeaker blaring a current George Jones song which went something like this: "I've got —and lovin' on my mind." Children of all sizes and ages were running alongside yelling and laughing. Every time it stuck, everyone jumped out and began to lift and push. We came to our car and it was removed from the mire by the sheer force of the numbers of pushers and pullers.

Eventually, we arrived back at the Timber Slough sandbar liberally bespattered with mud and black oil and there we met up with Ernest and his musicians. They had been detained. It seemed the fiddler, Blackie Roberson, had had an accident and almost cut his thumb off. It had been repaired at the local emergency room and, since luckily it was on his bow hand, they continued their original purpose, and regaled us with music.

We stood about on the sandbar: a vast expanse of white sand with large willows draped over it at the woods' edge and a full moon over the water illuminating the scene. Two Holifield cousins, Gurney and Benny Lee, had a campfire on the bar and were lounging about drinking beer. It was an impressive moment as the music echoed from the forest across the water, and the artist said, "I don't think I have ever witnessed such a beautiful scene."

I have been on this sandbar many times and that scene always comes before me: a happy time. The National Park Service has designated it as a recreational area and will someday develop it as a campsite.

Meanwhile, news of the purported ivorybill sightings had reached round the world and, since my name was mentioned in both publications, I was besieged with requests from as far away as Germany, Mexico City, and England to guide birdwatchers into ivorybill territory. No matter how I argued that their chances of seeing the bird under the best of conditions was perhaps one in a million, they WOULD come.

My experiences with these nuts would fill a book, but I will give only one example. There was this priest from Mexico City who had called and against all my reasoning, engaged me for three days. I explained that I had many demands for my time and expressed doubts that he could keep the appointment from so far away. He assured me that he would keep his word. "I am a MAN OF GOD,",he insisted. "You can trust me."

I hired a babysitter for my children and at 7:00 A.M. on a sleety winter morning met him, black habit, reversed white collar and all, at the Pinewood Inn. While waiting for him to finish preparations—packing camera, thermos, etc.—I explained how careful we must be that the wrong type of person not pursue the rare bird, as there were still people who would shoot the last surviving ivorybill to add it to their collections. He repeated that I could trust him for he was a MAN of GOD.

The Man of God brought out topographic maps and asked that I show him where Armand and John saw the ivorybill. At each site, he asked about access and the conditions of the roads. As I would say, "You can only get in there by boat," or "That will require a half day's walk through difficult terrain," he would mark his map. As I had already taken him into Cypress Island by boat, he concentrated his interest on two sites: The Forks of the River and the Sternenberg Preserve. "Those are easy to get to. There are paved roads to them both," I said. He carefully marked them on his topographic map, raised his head, looked me in the eye and said: "I have decided not to go out today. The weather is too bad."

I was stunned by such flagrant duplicity—especially from a man of the cloth, but found myself saying, "Well, you will have to pay my fee, anyway. I turned down a lot of people to reserve these days for you and have hired a babysitter." He argued and bargained with me as if he were at a Mexican marketplace, and finally paid me eight dollars for the three days. A few minutes later, sitting in the office of the Pinewood Inn drinking coffee with its owner and my good friend, Helen Barefield, I saw the "Man of God," all bundled up against the weather, headed out to visit the sites that I had so carefully located for him. No wonder there are so many atheists in the world.

One of the most exuberant groups coming into Big Thicket with hopes of ivorybill watching was the Dallas Audubon Society. These people were not only birdwatchers but dedicated environmental activists as well. Ned Fritz, Geth Osborne White, Maxilla Evans, and others jumped into the fight to save Big Thicket with all the resources at their command.

Geth Osborne and Ned Fritz organized groups of influential people to come and see the Big Thicket for themselves. One day, Geth got together a group and chartered a plane to come down for a day of hopefully viewing the bird. While I was waiting for them at the Hardin County airport, they were waiting for me at the Temple-Eastex landing field at Evadale. The pilot had become confused in the haze and selected the wrong airfield. Eventually, we got together and I drove them into the river bottom to the cabin on the bluff. Geth organized the group, stationing them at intervals in the forest with binoculars and cameras, ready for action. One of the group had to be in Houston that evening, so I took him out where he could rent a car and be on his way.

Before I could return to the river bottom, it came a gullywasher of a rainstorm and the Timber Slough road became impassable. Desperate, I called a friend who worked for the oil company then operating at the end of the road to seek his advice. He referred me to James (Son) Gordon, who lived on the hill at the edge of the bottom and gave me his phone number. Son Gordon offered to go into the bottom with me and retrieve my party, so here we went, me slipping and sliding and praying, from one side of the road to the other, he behind in his specially equipped pickup ready to pull me out if need be.

Halfway there, we met Ned Fritz, who had started walking out for help. The rest of them were at the cabin, drenched to the bone. Poor Geth had been caught out in the woods in a lightning storm and was almost in hysterics. They opened the bottle of champagne with which they had planned to toast the ivorybill, and were soon warmed and ready to return to civilization. We made it out with Son Gordon's help and when everyone tried to force money on him, he resisted in his slow, quiet voice: "Nope. Glad to help." This began a friendship between Son and me that has lasted all these years. I've turned to him and his grandson, James, whom I made a Junior Park Ranger, many times and they have responded in the same manner as the first time. Son Gordon has all the qualities which the men of Caney Head have, both to survive on the land and river and to use the commodities of the machine age, but not in as flamboyant a manner as the Easons. They are all individuals out here.

There were also serious scientists involved in the search for the ivorybill. Several professors from Baylor University came and I took them to the Boat Lake area in the bottomlands on the east side of the Neches where John Dennis had seen the bird. It was the first week of deer season, the area had been leased by a hunting club, and, since I knew that the woods were full of hunters who only held a gun that one week of the year, I devised red covers for their chests and we drove into the bottoms. There were literally traffic jams on the jeep trails and it sounded like a full-scale war was going on. The scientists gaped in amazement: "Do you mean to tell me that this is the habitat of the world's rarest bird?" "Yep!" I replied.

The Bureau of Endangered Species sent a young man, Paul Sikes, to spend two weeks in the Big Thicket area to settle once and for all whether the ivory-billed woodpecker was extinct or not. He brought with him James Tanner, an ornithologist who had done his master's thesis on the last colony of ivorybills in Louisiana. Tanner, in his published work, claimed that ivorybills had to have virgin hardwood forests to survive. He and Sikes spent a week looking for virgin hardwood forests and found none that they could be certain had never known the axe or the saw, so they went home and reported that the ivory-billed woodpecker was indeed extinct .

Conversely, I received a copy of a letter from the Bureau of Endangered Species to a Dr. Smith stating that the tapes made by John Dennis in the

Sternenberg Preserve had been authenticated by the Cornell Laboratory of Ornithology.

I. C. Eason and his son, James, having been told by a Dallas birdwatcher that he would pay them a thousand dollars to show him an ivory-billed woodpecker, devised a plan to capture one. They knew where a bird, which looked exactly like the picture shown them, roosted in a hole in a tall, dead pine tree. Shinneying up the pine at night after the bird had gone to roost, they fastened a fish net over the hole and next morning, had them a bird. I was called to view it but had to dash their hopes, telling them that it was an immature pileated woodpecker. Is the ivory-billed truly extinct? Or does it still haunt the deep forests and cypress swamps of the vast Neches River bottomlands? I'm not trying to persuade anybody. I don't care what anybody else thinks. But I do know what I have seen with my own eyes. In a later chapter, I will tell how David and I saw a family of ivory-billed woodpeckers on Pine Island Bayou.

TIMBER SLOUGH AND PEACH TREE RIDGE

River Mile 72

The big sandbar where Timber Slough enters the Neches evoked many memories as it has been the scene of encounters both pleasant and unpleasant for me, but I did not stop, having already explored this area thoroughly and often.

The upper reaches of Timber Slough pass by an unusual topographical feature called Peach Tree Ridge. I had heard so much about it that I asked James and Leslie Eason to take me there. So one afternoon we took off on their four-wheelers to explore. We left the vehicles at the McGallion Lakes. These lovely, cypress-fringed, deep, black-water lakes are two of the string of abandoned channels of which Tater Patch Lake and Black Creek form a part. We walked southward along the bank through lovely beech-magnolia woods until, reaching a narrow place between the two lakes, we jumped across and proceeded northward on the east side. I always wondered why this ridge was so named, for I couldn't envision peach trees growing in the river bottom. Arriving there, I saw that it was crowned with a dense growth of Carolina laurel cherry, locally called wild peach. How or why it is so called is a mystery, for it bears no fruit resembling peaches and its evergreen leaves are a dark, rich, glossy green unlike the limp, lighter green of our cultivated peach. It is, however, a member of the same family, the Rosaceae.

I should have suspected Carolina laurel cherry, which is evergreen, for the backwoodsmen marvel that in the winter, the ridge is always green and stands out against the grays and browns of the typical bottomland hardwood forests.

Due to the dense canopy of surrounding trees, it is not apparent that the ridge is so high until you begin to climb it. It is elongated, roughly about two to three hundred feet long, a hundred feet wide, and rises a dozen or so feet higher than the other ridges of the bottoms. I assume that it was once part of the upper terrace and was cut off when the river changed to the Black Creek course. After the lumber companies clearcut all the bottoms above the preserve boundary, I noticed a few other such ridges which stand out prominently above the surrounding land.

I.C.'s Indian grandfather brought him here once and told him how the Indians lived on the ridge since it was high above floodwater, there was a source of fresh water nearby, and the river could be reached by dugout via Timber Slough, which ran at the north end of the ridge. The grandfather told how they would beat their drums and dance around the campfire here in his boyhood.

We descended the ridge on the north slope and jumped the nearly dry slough to return around the north end of the lakes. As we reached the top of the bank, James, who had his compass out, suddenly stopped and exclaimed, "Hey! Looka here!" The compass needle was spinning around. He moved to several different locations, but only at that place did the compass go crazy. He made an X with two limbs at the spot and determined to return later and do some digging. If he did or if he found anything, I don't know. The Easons can be pretty closed-mouthed about some things.

That there could be buried treasure here is not so unbelievable since the Old Wagon Road, which was once an Indian trail and later used by French and Spanish traders and early settlers, runs nearby and tales of lost treasure in its vicinity abound. Son Gordon told me a story about a Dr. White who came to the area looking for Timber Slough because he had a "waybill" (map), indicating the location of buried treasure at certain places on the map. He said the doctor had every kind of gadget to detect the presence of metal in the ground, including a witching rod. Son helped him locate the sites and they turned out to be Timber Slough and Peach Tree Ridge, a site just above Franklin Lake, and Trull Hummock. All these places are on old Indian trails. An eight-foot-long copper chest and an iron pot were supposedly buried at Timber Slough and Peach Tree Ridge. After Son had shown the doctor the sites, the doctor said he wouldn't try for the gold because he distrusted their "company," which happened to be Cat Eason and a man from Liberty. Later, Son said he returned to the site near Peach Tree Ridge and found the perfect shape of an iron pot where someone had dug a shallow hole.

Esker Goins and his boy were cutting ties around Timber Slough when an Indian came through the woods. He admitted that he had a map showing the location of buried gold and when he left them, he was heading toward Peach Tree Ridge. The Indian could well have been a relative of the Easons, an Indian chief named White Eagle, who had reason to believe there was gold buried in the Timber Slough vicinity and came with his son to find it. He had a map drawn on a buckskin and gold was found, but it caused an argument between them, and the father killed the son. Then, of course, there was Bony Gore's "gold hole" where the old Wagon Road crosses Timber Slough. Napoleon Buonopart Gore located a treasure site and proceeded to dig for the treasure. As he dug, the loose sand fell into the hole as fast as he could dig, so he went to Woodville in his wagon and got a section of metal smokestack from an abandoned sawmill to use as a curb. There are various tales as to what he found or did not find, but the top of that curb can be seen to this day. This area where the Old Wagon Road goes through the Open Gap and passes by Timber Slough through the magnificent forests that the Eason boys saved is rich in history and legend.

There is often a touch of the supernatural in these lost treasure stories. Son Gordon also told me how Aunt Viney Jackson looked off toward the baygall one evening, saw a strange ball of light, followed it, and found a pot of money.

The Eddings boys found gold at Trull Hummock and Elbert Eddings drowned by falling out of a boat with a tow sack filled with gold, which was not recovered. Eddings was well known as an expert swimmer and it was a great mystery that he could have so easily drowned. Still another source said the Eddings boy died as the result of a shoot-out over a woman: all of which makes these tales so intriguing to a researcher. A bit of information, embellished and distorted by time and bad memory, is enough to make you want to get to the truth of the matter and know whether to assign the tale to history or legend. A treasure hunt for truth can be as addictive as gold fever.

These are just a sample of the many stories told around the fireplace in winter evenings or the front porch in summer. Daddy had his own collection of buried gold tales. I once did a collection of them and planned to publish a book on the Lost Treasures of the Big Thicket, but never got around to it.

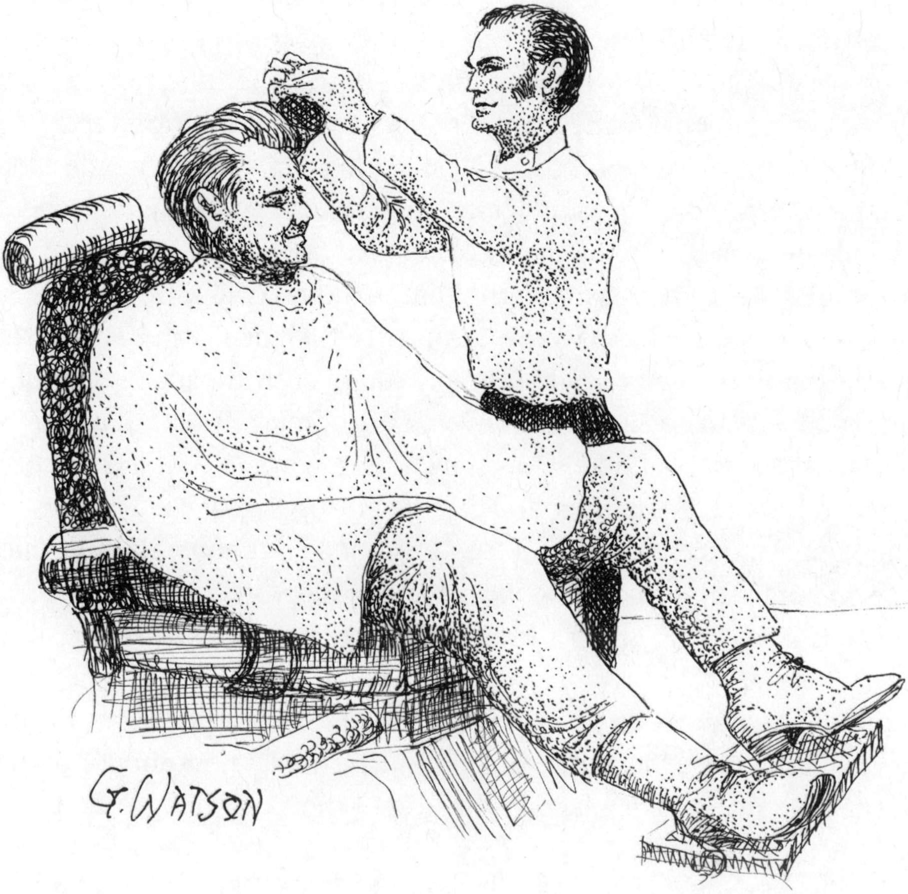

ERNEST SPELL

Throughout this book, from Town Bluff all the way to Beaumont, I have made references to Ernest Spell. Without Ernest, there would be no book and probably no Jack Gore Baygall, Neches Bottom, nor Neches Corridor Units, though he would be the first to disclaim it.

Ernest's seat of power where he held forth and received and dispensed information as to what was going on in Caney Head, was his barbershop. Once, when I was visiting Jeanette Gore, her husband, Marvis, said: "Well, I'm going down to the *Hardin County News*." I looked questioningly at Jeanette and she laughed and explained, "Ernest's barbershop." Spell's barbershop was a one-room affair on Highway 92 practically on the edge of Jack Gore Baygall. On the wall hung guitars and other musical instruments with which he wiled away the time between customers, or the customers amused themselves while waiting their turn. He was always in close touch with the many talented musicians of Caney Head, and numerous times when we needed to impress visiting television documentarists, newspaper and magazine writers, etc., with our local folk culture, Ernest supplied the performers.

Ernest spent his time and energies helping us to preserve the land on which he was born and bred and, after the preserve was acquired, spent his time and energies stirring up the locals to give the Park Service a hard time. Ernest thought, and he may be right, that without constantly reminding the Park Service that the natives were here and that their needs and desires should be taken seriously, they would be simply run over by the juggernaut of government bureaucracy. Since they have no economic or political power, their only recourse is to continue life as they have always lived it in spite of government rules and regulations, and pay the fine or go to jail if they are caught by the Rangers. In other words, if they give the Park Rangers a hard-enough time, someone, somewhere is going to take notice.

Cutting hair wasn't Ernest's only profession. He did a number of stints on oil rigs in Saudi Arabia, in Iraq, and on the North Sea. And, at one time, he worked the high steel on Chicago skyscrapers. He had been an insurance agent and probably a lot of other things which I don't know about—or that he didn't talk about. But his place in the great scheme of things had to be his barbershop.

I first met Ernest through Gene Barrington, Silsbee lawyer, who was probably his best friend. Gene recognized that Ernest was more than ordinarily intelligent and inspired him, as he did everyone else, that he could take his destiny into his own hands and change the course of history. They both believed that the people should rule themselves, not be ruled by the multinational conglomerates that control the land, or a far-away government body that neither knows or cares anything about local conditions, and they proceeded to join Houston Thompson in setting rebellion in motion. Since the successful establishment of a Big Thicket National Preserve would take the land from the lumber companies and the hunting clubs, their enemies, the river-bottom people threw all their resources behind us. Whatever was needed—boats on the river, guides, etc.—a call to Ernest was all that was needed.

During my wanderings, I had come to know the roads to the river fairly well, but had done no exploring of the vast woods and swamps in the Neches floodplain, so one day when I stopped by the barbershop, Ernest put his Closed sign in the window and said, "Come on. I want to show you something." So we drove to the edge of the upland, down an old abandoned road, got out, and walked a short distance into a beautiful beech grove at the edge of a baygall fringed with luxuriant ferns. This was my introduction to Jack Gore Baygall and I took many influential people to that spot in later years. This was also my introduction to the Old Wagon Road. He was always showing me something special.

One of my favorite pastimes was sitting in the barbershop on a Saturday afternoon when everybody came in to get haircuts, maybe hear a little music, and catch up on the latest gossip. I swear I think the originators of the television show *Hee Haw* must have passed this way, heard music, stopped in, and said to themselves: "Here's a knockout idea for a television show!" Sometimes the little building rocked with music, and always witty badinage and banter passed back and forth. No matter what the subject, Ernest had an amusing, appropriate adage. Once, when he was being interviewed for a television documentary on pioneer life in Southeast Texas, after telling how happy and pleasant life used to be in the backwoods, he concluded with: "But that's all water under the bridge now." And that's how they ended the documentary: Ernest saying, "That's all water under the bridge." He was never at a loss for words and, like all the other habitues of the shop, wouldn't hesitate to say what he thought about a matter, whether you liked it or not. Not to be rude or insulting—just everybody has an equal right to express his opinion, which shouldn't make anybody mad.

My and Ernest's friendship really stood some acid tests. The most acerbic could be the time I brought to Ernest an Associated Press writer, who was doing a series of articles on the Big Thicket to be published in newspapers throughout the country. We really catered to those guys in those days, for we needed all the publicity and support we could get to push our bill through Congress. Anyway, I pointed out to the writer a book on folk medicine that had been owned by Ernest's grandmother. As was usual in such books, (I have one owned by my grandfather) the remedies were a mixture of medicinal plants and incantations. It also included some useful information for those who wished to put a hex on an enemy.

Talking about outlaw hunting, the writer asked Ernest if he were an outlaw and, typically, Ernest gave a joking reply, ending with, "I don't hunt deer." The series appeared in the *Beaumont Enterprise* newspaper and I was appalled. The writer had twisted everything we had said into something outrageous, and it appeared that I had insulted everybody I knew. Not only was Ernest an outlaw hunter but, the writer suggested, "There are those who say he is a warlock!" Also, when discussing who shot the herd of pet deer in someone's yard in Saratoga, I said: "There's some of the meanest people in the world in Saratoga." This came out as "The people of Saratoga are the meanest people in the world." I called the editor of the paper and protested vigorously, telling him that the entire article was either a lie or a distortion of facts, and that it would severely damage our Big Thicket cause if the remainder of the series were published. The editor stated that it was just the sort of thing the public likes to read and that he intended to publish it all. When I threatened to sue him, he laughed and said I didn't have enough money.

All I could think of was Ernest's children who attended Silsbee schools and what they must be suffering over it. I didn't go to Ernest's barbershop for a long time and when I finally got the nerve to approach him and apologize profusely with tears, he had a good laugh over it. When the kids at school told his youngest son, Daniel: "Yaa yaa! Your daddy's a witch!" Daniel replied, "You bet he is and you had just better watch out!" A true Spell!

I guess we all, when we go to die, would like to think our lives had stood for something and that we made a difference for our having been here. Aside the fact that Ernest saved the Jack Gore Baygall Unit, that he gave courage and spirit to those without it, and a lot of free haircuts to those who couldn't afford them, you can certainly say that he gave joy and merriment to all who came his way.

Postscript:

One of the saddest things about updating this manuscript prior to publishing, has been changing the "is" to "was" in the account of Ernest Spell's life. An automobile crash almost killed him and he spent his last years in a totally helpless state hooked up to tubes and machines. After a disastrous stay in a nursing home, his daughter, Sabra, took him to her home to care for him. I visited him there and Sabra raised his eyelids to look at me, insisting that he knew that I was there. She kept his favorite music playing, read the newspaper to him, and did all the unpleasant things necessary to keep an invalid clean, comfortable, and alive. I was appalled. I simply could not equate those bones with white, dry skin stretched over them and that gaunt, blank face with the strong, vibrant, laughing, life-loving man I had known. When he finally died, I missed the funeral, not seeing the obituary in the paper.

Since my phone is unlisted, Sabra couldn't call to inform me. I must say that I was more glad than saddened that he was gone, for I felt that his spirit had left that bed and was again roaming the river and the beautiful forests he had saved.

RIVER FLOAT TRIPS

River Mile 72 12:30 P.M.

I passed the Timber Slough sandbar right after noon but didn't pause, as I wanted to lunch at my favorite stop, a big bar by a recent cutoff a short distance downstream. Timber Slough was the point from which I launched my one-day float trips back in the early 1970s and the big bar was our first rest stop. I had enrolled at Lamar University and didn't want my poor husband, who was the sole support of our home and five children, to pay for my expenses, so I hired out as a guide for birdwatchers and general nature lovers. As most of my clientele were inexperienced older people a little on the overweight side, it was too risky to put them and their expensive cameras and binoculars into tipsy canoes, so I used l2- and 14-foot aluminum flat-bottom river boats, paddling from the bow just enough to keep in the current.

This was a beautiful route with wide expanses of snow-white sand, graceful bends of the river, and deep forests that the lumber companies had not yet ravaged. We stopped for coffee and snacks and to explore a bit of woods in the middle of the morning, and lunched on the large sandbar of an island which had been cut off by the river. This big bend was once called Gourdvine Eddy. (An eddy is a whirlpool.) A few bends below this sandbar at River Mile 67.9 is Trull Hummock, where an Indian trail from Franklin Lake crossed the river and proceeded west. I'm told there was a trading post here in ancient times and there are many legends concerning it. I don't know if it was one of the hideouts of Jesse Trull during the Civil War, but that is possible.

Clark's Camp just below Bear Man's Bluff was my point of debarkation. Under normal conditions, the trip took about eight easy hours and my fee was $10 per trip—good money in those days.

There were pleasant experiences, amusing ones, and frightening ones. Once four dear ladies from a college in South Texas engaged me for a day on the river. David assisted and we proceeded down river, he and I at the prow and two ladies sitting in each boat, smiling upon the world, each with her fancy parasol and dressed as though for an afternoon tea party (even though

I had stressed outdoor attire). We made quite an impressive procession as we floated past river people tending trotlines. Guess we gave them something to talk and laugh about for some time.

Then there was the group from Dallas—all extreme political conservatives save one who was an outspoken hippie pacifist named Ruth. While we were moving serenely down the river some military planes passed overhead. Ruth jumped up, almost capsizing us, and shaking her fist, screamed: "You s—of b———s! How many babies are you going to kill today!" That night at dinner, she sweetly asked one of her fellow guests, "What would you do if someone approached you on the street and handed you a flower?" The addressee was so completely flustered she couldn't formulate an answer, so the hoped-for confrontation was averted. Later, two ladies discussing the situation came to the conclusion that Ruth was a Communist sent to spy on us. Whatever a group of birdwatchers on the Neches might do or say that could interest the Kremlin or Hanoi, I have no idea, and doubt that our little expedition had any impact on the outcome of the ongoing war in Viet Nam.

Though all excursions were accomplished without mishap, there were some scary moments. There was the time when the weather was bad and the river in flood, but the couple who engaged me insisted on making the trip. My husband helped me drop the boat off into the churning, muddy waters. We put the couple aboard and I climbed in, so terrified my knees were like rubber and my stomach was in my throat. I commended my soul to God and off we shot into the current. Uprooted trees lunged by on the swift current and it looked as if we were going to be swept into limbs extending from the banks or logs and snags in the water. After I learned to avoid the debris, it became an exhilarating ride. In fact I became disgustingly conceited as I adroitly guided my vessel down the crest of the flood with dash and verve, impressing my passengers no doubt with my total command of the situation. (Little they knew.) Due to the speed of the current, we made the trip in half the time and I decided after that there wasn't much that could scare me.

The most memorable trip I ever made down this section of river was with Edwin Waye Teale the Pulitzer Prize-winning nature writer, and his wife, Nellie. Edwin was here to get material for an article on the Big Thicket for the *Audubon Journal* and I was their hostess. While we were sitting on a bank eating lunch, a luna moth, its silvery pale green wings shining against the dark forest background, floated across the river. We were enjoying the rare treat (they are usually nocturnal creatures) when suddenly a dragonfly swooped down and captured the large moth and carried it away to eat. Later, paddling in the strong current close to the cutbank side of the river, I heard a loud splashing sound ahead. Looking up, I saw that the bank at the base of a large tree was collapsing. The tree slowly began to fall across the stream, directly in our path. "Grab a paddle!" I yelled, desperately trying to cut across the current to safety. Instead, Edwin grabbed his camera and began recording the event. The only thing that kept us from being crushed by the tree and its huge spread of branches was this: the top branches were laced with tough muscadine vines that tied them to other trees on the high bank. The tree fell, the vines held on, and it gradually angled down parallel with the bank instead of across the river and onto us.

What a privilege to be with Edwin and Nellie Teale! I can honestly say that I have known two people who were truly "as one." As each discovered a small bit of beauty, they would call to the other: "Oh Edwin! Come and see!" Then they would discuss every facet of what was being observed. They saw beauty and wonder even in the smallest, most commonplace things and shared it with a smile and knowing look into each other's eyes.

This stretch of the river has changed since those days. Much of the beautiful mature, closed-canopy forests was cut and there are now impenetrable brier and brush thickets. Some of the deep bends have filled in, and some cut through, changing the river's course. Which is all right—these are natural changes. I can accept them, even enjoy watching nature's work. The loss of the deep woods is something else, though. I feel anger, sorrow, despair, and hopelessness. These woods are owned and controlled by powers which in my experience have shown no feeling, no sense of responsibility for the future, no loyalty to people or country. What can one expect?

GOURDVINE EDDY

River Mile 69.6 1:00 P.M.

The big sandbar and cutoff island where I stopped for lunch was once a big bend in the river. I remember when the river cut through and created the island. The bend was called Gourdvine Eddy. When the current rushes into a bend, it hits the cutbank, and is thrown back. The oncoming water forces it back again, so it circles around. The incoming water on the surface is sucked down to river bottom and rises again downstream. This action removes sediments from the bottom so the bends are sometimes 40 to 50 feet deep. The ejected sediments are piled up at the downstream end of the bend, creating a barrier that forces the bottom water back to the surface. I have seen whole bends filled and the river cut another channel to avoid the blockage.

While there are hydrologic laws that predict the behavior of streams, one can not always rely on them. I once saw a whirlpool create in the center of the bend a cone of sand which built up until it resembled an upside-down ice cream cone and filled the bend so the river moved to another course. This is a rare thing.

I often wondered what I would do, not being a strong swimmer, if I should fall into a whirlpool—possibly just hold my breath, sink to the bottom and let the current throw me up downstream. Fortunately, none of the whirlpools on the Neches seems very strong and the vortex is simply a dead area which holds your boat in place. At first, I thought I was saving time and effort by cutting across the center of these big bends but found that I had to paddle like the dickens to get out of them. I learned that the fastest route was with the current along the cutbank side.

Most of these bends and sandbars in the river have stories to tell. It is said that Bonnie and Clyde, the famous outlaws, hid out on the river at Gourdvine Eddy for two weeks as guests of Grandpa Ard who later, quite surprisingly for it was well-known that he didn't have a dime, turned up with a brand new Ford auto. The Mosses were also friends of Bonnie and Clyde and many Caney Headers have experiences with them to relate. I remember how thrilled and excited we all were when it was known that they were passing through Tyler County. They were folk heroes, for they robbed the banks which, during those Depression days, foreclosed on many a home and farm. Law enforcement officers found they had emergencies that required their presence on the other side of the river when Bonnie and Clyde passed by. You couldn't say these outlaws were modern-day Robin Hoods, for, even though they stole from the rich, I don't know that they distributed the wealth among the poor, unless the tale about Grandpa Ard is true.

Somewhere along here is a sandbar known as Jenkins Sandbar because a fellow named Jenkins had a camp here. Jenkins was a very fat man and one day he was lying out on the sandbar in the sun taking a nap when a man not native to the area passed by in his motorboat. What he thought he saw was a bloated drowned victim washed up on the shore, so he rushed in to alert the authorities. Let us hope all those involved in the "rescue and recovery" operation had a sense of humor.

CANEY HEAD AND THE DOG PEOPLE

Caney Head is a community in the Jack Gore Baygall area between Highway 92 and the river and somewhat south of Fred and north of Silsbee. It includes upland, slopes, terraces, and river bottom. There were once extensive cane brakes in East Texas before excessive grazing and over burning exterminated them. (This is switch cane, a bamboo and member of the grass family.) At the head, or beginning, of small spring branches are seepage areas called brakes. Because of the moisture, fire from the uplands did not often reach there and cane grew luxuriantly. Apparently, in the early days there was such a cane brake here and it gave the community its name.

There was also a small, now forgotten community called Wiley Mae at the southern end of the area. While Mormon history has concentrated on the adventures of Joseph Smith and Brigham Young in Missouri and Utah, it has overlooked the smaller settlements over the country. There was such a settlement and a Mormon church here at Wiley Mae in the far dim past, and another on Beech Creek in what is now the Beech Creek Unit of the Big Thicket National Preserve. It is a curious chance that both sites are now under national preservation. These Mormon communities have a fascinating history, that is remembered and cherished by the present generation.

There are few places in the United States where almost all the residents are descendents of the original settlers and where pioneer ways are still kept. The settlers trickled in before the Texas Revolution and came in the waves of migration following the Texas Revolution and the Civil War. The majority of the inhabitants of Caney Head are of Protestant, Scotch-Irish descent. Many of them were well-educated people with a high standard of living who kept up with national politics and world affairs, but as time went on, it was necessary to adjust to a pioneer lifestyle, so their keen minds and senses turned from a knowledge of the outside world and its past and peoples to an intimate knowledge of their own personal world of the river.

There was at one time, a school in the north end called Hare School, and another at the south end within the Jack Gore Baygall Unit called Wiley Mae. All that remains of the Wiley Mae school are the concrete foundations of the sanitary toilets that Roosevelt's public works crews constructed during the Depression. The Old Wagon Road passed by it. In the 1930s, the school, books, desks, and all were burned because the teacher had tuberculosis and the people did not know how to disinfect things in those days. Some time in the late 1930s, the rural schools consolidated, and the Caney Head children were bussed to the school at Fred. They were referred to as "the swampers," while the swampers retaliated by calling the children of the uplands "the pineywoodsers." Perhaps this prejudice is one reason why so many river people of that generation do not read or write today. Many of their associations with education were unpleasant while they felt at ease in their own world of the woods and the river.

Most homes were simple one- to two-room log houses with hard-packed clay floors and a few pieces of hand-made furniture. Cooking was done at the fireplace with its mud-daub chimney. There were no window screens, so on summer nights, hordes of mosquitoes from the swamps were kept at bay by smudge fires and those who could afford it used cheesecloth netting. Nevertheless, malaria kept many in a constant state of malaise. Large families and high infant mortality were the rule, and diet was restricted to whatever was available. In the winter, collard greens, sweet potatoes, dried beans and peas, and cornbread were standard fare while summer offered a wide variety of fresh fruits and vegetables. But most important were the fish from the river, game from the woods, and the feral hogs that kept the smokehouses filled.

An Englishman, William Kennedy, wrote a book for prospective immigrants to Southeast Texas, and summed up the difficulties the pioneers encountered:

> To hew out a farm from the heart of the primeval forest is a ponderous and life-consuming task, even for the American backwoodsman, accustomed to wield the axe from boyhood, and to trust for subsistence to the unerring rifle. Alas! For the European, if above the condition of a daily laborer, who is constrained to engage in the unwonted and depressing toil.
>
> Years may follow years and find him struggling with difficulties which he is destined never to overcome. By dint of the severest and most irksome drudgery, he is enabled to reclaim a mere patch from the wilderness, and that overspread with unsightly stumps, and encircled by the burned and blackened trees. In this disheartening pursuit, he wastes the flower of his manhood.
>
> Where the vegetable accumulation of ages are suddenly exposed to the beams of a scorching sun, and where heaps of leveled timber are left to rot upon the ground, the atmosphere is inevitably tainted with noxious inhalations, which soon blanch the ruddiest cheek and palsy the most vigorous arm.

A woman, writing to her family back East, lamented that she had to "watch my children die from the fevers and lay their little bodies to be food for worms in this cursed soil." It was often said in those days that Texas was heaven for men and dogs but hell for women. Apparently, from the opinion of the Englishman Kennedy, the men didn't have it so easy either.

In the 1850s Frederick Law Olmsted toured the South and described Southeast Texans as lazy, dirty, and mean—but then he was an urbane Yankee gentleman with generations of civilizing behind him. Another writer commented, "These frontier folk knew loneliness and poverty and dirt, suffered much from the forest fevers and malnutrition, commonly had a lean and sallow look, yet they were on the whole remarkably proud, bold, and independent. They were half wild and wholly free."

I love that last phrase. It describes the Caney Headers perfectly. The older inhabitants who lived the pioneer life speak with nostalgia and longing for those times which they describe as happy, happy days. Perhaps before television and the modern communication media, that life was all they knew and they chose to be happy rather than grouse and gruntle and lament. That they met these overwhelming obstacles with vigor and good cheer and triumphed over them testifies to their indomitable strength and courage.

With the coming of the sawmills, the vast timberlands of Southeast Texas finally had economic value and forces were set in motion which would change the Caney Headers' bucolic way of life.

Enter upon the scene John Henry Kirby, sometimes styled "Prince of the Pines," but more aptly "Robber Baron," for he was one of the entrepreneurs of that day who exploited the natural resources of the country and the cheap labor of immigrants from foreign countries to build financial empires of enormous economic and political power. John Jacob Astor controlled the fur trade, Cornelius Vanderbilt shipping, Andrew Carnegie the steel industry, Jay Gould the railroads, and John Henry Kirby went after the forests.

While many of them feigned to be religious and built cathedrals, their real religion was Capitalism, or Economic Darwinism. They believed that the natural law of survival of the fittest and rule by the strongest would result in economic and national progress, and, of course, keep them on top. There were no laws, either moral or legal, which stood in the way of their getting what they wanted and Profit was their God. John Stricklin Spratt, in his book, *The Road to Spindletop*, described it thus: "The corporation—the essence of greed functioning without soul or feeling."

The tentacles of this giant capitalism reached down into Southeast Texas and touched the forest, the river, and the lives of all the people.

John Henry Kirby was a lawyer who represented some Easterners in a case involving title to three leagues of land and, in 1886, their association resulted in the formation of the Texas and Louisiana Land Company and the Texas Pineland Association. For quicker and easier access to the timber of his holdings, Kirby began construction of a railroad system called the Gulf, Beaumont, and Kansas City Railroad, and taking advantage of the economic "panic" of 1893–1896, he continued to acquire land and expand the railroad. At Silsbee in 1896, he built the first of a chain of twelve lumber mills and expanded operations into ten logging camps, employing 16,500 men.

Kirby's control of the people, the resources, and the land was complete. I could fill volumes of stories by the oldtimers of how they lost their land to him. His empire was divided into three main divisions: Kirby Lumber Company, which exploited the timber, Houston Oil Company, which went after the minerals, and Southwestern Settlement and Development Corporation to sell the land (minus the mineral rights) after the timber had been removed. Land sales ceased after tree farming began.

Even after Kirby's demise, the forest products industry continued to control Southeast Texas: the law, the courts, the economy, and the social structure. Since the dissolution of Kirby's empire, Santa Fe Railroad owned Kirby and thus controlled the land along its route, and would allow no competing industry to locate in the area. This was before the trucking industry made rail transportation practically obsolete. You don't dare oppose the "powers that be" in such a one-product economy, or you and your family will be faced with social ostracism and more than ordinarily close scrutiny by law enforcement personnel. I won't go into what my family suffered during the ten years we were fighting for a Big Thicket National Preserve, which the forest products industries bitterly and ruthlessly opposed. That, too, would take volumes.

Land ownership in Caney Head was complicated. Under the Spaniards and continuing under the Mexican Colonization Act, a "head of family" was granted a "league and a labor" of land. A "labor" was 177 acres, and a league 4428. After the Texas Revolution, the Anglo-Americans were anxious to fill Texas with their own kind, and were very generous with state land. Under the Constitution of 1836, all heads of families living in Texas on March 4, 1836 (excepting Africans and Indians), were granted first class headrights of a league and a labor (4,605 acres). Single men seventeen years or older were granted a third of a league. Those who immigrated during the year following the revolution were given second class headrights of 1,200 acres, and single men, a section of 640 acres. Third class, fourth class, etc., were granted for later arrivals. On top of that, colonization contracts were granted to individuals to bring in groups of colonists, and the Congress of the Republic passed the Homestead Act allowing anyone to settle on any vacant land with the right to buy 320 acres. Both the Republic and the state, after joining the Union, gave bounty and donation grants of 640 acres to men who had served in the military during the war of independence. After the Civil War, grants were offered to Texans who had served in the Union Army, but no one applied for them.

Those who benefited most from this great give-away were the railroads. They were given a certain amount of land for each mile of track laid and were granted 32,153,878 acres, one-fifth of the total area of the state! Over three million acres were given for the building of the state capitol. There was enormous waste of public lands during the period between 1850 and 1875, with unscrupulous speculators, and fraud, graft and corruption rife. During this time, there was a lot of paper shuffling going on in the country, and when it was over, many people who thought they owned land, didn't.

Caney Headers had acquired land under all these provisions, some of the late comers either buying from owners or settling on open land under the Homestead Act. Due to the large families, multiplication of heirs further complicated land titles. Land was so little valued that Law Scott, on the Jasper County side of the river, traded an entire section of 640 acres for a pair of oxen. William Withers, who owned and farmed a section in the Reddick Survey, abandoned it after losing crops and fences to floods, so when Kirby took it over, Withers didn't fight for it. As late as the 1940s, the Withers family sold 500 acres for $5.00 an acre. I once asked Austin Withers how that family had managed to retain so much of their land while others had lost all to the lumber companies. He said it was because the Withers family stuck together. In other families, the company lawyer would get one man in a family to sign title transfer papers and he would be "well taken care of." Usually, the rest of the family didn't even know of the transaction until many years later.

It wasn't hard for Kirby, with his battery of lawyers, to acquire title to much of the land in Southeast Texas, and few locals knew or cared. As long as the lumber companies only did a little selective cutting in the bottoms now and then, they saw no need for alarm. Few cared even that they no longer owned the land. They didn't have to pay taxes on it, there was open range grazing for their stock, and their hogs could grow fat on the mast of the bottomlands. They could even cut firewood and building wood with no one to hinder. This all came to an end with the closed range laws in the 1950s, and the forest products industry's practice of "multiple forest use" administered the coup de grace to the free life of the open woods and river.

All this history is to lead up to Houston Thompson, Gene Barrington, the Dog People, and the Hardin County political wars of the late 1950s and early 1960s, and the closing off of the woods and the river roads to the local people.

Since the pulpwood industry had entered the picture, natural forests were clearcut, the land bulldozed and planted with slash pine, a Florida species which grows faster and fatter than the native pines. The land was leased for grazing, for oil operations, and to hunting clubs. The latter was the straw that finally broke the camel's back and the backwoodsmen rebelled.

A local businessman, Howard Hargrove, organized a hunting club called the East Texas Wildlife Conservation Association, and leased the entire river bottom from Sheffield's Ferry down to Evadale. Hargrove's motives were good; he hoped to restore the game animals in the Neches bottoms by strict rules and regulations. These rules were rigorously enforced, but the wardens selected to enforce them were harsh and ill qualified for the job and so a lot of bad feeling was engendered. The last time Daddy and I went down the river in a paddleboat, we pulled up on the Clark's Camp sandbar and a warden put a gun in our face and told us if we as much as put a foot on "their" sandbar, we would be fined and hauled off to jail. I knew the laws regarding riparian rights, but you don't argue with a man with a gun pointed at you.

Hargrove tried to make it possible for the poor backwoods people to join his club by allowing them to work on roads and fences to pay for membership, but the highhandedness of the club and its wardens, and most importantly, the ban on hunting with dogs, so disgusted the local people that they withdrew. The hunting club derisively referred to the locals as the "dog people," since they insisted on hunting with dogs, but they were proud to accept the designation and the name stuck.

One of the stipulations of the lease required of the hunting club by the company was that the club build roads and bridges and fence the entire lease. This cost a lot of money, so Hargrove advertised in the city newspapers for members. The fee was minimal so hunters responded in droves. Imagine the chagrin of the man sitting on his porch at the edge of the bottom, watching city people drive in to hunt in his territorial hunting grounds where he, his father, and many fathers before them had hunted. To further enrage the locals, the traditional roads to the river were fenced, gated, and locked. Going to the river was the only form of recreation for young and old and they were cut off from the only thing that gave meaning to their lives. It was at this point that Houston Thompson and Gene Barrington, law partners in Silsbee, got involved.

GENE BARRINGTON

The skies turned black and there was an ominous stillness in the air. Then bedlam broke loose. A small tornado dipped down and torrents of rain and wind lashed the little town of Kountze. A hound, skulking at the doorway of Pace Funeral Home, let out a lugubrious howl, and then the sweet strains of a duet could be heard:

Just as I am without one plea
But that Thy blood was shed for me
And that Thou bidst me come to Thee
O Lamb of God, I come. I come.

Family, political friends and foes, loved ones, business and professional persons, and the "dog people"—in fact, just about everybody in Hardin County—had come to pay respects and say goodbye to Eugene Barrington. The long cortege wound its way to a little cemetery on a bluff overlooking the Neches River bottomlands, and Gene was buried in the area in which he had made such an imprint on the land and the people.

Just 34 years old! Six feet, six inches tall with black wavy hair and blue eyes, he was very good looking and had a brilliant mind. Gene got his law degree at the University of Texas and set out to change the world, right wrongs, secure justice for the poor, and return to the disenfranchised the power over their lands and their lives. Now he was dead—killed in a one-car crash on Highway 105 when his automobile left the road and plunged head on into a tree.

There was no autopsy and no investigation. The sheriff, Gene's bitter political foe, blamed it on drunk driving, but the mortician, who had many years of experience with such things, said there was no post-mortem emission of gasses, a common result of intoxication before death. The fact also that facial and body cuts inflicted by broken glass did not bleed led him to conclude that Gene had been killed hours before the crash from a blow at the base of the skull, which could not have occurred as a result of the crash. Gene's brother, Sam, and his best friend, Ernest Spell, examined the wrecked car and found evidence that it had been tampered with. The throttle had been opened full and the car apparently aimed down the road and turned loose with Gene's body inside.

In the absence of legally documented facts, many theories evolved. None doubted that Gene was murdered. Too many people had motives. Gene and Houston Thompson had taken on the powers that had been godalmighty since the turn of the century and that intended to keep Southeast Texas in the firm grip of their iron fist.

Gene was hard to let go of. He represented hope to people who were resigned to hopelessness, and power to those who had no control over their lives and destinies. The people of the Neches bottoms were still like their

Indian ancestors in that they were extremely individualistic. Gene inspired and led them to work together to claim and hold their rights. He could be all things to all people. The elderly blacks whom he represented absolutely doted on him, and the backwoods people idolized him. How he loved people! And how he loved life! He would whoop with delight when he would best me in one of our long, good-natured, philosophical confrontations. It has been many years since he died and those of us who knew him best still miss him.

Most of those who fought to save these woods are gone. Gene and Houston, Ernest Spell, Clyde Scott, I. C., and Deacon, are all gone and I walk the Old Wagon Road alone—but sometimes I am almost certain that they are with me. Others share this feeling for I've been told by some that Gene has walked the woods in the bottom with them after he departed this life. In the spirit—in their hearts and minds? Who knows.

HOUSTON THOMPSON

Houston Irving Thompson was born and grew up in Hardin County and went to Silsbee public schools. His family was poor, it was the Depression and, like other men of that time, his father did what he could to feed his family from bootlegging to selling Watkins products door to door in the backwoods and the farms. Since money was scarce, he was usually paid in chickens, eggs, and smoked pork. Houston often accompanied him on these expeditions so he got to know the people quite well and developed an understanding of them and empathy for their woes. He was especially intrigued by their love and talent for music.

Houston had a brilliant mind so he found his way through hard work and scholarship to Texas A & M University where he majored in sociology. He had graduated from high school at 15 years of age and from college at 18. With masters degrees in rural sociology and education, he sought a job teaching school, but when some of the students were older than he was, he was deemed too young for the job. Unable to secure a teaching position, Houston returned to school where he pursued a degree in law at Columbia University. At A & M, he had become close to one of his professors, Dr. William Owens, who had come from the same sort of background. Dr. Owens was in the process of collecting and recording Texas folk music, so Houston took him to Caney Head where he recorded many of the people there, such as Doc Eason and Rod Drake, singing the traditional songs of their people. Many of these ballads had come down from Elizabethan England, from Scotland, and from

Ireland, across the mountains and rivers of America and were still being sung with little change.

The Caney Head community, also called Sandy Creek, was an isolated pocket of culture in the 1940s. No one had an automobile or a radio, many people still lived in one- or two-room log cabins with hard-baked clay floors, and the language, a form of early English, was almost extinct in America.

Dr. Owens persuaded Houston to take this community as a subject for his masters thesis in sociology, so Houston came and lived among them for a couple of years around 1940, and while there, learned firsthand how they were exploited and defrauded and how powerless they were to defend themselves. When Houston earned his degree in law at Columbia, instead of going to the city where he could get rich and live the good life, he came back to Hardin County and dedicated his entire life to helping ease the onerous burdens of the poor. He knew all the stories of how the lumber companies had stolen their lands one way or another and bided his time to set things right.

WAR IN THE BOTTOMLANDS

The time came when Houston Thompson decided to begin his long-planned effort to bring about reform and he started with the county court. The county judge, in office for 24 years, was on Kirby Lumber Company's payroll as legal advisor, and the members of the commissioner's court were all establishment men. If you had a boundary dispute with a lumber company in court, there was no doubt of the outcome. There was also a great disparity in tax evaluation. Friends of mine had 30 acres of woodland which were evaluated at $3,000 an acre, while Kirby's land alongside was evaluated at seven dollars an acre. Diversification of industry was discouraged, as other industries might pay their employees higher wages or give better benefits and thus force Kirby to compete for labor. Wages were the lowest in the state excepting those for migrant farm workers. Most industries relied on access to rail transportation and, since Kirby owned all property along the railroads (Kirby at that time was a subsidiary of Santa Fe, Inc.), there was no available land. There are many advantages to being the only industry in a one-product economy and Kirby saw to it for many years that it remained that way in Southeast Texas.

Every cause needs a voice so Houston became owner and publisher of a weekly newspaper called *The Pine Needle*. Gene Barrington's wife, Peggy, a tall, beautiful blonde, was the editor and Gene wrote editorials. Together they proceeded to arouse the citizens of Hardin County to the need for change.

At about that time, the Big Thicket movement began and I wrote a letter to the editor of the *Beaumont Enterprise* newspaper promoting the preservation of the Big Thicket. Houston read it and telephoned me and asked that I come down to his office and talk, which I did. He spoke of the condition of the poor in Hardin County, how they were victimized, and of unequal justice. He spoke of the evils of a one-product economy and his hopes to bring new industry into the area. He was quite honest in explaining that he was no nature lover and had no knowledge of nor interest in the biology of the Big Thicket, but that he saw it as the nucleus of a new industry for Southeast Texas based on tourism with the Big Thicket a main attraction.

Since I had been raised on Dickens, Hugo, Jesus Christ, and the modern poets, Houston spoke to my heart. He said that I had talent as a writer and he would like for me to contribute regular articles about the Big Thicket to the *Pine Needle*. Thus began my career as a researcher and writer and "The Big Thicket—Past, Present and Future" became a weekly column in the *Pine Needle*. Houston promised me: "Believe me, it will change your life. Your life will never be the same again." Prophetic words! It indeed changed the course of my life for then and always. I had been a civic do-gooder, member of the library board, organizer of the Silsbee Art League, Sunday school teacher, and keeper of the home for my husband and five children. I also had been collecting plant specimens for Dr. Donovan Correll of the Texas Research Foundation for the taxonomic encyclopedia *Manual of the Vascular Plants of Texas*.

From then on, I was caught up in a burning cause. I enrolled at Lamar University to learn all I could about the natural world and man's place in it. This was in the early 1960s and the hippies of the universities took up the Big Thicket fight. Since I am an avid believer in Christ's message of love, peace, and brotherhood, they also spoke to my heart and I became very close to that generation of young people. It was a golden age when people cared for the earth and for one another and we thought we were going to change the world.

The Pine Needle newspaper enjoyed a wide circulation. People all over the country who were interested in politics subscribed to it to follow Houston and Gene's quixotic tilting at the giant windmills of the lumber industry and its political machine in Hardin County. As a result they also became interested and involved in the Big Thicket movement.

Hardin County took sides and it was the classic confrontation: liberals, intellectuals, and the poor vs. conservatives, the well-to-do, and the ignorant. Archer Fullingim's *Kountze News* and Howard Hargrove's East Texas Wildlife Conservation Association were the voice of the opposition, though I will say to Archer's credit that he later became an ardent supporter of the Big Thicket cause.

Gene and Houston took up the cause of the backwoods people against the East Texas Wildlife Hunting Club, organizing them into a group called the Hardin, Tyler, Jasper, Polk County Dog and Wildlife Protective Association. (I still have my honorary membership card in the H.T.J.P.D. & W.P.A.) Organizing them was no easy matter, for these people value above all their individuality and freedom—nobody is going to tell them what to do—so they are not "joiners." The hunting club dubbed them the "dog people" in derision because they hunted with dogs, but they were proud of the designation and the name stuck. Gene stirred them up by writing a pamphlet called *The Raw Deal,* outlining how they had been cheated of their rights and freedom by the big companies.

The roads to the river—Bush Lake, Timber Slough, and Clark's Camp (Bear Man's Bluff)—were declared by the dog people to be public roads, and Ernest Spell, president, announced that he intended to open the Timber Slough Road on a certain date. When it came time to do the deed, however, no one showed up except a childlike young man who was scared to death. Ernest, nevertheless, shot the lock off the gate and flung it open. When the Park Service puts up a big iron gate across a road customarily used, the children of the dog people, now grown, merely winch it off, carry it to the nearest slough and drop it in.

To show their defiance of the hunting club, the dog people hunted in bands wherever they chose in the bottomlands and the hunting club wardens took care to be on the other side of the river. I'll never forget my first encounter with the denizens of the river bottom. The dog people were going to have a big barbecue on the river to celebrate the opening of the Timber Slough Road and Gene had never been there. Since I knew the road well, I offered to take him there to scout out the area. We went in my little red Volvo and were navigating the curves in the sandy road when suddenly there was standing in the road ahead an armed band of desperate looking men surrounded by a pack of dogs. I stopped and they looked at us with narrowed eyes and tight lips, holding their rifles in a position that indicated they would be ready if action should be required. I said, "Oh Gene! They must be those outlaw hunters people are talking about!" Gene started to unfold his long legs and get out the door when someone yelled: "Hey! It's Gene!" And then we were swooped upon with everybody laughing and talking all at once. I was introduced and each solemnly shook my hand, and because I was Gene's friend, they became mine. From then on, I was trusted because Gene said I was all right, and so it is until this day.

Not only had the Caney Headers suffered exclusion from their traditional hunting grounds, but they had to watch thousands of acres of forests bulldozed to raw earth and pine trees planted in place of the oaks, hickories, and beeches on which the wildlife depended for food, nesting, and cover. When environmentalists came in and talked of saving these bottomland forests, some of the Caney Headers joined them heart and soul. I. C. Eason said he would rather see all the Neches bottom become a National Preserve, even if it meant he would never hunt or fish it again, than to watch it destroyed.

With a great deal of help from the dog people, some ground was gained. Control of the commissioners' court was accomplished and Kountze businessman and farmer/rancher, Howard Barrington, Gene's father, was elected commissioner of the district that included the disputed land along the Neches River. Emmett Lack, an ex- union official and former state representative, was elected county judge. One of the first things Emmett did was hire an out-of-the area appraiser to re-appraise Hardin County property for tax purposes. This did little good. Since the lumber and oil companies were the only industries and the chief land owners, the bulk of taxes came from them and they simply refused to pay anything. The county took them to court to force them to pay their taxes, but the companies had unlimited financial and legal resources while the county had no money even to pay its employees, let along carry on a court battle. Finally, the companies told the county what they were willing to pay and the matter was settled.

It was a dirty business. The office of the *Pine Needle* was firebombed. Houston was beat up in the courthouse lobby, was thrown in jail, and attempts were made to have the American Bar Association disbar him from practicing law. Gene was beat up in the Kountze bank lobby and his little daughter, Denise, could not even go to Sunday school or to children's parties because of threats toward her.

The word of mouth, or rumor mill, spread the word that Gene was a womanizer, and that Houston was a card-carrying communist, a homosexual, and had been married to a black woman while a student at Columbia University. Along with being a homosexual, he also was supposed to have broken up some homes by seducing innocent wives. I won't even go into what my family suffered during that period—it would take a book by itself. A retired lumber company official later confided to me: "If you could have sat in on some of our executive sessions, you would have taken your family and left the country." I said: "Thanks a lot for telling me—now." Since the political campaign had become a "moral" issue, the churches got on the conservative side. Nothing from the pulpit, of course, just the whispers and gossip. In my 70-plus years, I have ever seen it thus: when an opponent is wrong and cannot stand up to the facts and issues, he resorts to emotional and moral charges, none of which can be either proved or disproved, but nevertheless get all the "righteous" up in arms.

In the next political campaign, Ernest Spell was defeated for county sheriff, Houston was defeated for state representative, and Gene was defeated for county attorney in an election unparalleled for dirt and mud-slinging, and Emmett was defeated in a later election fraught with bribery, violence, and fraud. Camelot disappeared like a puff of smoke. Houston went back to trying to get justice for individual clients in a courtroom usually prejudiced against the poor and the black and Gene continued to fight to regain lands taken from the local people by the lumber companies.

They had not lost everything, however, for Gene had taken the case of opening the roads to the river to an out-of-county court and the three roads, Bush Lake, Timber Slough, and Clark's Camp, were declared public roads. In an effort to persuade the people that they didn't need a national park, the timber companies set aside several "parks for the people." (Postage stamp-sized areas with fences and posted signs around them.) Kirby alone, due to the influence of their public relations man, Jim Webster, set aside a sizeable tract which later became the gem of the Turkey Creek Unit of Big Thicket National Preserve. Jim Webster will always be a hero to those of us who know and remember. It takes foresight and courage to do what you know is right at the risk of your career.

Three of these parks for the people were placed on the river at Bush Lake, Timber Slough, and Clark's Camp, and donated to the county, though the land, being sandbar and woods edge, was already public domain. The county had neither the money nor the personnel to take care of the "parks" and they were quickly trashed and dominated by the worst element.

Gene Barrington had complete confidence that the Big Thicket would be saved and was fond of quoting Hugo: "No army can stop an idea whose time has come." "The time has come," said Gene, "for the Big Thicket." And he was right. Gene's goal now was to reclaim family land from the companies, and he was having success by taking his cases to courts out of the county. This, most believed, was the cause of his death. After the funeral, I was reminded of the attitude of Christ's disciples after his crucifixion: "I go a'fishing." Unfortunately, for the dog people, there was no resurrection.

NATIONAL PARK SERVICE IN THE BOTTOMLANDS

One might say, "Well, we now have a Big Thicket National Preserve in the Jack Gore Baygall protected by the National Park Service. The local people should be happy." Unfortunately, it didn't quite turn out that way. The bill creating the preserve allowed hunting to be conducted in accordance with state game laws, but it was the first time the Park Service had ever managed a hunting program, so mistakes were made and so were enemies.

First, it was decided to have everyone who wanted to hunt in the preserve come to the Park Service office in Beaumont and fill out an application for a permit. These applications were then processed by a computer which randomly selected certain ones to receive permits. Sounds fair. To begin with, the Park Service advertised free hunting in the Big Thicket National Preserve in the city newspapers and people were allowed to apply for permits by mail. The result was far more applicants than the units could accommodate. Some of those from distances who applied by mail and received permits, didn't bother to come and hunt at all. Also, most of the local people did not (some COULD not) read the newspapers and didn't know the time and place for signing up, and those who did were confused by complicated forms and made mistakes, thus causing the computer to throw their applications out. Imagine the feelings of a man sitting on his porch on the edge of the preserve, watching the city people drive by to hunt in his family hunting grounds. It was the East Texas Wildlife Hunting Club all over again.

The main problem with park service people is that they, like most everybody else nowadays, are rootless. America is a mobile society, constantly on the move. It is difficult for outsiders to understand the instincts of territoriality deep in the bone, muscle, sinew, heart, and soul that governs a person who walks the same ground his ancestors walked, who derives his living, and all his pleasure and recreation from that ground, unless they have had the same experience. It is difficult to see how anyone could have a love of country or a willingness to fight for it if they cannot feel that they belong to a piece of the land and it to them.

Territoriality is an instinct stronger than the need for food or sex. It has been found that among animals, one on his home ground can defeat an invader many times his size and weight. The invader knows he is off his own territory and onto that of another and is thus at a psychological disadvantage. Much has been hypothesized about the cause of the U.S. defeat in Viet Nam. The answer is simple. A man with his back to the wall of his home which houses his wife, children, and possessions, will fight like ten men, even to the death. A man who is, psychologically "out in the open" has nothing to fight for except his own life and he will turn and run to save it. Unfortunately, few of the Viet Nam soldiers turned and ran. They just stood and died by the thousands. Ah well!

There was also confusion and misunderstanding because of the difference between the rules and regulations of the various agencies involved with enforcement of fish and game laws, and the Federal National Park Service and its rules and regulations. One young man killed a bobcat and carefully skinned it so his son could hang the skin on his wall. He met a park ranger on the road, and proudly showed the cat. "Looka here! I got me a fine cat!" The ranger said: "Uh-oh! We have a problem here." It seems bobcats were not on the list of animals that could be killed, so the young man who thought he would be praised for having killed a "varmint" was fined $500. He happened to be out of work at the time, had a wife and two children at home, and hoped to get some squirrels to eat. About that time, someone spread roofing nails on the road that the rangers patrolled and a park service vehicle wound up with four flat tires out in the middle of the bottom. The young man was terrified that the park service would assume that he did it out of retaliation for the fine, so he asked me to intervene. I took him to talk with Chief Ranger Ken Tiege, who advised him to go before the federal judge rather than just lay out his fine in jail, for the judge himself was an old dog hunter and would understand. When he appeared before the judge in Beaumont, his fine was reduced considerably.

I went out to California once to visit a son and while there, received a phone call from one of the backwoods people. "We want you to know we don't have nothin' against you but just don't come into the bottom with those yankee wardens. Somebody's gonna get killed and we'd hate for you to be mixed up in it." He explained some of their complaints, so I told him whatever they did to NEVER shoot a federal law officer, which the rangers were. They would certainly be caught and be executed or in federal prison for life. I assured him that most of their problems could be worked out, that I would be home in a few days and we would go to the park superintendent and talk about it. But, above all, they must do nothing until I got back. Sure enough, those particular problems were solved by opening communications, but they were just the tip of the iceberg. Strangely enough, the call came when my son was trying to convince me to move to California and live with them and I was seriously considering it. I would have to do nothing but lounge by the pool and Jacuzzi on the terrace, go into L. A. for the opera or to the museums, hike in the beautiful arboretum nearby, and have nothing to worry about the rest of my life. The call reminded me where my place was and what my duty was. As you grow older, it's nice to think you might be needed by someone and that your life makes a difference.

In order to clear up some of the misunderstandings, the park service let it be known among the locals that they would meet with everyone who had an interest in the Jack Gore Baygall Unit on a certain day by the preserve entrance on Timber Slough Road to discuss their concerns. It wound up with the park service explaining their rules and regulations, which didn't solve many problems. One young man said: "We just want to know one thing. How much are you gonna fine us IF you catch us." From that remark, the park service knew they were going to be faced with serious law enforcement problems if they didn't make some changes.

Preserve personnel were sincerely trying to do what was fair for everybody and still comply with the guidelines and restraints placed on them by congress. Each year, changes for the better were made in the hunting program. Registration was held in a public school nearest the unit involved and permits given on a first-come, first-serve basis, which gave the locals an edge. Aside from a few diehards who want everything to be as it was in the old days, people seem to be satisfied with the program. Even those who bitterly opposed the creation of the preserve are now looking on with horror as all the forests around them are falling, and are appreciating the fact that at least the national preserve land is protected.

I have believed in and fought for the premise that those who have lived in and around the preserve for generations have moral rights which outsiders don't have. That might be true, but the tax money of all Americans bought the preserve and all Americans have equal rights to use it and the park service is bound to manage it for ALL the people. Imagine what a time they would have trying to sort out and select the "rightful" users. Why the descendants of the Gores, Holifields, and Easons alone would overrun it. Their logic always overrules my views on "how things should be."

All I know is that without Houston Thompson, Gene Barrington, Ernest Spell, I. C. and Deacon Eason, Son Gordon, and a few others of the dog people, we would not have the Jack Gore Baygall Unit, the Neches River Corridor Unit, or Neches Bottom Unit of the Big Thicket National Preserve. It's easy to be a hero with an army behind you, but with the mighty powers of industrial giants like Time, Inc., and most of the people against you, it takes courage to fight for what is right. I once asked Ernest why these people took the risks they did to stand with us and his reply was this: "You can afford to take risks when you've got nothing to lose, and we've already lost it all."

Many of those who worked and sacrificed to save these beautiful woods are gone, but the National Park Service is still here and it is on them we must rely to take care of them. I just wish they could really know and understand what so many of us endured in order to turn it over to them.

THE HOLIFIELD FAMILY

Among the Caney Head families I came to know well are the Holifields. In the early days, when I needed guides to take influential visitors to bottomlands unfamiliar to me, cousins Benny Lee and Gurney Holifield, teenagers at the time, were called on. As I recall, Gurney wasn't above pretending to be lost just to give the city folks an interesting experience. Later Benny Lee and his brother Tommy worked on a carpenter crew with my son, Marvin. Incidentally, many names in the South include "Lee," originally in honor of the great Confederate general, but few now make the connection. Names are just passed down in families.

Benny Lee is, as are most of the Holifields, the tall, blond Viking type. Once, a young woman park ranger and I, while on duty in the Jack Gore Baygall Unit, met him and stopped to chat a moment. Benny Lee stepped out of his pickup, dressed only in a pair of jeans, and his long, wavy blond hair falling about his shoulders. His green eyes looked the young ranger up and down from under long dark lashes and he drawled "Howdy." As we drove away, she finally let out her breath in a long whistle and said, "Whooo!"

Now grown men, these boys still come to my assistance when needed. Just recently, I had a devastating fire at my home in Silsbee, and since my husband had died and all my sons had moved away, Tommy and Benny Lee came and did a professional job of repairing and rebuilding. A cousin, Donald Roy, (named for one of the original Holifield settlers) did complete electrical rewiring of the whole house—passed inspection, too. Like most of the Caney Head people, the Holifield boys can do just about anything.

Since Donald Roy didn't have a phone, whenever I needed to talk with him, I had to drive out to Caney Head where he lived with his father, Lester. The first time I was there, I was captivated by a child's swing hanging in a tree in the yard. It had been made from an old tire and cut to form a swan. As the device swung on its long rope, there was a strong impression of a graceful swan riding the waves. I coveted that swan, and the more I saw it, the more I wanted it. Finally, one day, I came right out and asked if he would sell it to me. With typical directness, or in jest—one never knows with these people—he said, "Well, I'm out of work, broke, and hungry. What will you give me for it?" After ten dollars changed hands, the swan was taken down, put in the back of my pickup, and was soon gracefully riding the waves under the oak tree in my own yard.

Later, sitting in his livingroom, I noticed a homemade settee created from one-inch by twelve-inch boards of what was obviously rose pine, an extinct species. I said: "If you ever get hungry enough, how about selling me this settee." "Oh no!" he hastened to say. "That is not fine enough. I'll make you a better one." He then explained how it had been made from planks taken from his parents' old house when it was demolished. Most early homes were made of logs, then later, when lumber became available, were covered with one-inch by twelve-inch rough-sawn boards, with one-inch by four-inch boards covering the cracks between. This was called board and batten siding. I was honest enough to tell him that he could get two or three hundred dollars for it at Larry's Antique Mall, but he didn't believe me. He sheepishly apologized for taking money from me for the swan. "I shoulda giv it to you," he said.

Lynn Holifield, another cousin, is an extremely talented artist. I saw a collection of his pencil sketches and was thrilled and excited. They depicted, in photographic accuracy, the life of the people, of the woods, and of the river, and all with a twist of humor. I wish they could be published, as they have value as an exposition of the cultural and natural life of Jack Gore Baygall, a portion of the National Park System.

One Holifield I could never approach was Benny Lee and Tommy's Daddy, Hannan Holifield, Jr., known only as Junior. A big bear of a man, Junior Holifield was and is a man "It just won't do to fool with," as the saying goes. Once he had a difference of opinion with Possum Warren in Jim Burns' beer joint, and to avoid a confrontation, left, and went home. Possum followed him and when Possum appeared in the doorway with a gun, Junior shot him between the eyes—"graveyard dead!" as Ernest Spell would say. On another occasion, when he turned and walked away from an argument, his opponent took the opportunity to slug him from behind and run away. Junior pursued him and, with his buck knife, partly severed his arm and shoulder. This is the typical frontier response when retaliations for "errors of judgment" were swift and prompt. No police called, charges filed, preliminary appeals, or the side with the most expensive lawyer winning. Just, if you hit somebody, you can expect to get hit back. Somewhere along the river, two families got into a fracas where guns, knives, and axes were employed. Some were killed and one young woman had her arm either cut or shot off. When the law came to sort things out, they were told: "This is a private matter. You aren't wanted here." I'm not advocating taking the law into your own hands, for the weak and helpless get the short end of the stick when the law of fang and claw takes the place of a judicial system. That's just the way it was in pioneer times—and still is in Caney Head. Junior Holifield minds his own business and doesn't bother anybody, but do him wrong and watch out! At any rate, he raised a fine family, or at least his wife did. His boys are ambitious, work hard, and have a lot of pride and self-confidence in who and what they are.

Another Holifield cousin, Hannan Rufus, lives in a 100-year-old log house along the Old Wagon Road. There was one of the biggest pecan trees I ever saw in the front yard but one day three bolts of lightning struck it and it didn't survive. The house had been used as a post office when that was a main route of travel through the area. I was always curious about its age and origin, but none could remember who built it and when. I was visiting with Hannan's mother, Rannie Calloway Holifield, when the subject came up and she gave me some information. She said that her grandfather, Mark Cunningham, had lived there and sold it to Bunkie Hare. Unfortunately, a Hare son, Samuel Andrew Jackson Hare, had a problem with the law and his mother sold the site and house to Hannan Rufus Holifield, the present owner, to pay lawyer's fees. It seems Sam had sent off for a mail order bride and subsequently, for what reason nobody seems to know, or will say, he killed her. As of this writing, Sam Hare still lives, a man who minds his own business, stays out of trouble, and is respected.

At one time, the Holifields owned most of the land between what is now Highway 92 and the river, but, like most of the early settlers in this area, lost most of it to the robber baron, John Henry Kirby. One of the Holifields, who a lawyer friend described to me as a tall, big, red-headed woman who was extremely intelligent, decided they could go to court and recover their land. Houston Thompson represented them and they were able to recover some of it. The Holifields have a reputation as pretty brainy individuals. I was also told of a family member who went away to college on a scholarship, got a master's degree in something or other, and then came back to live his chosen way of life—that of the woods and river.

While I was talking family history with Lester Holifield one day, he remarked that he had an old book on the family somewhere. At my interest, he scrounged around and came up with—voilà!—a superb family genealogical study, done by Harlan Huddlin Daniel, son of Amy H. Holifield, which went all the way back to Essex, England, in the twelfth century. The part that dealt with the Caney Head Holifields was picked up in South Carolina in 1769 where one John H. Holifield got an itching foot and moved south and west with his family. John H. had such a happy cheerful disposition and such a ready wit, that it was talked of in family circles for generations.

The history books claim that westward expansion was due to a spirit of Manifest Destiny, but families multiplied so rapidly, there was not enough room for all of them to make a living, so population pressures and land worn out by cotton and tobacco farming pushed the more-adventurous ever westward onto unclaimed land. Most of the settlers on the frontier came as family groups: sons, brothers, and cousins. Some came, sent back glowing reports and were joined later by other family members. John's first son, Moses, moved to Jones County, Mississippi, in 1830 and John W. followed in 1850 with the rest of the family. They lived in a community in the "gallberry flats" (baygalls) called Laurel and proceeded to develop it culturally and economically with schools, churches, and businesses. The Holifields owned all the town and surrounding land in those days. Some entrepreneurs wanted to put in a sawmill at Laurel, but the people would not allow it because the smoke and cinders would foul the air and it would attract a rough sort of people. Imagine! The Holifields were environmentalists in the 1800s.

The Holifields were also pacifists, at least where the Civil War was concerned. They considered it a "rich man's war and a poor man's fight." They withdrew Jones County from the Union, called it the Free State of Jones, elected a president and fought both the Yankees and the Confederates. After the war, they rejoined the Union.

Moses Holifield had a son named John C. who was called Cow John because he bought and sold cattle and had more cows than anyone else in the territory. Cow John was quite prosperous and owned a store, grist mill, and cotton gin. His life and character were the stuff with which grandchildren were entertained before the fireplace on wintry evenings.

Cow John had three wives, one at a time, of course. One of his first marriages failed for the following reason: His wife's brother came out to the field where he was plowing and told him that his wife was trying to poison him by putting spiders in his beverages. Cow John stopped the mule, went to the house, told her to pack her clothes and that they were taking a trip. He took her to her parents' house and told her father, "I've brought her back just like I found her," and left her there.

Cow John had 20 children and lived to 80 years of age and, according to the records, his last child was born after he died. Before he died, he had a stroke and couldn't speak. He kept frantically pointing to the fireplace, but the family thought that he was delirious. After his death, the family money was not to be found and the once-prosperous family fell into destitution with the wife reduced to taking in washing for neighbors in order to live. (What I would like to know is where were all those twenty kids when the old woman was stooping over that rub board.) Much later, a man demolishing the house found the horde of gold behind a stone in the fireplace.

I love these family histories, for seldom are the graces and accomplishments of the majority of the family mentioned, only that which was unusual and astonishing enough to be talked about for generations. For instance, it was reported that one member of the family had been killed and eaten by wild hogs.

The Moses branch of the Holifield family remained in Mississippi, while John W.'s son, William, with his sons, Hannan and Leroy, migrated to Texas. John W.'s sister, Sally, with her husband, John Moss, moved to Louisiana in 1865, and from there to Texas where other members of the Moss family had already come. When the party reached the Mississippi River, Hannan's wife said: "I'm not gonna cross that water!" She stuck to her guns, so Hannan went off and left her there, proceeded to Texas and married another woman. His abandoned wife returned to her family in Mississippi. Apparently, she took the "til death do us part" marriage vow seriously, and viewed the Mississippi River as its possible equivalent.

My present friends, Lester and Donald Roy, are members of the Leroy family branch, while Junior, Tommy, and Benny Lee are from the Hannan branch.

Caney Head families who intermarried with the Holifields include the Eason, Gore, Smart, Cunningham, Moss, Calloway, Gilmore, Jenkins, and Craven families. Records show that back in Mississippi, they were marrying Gilmores, Jenkins, Mosses, and Cravens even then. In Caney Head, everybody is kin somehow to everybody else, though the kinship might have branched off three or four generations ago. I know of Gores who don't claim kin to other Gores, but it's safest just to not say anything derogatory about anybody to anybody—they're bound to be kin somehow.

When a man has 20 children and each of them has at least 10, with similar names in each family, one understands the dilemma of the genealogist who commented: "Part of John's family is a little confusing. James M. Holifield's second wife was Cornelia Azaline Geiger (half sister to William H. Holifield, stepdaughter of Mark Holifield). After James M. died, she married Albert H. Holifield when Albert's first wife was a sister to James M. Holifield (Sarah Jane.)" ? ? ?

JIM BURNS' BEER JOINT

History of Caney Head and its inhabitants wouldn't be complete if it didn't include the ways the people amused themselves. In the old days, there were Josie parties and country dances for the young and lighthearted, and, for the more spiritually-minded, nightly (that's right—seven nights a week 'til midnight) church services of a purging and emotionally satisfying nature. But there were some who preferred to ease their tensions and anxieties by whooping it up at Jim Burns' beer joint. This establishment was located on Highway 92 near the Tyler/Hardin County line for the convenience of Tyler Countians who wanted to keep their area uncontaminated by the demon drink but didn't hesitate to pollute their neighboring county with said demon and bestrew the highway thither with their wrecked cars and mangled bodies. There was a song of that day called "Wreck on the Highway," popularized by Roy Acuff, which might have described a typical gruesome Saturday night scene on Highway 92 where bodies lay in whiskey and blood and broken glass. A typical stanza went like this:

> I heard the crash on the highway
> I knew what it was from the start
> I went to the scene of destruction
> And this picture was stamped on my heart

Jim Burns was a big man and carried a .44 pistol in his belt. He was THE law on his turf and whenever Billy Payne, the local sheriff and a native son, was called in because of a shooting, knifing, or other bodily injury, the sheriff would call the hospital or Farmer's funeral home, as the situation required, and write the incident off as "justifiable homicide," or "self defense."

Junior Holifield and a buddy always went to Jim Burns' on a Saturday night in the hope of finding somebody to fight with. That failing, they would fight each other. Seldom, however, was the place lacking in excitement. Bradley Gill, another ex-habitué of Jim Burns', did some plaster work for me recently and I asked him about the old days at Jim Burns' and I almost didn't get my ceiling plastered, there was so much to tell. Like all Caney Headers, Brad Gill is loquacious and can do ample justice to a story.

Another gladiator, or I should say gladiatress, of the Jim Burns arena was Sugar Bowl Eason who could hold her own with any man, whether it was riding, shooting, or fighting. And I'm not talking scratching and hair pulling—I'm talking knock-down-and-drag-out fighting. We hear a lot about Belle Starr and those other tough ladies of the Wild West, but they have just gotten a lot of press. Our Sugar Bowl would be a legend in her own time if she got the publicity they did. I once took some Cornell University friends, Dr. Peter Marks and Dr. Paul Harcombe, to a dance and fish fry benefiting a local hospitalized resident. It was held at one of the clubs on Honkytonk Road. Sugar Bowl was there having a better time than most and every so often would express her good feelings by letting out a whoop: "Hooooohaw!" It just delighted the heck out of those Yankee professors and that's all they talked about afterwards.

Sugar Bowl was the daughter of Doc (Barefoot) Eason who was also somewhat of a legend in his own time. He was another of Lum Eason's boys, each of whom was unique in his own way. Doc got his other nickname because he only wore shoes once in his life and that was the day he got married. He was taped singing the traditional folk songs of the community by Dr. William Owens, then of Texas A & M University, and is cited in Dr. Owens' book *Texas Folk Songs*. I once sat on a bank of the Neches with Doc and we compared our versions of the songs, which had been passed down in our families. He and his wife were both well diggers in the day before drilling machinery was built. I liked Doc and I liked Sugar Bowl and the rest of his kids. They dare to be themselves and feel no need to conform to anybody else's standard of life.

But back to Jim Burns—he finally died of natural causes and the establishment was closed. A daughter inherited it and sold it, but before it could be reopened, it was burned to the ground under suspicious circumstances. There were plans to rebuild, but the good church people of the community called an election to decide whether north Hardin County would be wet or dry and the dries won out. Most of Jim Burns' patrons didn't even know there was an election—part of them couldn't read the notices and, besides, if it was hunting season or the fish were biting, they wouldn't show up for Judgment Day. The church people were well organized and transported dry voters to the polls in busses, so they won a resounding victory. A couple of years later, a subsequent election restored alcohol to north Hardin County, but only as takeouts. The good people of Caney Head had good cause to deplore the easy availability of alcohol in the community. The carnage on the highways was not the only aftermath of a night of drinking at Jim Burns' beer joint. The inebriated who were too weak or cowardly to fight other men staggered home to take out their frustrations on wives and children. Some of these pitiful victims, now grown, have told me of the nights of terror when mother and children would run from the house into the woods in all kinds of weather to escape the violent ravings and beatings. Another told how her sister, just out of the hospital with major surgery, was kicked out the door and down the steps by a drunken husband while her grown sons looked on and did nothing.

Apparently, alcohol rouses the anger and violence in a man without giving him the courage to take it out on someone who might fight back. Wife beating has been accepted as normal in the past, and especially excusable if the man was drunk. I know of a man who killed his wife in a drunken rage and was judged innocent of murder because "he was drunk and didn't know what he was doing." This reflects the attitude in the past when a wife and children were property to be used as the man saw fit. This premise has disappeared legally, but wife and child abuse persists today—not just in the backwaters of society, but as far up the socio-economic scale as one wishes to go.

Eventually, the alcohol turns on the drinker himself. Recently, while I was waiting for a friend in the emergency room of the local hospital, a man was brought in with the D.T.s (delirium tremens) and it took all the personnel of the E.R. plus a few onlookers to subdue him. He was fighting snakes, which were crawling all over him and biting him. A high price to pay for whatever benefit he derived from drink.

There are no more beer joints in Caney Head where one can go on a Saturday night, quaff a few beers, and exchange a few blows. Junior Holifield has been laid low with a stroke and the recompense of a wild life. It is the end of an era. But, then, most everybody in Caney Head had a pickup and could go down the road a piece to the Starlight Club in Honey Island. It wasn't the same, though. After my cousins, Jerry and Herb Stutz, took it over, cleaned it up and made it a nice, quiet, safe place to enjoy an evening of music, dancing, and wholesome recreation, it just didn't have the appeal that the raucous, free-wheeling life of Jim Burns' beer joint had. Jerry and Herbie retired, and the last I heard, the Starlight Club building had been taken over by a church. Ah well! All things change.

Indians
Drawing by Regina Watson

INDIAN PINEY WOODS

The Indians who used the Neches River for transportation and fishing lived on bluffs and hummocks out of reach of the annual floods. Some of these were on the bluff banks of the river but most were back on terraces. Probably the largest habitation site between Dam B and Beaumont was what is called by locals, Indian Piney Woods. Located between Timber Slough Road and

Bear Man's Bluff Road, it is a large hummock of sand half encircled by Jack Gore Baygall on the southwest side. On the eastern side, the hummock drops off into the lower floodplain and Franklin Lake, a cypress slough, borders it and provides water access to the river. The hummock was formed as a pointbar deposited perhaps 5,000 ybp and was once thinly forested by giant longleaf pines. The forest products company who owns the land clearcut the area and planted it with slash pine, which they thought would be a faster-growing, more profitable species. It has proved to be disastrous as the slash pine was not suited to the arid condition and the area is now a spotty stand of trees which are stunted, fork-stemmed, and infested with fungal diseases.

There is abundant evidence of the Indian presence here in the many artifacts collected by locals, and people still living speak of their grandparents' relationships with the Indians. I. C. told me his grandfather taught him Indian wrestling and showed him an area on Ard hummock, another pointbar just across Maple Slough from Indian Piney Woods, where a bare circular depression had been worn into the ground by the Indians dancing around their campfire. Incidentally, I. C.'s brother, Cecil, told me this grandfather himself was an Indian named White Eagle.

Apparently, there were no large, organized villages between the Hasanai village at the Forks of the River (Neches and Angelina) and the Attakapa villages on both side of the Neches at Beaumont (at least none have been reported), but there were many related family groups, each living where they chose on permanent sites. There was a system of trails connecting these living sites, and the Indians traveled them to visit one another and, no doubt, attend the important festivals like the annual Busk, or New Year Celebration, at the large villages. Maybelle Ard told me of her grandfather's talking about the Indians who walked past their house on the Old Wagon Road.

Everything published on the Indians of the Big Thicket states that no Indians lived here, that they only came in to hunt. This assumption is based on Dr. Francis Abernethy's book, *Tales From the Big Thicket*. Dr. Abernethy was speaking of an area in the Little Pine Island Bayou watershed known as the "Traditional Big Thicket," located roughly within the triangle between Kountze, Sour Lake, Saratoga, and extending north to Segno. The Traditional Thicket was an area of dense thickets of palmetto, titi, and gallberry holly, baygalls and swamps, bears, panthers, alligators, and cottonmouth moccasins. Aside from the removal of the bears and panthers and most of the alligators, it hasn't changed much.

The area known as the Ecological Big Thicket consisted of open parklike forests: longleaf pine on the uplands, beech/magnolia/loblolly pine/white oak communities on the slopes and hummocks, and oak/gum forests in the floodplains, all interspersed with dense thickets, sloughs, and baygalls. It was a literal heaven for Indians, with its many streams and springs in flood-free sites, clay for pottery, a few open areas for farming, native fruits, nuts, and vegetables, and plenteous game and fish.

Most land in this area is acidic—poor ground for growing corn, the staple food of Indians from Maine to Tierra Del Fuego. This could be why there were no large villages in our area, but there were patches of rich bottomland, especially where exposures of the Fleming geological formation provided lime-rich soil. The Indians grew corn, beans, squash, melons, pumpkins, sunflowers, and tobacco. Corn and beans were grown together, apparently because they knew what agronomists now know, that legumes replace the nitrogen corn takes from the soil. They also buried a fish on each hill of corn and, perhaps they, like the Chinese, used human excrement to fertilize their crops. A type of crop rotation was practiced in that they grew corn on the ground for several years, and abandoned the field for ten years. Then they burned the weeds and brush and started the cycle over again. Fire was an important tool to these Indians. They might not have known that the ashes provided potassium, phosphorous, and other minerals necessary for growing crops, but they knew, after a thousand years of experimentation and observation, that crops grew better after fire and that insects and plant diseases were less of a problem. Women did the farming while men hunted and fished. When asked by a mission padre why this was so, an Indian woman said it was only natural that women, who were fruitful and produced life, should be the ones to bring life from the seed and soil. They did not perceive farming as onerous toil, but a joyful task which gave them pleasure and food. They worked together in unison, doing the cultivating to the rhythm of stamping and singing. Small boys sharpened their skills with bow and arrow and sling by ridding the fields of the small animals, coons, squirrels, etc., which ravaged the gardens.

Fire escaping from the cooking fires and from farming no doubt was responsible for the stands of longleaf pine and other pyric species on these hummocks as the areas are not large enough for the chance of lightning ignition. Surrounded as they are by water and wetland, spreading fires from the uplands couldn't have reached them except during the very rare severe droughts when slope, baygall, and slough were powder dry and fires from the uplands swept across them. Even these fires weren't destructive of full-grown trees since the frequent fires prevented an accumulation of fuels.

Most of the food—roots, nuts, fruits, berries, and greens—as well as medicines and building materials were found in the native plants. It is said that the Indians wove beautiful mats for floors and walls, and dishes and bowls from reeds and fine roots, especially the roots of willows.

Plentiful game included deer, squirrel, coons, possums, and rabbits, as well as many kinds of water birds. Stationing himself behind a tree beside an animal trail to water, a hunter could easily kill as much meat as was needed. Fish was abundant in all the streams and sloughs, and the Indians were adept with hook and line, spear and net. Fresh water clams were also plentiful along these waterways, as were frogs and turtles.

Food was prepared early in the day so as to be available at any time for anyone, including the wayfaring stranger, whenever they felt like eating. It was served on decorated pottery or beautifully woven grass plates and eaten with the fingers. Along with the farming and the cooking of food, Indian women had many other chores. The preparation of skins to be cut and sewn into garments, the weaving of baskets for food gathering and storage, and the making of pottery. They still took the time to make sure that these items were not only useful but decorative. Intricate designs were pressed into the damp clay and varicolored clays were used to paint the patterns on the pottery. Fragments of their pottery can be found many places along the Neches. Also plentiful are flakes of flint where tools and missile points were made from flint brought by traders from deposits in Northeast Texas.

While fields, storage, and living quarters required a permanent habitat, hunting, gathering, and visiting relatives in other villages resulted in a mobile society. Their system of trails connecting villages, watering springs, and distant sources of shells, copper, flint, and salt, followed high ground and crossed streams at the best fording places. Later, French and Spanish explorers and traders found these trails useful and they were widened to accommodate pack horses and mule carts. As Anglo-Americans moved into Texas, these same trails were widened even more to wagon width. Today, many of our highways follow these routes. Ed Parmley, of the State Highway Department, had an extensive collection of artifacts picked up as road scrapers widened highway rights-of-way.

Travel by water was common, too. Dugout canoes were made by gouging and burning logs into shape. Indian Piney Woods not only had water access to the river by way of Franklin Lake, but there were a number of trails radiating from the hummock to other residential sites and to major trails. Anglo settlers used these trails and many of them are still traveled. I can remember myself when these trails could be located by the large beech trees with Indian signs and French and Spanish words on them. These signs usually gave information about the trail ahead. Another method of marking a trail route was to tie the tops of young, pliant hardwood trees to the ground with three of them pointing in the same direction. I have found these old trees with their topside limbs grown to tree size. Widening of roads and lumbering have eliminated all these old trail markers. The last one I saw hung over Cairo Springs near Austin Withers' place, but when I passed that way later, the woods had been cut, so the tree is probably gone.

I have tried unsuccessfully to find out who these Indians were who lived in Indian Piney Woods. Artifacts found in sites along the Neches are relics of the Paleo Indians, aboriginals who lived here 12,000 or so years ago, as well as the Attakapas who moved through here from Southwest Louisiana about 2,000 years ago. The later residents were probably members of the Hasanai Confederacy, a related group of East Texas Indians. Incidentally, the word Hasanai means "our own country." Those Indians remembered by local people were no doubt remnants of the East Texas tribes—some of whom refused the move to the Brazos reservation in 1855 and therefore missed the flight to the barrens of Oklahoma Territory and the final massacre. Scattered family groups of the Eastern tribes, Cherokee, Creek, etc., emigrated here and avoided oppression by selecting the least desirable areas in which to live. The Cherokee were civilized farmers who were driven out of their ancestral lands in North Carolina and Tennessee. In 1817, around 20,000 of them were moved by soldiers through the mountains in midwinter and nearly 7,000 of them died on the way. The route became known as The Trail of Tears.

Some of the Alabamas left the land given to them on the east of the Trinity River during the Runaway Scrape of the Texas Revolution, and returned to find their homes and farms taken over by Anglos. They wandered homeless for 16 years ,when they were located at the Fenced-in-Village on the Neches. Losing this, they finally joined the Koasatis on the 4,351-acre reservation on Big Sandy Creek in Polk County acquired for them by the efforts of Sam Houston in 1854.

The end of the gentle, friendly Indians of our woodlands is so unbelievably tragic, so sad, I can't bring myself to tell it. Could we, all born and bred to the Christian religion of love, brotherhood, and peace, have done this incredibly cruel and inhumane thing? We shudder at Hitler's murder of six million Jews, truly a crime against humanity, but how many millions did our ancestors kill: the men, women, little children, and old people who once walked these trails, rode the currents of these streams, grew their simple foods and didn't wear out the soil, poison the air, or pollute the water. Nor did they destroy the forests or deplete the game to extermination. "But that was long ago," you say. "We are not responsible for what our ancestors did." I could buy that if we were not still at it—in any part of the world where our greed and avarice take us. We are a people who take what we want and justify it by declaring that the owners are only savages, or we must protect "our national interests." Ah Well!

What has happened to the people of Indian Piney Woods? When I posed this question to Ernest Spell, he answered: "Why we ain't gone nowhere! We're still here!" In talking with most of the oldtimers, they say: "My grandma was an Indian!" So their blood still courses through the veins of those who live here today. Half of Caney Head claims Indian blood. Ernest Spell explained it this way: The pioneer way of life was so hard on white women that a man might wear out three or four wives in his lifetime. The Indian women were tough and accustomed to hard work, so more and more Anglo men took wives from the Indians. This is logical and probably true.

THE OLD WAGON ROAD

The Old Wagon Road through the Jack Gore Baygall Unit goes from Yellow Bluff on the river, westward, skirting the west side of the baygall to where it meets the Old Spurger Highway at the Old Maids Road. It is a part of an intricate network of Indian trails which connected habitation sites and river crossings. In my wanderings over the baygall and its environs, I have come across remnants of this old road and have wondered where it came from, where it went, and who traveled it. Finally, after I went to work for the park service, I traced its entire length through the unit with the help of local people. Maybelle Ard said she used to sit on her porch and watch the oxcarts and horses and buggies pass on the old road beside her house. Marvis Gore's grandpa told about the Indians who passed his house on the old road with their babies and their goods strapped to the backs of the women.

Son Gordon took me on the upper fork over which he drove his own wagon and team to the river before the park service closed it off. I rode the

last section of it in I. C. Eason's hoopie, Huldy (a pickup modified by him for navigating the rough bottomland roads), a wild, rambunctious ride over the ridges, down the swales through the sloughs to his camp on the river near Yellow Bluff. In the 1970s, Ernest Spell took a machete and hacked out a pathway through the rough where it intersects the old Spurger highway so I could drive my auto down a section of it, but it has since grown up again and is quite impassable except by foot. Some Junior Rangers from the area and I cleared another particularly scenic section of it, but the park service had neither money nor personnel to maintain it so it also has returned to a brushy state. It is my dream that it will eventually be maintained as a historic trail by the park service in that perhaps dreamtime when the government recognizes the aesthetic and cultural values of our land as well as its economic values and will allocate funds to take care of it. Ah well!

The old road intersects the paved Spurger Road on the shortleaf pine upland at the southernmost end of the Jack Gore Baygall Unit. At the very beginning, the old road struggles for a quarter of a mile or so through dense brush. Someone bought about 50 acres here about 20 years ago and clearcut it but didn't keep it up so it immediately began the first stage of ecological succession (the weed/brush/sapling stage) to return to the open, closed-canopy forest it once had been. This tangle abruptly ends and one enters a beautiful, parklike, gently, sloping forest of huge beeches, magnolias, loblolly pines, and white oaks. On the right is the baygall, its edges rimmed with lush colonies of ferns, jack-in-the-pulpit, and some species of orchids. On the left is upland that is frequently cut and perpetually in an early successional stage. It is impossible to get lost on this trail provided one has the sense to stick to the open woods and not enter the baygall with its endless maze of shallow black water and little hummocks of roots, ferns, and mosses, or, of course, the dense thickets on the upland.

The ruts of the road can be easily followed most of the time except where the canopy trees have been cut and the light causes thickets to grow. It follows midslope, but where a homestead stood at the top of the bluff, the road turns up slope and there is a short loop there. My guess is that this route was chosen to avoid the deep sand of the uplands and the boggy soils at the base of the slope. Being an old Indian trail, it would naturally go from one water spring to the next. Anglo settlers found this convenient as toiling teams of mules, horses, and oxen as well as the laboring men, would need drinking water.

There are numerous seep springs along the route between the Spurger highway and the Timber Slough Road, and at least three boiling springs. The springs at the base of the slope feed little streamlets with wild azaleas, ferns, and mosses along the bank. They wind their way through open, parklike beech/magnolia/loblolly forests until they spread out into the flat surface of the baygall.

To walk the trail is easy and pleasant. There are flowering dogwoods and azaleas in spring, and the trail is cool and shady in the summer, and a joy in the autumn with the mixture of colorful hardwood leaves and the dark green of pines. Winter is good for birding, as the leaves have fallen and the many birds that migrate through at this season can be easily seen. Woodpeckers are especially plentiful because of the many mature trees.

After about an hour of strolling, one comes upon the most beautiful of the springs: three pools called the Blue Springs. They are at the edge of the baygall at the base of a long hill, at the top of which was the home of John Gore, one of the early settlers. The park service once had a plan to restore and clean Blue Springs and clear the brush around it, but nothing came of it. The Blue Springs will (could) be one of the star attractions when (if) the trail were opened to the public.

Just past Blue Springs, the trail forks, one fork turning east and crossing the baygall at a narrow point, it goes over the sand hill to Indian Piney Woods and Franklin Lake. The left fork goes through a brushy area to the top of the rise, as the slope is too steep for a road and the base is too boggy. Perry Gore has two pastures at the top of this rise which he mows occasionally. I understand that they once belonged to Bony (Napoleon Buonopart) Gore who had a cabin here. The road descends the north side of the slope and crosses some small spring branches. Unfortunately, the spring which fed them has been covered. Oil operations bulldozed tons of earth to the bottom of the slope in order to level an oil drilling pad on the upland. Frequently, the water in the streamlet tastes and smells of oil and salt.

Once I was walking along this section of trail when I noticed something a little unusual out in the woods. Rising above the mulch of fallen leaves was a moss-covered mound two or three feet diameter. In the center was an arrangement of baby's toys: a clown, a rubber ball, and a duck. The colors had long since faded so it was hard to tell how long it had been since they were placed there. I looked about for the rest of what I thought must have been an old trash pile, but found nothing else. It could well have been the grave of an infant whose parents could not afford the services of the local funeral home, so they gave it the best burial they could, and, as is the way with primitive peoples, they placed his favorite toys on the mound to console his little spirit left all alone in the dark woods.

While the road continues at a lower level, our trail rises again to the upland so the hiker can view something truly rare in Big Thicket Country: Caney Head Canyon and waterfall. The "canyon" is a deep gully into the upland where a small spring branch has eroded the rocklike red clay to the level of the floodplain. Its steep walls are forested with dogwood, beech, and magnolia with wild azalea and Christmas ferns festooning the lower areas. A little streamlet enters from the upland where runoff forms a lateral erosional gully and drops over a horseshoe-shaped edge about 15 feet into a blue pool, then again drops about six feet into a smaller pool where, via a little streamlet, it joins the spring branch of the main canyon.

At one time, Indians lived in a cave dug into the rocklike clay of the canyon. People my age saw the clay pots and basketry and the flint tools that were left behind when the Indians left, never to return. An oil well was drilled nearby and in leveling the pad, clay was bulldozed over the cave mouth and a pipeline laid directly over it. Some Caney Head residents have artifacts collected at the site.

After crossing Caney Head Canyon, another trail branches to the east, crossing the baygall at a narrow place. An oilfield road follows the trail now, connecting oil well pads in the baygall. Locals call it the Shell Road because it has been paved with oyster shell. Park rangers call it the Zig-zag Road because of its angled configuration. Where the maintained oilfield road stops, the old trail continues through the woods to Indian Piney Woods on the sand hill and thence to Franklin Lake, and then to the river where it is said there was once an Indian trading post.

From the shell road, the original wagon road went upslope past Junior Holifield's house and through what is now an extremely dense brier/vine/brush thicket. All the trees were cut here about 20 years ago and it will take some time for the forest to recover a closed canopy stage. In the meantime, I have routed the trail down slope from the original route through open woods. Where my trail joins the original, there are some of the biggest and finest beech trees I've ever seen. Also, here is where sugar maple begins to share dominance with beech and there are some magnificent specimens here. This seems to be the southern limit for sugar maple as it is not found below this point.

The old road divides again, forming a loop—one loop going upslope to Hannan Holifield's place. He lives in a squared-log building which is over a hundred years old. It served as a post office when the Pony Express brought the mail around and all travelers stopped here to water their teams from the well. The road takes two alternate routes downslope back to the lower road. One goes directly downslope past huge beeches, magnolias, hickories, and oaks. Here, the rare and strange orchid, *Hexalectris spicata*, was discovered by Dr. David Snell and Joe Ligio. It is saprophytic, meaning it derives nutrients from decaying organic material with the help of friendly microscopic fungi in the soil and without the help of sunlight. The fleshy, leafless stem is a grayish pink and the several 3/4-inch orchid blossoms at the summit are yellow-lavender with maroon stripes and spots. Not spectacular, but very interesting. Joe Ligio featured it in his very beautiful and scholarly book on Texas orchids.

The lower route has a beautiful display of azaleas during the spring. The upper route goes by Sambo Gore's place then downslope to join the other road before it crosses the lovely streamlets that come from the big spring at Sambo's place. Here between Sambo's place and the baygall, ringed by spring branches, is a ridge where Indians lived. Sonny Yawn, who with generations of his family lived nearby, has a collection of artifacts from this site. At this point, a lateral trail crosses a narrow place in the baygall which I call Sam Hare Ford because it leads to Turkey Hummock where old Blind Sam Hare (one of the innumerable Samuel Andrew Jackson Hares) had a cabin. This trail was part of the network of Indian trails through and around the baygall.

Back behind Sambo Gore's place is a hummock of open woods on the edge of the baygall. I saw a strange sight here a few years ago. A circle about 50 feet wide was blazed with an axe on large beech trees. On one side of the circle, a pole about eight feet high had been put in the ground and on it was mounted the skull of a cow. On the opposite side was another pole, this one with the skull of a horse. In the center lying on the ground was a cross formed by two limbs tied together by a man's shirt. Ten or fifteen yards away was a bare patch of ground around three by six feet in size. Returning to the park service office that evening, I described what I had seen to Ken Tiege, our chief ranger. He and ranger Dave McHugh were intrigued and insisted on viewing the scene. We went, taking along a shovel to see what might be buried at the bare spot. Our shovel turned up nothing, so the intent and purpose of the arrangement is still a mystery. There are many mysteries in and around this baygall. Among these people, there is a strong belief in supernatural powers. This could have been a hex worked against some enemy. Who knows?

For some distance, the woods are lovely and the road plain, but the route becomes confusing. It appears to go up the end of a ridge and into a dense, cutover, thickety woods to the back fence of the Ard place. Because the Ard land is grazed, it is clear and open, but I couldn't continue the trail, as the park service boundary followed the corner of the Ard property and the old road cut across this corner. Also in this corner was the beautiful Caney Head Springs—another boiling spring gushing from the base of a great beech tree—a jewel in a setting of lush ferns and flowers with a streamlet flowing from it through banks fringed with ferns, mosses, and violets. The streamlet enters an inlet of the baygall at the base of the slope and is divided into a braided pattern with titi, gallberry, and other large shrubs forming a somewhat canopied thicket. This spring is where Maybelle Ard, who lives on the top of the rise, used to do her washing.

Maybelle Ard was somewhere between 60 and 70 years of age. Her blue eyes and sandy-colored, curly hair showed her Scotch/Irish heritage, but high cheekbones and romanesque curve to the nose were evidence of her Indian blood. Her simple clapboard house and way of life were definitely of the people, but Maybelle Ard was a great lady. I met her many years ago when our husbands shared a hospital room in Beaumont. I recognized Mr. and Mrs. Ard as two people I had once met and photographed as they were coming down Timber Slough Road to the river in a horse-drawn wagon. Mrs. Ard needed to go home for some reason and, since I had a vehicle and she didn't, I offered to drive her there. We were friends until her death. When I had park service business in the area, I always stopped by Maybelle Ard's for a cup of coffee and conversation. Her home was surrounded by pastures where her son's horses, miniature mules, and her cow grazed, and a fair-size field (for this area) perched on the edge of the upland bordering the baygall.

The Ards married young and had three sons, then tragedy struck. He developed an illness which caused him to be paralyzed in his legs and it fell on her to work at whatever she could do to feed and school her sons. It was probably polio, but what medical help that was available had no name for it so they treated his legs with home remedies, even to soaking them in kerosene! The oldest child quit school to help, but the brunt fell onto her shoulders. She farmed the land with mule power, raising corn, peas, and vegetables. She also did farm work for other people, working in exchange for food. After the crops were laid by, she hitched up the horse, packed enough food to last a month or so, and they went to the river where they had a semi-permanent camp under the big trees at Timber Slough sandbar. Everywhere they went, she had to pick him up and carry him. She carried him to the wagon, but he drove the horse. She carried him to the boat, and he operated the motor and ran the boat. Together, they set out trotlines and ran them, putting their catch in fish traps, which were cages constructed of cypress slats and kept in the water so the fish would remain alive until needed. After the traps were filled, Maybelle would take the fish out to Cunningham's store on the Spurger highway and sell them for money to buy clothes for the children.

Mr. Ard died after many years of invalidism. She spoke fondly of those days in which she cared for him as being the happiest of her life. She told how she and her sister would take the dirty clothes down to Caney Head Spring and wash them. How they would laugh and sing as they bent over the rub boards scrubbing the clothes and together would carry the tubs of cleaned clothes back up the hill to hang and dry in the sun. Most people would look back on such times of unremitting trouble, toil, and desperate hardship with sadness and bitterness, but she looked back with wistful nostalgia. She had those she loved about her and had the forest and the river and a way of life which was familiar and for which she was fitted. "We wus so happy!" she said. I have known some really fine women in my time—Lady Bird Johnson, Barbara Jordan, Maxine Johnston—and I rate Maybelle Ard with the greatest. Good Lord! What a woman!

The trail crosses a bit of baygall, goes up slope and joins the old road as it crosses Timber Slough Road, leaving Big Thicket National Preserve land. Timber Slough Road is the north boundary of the baygall.

Past Timber Slough Road, the Old Wagon Road goes up slope past James (Son) Gordon's house. I have referred to Son and his grandson, James, throughout my meanderings many times. His daughters used to sing the old folk songs for the city folks I would bring into the Neches bottom. Son typifies all that is best in backwoods East Texas men. Coming from generations of Caney Headers, and kin to practically everybody here, he knows all the lore and loves to talk about it in his low, slow drawl. What a storyteller he is! I could listen to him for hours.

But back to the Old Wagon Road—past Timber Slough Road, it forks with one fork proceeding north toward Fred and Town Bluff, the other circling around Maple Slough, crosses Black Creek and skirts the north boundary of the Jack Gore Baygall Unit, and proceeds across the river bottom to Yellow Bluff. The section of road over the upper terraceland is still passable, but after it reenters national preserve land, the road has been closed.

Between the road and Maple Slough, I found what appeared to be a memorial grove of big beech trees. Tombstone shapes were cut into the smooth bark and on each was inscribed: "BROTHER" and the name of a deceased member of the Eason clan with a date. Where better than in the woods that they roamed as boys and men and which they loved, rather than in a crowded cemetery beside a noisy highway?

The road circles around the rim of the deep sand of Ard Hummock, where there was another Indian settlement and a large spring, proceeds northward alongside the McGallian Lakes, a string of enlargements of Black Creek which follow the base of the bluff line of the upper terrace, and crosses at what is called the Gap to enter the lower floodplain. Here it again enters park service land. The floodplain is ridge and swale topography with open woods of magnificent oaks and gums. It is alongside one of these swales that Bony Gore's gold hole is located.

The legend of Bony Gore's gold is of recent origin—that is, about 75 years ago. In those days there was no radio nor television, and people entertained one another with stories of the past, and many buried treasure tales were passed around. Somehow, Bony Gore got into his possession a "waybill," that is, a map with instructions supposedly passed down by people who were involved in hiding treasure. He located the site and began to dig. It is said that he found a chest but could not raise it in the wet, quicksand-like alluvium of the bottomland. So, he took his wagon and team of mules and went all the way to Woodville and bought some sections of iron smokestack pipe from an old sawmill. As he dug, he sunk these sections into the ground as a curb. The treasure still eluded him, so they say, and he gave up the search. Some say, however, that he did find it and quietly reburied it one dark night near his house. He must have seen some concrete evidence to have gone to such heroic measures. Trips to Woodville might have been undertaken over the slick clay or deep sand roads of that time once a year or less frequently. Some say that his obsession with the lost gold unhinged his mind and that disagreements over it caused a permanent falling out or rift between him and his sons.

Another gold story involving the Old Wagon Road was told to me by Ernest Spell and is verifiable, for those involved are still alive. It seems two young men were riding horseback along the old road. It was getting late, they were in a hurry, and they got off the road. One of the horses stumbled in a hole and fell and in trying to right itself, kicked up quite a bit of dirt and humus. Seeing something shining in the hole, the young men picked it up and it was a shiny, bricklike object. Taking it home, they found it was solid gold so, naturally, they took lanterns, and shovels and hurried back to the site where they unearthed thirteen gold bars and the complete skeleton of a man minus its head. Knowing nothing about how to convert this gold into usable money, they took it into Silsbee and consulted an educated man, a doctor, who gave them, if my memory serves me correctly, $300 for the gold bricks. The story did not have a happy ending, for the young man who first discovered the gold and uncovered the skeleton was haunted by a white dove, which followed him everywhere, beating on his window at night or even sitting on the foot of his bed if it could get into the house. They say it almost drove him crazy. Such are the tales one used to hear around the fireplace on cold winter evenings, or at Ernest's barbershop on a Saturday afternoon.

In the upper Jack Gore Baygall Unit, the road winds through magnificent floodplain forests, following ridges and past cypress sloughs to Yellow Bluff, which was the main steamboat landing for the area. I have mapped the trail and named each segment according to its outstanding feature: Blue Springs Trail, Azalea Trail, Sugar Maple Trail, Waterfall Trail, Gold Hole Trail, etc. Perhaps someday the park service will be allowed enough money to develop and care for this beautiful trail before it is totally lost to living memory and the public will be able to enjoy it as I have. I would also like to see the section of the old road that is in timber company possession donated to the park service so the Old Wagon Road Trail can be made complete. Ah well! This is another cause in which people with time and money on their hands can become involved. I no longer have either.

JACK GORE BAYGALL

River Miles 64–71

Jack Gore Baygall was named (of course) for Jack Gore, who lived on the edge of the baygall. He was the son of John Gore, the original settler. In every Gore family there is a Jack so the name continues. The baygall begins on the south side of the Timber Slough Road and follows the old Neches bluff line to the Old Maids Road. It has been published that Jack Gore Baygall is the largest of its kind in the world, but I doubt it. The claim was made by someone who wanted it included in the preserve.

Divided from Jack Gore Baygall by a meander ridge on the north is an extensive baygall called Maple Slough. Timber Slough Road follows this ridge from the upland to the river. South is another ridge, followed by the Old Maids Road, which divides Jack Gore Baygall from Deserter's Baygall.

Several thousand years ago, the Neches River was much larger than at present, with a wider floodplain. The meanders of the ancient river were

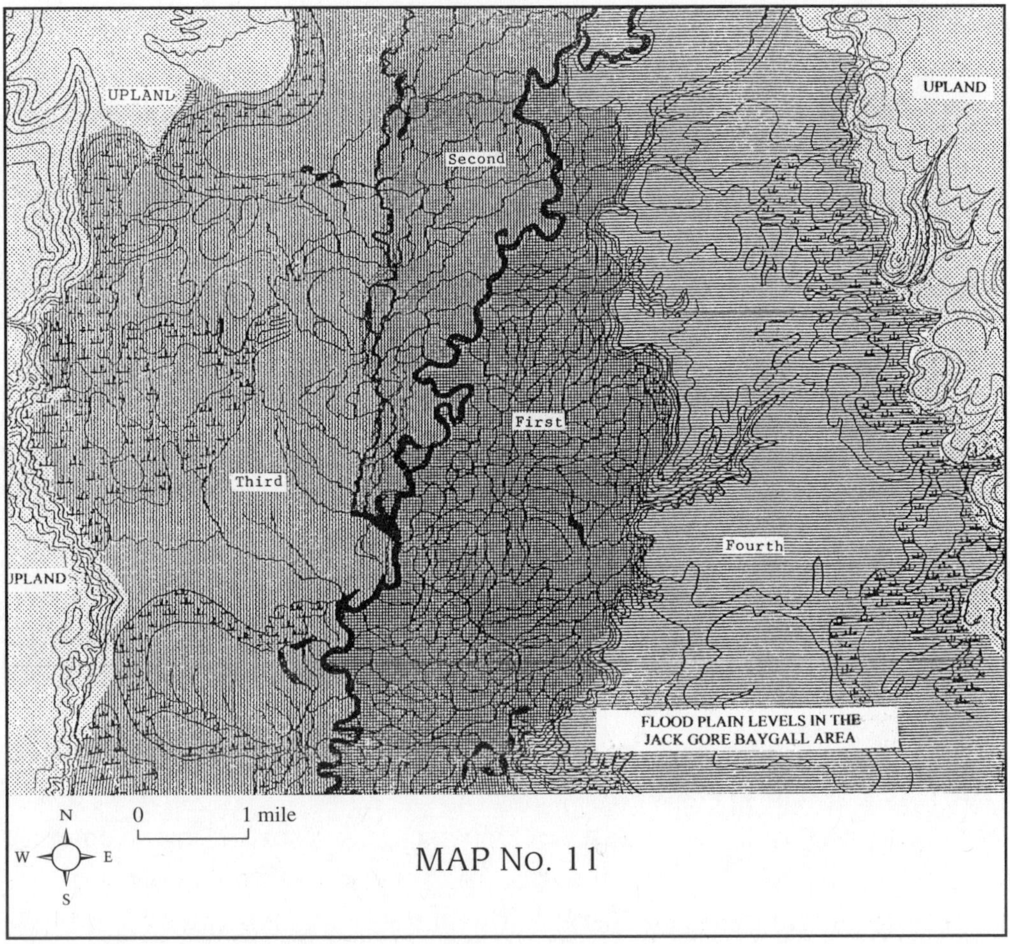

MAP No. 11

much larger than at present, and, in its meanderings, changed course many times, leaving behind deep oxbow lakes that were periodically flushed by the flooding river; however, when the climate changed and the river became smaller, it no longer flooded these upper terraces, so the abandoned channels began to accumulate organic debris, fallen leaves, and dead limbs and trees, until they were almost completely filled. The old floodplain had a ridge-and-swale topography, and developed a forest of less water-tolerant trees. Beech, magnolia, white oak, and loblolly pines colonized ridges, while the acidic swamps of the meander depressions acquired a community of water-tolerant vegetation: copses of white bay magnolia, wax myrtle, gallberry holly, and various heaths. Many species of mosses, chiefly sphagnum, and ferns occupied the small hummocks within the swamps.

A baygall receives its name from the dominant shrubby species, bay and gallberry holly, although, I have also been told that the term comes from an old French word meaning "scar in the earth." And, incidentally, the difference between a baygall, a slough, a marsh, and a swamp is this: A baygall is a closed-canopy, acidic, low-oxygen swamp cut off from outside sources of water except seepage from the uplands, and the water is clear and black with tannic acid. A slough is in an active floodplain, is replenished by periodic flooding, has a higher pH and oxygen level, and the water is yellow and murky. A swamp is a forested, shallow, water-filled depression; and a marsh is an open shallow, water-filled depression. Baygall communities can develop on upland seepage slopes where fire is suppressed, but usually, they occupy abandoned channels on stream terraces.

The vegetative composition of baygalls is mostly shrub species, for large trees do not remain upright due to the wet, unstable nature of the soil. They fall when they begin to grow tall, which allows sunlight to the lower levels and encourages the shrubby species to grow dense. Some trees, such as black gum, cypress, and white bay, develop prop roots which branch out and support the tree so most baygalls have a closed-canopy, shaded openness.

When the ancient river was filling its valley with deposits eroded from the upper watershed, the climate changed and it ceased filling, leaving the old floodplain lower than the adjacent upland. The boundaries of the upland do not correspond to an abrupt drop, but are eroded into irregular slopes of varying degrees. At the base of these slopes, seepage from the upland emerges in springs and bogs. (This is a true "acid bog." Some refer to pine savannahs as "acid bogs" but this is erroneous.) The larger of these springs are named, the most famous being the Blue Springs. There are three 8- to 12-feet round pools, crystal clear and so deep they are blue. These springs were important to the people and animals traveling the Old Wagon Road. Rare plants such as jack-in-the-pulpit, cranefly orchid, and the rare lady's slipper orchid grow around these springs and in these bogs. They and the baygall are fringed with luxuriant ferns and mosses. This seepage, together with that from the large pointbar sand hummocks which the baygalls encircle, supplies the water which moves very slowly through the baygalls, and, reaching the lower terraces, coalesces into black-water creeks and then flows into the sloughs and river. In the case of Jack Gore Baygall, drainage flows around Indian Piney Woods hummock and, on the south end, flows into Little Black Creek and thence into Bear Man's Lake and the river. The upper portion drains into Franklin Lake and Black Creek, some into Black Creek Lake, some into John's Lake, and some into a swampy area between John's Lake and Bear Man's Bluff known as Devil's Pocket, thence to the river.

Another climate change caused the river to become smaller, so it abandoned the wide floodplain and began to cut a smaller one. These different floodplain levels are called terraces.

The topography of the lower terraces, the present, active floodplain of the river, has smaller meander scars, deeper abandoned channels, water-tolerant vegetation, and sloughs instead of baygalls, which are flooded frequently by the river. Basket oak, sweetgum, and blackgum are the dominant trees on the ridges while cypress and water tupelo are in the wet swales. Underbrush is sparse due to the closed canopy and frequent inundation and dominant species are deciduous yaupon and arrowwood viburnum.

On the slopes of the old bluff, and on the ridges of the terrace that Jack Gore Baygall occupies, are closed-canopy, parklike forests dominated by beech, southern magnolia, loblolly pine, and white oak. In the spring, dogwood and redbud understory trees and pink wild azalea shrubs create very beautiful and fragrant scenes in the forest, especially along the Old Wagon Road Trail, which follows the bluff line.

Many people are afraid to go into the baygall for various reasons, superstition being one of them. I had an English professor named Lily Kreisher at Lamar University with whom I became friends and who often went on excursions with me. Lily was deeply into metaphysics and the occult and she decided she didn't like Jack Gore Baygall, insisting she got "very bad vibes" there and could hear moaning and wailing, that it was a place of evil or unsettled spirits. On the other hand, she heard "astral music" in the Sternenberg Preserve and declared it to be inhabited by good spirits.

I did have a rather strange experience in Jack Gore Baygall once. I had gone with my dog Little Wolf, a tough, big chow-samoyed mix, to the baygall to botanize one day and, as usual, stopped at Ernest's barbershop to let him know where I was going and when I expected to return, so if I didn't show up by closing time, he would know where to start looking for me. My dog always made wide circles, exploring and periodically coming back to me. When I was ready to return, I was aware that Little Wolf had been gone some time. I sat on a stump and waited, then began to call. I heard him far off in the baygall, but his barks were unusual, more screams than barks. The sounds came nearer until he appeared, but seemed so completely disoriented and panic-stricken, that he rushed right by with me yelling and calling to him. I couldn't believe it! NOTHING frightened Little Wolf! I finally recovered him and calmed him down, and hurried to the vehicle so Ernest wouldn't be worried about me. It was almost time for him to close the shop. Rushing into the shop, I began an explanation for my delay, of my dog's hysterical behavior, and saying I just had to wait for him, that no way would I go out into the baygall looking for him. Then, I noticed sitting in the corner, a little old Negro woman. She said: "Honey, it's a good thing you didn't go in that baygall!" "Why?" I asked. "That baygall's hainted. That dog. He knowed!" "Why?" I asked again, my interest really piqued. Then Ernest went into several stories of hidden treasures, Spanish gold, and ghost stories—all supposedly true. I would say more about the presence of the little old Negro woman there, but that is a long story by itself.

Be that as it may, I spent a lot of time in that baygall later and was never carried off into nether worlds. Probably the only "evil spirits" there were the cottonmouth moccasins and they didn't bite me either, though given ample opportunity.

Ernest Spell showed the baygall to me the first time, taking me down the Old Wagon Road almost to Blue Spring in my Buick station wagon, and Gene Barrington took me to his favorite spot, which was a grove of huge beech trees on a large fern-fringed knoll partly surrounded by the baygall. If it were not for those two incidents, the Jack Gore/Neches Bottom Units and Neches River Corridor Units would never have been added to Big Thicket National Preserve. That was the beginning. Not that I had all that much power, but I knew a lot of people who did.

JACK GORE BAYGALL UNIT

River MileS 74.8–64.9

The north boundary of the Jack Gore Baygall Unit of Big Thicket National Preserve begins at the Hardin County Line. On the east side of the river, it extends eastward to include Sally Withers Lake, and to the west past Tater Patch Lake, then southward. As with all the units of the preserve, the boundaries are drawn along property lines, pipelines and roads, and not according to ecological or topographical principles. The proposed unit boundaries were delineated by environmentalists, chiefly Bill Hallmon of Dallas, who spent many long and at times dangerous hours walking the area, and talent and expertise in drawing the unit maps.

When the bill was passed creating the preserve, Tom Lubbert, the first superintendent, had limited time and practically no staff, so he used Hallmon's maps for the official maps, simplifying them as described above. More dam-

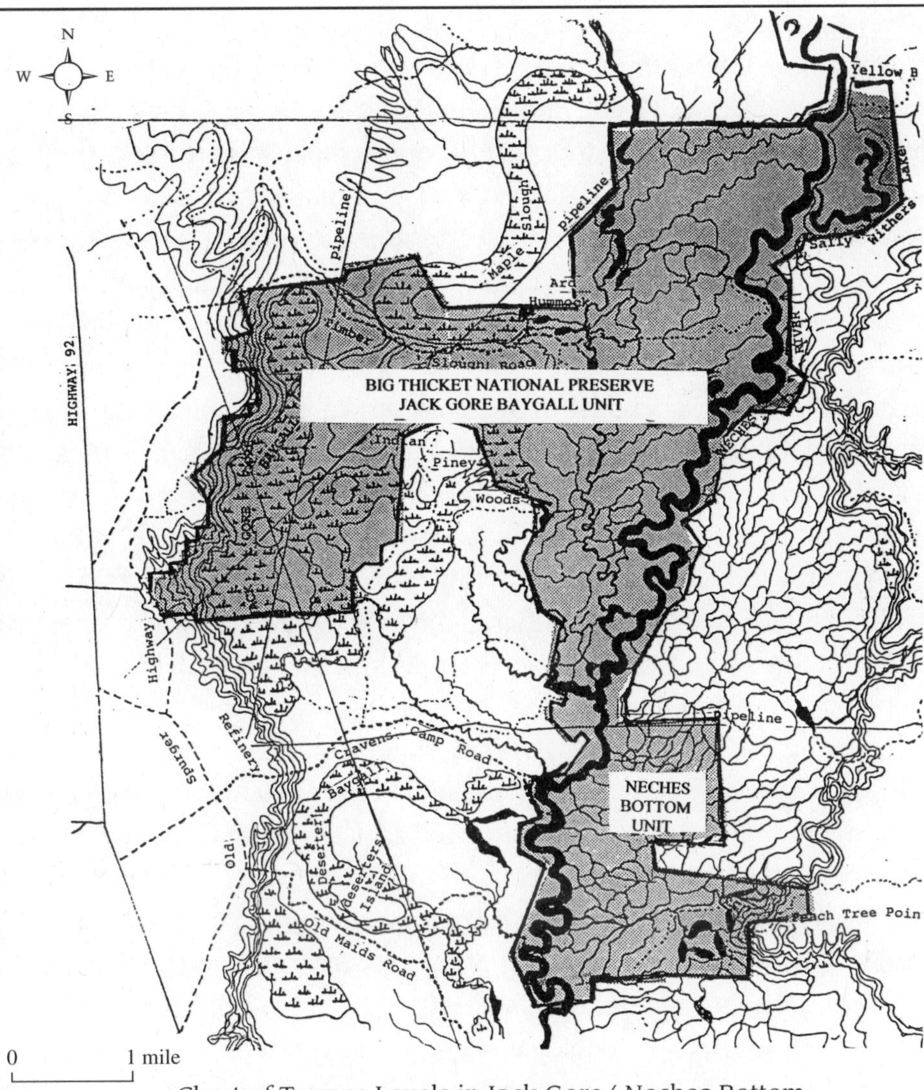

Chart of Terrace Levels in Jack Gore/ Neches Bottom

MAP No. 12

aging than the limited time were the limits imposed on the acreage. Many features important to the ecology of the unit were either excluded or cut in half. The large pointbar sand hummocks, Ard Hummock and Indian Piney Woods, from which the baygalls receive much seepage moisture, were excised, partly because few people recognized the value of the xeric plant communities found on them, but largely to cut acreage. Much of Jack Gore Baygall itself was excised, as was two-thirds of Maple Slough baygall. The western boundary included no upland at all and that is from which the springs at the base of the slope receive their moisture.

There is much to be said in criticism of these boundaries, but that will suffice to show that it is extremely important, if those attributes which made these units worthy of preservation are to be protected, that these boundaries be re-examined and adjusted according to topographic and ecological principles.

The Jack Gore Baygall and Neches Bottom Units are of great ecological significance as they exhibit an east/west cross section of the river and its floodplain terraces. There are several different terrace levels, each with its own vegetational structure. The baygalls are located on the oldest and highest terrace and occupy meander scars of the ancient Neches. Adjacent to the baygall and on the edge of the upper terrace are deep sand deposits laid by the ancient river when it flooded its banks and dropped its load at streamsides. These are called stream levee deposits. On these dry, sandy sites are many rare xeric, or desert, plants. These xeric sites are disappearing in the Jack Gore Baygall Unit because they were planted to pine plantations by the forest products industry before the National Park Service acquired the land. Detritus from the trees and shading, with fire suppression, allowed a more mesic community to become established and replace the former xeric plants on the site. It took the park service ten years to be convinced that fire management was essential to preserve the diversity of the Big Thicket. Then when resource manager Jim Woods and fire ranger Dave McHugh did develop a fire management plan, it was seriously hampered by a few misguided environmentalists and lack of money and personnel to carry it out. An environmental lawyer who had a personal bias against fire, threatened to take the Park Service to court to stop the burning, so Resource Management had to come up with a fire program that was "legally defensible," not necessarily "ecologically defensible." Meanwhile whole species and communities were disappearing.

The unit has an interesting history and since the descendents of the original settlers still live and recall the tales told by the old ones, its history is still alive. The Old Wagon Road that runs the entire western edge of the unit should be officially delineated, marked, and maintained as a historic trail before those who can give accurate information are gone. The excuse is "No money!"

NECHES BOTTOM UNIT

River Mile 60.9 to 64.9 4:13 P.M.

Just below John's Lake is a pipeline that marks the north boundary of the Neches Bottom Unit of the Big Thicket National Preserve. This point brought back many memories of the times I used it as an access point to take influential visitors into the Neches bottom so they would support its inclusion in the preserve. A short walk through these awesome forests was enough to convince anyone.

This forest is on the lowest terrace level of floodplain in a cross section from east upland to west upland and is frequently flooded—sometimes 10 or more feet. The terrace is laced with sloughs. Some of them, Sand Slough and Deep Slough, are major waterways which rival the river in size, depth, and current when water level is high; and some widen into deep, abandoned-channel lakes such as Clear, Boat, Buck, Lone Pine Ridge, Side-Pocket, Big Pine Hammock, and Pool Stave Camp Lakes. I have no idea how Side-Pocket Lake got its name but I do know that Pool Stave Camp Lake was named that because timber cutters who were harvesting basket oak to make barrel staves camped there while working the Neches bottom. The best white oaks of our Southeast Texas forests went to make barrels for the wine industry in France around and after the turn of the century. My great-grandfather, James Polk Lunsford-Wilson, worked in a stave mill as well as keeping up a farm.

This was probably one of the best-managed forests under forest products industry control. Temple Industry selectively harvested the best trees with long periods in between and the forest had recovered to the point that many declared it to be a "virgin" forest when promoting its preservation.

Deep sloughs are ringed with cypress trees while those that are relatively shallow are canopied cypress groves sometimes with a midcanopy of water ash and water elm, while water-tolerant oaks and gums inhabit the ridges. Dr. Charles Mohler, Cornell University scientist, spent a few years studying these forests and was amazed at the change in species composition only a foot or two elevation makes. Swamp post oak and overcup oak prefer swales which don't hold water continually, while on the ridges are sweetgum, blackgum, and basket oak. Where the overhead canopy has been opened by the removal of a giant tree, either by cutting or windthrow, deciduous yaupon and ironwood form thickets which gradually thin to form a midcanopy. These ridges are beautifully parklike, and shading the leaf-carpeted forest floor are widely spaced, thick-buttressed, broad-branched basket oaks with towering sweet gum, and water and willow oaks in between.

Rising and twisting high upward from the forest floor like the magic ropes of Hindu fakirs are giant muscadine and summer grapevines striving to reach the life-giving sunshine atop the canopy. It was always a mystery to me how they managed to reach these high branches with no visible aid until I found one with the dead remains of a slender sapling in its coils. The vine grew upward with the sapling and when the sapling reached the overhead canopy, the vine grasped hold of the nearest limb and, growing stronger, its coils choked the flow of nutrients and water from the sapling, thus eliminating it as competition by strangling it to death.

The best and easiest way to see the Neches Bottom Unit is, unfortunately, inaccessible to the public. On the east side of the river, a road exits from the Antioch Church Road, winds over what was once pine savannah, and drops abruptly into the bottom. The river had cut all the way across its floodplain into a high terrace and the bluff line is precipitous. A deep slough follows the bluff line closely and the view of cypress grove waters from the beech-magnolia bluff forest is superb. This promontory is called Peach Tree Point. An oil company developed an oilfield in the middle of the floodplain and, in order to reach its operations in all kinds of weather and keep its facilities above flood level, they undoubtedly expended an enormous amount of money, time, work, and dirt in building elevated roads and drilling pads and constructing sturdy bridges over the sloughs and cypress swamps. Some of the roads have been abandoned and fairly large trees have colonized them. These elevated roads and bridges make a marvelous hiking trail where one can view the floodplain forests and waters dryshod. It also provides great birdwatching as one has an eye-level view of the treetops. Hopefully, someday a more environmentally conscious government will acquire access to this area, for which our tax money has already paid, and it can be made available for us to enjoy. Ah well! I can dream, can't I?

The road from the upland splits at the Peach Tree Point bluff and, while one follows the elevated roads into the bottoms, the other goes to Boat Lake and follows the line of lakes and sloughs south-westward. This area brings back many memories to me, as my family used it as a base for many camping, hunting, and fishing outings as Daddy's family had done in his boyhood. Mother constructed a large, square enclosure of cheesecloth for protection from the swarms of mosquitoes which rose at dusk, and we all put our sleeping pads beneath it.

The Neches Bottom Unit evoked other memories—searches for the ivory-billed woodpecker, confrontations with hunting club wardens, of being lost, of following Daddy while he fished the lakes for bass. I didn't get out of the boat and explore the woods of the Neches Bottom Unit on this trip; I had done so many times in the past and, besides, I wanted to get below Bear Man's Bluff for my evening camp.

The current had picked up swiftly at John's Lake and the course was rather straight with few sandbars. It was obviously a new course, the old having abandoned the John's Lake and Bear Man's Lake courses in the past and, even more recently, the many abandoned channels in the Neches Bottom Unit. Where these broad lakes entered the river, the current formed giant whirlpools with large areas of dead water in the center. A knowledgeable person on his toes will follow the current close to the bluff and avoid being swept toward the center. I, of course, being tired, tried to cut through the shortest route, then had to paddle like the dickens to get out of the doldrums and fight the upstream sweep of current to get out. An exhausting business. I had no trouble getting to sleep that night.

THE LAST BEAR HUNT IN JACK GORE BAYGALL

River Mile 63.8 to 64.5

Between John's Lake and Bear Man's Lake is an area so dense and swampy that it is called Devil's Pocket. I know of several Devil's Pockets in the area: one between Highway 87 and the Sabine River east of Evadale and another a few miles north of Kountze on an extension of Road 420. It seems that any area so unpleasant that no one wants to go there gets that name. Anyway, the Devil's Pocket on the Neches was the scene of the last bear hunt in the Neches Bottom.

Stanley Gore, an elderly lifelong resident of the area told Jim Cosine, a historical researcher, about the last bear hunt in Jack Gore Baygall:

A bear caught a hog back by our fence there one evening about dark. We could hear that hog squealing. My father, Jack Gore, knowing the bear would come back to the dead hog, poisoned the carcass and left it there. A neighbor had some dogs and he told my father, "If you want to catch that bear, I believe my dogs will find him." So they used the dogs. One of his dogs was so afraid that if he should see an old black stump he would get behind him and his tail would just swell up, he was just that scared. They never did jump that bear. About two or three days later, we had a field back there of about 31 acres and we had some hogs in there. So the bear bit an old sow down in the back but he didn't kill her. So him and a feller named Kirkendall went into there but that bear had drifted down toward Bear Man's Bluff near Craven's Camp that used to be on the river. They jumped that bear and killed it, but he killed one dog. That bear just crushed that dog. That was the last bear that was killed here and that's been a long time ago.

Talk to the oldtimers and they will eventually get around to admitting that their ancestors came to Southeast Texas for one of two reasons (sometimes both): to escape the results of rash actions back East, and to pursue the bear.

As human populations increased, bear populations decreased and rapidly moved westward. Pioneers depended a great deal on the meat, oil, and skins of bears as well as on deer and wild hogs.

Bears were killed, not only to provide meat, oil, and hides for family use but to sell. Aboriginal man took from the environment only what he needed for that particular day. The white man took what he needed and everything else he could get his hands on to sell and thus acquire more possessions. As long as the bears lasted, bear meat was featured on the menus of many restaurants, hotels, and riverboat tables.

Bears are crepuscular. That is, they feed at dawn and at dusk and establish their range according to availability of food. The omnivorous black bear has quite a menu in the Neches bottom: grasses, forbs, and roots in the spring, fruits and berries in the summer months, hickory nuts and acorns and other mast in the autumn, and small animals, larvae, and insects from downed and rotting trees throughout the year. With the demise of the bear, wild hogs, once their favorite food, are making a strong comeback.

Biologists say there are no bears left in East Texas, but I have reason to believe otherwise. Along with the word of reliable witnesses, I know what I have seen with my own eyes. In the 1970s, a team of scientists and students from Cornell University were down here and we went into the woods near where Beech Creek enters Village Creek. We found a bear lying dead. It had apparently been shot by night hunters and had run off into the brush and died. Its carcass had not even become stiff, it was so recent. A mammalogist with us estimated the bear to be about two years old. The year before, a pulpwood cutter had told me about seeing a she bear with two cubs in the general area, so this could well have been one of the cubs. I went back later and collected the bones.

I. C. Eason claimed to have seen a she bear and cubs up around Joe's Lake and others occasionally report seeing them also. A man from Segno once called me and said that he was investigating a ruckus in his barnyard the night before, and rushing out with light and gun, saw a bear, which reared up on a tree and scratched it and disappeared into the woods. I didn't go and view the scratch marks, though earnestly invited to do so.

BEAR MAN'S BLUFF

River Mile 63.8 4:40 P.M.

After a straight stretch with no sandbars, the river becomes broad and placid at Bear Man's Lake. In fact, the lake itself is broader than the river. It is a remnant of the river when the stream was much larger than at present a few thousand years ago. The river moves westward in its meanderings, cutting into older, higher terraces and leaving the eastern side a broad, low, slough-laced bottomland. Because the cutbank side is above normal flood level at Bear Man's Lake, people have always lived here.

The Kirkpatrick family lived for some time at Bear Man's Bluff. George Pleasant Montgomery Kirkpatrick and William Riley Kirkpatrick, brothers, came there in 1859 from Alabama. William died in the Civil War and his widow, Violet Rebecca Williams Kirkpatrick, married the brother. Their son, Henry Walter, moved to Evadale in 1915 and lived in what was then a sumptuous house on a bluff overlooking the river. There is more about this family in the Evadale section.

The bluff has been called Bear Man's Bluff since Civil War times because local "conscientious objectors," "deserters," or what have you, whose hideout was in the nearby baygalls, would leave bear meat and hides at the steamboat landing on the bluff, and the riverboat captain would take them and leave such goods as coffee and gunpowder in their place. The men were never to be seen and would pick up their trade goods after the boat left. The riverboat people began to call the bluff Bear Man's Bluff.

Few people of the lower Neches had slaves and couldn't very well get into the spirit of the Civil War so they hid out until the war was over. The conscientious objectors of Bear Man's Bluff were probably the band led by Jesse Trull, which included the Tantons and Hares. I haven't been able to determine whether these men had been in the army and deserted, or had failed to show when drafted, but stories have been handed down how the army sent men into the bottoms to capture the band and were seen or heard from no more. The captain of these army forces began to harass Jesse's wife, Rebecca, who was pregnant at the time. She was at the spinning wheel when the soldiers grabbed her, tied her to the well rope by her thumbs (?) and hung her over the deep well, threatening to drown her in the well if she didn't tell them where Jesse was hiding. "Just let me drop, boys, you won't get anything out of me," was her reply. Obviously, they didn't carry out their threat, but when the incident was told to Jesse, he determined to pay the captain for the mistreatment of Rebecca. The army men were camped out on the edge of the baygall. Jesse and his men crept up on the encampment at night when the soldiers were gathered around the campfire and, taking aim at the captain from a long distance, Jesse said, "See where his suspenders cross? That's where I'll get him!" The captain was shot where indicated and killed.

There were loyal Confederates in the area, even among the kin of the deserters, and someone turned Jesse in and he and his men were captured. They were made to dig a trench and stand beside it and were shot into it. Jesse's brother, George, escaped and, later, Jesse's family went to the mass grave, dug the men up and buried them at Cunningham Cemetery. Rebecca later married a Kirkendall, then a Carroway, but her first child, a girl, was named Jesse Jane and practically everyone in Caney Head can trace their lineage back to Jesse Trull, a hero who fought for freedom. Jesse Jane first married a man named Bush who hired a handsome young half-Indian named James B. Eason. Jane and James fell in love, so the husband left and the two were married. They had four children: Christopher Columbus (Lum), Addie (Gore), Bertie (Denman), and Clerie (Spell). Jesse Jane died in 1947 and James B. died in 1958. Lum was the father of I. C., Deacon, Doc, Cat, Cecil, etc., and Clerie was the mother of Ernest, Floyd, and two sisters.

Rebecca's second husband was called Big Daddy Carroway. His mother, Patsy, had come from the East, no one knew exactly where, with her sons and a fine Tennessee walking horse, and went into business raising and trading horses. Many stories are told of her. She would go all the way to Beaumont on horseback to do business and take jugs of milk along so the motion of the horse's trotting would churn the milk into butter along the way. In Beaumont, she would sell the butter and buttermilk. Once, upon reaching Village Creek, she found the creek in a raging flood and the ford impassable. There was a man in a fine suit pacing up and down, wringing his hands, and saying: "I don't know what I'm going to do. I must be in Beaumont and this creek is impassable. I just don't know what to do!" Patsy said nothing, just got down off her horse, took off her petticoats and tied them behind the saddle, grabbed the horse's tail, gave him a whack and off they went, swimming across the swollen stream. She looked back and yelled: "I feel sorry for a man who don't know what to do!" Patsy's daughter-in-law Rebecca is remembered as Aunt Beck and Beckie Lake in the Jack Gore Baygall Unit is named for her.

The Carroways were successful and owned a big two-story house, a symbol of having made it in those days. Big Daddy was a legendary figure and feared, a powerful man who carried a whip with him everywhere he went. He had taken a half-Indian orphan boy named Moss "to raise," and was mean to him. One day, when the boy had reached his midteens, Big Daddy decided to chastise him with his whip. He cracked the long whip and wrapped the end around the boy's waist. The boy pulled his knife from his belt, stuck it between his teeth, and began to "climb" the whip. Before Moss reached the haft, Big Daddy dropped the whip and ran—the first and last time anyone had known him to do so. It was also the last time he whipped the Moss boy.

The Carroways are still a prosperous family in the area, though they switched from horse trading to car trading. Clifton Carroway had an automobile dealership in Silsbee when the energy crisis hit and everyone turned to small cars. He had had the foresight (or luck) to obtain the Toyota dealership, and got rich practically overnight. His success was due also to his wife, Rowena, a smart businesswoman, and the folksy T.V. commercials featuring his little daughter, Susan. Several Carroways have been prominent in Hardin County politics and served honorably in various offices.

I have been told that a son of Tom Carroway became one of Kirby's land men and assisted Kirby in taking over his neighbors' land, and that he, and others who were willing to swear in court to anything to Kirby's advantage, were "well taken care of." But then there was a lot of that in those days.

There are many descendants of those Carroways, Hares, Trulls, and Tantons still in the Jack Gore Baygall area. Some have continued the simple life of their ancestors while others have come up out of the bottoms and "made it big." Strangely, all these descendants remember the soldiers who harassed their ancestors as "Yankees" when actually, they were Confederates rounding up deserters or draft dodgers.

Part Two

Day 5

GORE LANDING

River Mile 61 9:48 A.M.

Just above Pearl River Bend was Gore Landing. I got out of the boat here and looked around, but found no evidence that it had once been an active and busy place. It was probably a summer port as the access road is across the multiple drainage pattern from Deserters Baygall and must have been a booger to traverse during wet weather.

Gore Landing Road follows hummocks through the bottom and joins the Old Maids Road near Gore Cemetery at the edge of the terrace. It then proceeds west along the ridge dividing Deserters Baygall from Round Pond Baygall to the Gore house on the Old Wagon Road where the terrace rises to the upland. The Old Maids Road was named for two sisters, Tina and Lisha Gore. Never having married, they lived in the family home after their parents died. I used to stop by and visit them—oh, it must have been in the late 1960s. They lived exactly as their forebears did and in the same house.

The Gore house was set back behind two big live oak trees and a hand-split rail fence, and several big mulberry trees grew along the fence row. There was a kitchen garden with the usual vegetables and several bushes of old-fashioned roses: big, white cabbage roses, pink moss roses, and others which have long since been replaced by hybrid varieties. I loved the oldtime roses. They had such a rich fragrance you could smell them all over the yard. I have had for about thirty years, with no spraying, pruning, or fertilizing, a rose bush that I grew from a cutting off a rose bush brought over from the East before the Civil War. It grows underneath my son David's window. Once, a tendril found its way through a tiny crack between the screen and window frame and, one day, he awoke to find a full-blown rose right over his head. How I wish I had taken cuttings from the Old Maids' bushes and thus perpetuated them!

The Old Maids' house was right out of the last century. A covered well at the end of the back porch permitted them to draw water without going out into the weather. A wood cookstove in the kitchen, a fireplace, and coal oil lamps provided heat and light. The house was plain but very neat and was furnished as country houses were a few years back. There was no parlor nor settees—just beds, a couple of tables, and a few chairs—just the necessities. The Gore sisters liked the old-fashioned way, wearing dresses down to their ankles and high-buttoned shoes. They chose to remain in the last century and let the world go by. Until shortly before they died, they had never ridden in a car, seen a doctor, nor listened to radio or watched television. I wonder if they lived in fear and dread of a world on the other side of that fence that had changed around them. Tina died in 1969 at the age of 84 and Lisha was taken to a nursing home in Silsbee where she died in 1972, also at the age of 84. What a culture shock! I wonder if she lived out her days wallowing in the luxury of bathtubs, indoor toilets, air conditioning, and served meals, and marveling at television showing her a world she never dreamed existed.

After they left, the house deteriorated rapidly, assisted by vandalism. The rough-sawn one-by-twelve-inch boards which covered the log walls lay on the ground half buried by leaf mould. I got permission from a family member and dug some of them up and took them home. After a good hosing and sanding, the beautiful rosy-gold of rose pine, an extinct species, shone and I made a Spanish chest, a cabinet, and hutch, and front doors for my house at Hyatt from them.

The rail fence is gone, as are the mulberry trees and a new modern brick house stands under the live oaks. What a giant cultural leap from the last family who lived on this site to the present one. Only one decade and it could well be centuries!

The Gore family is well represented in Southeast Texas by four main branches. In the 1850s, James (Jim) Gore and wife, Betsy, brother Calvin, and cousins Charles and Shadrack (Shad) left North Carolina and headed for Texas. Their inspiration was the same as most new Texans of the day: trying to keep a step ahead of the law. Not that Jim Gore was a criminal—the family was well regarded in the area. The story passed down in the family is this: In pioneer communities, entertainment and recreation were limited, so the young men would engage in horse racing, foot racing, fist fights, and Indian wrestling. A man named Boggs challenged Jim to a foot race. The practice was for the racers to join hands, start running, then break apart at the firing of a gun, thus insuring an even start. Instead of turning Jim's hand loose, Boggs jerked him down and won the race. Jim insisted on a rematch where they held a stick and dropped it to start the race and this time, Jim beat Boggs badly, whereupon Boggs jumped on him and a fist fight ensued. Boggs was a dirty fighter as well as racer and when he attempted to gouge Jim's eyes out, Jim pulled out Boggs' eyes.

Pioneer justice ran along the "eye for an eye, tooth for a tooth" line, so the sheriff told Jim: "Boggs is no good and nobody has any use for him. He deserved what he got, but his family is bent on getting even, so you had best head for other parts." Deeming this wise advice, Jim headed west. They went from North Carolina to Pike County, Georgia, where they stayed a year and made a crop. They moved on to Louisiana where they stayed two years and grew crops—probably for food to sustain them on their journey—then from there to Southeast Texas and the Neches River. Shad Gore built a cabin by a cutoff lake called today Shade Lake (named after him, but with an "e" added by the mapmaker) and Jim built his cabin by another a short distance southward which is now called Gore Lake. These lakes were on the edge of a terrace hummock where they built shelters. I have visited these sites with Jeanette Gore, wife of Marvis Gore, great, great-grandson of Jim, and it is truly a beautiful site with huge hardwood trees on the hummocks and cypresses rimming the clear waters of the lakes.

In 1858, Jim Gore moved to the uplands on the east side of Beech Creek near a place called the Thick and, believe me, today, it is still thick. He stayed there a year before building a nice house on the hill above Blue Springs on the Old Wagon Road. The well curb can still be seen there. The house was said to be a fine house with carpets on the floor. Jim Gore gave his children the choice of going to college or taking land to become farmers. There were some of both persuasions. His son, Andrew Jackson (Jack) Gore, for whom the Baygall was named, built a house near where the Old Wagon Road and the road to Town Bluff forked and where there was a fine spring of water. There is a large brick house there now.

When the Civil War came, local people were divided in their loyalties, and Jim Gore was one of those whose heart and soul wasn't set on dying for Old Dixie. Toward the end of the war, heavy casualties and desertions were depleting the Confederate Army. Most Southeast Texans served east of the Mississippi with Terry's Texas Rangers, which lost more than two-thirds of the company, including Terry himself.

The Confederate Congress passed a Conscription Act that called for men 17 to 50 years to join the army, but if a man owned a certain number of slaves or had enough money to pay a substitute, he was exempt. Desperate for cannon fodder, the Confederate Army sent "Jayhawkers" (one of the names given soldiers who routed out the deserters) to scour the woods for the men and Jim Gore was captured and taken to the prison on Galveston Island. There was no food and yellow fever was rampant, so Jim, along with Allen Blair and another area man, decided to come home. They escaped and swam across Galveston Bay to Bolivar Point. Apparently, Jim couldn't swim so they made a raft out of a door and Allen Blair pushed him across. It was a fearful night for a huge "fish" kept trying to upset the raft and Jim was almost dislodged and drowned. No doubt it was one of the playful porpoises that abound in the bay. It took them three days to walk home, during which they only had a small sack of corn meal to eat. Arriving home, they hid out on a high hummock in the river bottom which is still called Deserters Island No. 2.

I was always confused by the conflicting stories of the Civil War incidents in the Jack Gore Baygall area until I learned that there were two separate bands of men: Jesse Trull's group, who hid out on Deserters Island No. 1, and Jim Gore's band on Deserters Island No. 2. These are hummocks surrounded by baygall. I have been to both places and neither is a spot where I would want to try to roust out desperate men who had spent their lives in these bottomland swamps.

There were conscientious objectors here during World War I also. Son Gordon told me how when Thomas Ard died and Son and Thomas' brother Dennis were digging his grave, Dennis remarked that this was the second grave he had dug for his brother. The first was during the war when he dug a grave-like hole beneath the horse trough so Thomas could hide in it when the authorities came looking for him.

After the war, Jim Gore farmed, hunted, and fished. He took deer hides down the Old Wagon Road to Concord, a steamboat port on Pine Island Bayou, to trade for supplies. That was before riverboat traffic was common on the

Neches. He and his children lived a good life in the wilderness and prospered by their hard work, intelligence, and good character. They had large families and today the area is rather heavily populated with Gores. (There are 118 Gores in the phone directory.) Some of them advanced economically and culturally and left the area, some advanced and stayed, and some chose to live the old ways and still do. There is usually a Jack Gore in every family and the other family names are perpetuated. I noticed in the 1959 Hardin County tax rolls, a Charles Calvin Shade Gore was listed—apparently his parents didn't want to cheat any of the original pioneers of any honor.

It has been my pleasure to know many of the Gore family, especially Jeanette, who has a lively interest in the local history and ecology. To say that my heart always lifts when I hear her voice on the telephone says a lot—I abhor the telephone—but she always has something to say worth hearing.

One day, Jeanette called and asked if I would like to go to Gore Cemetery next day. I had expressed a desire to do so but it is now a posted area. We walked a few hundred yards from where we parked our car onto a terrace hummock overlooking Gore Lake. Apparently, this was the site where Jim Gore first lived. It is a beautiful spot and the cemetery is well kept though few were buried there after the people moved to the uplands.

People living in the wilderness buried their dead nearby, usually on high ground, and the site became the family cemetery. Than, after church buildings were built, cemeteries gradually surrounded them. There was a practical reason for burying the dead close to home and in haste. In our warm, humid climate, a body begins to deteriorate immediately after death and there were no morticians or embalming in those days. I can still remember the odor of death in a home where the deceased was "laid out" in a hastily constructed pine coffin in the front room. There were no flowers as there were no florist shops or money to pay for them.

There was always plenty to eat in the kitchen, for neighbors and friends brought enough food to sustain the family during the illness, death, and funeral. Several would stay with the family to sit up with the corpse its last night on earth. The next of kin met at the door those who came to pay their respects. After handshaking, hugging, and crying, the visitor was conducted to the casket to view the remains. If the visitor was a female and close to the family, she would shriek, cry, throw up her hands, and sometimes fall to the floor in a faint.Those standing near would catch her in midair, (which she probably was counting on) and there would be much rushing about, slapping her face, and applying cold cloths. When revived, the mourner was led into the kitchen where she was soon eating, drinking, laughing, and talking. Pete Farmer, whose family has been mortician to this area for generations, and I had a private chuckle over a lady who went to all the backwoods funerals and never failed to fall into a faint. She weighed about 350 pounds and, believe me, nobody caught her. They revived her where she lay.

Funeral services were held either at the local church or at the grave site. During the funeral service, between the prayers and the eulogy, sad songs were sung and the wailing and crying began in earnest. Hysterical grief reached a crescendo when the loved one was lowered into the grave; some mourners would try to throw themselves into the grave crying, "Take me with you! I just can't let you go!"

After the funeral, the family was accompanied home by friends who consoled them and polished off the remains of the food. Afterwards, everyone went about their lives as before, their grief fully and completely expressed.

When the Eason patriarch, Christopher Columbus (Lum) Eason died, I attended the funeral at the Wiley Mae Pentecostal Church near Jack Gore Baygall. There were literally hundreds of descendants there. As each of his grown children entered the building and saw the casket at the altar, they paused, wailed, and gave a lament, each according to his own experience with his father. One son eulogized his father thus: "Oh Daddy! You took me to the river and taught me to fish when I was just a little kid! Oh Daddy! I had to go away to war but I come home to you. Oh Daddy! We walked the woods together many a year." Etc., Etc. One son eulogized his father thus: "Oh Daddy! You took me to the river and taught me to fish when I was just a little kid! Oh Daddy! You taught me to hunt and let me use your gun. Oh Daddy!" One daughter was so overcome that she began wailing like a steam whistle and ran off into the woods. Lorine, I. C.'s wife, said laconically, "Somebody'd better go after her."

Those close to the deceased are expected to kick up quite a fuss. Most go to funerals for the "show," craning their necks and ogling at each outburst and would be disappointed if the mourners exercised restraint and self-control. After the services, the old ladies stand around and talk about how various family members "took it," whether or not "he left her well-fixed," and what they wanted to wear and what songs were to be sung, at their own funerals.

I attended another Eason funeral once. H. C., a son of Lum, died of a heart attack, leaving a wife and several children. Ned Fritz, the Dallas attorney, had become friends with the Eason boys and, since he was in the area, accompanied me. Coming from a Methodist-Eastern-Harvard background, he was quite agog over the emotionalism exhibited and, forgetting himself completely, stared open-mouthed at the beautiful, hand-tooled leather wallet clutched in the hands of the corpse. He whispered: "Is he, in effect, saying: 'Don't tell me I can't take it with me'?" The fact was that his little girl had made it as a surprise Christmas present and wanted him to have it.

I do not relate these things to cast aspersions on these people or suggest they show bad taste in the way they deal with death and the loss of those they love. Perhaps it is a far healthier custom than our modern way of following a formalized funeral ritual, orchestrated by an unctuous mortuary director, maintaining strict control (usually with the help of a strong tranquilizer), and trying to convince ourselves that death has no power over us.

No longer do friends come over to help wash and prepare the body, build the casket and dig a grave in the community burial ground. The hospital calls the funeral home immediately after a person dies, and the mortician does all the necessary chores, taking all the unpleasant reality of death away from us, usually for a mind-boggling price. Ah well! I'm not going to argue that point. People of all cultures feel that they must do what they must do, particularly since they can do absolutely nothing about the real cause of their grief: the inescapable fact that we all are going to die, like it or not.

In a local cemetery, there is a large tombstone with the name "Tom Cravey" inscribed. A small tombstone beside it says: "Tom Cravey's arm." It seems Tom Cravey lost his arm some years before the rest of him died and he gave it a decent burial.

RIVERBOATS

River Mile 60.9

After Bear Man's Bluff, which was easy to recognize both on site and on the topographic map, I counted bends with care because I wanted to be certain of my location when I came to Pearl River Bend. I reached it midafternoon. This was where the steamboat, the *Pearl River*, was wrecked. It was one of the larger boats, carried 1200 bales of cotton, and was piloted by Capt. William D. Loving.

Accidents were common. The river had many sharp bends, the current would shift sunken trees so that snags might be just under the surface of the

The Laura

water today where there were none yesterday, and sandbars would shift with each rise of the river. The pilots took advantage of high water so they could navigate far upstream and over shoals, but the currents in flood were swift and a moment's inattention might sweep the vessel into danger. In the early days, riverboats were the only means of getting produce to market or supplies from outside. Travel by land was just too long and too hazardous. One might be stuck in the mud one moment and stuck in the sand the next. Then there were the many streams, swamps, and baygalls to cross. The advent of the riverboat raised to a high level the standard of living of the folks in the Neches valley. A steamboat was too valuable to just abandon if it were sunk or grounded on a bar, so two maintenance barges named *Rab* and *Nab* patrolled the river to raise and repair wrecked boats.

Each steamboat had a distinctive whistle which could be recognized and there was a "language" of the river. If a boat were in trouble, it gave three blasts on the whistle. If another steamer were in hearing distance, it answered with a blast. Each blew once alternately until rescue was effected.

This same system was used to locate someone overdue from hunting or fishing. Everyone carried a horn made of a cow's horn. To locate a lost person, one long blast was given followed by two which asked for an answer. If the lost person heard, he answered once and they alternately blew once each until the person had followed the sound out of the woods. If the person were injured or in trouble, he blew three blasts which meant, "I need help." People who lived on widely spaced farms kept in touch with one another by the use of these horns. Each morning, the farmer went out on the porch and gave a long blast on his horn. His neighbor, several miles away, too far to hear a holler, gave an answering blast and so on down the line. If someone failed to answer, his neighbor went to see what the problem was. Housewives also blew the horn to signal the husband, working in a far field, that dinner was on the table.

The first crafts to carry cargo down the Neches were rafts and flatboats. They were made of logs or rough lumber, put together by pegs and ropes and steered with poles and a long hand-held rudder. A tent in the middle housed the cook and had sleeping space for the crew. They were borne downstream by the current, and, of course, couldn't go back upstream, so they were dismantled and sold for the lumber, which was in great demand in Sabine Pass, surrounded as it was by coastal marsh and prairie. The crew came back either by horseback or walked.

Flatboat crews had a reputation for being rough and rowdy. After a month or more on the Neches, they went wild when they hit the saloons and bordellos of Sabine Pass and Galveston. They were not known to be dependable and only made a trip when the money was all spent from the last trip.

One of the more responsible river men, Andrew Smythe, saw that much profit could be made from bringing goods up the river to the backwoodsmen, so he designed and built a keelboat. Its home port was Bevilport and it was named the *Jasper*. Keelboats have been described as compact Noah's Arks. With an oval shape and pointed bow, the keel cut the water and the boat was much faster and more maneuverable than the flatboat. It was also a bit more convenient as it had a rude cabin and a hold where merchandise could be kept out of the weather. One keelboat was described as being 110 feet long, 24 feet wide, and could carry 600 bales of cotton in three feet of water. Another advantage was that they required no machinery and no fuel. The keelboat depended on the current for power which was fine going downstream. Going back was a different matter. Four or five men walked along the banks pulling the boat by long ropes. When conditions prevented this, poles were used to push their way upstream. This was grueling work but folks in those days were used to hard work. They made the best of it with a sense of humor, singing, prank-playing, and yelling banter (usually of a lewd nature) at passing boats and people. When keelboats met, they tied up at the bank, built a big campfire ashore, had a feast, and spent the night laughing, telling tall tales, and singing.

Around 1860, Governor Sam Houston initiated a river improvement project which included the Neches and Angelina. Dredging of sandbars, widening at sharp turns, pulling out snags and fallen trees—all done by slaves and teams of mules. When loggers began to float large log rafts down river, occasional pileups at sharp bends would create log jams which were a barrier to river navigation. These were broken up either by pulling out key logs or by blasting them out with dynamite. With the river thus improved, steamboats began to ply the Neches and the Angelina. Captain Weiss took a 400-bale boat up the Angelina as far as Platonia in Nacogdoches County, and the steamer, *J. J. Warren*, 1400 bales, went up the Angelina to Townsend's Bluff in south San Augustine County. Travel up the Neches to Fort Teran was common in times of high water.

The better-known steamboats with their cotton bale capacity were as follows:

Angelina – 350	*Pearl Plant* – 450	*Mary Falvey* – 450
Sunflower – 600	*Dr. Massie* – 400	*Grand Bay* – 600
Era No. 8 – 650	*Flora* – 300	*Florida* – 2500
Uncle Ben – 900	*J. H. Bell* – 1200	*J. J. Warren* – 1400
Emma O – 200	*J. L. Graham* – 400	*Cora* – 900
Tom Parker – 200	*L. C. Lamar* – 1400	*Pearl River* – 1200
Adriance – 200	*Stonewall* – 600	*T. J. Emery* – 300
T. J. Smith – 3,550	*Sabine* – 450	*J. L. Webb* – 450
Roebuck	*Camorgo* – 350	*Tub Kate* – 75
Pelican State – 150	*Orleans* – 600	*Early Bird* – 800
Rough & Ready – 500	*Juanita* – 400	*Laura* – 600

Neches Belle – 1000
Toby Hurst - number unknown
Hooker – number unknown
The Bertha – number unknown
Bush Kirk -number unknown
Charles Lee - number unknown
Perch, *Vicksburg*, and *Dixie Queen* – numbers unknown

Well-known captains were :

Simon Weiss	George Jolly	A. H. Granger
George Harper	Ben Granger	W. E. Rogers
W. A. Fletcher	William Weiss	Napoleon Weiss
James Dalton	Tom Pickle	Benjamin F. Granger
E. I. Kelley	Cave Johnson	Press Work
Allen Nieland	Sherwood Perch	Aaron Sheffers
Mr. Moore	Mr. Postervan	Mr. Crask
Mr. Burr	Mr. Burley	

Benjamen Granger was the last man issued a river pilot's license in 1916.

The most important landings from Beaumont to Bevilport were:

Tevis Bluff at Beaumont	Pearl River Landing
Work's Bluff	Concord on Pine Island Bayou
Gore Landing	George Smythe's landing
Weiss Bluff	Bear Man's Bluff (once West's Bluff)
Ford's Bluff at Evadale	Yellow Bluff (Withers Landing)
McQueen's Landing below Town Bluff	

(The above information was taken from William Seale's *Texas Riverman* as well as other sources.)

There were landings on practically every bluff that was above flood level. There were ferries at most of these sites as, being on high ground, they were points of access from upland to river and to and from communities on both sides of the river. Those who did not have their own landings, took their produce to the most accessible ones where cotton and perishables were kept in warehouses until the steamboat arrived. Orders were left for goods to be purchased in Sabine Pass or Galveston and brought back upriver, for a fee, of course. Some of the landings also had stores where they kept a stock of goods most needed by the backwoodsmen: wheat flour, coffee, sugar, tea, calico and unbleached domestic cloth, needles, shoes, iron tools, and utensils. Produce taken downriver to Beaumont and Sabine Pass to be sold there or loaded on ships bound for New Orleans or Europe included cotton, shingles, staves, lumber, hides, wool, pelts, horns, mules, beef cattle, leather, deer skins, potatoes, beans, tobacco, bear skins, rice, tallow, Sour Lake water, otter pelts, salt, and tools. Not many people are aware that there are salt deposits on Pine Island Bayou and the Upper Neches which have been utilized by both Indian and white man.

The mansions erected by the wealthy merchants and entrepreneurs at Galveston were built from East Texas virgin heart yellow pine (longleaf) and cypress, while the beautiful paneling and cabinetry were made of walnut, cherry, curly pine, and cedar. East Texas still had a wealth of natural resources and rich productive farmland while the rest of the world had just about depleted all else, and farmland was worn out by overuse and abuse. Cotton and tobacco had drained the lifeblood from Eastern soils by this time, so there was much wealth to be reaped from the East Texas forests but only if it could reach markets. The steamboats on the Neches saw that it did.

The riverboats facilitated the movement not only of commerce, but also of people. Trips to back home in the East were arduous and took a year overland, but perhaps only a month by boat and in, for that day, pure luxury. The steamboats had accommodations for passengers, and some were quite elegant. Captain Smythe's *Laura*, which he purchased in 1872, was 115 feet long, 32 feet broad, had two deck levels, and was painted a sparkling white. On the upper deck were ten passenger cabins and a lavishly appointed saloon with a bar, mahogany sideboard, grand piano, sofas and chairs, pictures, and mirrors. The diningroom served an abundance and variety of foods such as venison, bear meat, turkey, chicken, fish, beef, pork, and all the accompaniments. The bar dispensed whiskey to the men and wine and brandied cherries to the ladies. Travelers dressed in their Sunday best on these trips and a party atmosphere prevailed. During the long trip, some of the men amused themselves with card games and whiskey drinking, but Captain Smythe saw to it that proper decorum was observed.

The cost of passage varied with the type of accommodation provided. A small but well-appointed stateroom aboard the *Laura* cost $15 for the 18- to 22-day voyage from Bevilport to Sabine Pass. Or one could sleep on the cotton bales on deck for a mere $6 to $8. Meals were about one dollar a day extra.

The *Laura* carried 600 bales of cotton, 1700 barrels, and several hundred boxes of merchandise. She was speared by a log once and sank right along about this site where the *Pearl River* went down. She summoned help with her whistle and a man on horseback rode to Yellow Bluff where the Withers family had a ferry and warehouse. The ferry was cut loose and brought down river and what could be salvaged of the *Laura*'s cargo was placed upon the ferry. She was pulled and poled to Yellow Bluff where the goods were stored in the Withers' warehouse. *Rab* and *Nab* raised the *Laura* and repaired her. By the way, the *Laura* was the first boat to navigate Buffalo Bayou to Houston, proving it to be navigable.

Another fancy steamboat was the *Neches Belle*. It was known for its deep-throated, mournful whistle, which could be heard for ten miles. It was a thousand-bale boat, had a grand saloon with a band, and was famous for its dining.

There were men, the riverboat gamblers, who rode the steamboats in order to take advantage of people who had time on their hands and nothing to do with it. My Daddy's Aunt Annie Scott married one. She said she was enthralled by his satin vest and gold watch chain. Uncle Joe Lizenby still cut a dashing figure as I remember him—tall, slim, and handsome with wavy, silver-gray hair. After the demise of the riverboats, he and his family sort of lived off the land and off their wits. He was a fine fiddler and the boys picked guitars and sang. They traveled about in a Model T touring car like gypsies, buying gadgets in the towns and trading them for hams, syrup, bacon, eggs, etc., which they would then sell in town. They also played music for parties and dances. The Lizenbys camped out wherever they happened to be, but spent quite a bit of time sponging off relatives. They always descended upon us like a plague of locusts after the crops were laid by and the vegetables ready to eat. We would see the overloaded Model T coming down the lane and Daddy would say with joy, "Here come the Lizenbys!" Mother would say, "Oh God! Here come the Lizenbys!" We children would dance around and shout as it always meant a break in the routine of summer vacation when they came. Word would get out that the Lizenbys were at our place and all the people around would come over that night. Furniture was moved, corn meal sprinkled over the bare wood floor, the Lizenbys would play and everybody would dance to all the old favorite tunes: "Under the Double Eagle," "Ragtime Annie," "Wednesday Night Waltz," "Red Wing," "Listen to the Mockingbird," "Orangeblossom Special," "Over the Waves," and, of course, the fiddle breakdowns like "Devil's Dream" or "Tennessee Wagoneer." The people would waltz, one-step, or just do the backwoods stomp if they didn't know how to do anything else. The Lizenby family spent a lot of their time camped out on the Neches or Sabine Rivers. Of Uncle Joe and Aunt Annie's children, the girls married well and turned out to be quite fine people. One of the boys, Howard was a small-time con artist until he got too old and he spent the last days of his life as a river rat on the Sabine. The other, J. R., a handsome young man with a fine voice and a simple mind, just had to steal. He stayed in the penitentiary most of the time. We got our first battery-powered radio so we could listen to cousin J. R. play and sing with the Huntsville Prison Band.

But, I digress. Uncle Joe was one example of many types of people who lived in, around, and off the riverboats.

The increasing movement of large log rafts downriver made riverboating dangerous and, with the coming of the railroads and improvement of roads, the riverboat era came to an end. Ferries were replaced by bridges. I remember when the first bridge on the Neches was being built at Evadale. It was finished around 1931 and so were the riverboats. They were beginning to get old and in poor repair anyway. If any sank, they were just left there. The *Laura* spent her last days tied up at the end of Pearl Street in Beaumont and finally sank there. The *Pearl River* went down near Gore Landing, the *Dixie Queen* sank near McQueen's Landing just below Town Bluff, and the *Neches Belle* went down at Logansport on the Sabine. There are probably more of them just below the surface of the river all up and down it, but many of them were tied up just north of Beaumont and left to rot. They can be seen now with their hulls all in a row when the tide goes out.

The last riverboat made it to Fort Teran on the Neches in 1925. I don't know its name. The people of the community threw a big party for the crew since it would be the last. The crew got drunk and didn't get back to the boat that night. When they finally did, the river had gone down and they couldn't get the boat over the shoals. It stayed there quite a while before the next rise in the river permitted it to leave.

PEARL RIVER BEND

River Mile 60.6

As I approached Pearl River Bend where that boat wrecked, I wondered, "Was the boat going downstream and the swift current swept it into these cruel snags just as it is trying to do to me?" Fortunately, my little boat was easier to maneuver than a steamboat and I avoided them. I thought, "How deep under the sand beneath me are the remains of the ship, or has the river shifted its course far from the site where it went down?" This bend has an unusual number of snags and half-buried logs and trees thrusting out of the water, and I was too busy dodging them to ponder further when I noticed one of

Pearl River remains

them was especially large and was jutting from the mud of the pointbar side four or five feet above water—and it was square! In between snags, I got a glimpse of the chiseled insets which showed it had been joined at right angles to another of its size! I fought the current with renewed strength to get to land before being swept past the bar and I made it! This was part of the frame of the *Pearl River*! About eighteen inches square and hewn from heart longleaf pine, it was still hard and had a strong pine odor when scratched. The rest of it, which scavengers hadn't salvaged, was buried beneath this mud. All the cypress planks and everything else useful, were stripped from these wrecked riverboats by the owner or the river people.

It would be difficult for anyone to understand the thrill and excitement I felt at discovering this relic, but I had heard and read of the *Pearl River*, its history and its captains and cargoes all my life and here it was! Just another snag a bit larger than usual sticking up out of the mud—but, Oh! What it portends!

The hands that made these hewed marks have long ago gone to dust, but their work is here for me to see. How could something so ponderous have been shaped and handled with muscle and primitive tools!

Then let the sounds of measured stroke
And grating saw begin;
The broad-axe to the gnarled oak,
The mallet to the pin!
Whittier "The Ship Builders"

Even the name of the owner who made great profits by its trips on the river, and the captain, who commanded such admiration and respect, are scarcely remembered if at all. The profits and honors vanished but the work of the laborer's hands is still here to speak of his skills and strength.

But enough! This stretch of the river where the *Pearl River* went down between John's Lake and Evadale commanded all my attention. It is a real booger! My little boat went through there like a speeding bullet, or rather like running a gauntlet. There was scarcely time to grab a pencil and log my time, and I don't know what kept my paddle from breaking—it sure bent a few times. The stream is very swift and fairly narrow along this stretch and, where a tree on the cutbank side is undercut and falls across the river, it nearly spans the width of it. Sometimes, it lies at water level and all floating debris catches on it and forms rafts. Usually, the water is deep enough that only the limbs protrude from the water surface. The sand in the current abrades the soft wood from the twigs and limbs until all that's left are hard, sharp fangs. This stretch of the river must have kept the snag-clearing crews and *Rab* and *Nab* pretty busy.

GOAT NECK BEND AND ALMOND HOLE

River Mile 56 to 59.8 11:00 A.M.

After Pearl River Bend, the river begins to make twists and turns that are confusing to a compass. Part of the time, the current runs north, as at Goat Neck Bend. The configuration of this stretch of river is in the shape of a goat's head, at least it appeared so to the river people who named it.

Downstream from Goat Neck Bend at about river mile 58 is a cutoff lake called Almond Hole, another descriptive term, for the lake is indeed shaped like an almond. I decided to take a look at Almond Hole so I pulled my boat upon the narrow bar and got out. There was a low berm separating the lake from the main channel and, as I made my way through the brushy fringe of willows and water elm at the crest of the berm, I heard the gabble of water fowl. Proceeding cautiously, I peered through the vegetation and saw a great number of mallard and wood ducks happily disporting themselves. Never one to leave well enough alone, I had to get closer, hoping for photographs, but my presence was detected and there was a flurry of fluttering and wild cries as they rose en masse and fled the scene.

There is no visible evidence here of the activities which once made the stretch of river between river mile 56 and 57 an interesting place. On the west side of the river is a cutoff called Round Lake and a ridge where Jim Gore and his band waited out the Civil War. Across the river on the east side is the mouth of Bean's Float Road. This route of deep water sloughs was once the bed of the river but it was, as were all the other sloughs of the bottomlands, abandoned as the stream cut westward into the alluvium of the old terrace. During the dry summer months, loggers cut a wide swath along this slough so that there would be no obstructions when log rafts were floated out during high water.

RABBITS

River mile 56.1

At river mile 56.1, a wide pipeline crosses the river. While all these pipelines certainly disturb and interrupt the continuity of the forest, the full sunlight allows lush grass to grow and so the pipelines are a banquet table for rodents and rabbits and also for the carnivorous predators on these small herbivores. Hawks prey on the mice which eat grass and weed seeds any time of the day, and in the cool of the evening, snakes crawl out from the shade of the forests and join the hawks in controlling the mouse population. Rabbits choose the evening hours to graze and are seized by owls, foxes, and the snakes. This doesn't seem to have too deleterious an effect on the rabbit population, however, for one can drive down a pipeline any evening and see a great number of them. Rabbit hunting after dark with a spotlight is not only great sport but one or two will furnish a great meal for a family, but that is probably illegal.

While the smaller cottontail is more common in the uplands, the large swamp rabbit inhabits the floodplains. This rabbit breeds year round and builds its nest on top of the ground, generally in the midst of a clump of dead grass and weeds which the rabbits pull around an inner cavity filled with fur. Rabbits practice an eating ritual called "copraphagy" (eating of excrement). This sounds repugnant to us, but makes sense to a rabbit. Two types of pellets are excreted: hard, brown fecal pellets and soft, green food pellets. The hard pellets are 60 percent nutrients and the soft pellets, which are eaten as they are excreted, contain vitamin B supplements. It seems nothing is wasted in nature.

Rabbits establish a hierarchy, much like that depicted in Richard Adams' *Watership Down*, to prevent young or weak males from mating with the females. One would never suspect that a story about a bunch of bunnies could be exciting, but *Watership Down* is a most interesting adventure story.

If someone should follow the pipeline at river mile 56.1 westward about a half mile, he would come upon Cow Marsh, a very broad, shallow, abandoned-channel lake which is in an emergent vegetation stage called a grass lake. It has many aquatic species typical of coastal marshes and not normally found in flat-woods ponds, baygalls, or sloughs. This makes me wonder if this area could have been a more recent embayment of the Gulf and its influence is still viable.

The first time I visited Cow Marsh was when I was working as a botanist with a group including NASA, the National Park service, and Rockwell International, planning a system of vegetation mapping by satellite. Topographical features which could be seen from miles above were located on topographic maps, investigated on the ground, and then numbers and descriptions fed into a computer, and Cow Marsh had been selected as one of the sites. We approached the marsh from the landward side, leaving Highway 96 at Lillard along a branch of what was once the Old Wagon Road and, turning eastward on the pipeline, a raised road crossed the marsh. Since it was made so easy for me, I headed toward the river and discovered the high hummock which turned out to be Deserters Island No. 2.

I remember Cow Marsh with a chuckle. Dr. William Cibula, who headed the expedition, and I were wading knee deep between clumps of sedges when he discovered he had lost the lens cap from his camera. He noticed something dark and round in the middle of a clump of sedge and, being extremely nearsighted, he lowered his face a foot or so from the object and peered into the open mouth of a tightly-coiled cottonmouth moccasin. Talk about levitating! The lens cap search was abandoned as his concentration was transferred to watching for cottonmouths.

EVADALE BRIDGE

River Mile 54 12:30 P.M.

With the Highway 96 bridge in view, I approached a slight bend in the river where there was once a large sandbar. I couldn't help but smile to myself at the recollection of the time I was hostess to United States Secretary of the Interior Walter Hickle. The Big Thicket was being considered for inclusion in the National Park System and the secretary came down to take a look at it, and, incidentally, to drum up votes for his fellow Republican, Richard Nixon, for the presidency. We didn't care about the blatant politics so long as we could impress him with the Thicket's qualifications for National Park status.

In order to show him as many areas as possible, a helicopter was used to transport the cabinet member from point to point. Ned Fritz and I were to meet his helicopter on the sandbar, along with the news media and all or any who might wish to rub shoulders with him. To reach the sandbar from Highway 96, one had to wade across the narrow, shallow mouth of a slough, so a county sheriff's deputy and I brought two large boards to span the gap so the fastidious could view the great man dryshod.

Along with the local law, there were federal law enforcement people and secret servicemen in their traditional trench coats to protect the secretary from the crowds. Actually, none of the river people knew or cared who Hickle was, let alone would they allow the occasion to interfere with really important stuff, like getting their trotlines baited and set for the night runs. A small contingent from the Hardin County Republican Party came and, swallowing their pride, asked me, a Democrat with "dangerous" liberal tendencies, to present them to Secretary Hickle, which I did, of course, with grace.

Ned Fritz gave the already nervous secret service men near heart attacks when he led the secretary off into the river bottom to view the lady's tresses orchids in bloom. The event was concluded without serious consequence, though I had had some anxious moments a few days previous. At that time, I had a lovely blue Buick station wagon with a sky-view roof, so I was to pick up the secretary when his helicopter landed at Howard Barrington's farm near the Sternenberg Preserve (now part of the Turkey Creek Unit) and drive him to the Preserve where we would walk the trail and discuss its merits. I made the mistake of leaving the car window open one night and one of the neighbor's cats (of which she had 38) crawled in and liberally left his territorial marks on the carpet. If there is anything that stinks worse than tomcat urine, I've been spared it, and I tried everything under the sun to remove the odor before chauffeuring the secretary. I was successful but don't remember what turned the trick.

Another helicopter trip that visited this sandbar did not turn out quite so successfully, however. Senator Ralph Yarborough, who had introduced a bill in the Senate calling for the creation of a 100,000-acre preserve, arranged for a National Guard helicopter to take several dignitaries, including the regional director of the National Park Service, and some news media people over the Thicket. It was to be strictly a "view-by-air" trip, following the Neches River and over to Village Creek, continuing on to the Indian Reservation in Polk County. To be certain the affair would go well, we did a dry run the previous day and everything went without a hitch. We all loaded into the huge troop-carrier type of helicopter with the whole side open. To start with, a big, fat news photographer appropriated the seat by the door and blocked everyone's view. I surprised even myself by shoving him out and saying: "That is the Senator's seat!" The Park Service regional director took a seat in the rear of the helicopter where he leaned back and went to sleep for the whole trip, for which I heartily despised him 'til the day he retired.

Anyway, when we became airborne, the pilot took an entirely different route from the one we had planned and executed the previous day, flying over the most populated and industrialized areas. When Senator Yarborough protested, finally reaching the pilot via an intercom system (the machine made such a roar, we couldn't hear anyone speak) the pilot claimed that the gyroscope had malfunctioned and he had to follow known land marks to avoid becoming lost.

A short time afterwards, there was a newspaper story regarding a National Guard general who was investigated, tried, and convicted of using National Guard aircraft to convey a party of timber company executives (our arch foes) and the general to a swank company lodge in South Texas for a hunting party. It apparently was a payoff for the general arranging to get us "lost" over the Big Thicket. Perhaps it was just a case of divine retribution or the fact that sooner or later everybody gets what he deserves.

I was still a few hours from Evadale when a nice thing happened. A monarch butterfly joined me for the rest of the trip. It would ride on the prow for awhile, then flit up and rest on my hand which held the top of the paddle and ride up and down with the movement. Sometimes on my shoulder, sometimes on my head, but it stayed with me the rest of the way. How often I have longed, "Oh, if I could only share the river with Daddy just one more time!" Since the butterfly represents the soul in myth and legend, dare I hope. . .? Naah! It was just a late straggler resting a bit before taking that long flight to Mexico.

Well, I made it to Evadale about a half day ahead of schedule. Actually, I thought it would take a couple of days to make this last stretch between Clark's Camp and Evadale, but wasn't counting on this sudden burst of speed. I radioed to Park Service Headquarters and had them call Regina to come pick me up, which she did. Aside from a slightly numb rear end and knees a little cramped from being bent so long, I was in great shape and ready to finish the last lap, so—a hot bath, a big salad, and several ice-cold coca colas, a night's sleep, and launch off again for Beaumont.

PART THREE

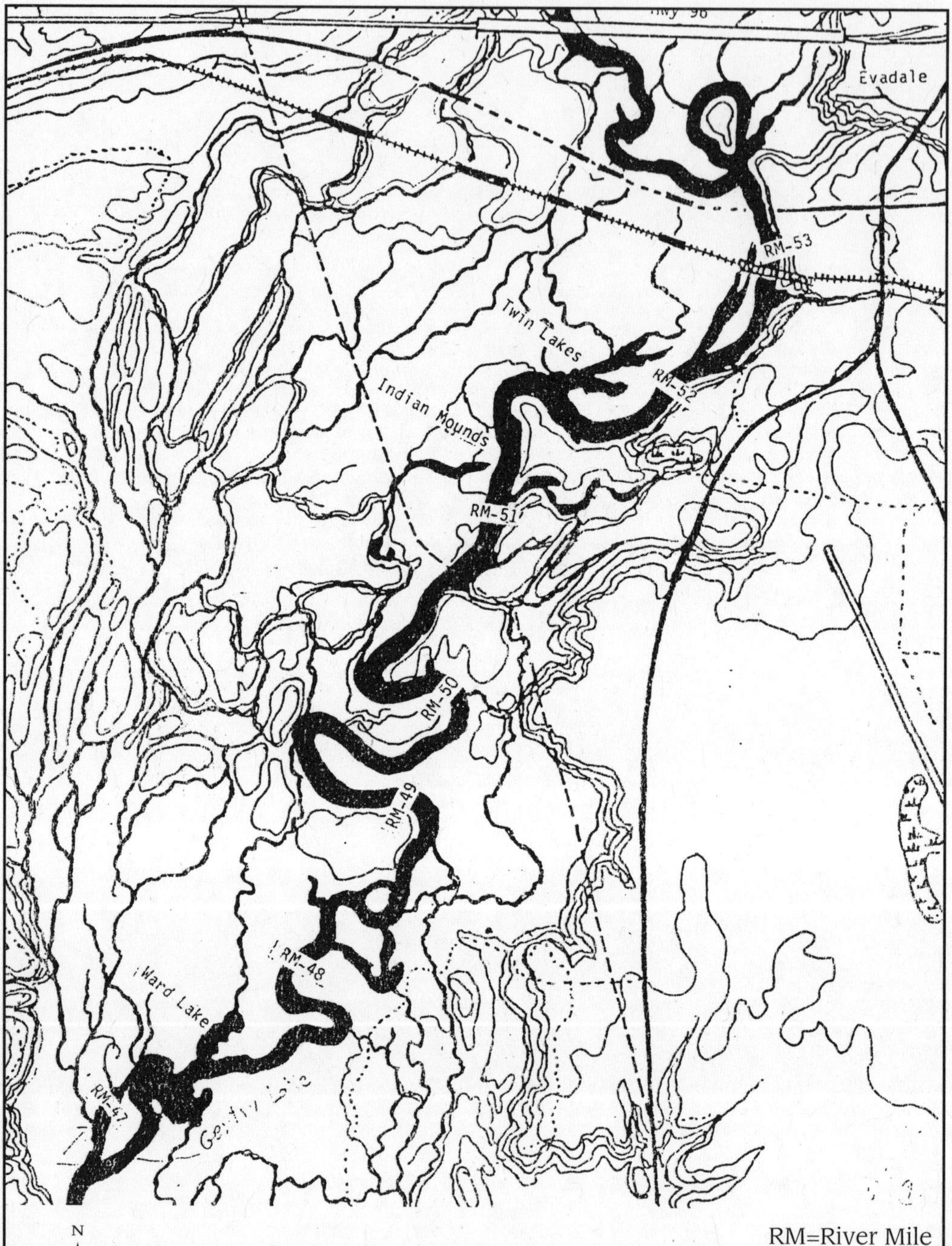
Evadale
RM-53
Twin Lakes
RM-52
Indian Mounds
RM-51
RM-50
RM-49
RM-48
Ward Lake
RM-47
RM=River Mile
N
W
E
S
0
½
1 mile
MAP No. 13

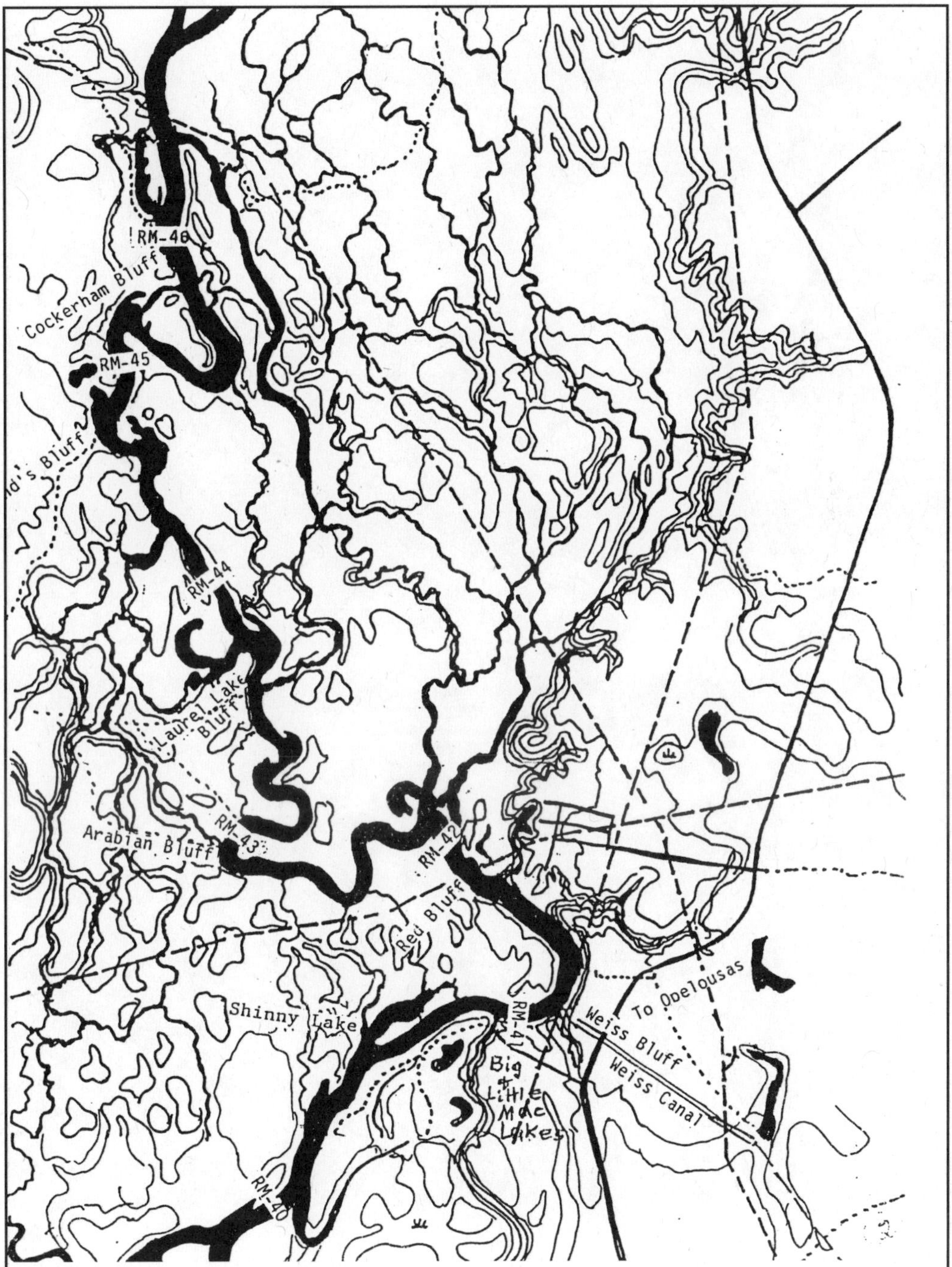

RM-46
Cockerham Bluff
RM-45
RM-44
Laurel Lake Bluff
Arabian Bluff
RM-43
RM-42
Red Bluff
Shinny Lake
RM-41
Big & Little Mac Lakes
To Opelousas
Weiss Bluff
Weiss Canal
RM-40
N
W
E
S
0
½
1 mile

MAP No. 14

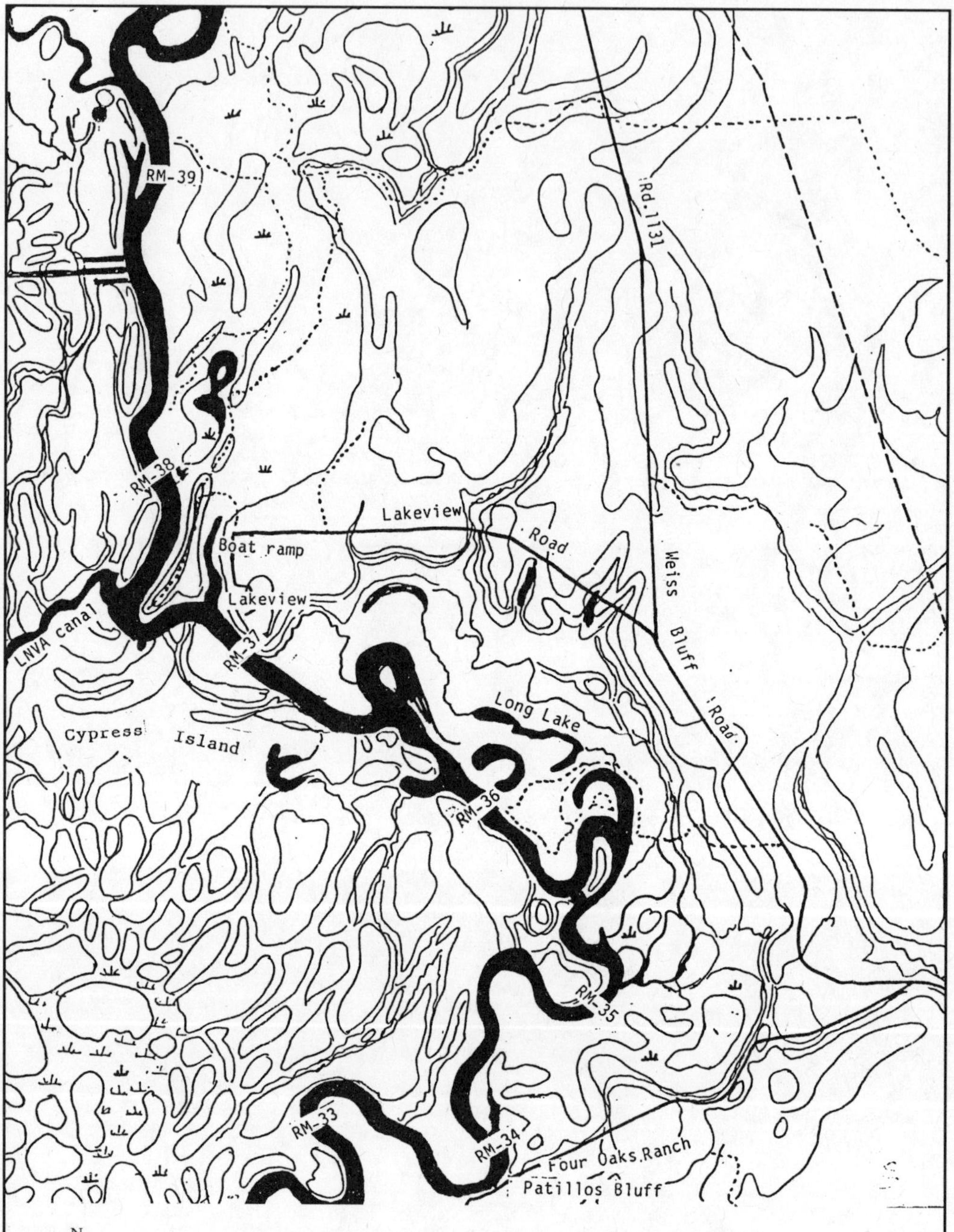
RM-39
Rd. 1131
RM-38
Lakeview
Road
Boat ramp
Lakeview
Weiss
Bluff
Road
LNVA canal
RM-37
Long Lake
Cypress Island
RM-36
RM-35
RM-33
RM-34
Four Oaks Ranch
Patillos Bluff
N
W
E
S
0
½
1 mile

MAP No. 15

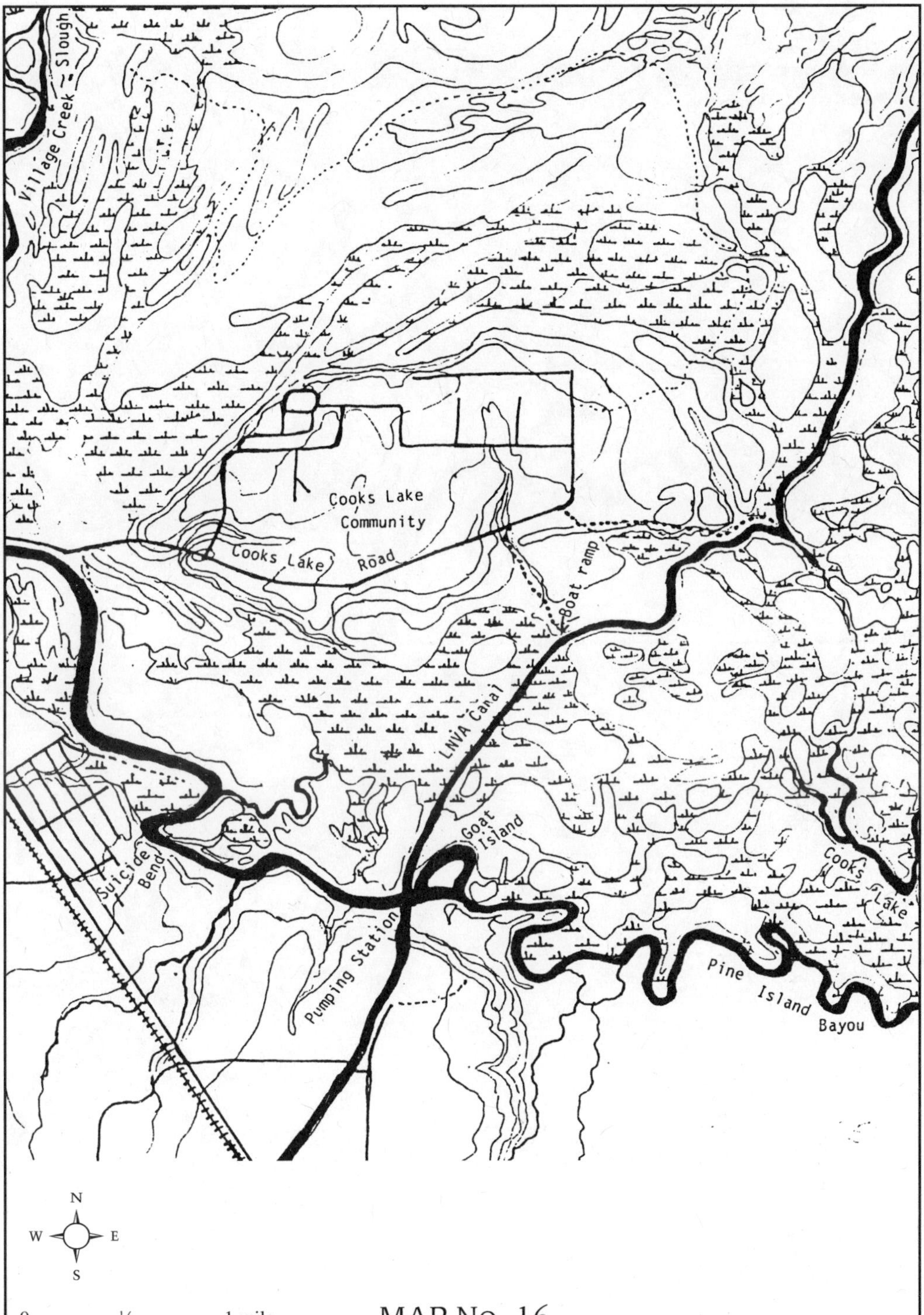

0 ½ 1 mile

MAP No. 16

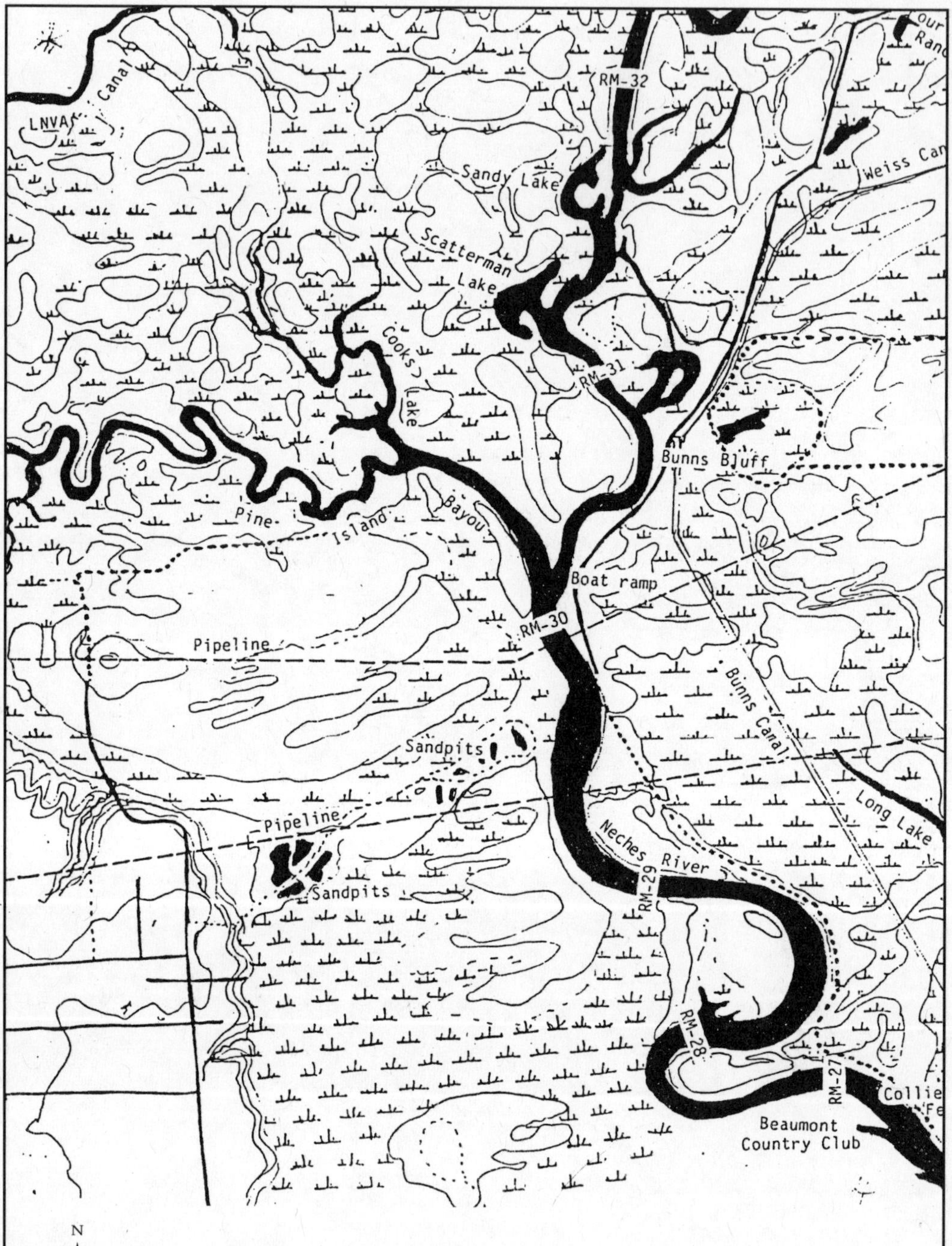

0 ½ 1 mile

MAP No. 17

Part Three

Day 1

EVADALE

Part Three, Day 1 9:00 AM

After a night of rest and revictualing, I took to the river again. The TV weatherman had warned about rain and thunderstorms, but I dismissed the possibility with the confidence born of the experience of seeing many a TV weather prediction come to naught. Regina drove my pickup home. We did not leave a vehicle at the landing site as I had the Park Service radio to notify her of my arrival at my destination. There was a good current, the sky was sunny, and my heart was light.

Shortly after leaving the Highway 96 bridge, I came to the site of the old highway. Its span over the stream has been removed, but the railroad bridge, picturesque with its framework of iron girders, is still in use. I remember when the old highway bridge was built around 1931! It was the first bridge to span the Neches River and its presence was the finish to the steamboat era. On the bluff, where the riverboats discharged and took on cargo, there were docks built of great pilings and large planks of virgin longleaf pine. One of my earliest recollections was going down to the wharves to see the steamboats. Daddy picked me up and carried me because I was barefoot and could get splinters in my feet from the rough planks.

The bridge was hailed as the greatest thing to come to East Texas in those days, but it quickly became obsolete after automobiles and trucks became larger and faster. The bridge was narrow and winding and built on high pilings above the floodplain, sloughs, and river. What a terror it was to meet a truck in midbridge! One vehicle usually stopped and let the other skin by. I used to cross it in the late fifties going to visit my parents who had a retirement home on the Sabine River at Deweyville. The present bridge was hailed with even more relief and pleasure than the old had been.

Before the first bridge was built, folks wanting to go from Hardin County to Jasper County crossed on a ferry. When we lived at Evadale in the late 1920s, (Daddy was planer foreman at the Kirby lumber mill there) the ferry was operated by Henry Walter Kirkpatrick, patriarch of the Hardin County family which has served the community in so many ways. Someone told me a fellow named Ira Graham ran the last ferry until 1935 and that the last log raft passed there in that year. The Kirkpatricks lived in a big white house that was considered grand in those days. It overlooked the river, and around it were great trees draped to the ground with Spanish moss.

Also near the river on a sloping grassland shaded by more moss-hung trees, was a "company" park. John Henry Kirby himself dedicated it and in his speech he promised that it was dedicated to the pleasure and recreation of the people for "as long as the sun shall shine and the river roll." Like the virgin forests and most of John Henry Kirby's promised benefactions, it is long gone.

Beside the ferry landing was a sort of shanty town called Cat Town. In my innocence, I always thought it was named for the catfish which were sold at a shack by the riverside. For those with as little carnal knowledge as I had then, if indeed there be any left, a "cat house" is a house of prostitution. Before everyone rushes to check out my story, like the company park, Cat Town is no more.

The river cuts into upland at this site, creating a high bluff where the town of Evadale survives and a humongous paper mill, Temple-Inland Pulp and Paper, sits polluting air and water. (Though to be quite honest, they are working hard to correct the problems.) The bluff has quite a history. In the early days, it was known as Richardson's Bluff for Benjamin Richardson who operated the ferry. He had acquired a league of land on the Lorenzo de Zavala land grant program and built a large log house on the bluff. The Richardson family still lives in the Evadale area, and their house on the old road is very well kept and has a Texas historical medallion on it. Daddy's Aunt Vivie Scott married Ben Richardson, probably the son or grandson of the original. My mother said he was known for the fine quality of the shinny he produced back in Prohibition days. I remember going to their house as a child and was much impressed with a huge kumquat tree loaded with fruit which shaded the kitchen porch.

The site later became known as Ford's Bluff for three brothers, John, Phillip, and Charles Ford, Yankee investors who bought the site for a sawmill in 1850. The death of Phillip Ford, who went to New Orleans to buy mill machinery and there contracted yellow fever, put an end to their plans. Depressed by their loss, they sold out and went back North.

Kirby put in a shingle mill in 1902 and a big lumber mill in 1904, with housing, school, churches, and all sorts of businesses for the employees. He named the town Evadale for Miss Eva Dale, a teacher of music at the Southeast Texas Male and Female College at Jasper. Daddy worked there in the mid-1920s, but didn't like carrying out what he considered Kirby's dirty work in employee relations, so he quit and went back to Doucette in Tyler County where he worked for Long-Bell Lumber Co. and where we spent the rest of my childhood.

It's hard to believe, as I survey what is now Evadale, that the town which was once there has been completely erased and replaced by other streets, other buildings, other businesses. I cannot even begin to guess where the house had been where we lived. There has probably been no other civilization where cities with their populations and their culture have come and gone so rapidly and so completely as the sawmill towns of the early 1900s—without the aid of a devastating war, that is.

The railroad track which crosses the river here is elevated over sloughs and floodplain for about a quarter of a mile. Maxine Johnston and I once decided to walk the track to the river, dismount, and walk along the river to a site called the Indian Mounds, not noticing a sign that warned pedestrians off. As we began our return, we saw to our horror a train coming toward us. There was no time to make it to the exit site and the track was too high to jump off into the slough, so we found a perch on each side about two feet square and there we cowered in terror. Fortunately, the engineer had seen us and stopped the train, allowing us to reach the exit, which we did in record time.

While that section of the old highway bridge that spanned the river is missing, the southern part which passes over the sloughs and floodplain forests can still be walked. It ought to be made an official trail, for there are few places so easily accessible where one can walk dryshod and view the plants, birds, and animals of the river bottom. It is a lovely walk of possibly a quarter of a mile and, because of its elevation, is much like walking in the treetops. Among the many species of trees and shrubs which have colonized its banks are dogwood and redbud which make it especially beautiful in the spring. Along with the contemplation of its beauty, it could give the canoeist the opportunity of stretching his legs and sampling some of the wares that Honkytonk Road offers.

HONKYTONK ROAD AND COUNTRY MUSIC

For those who would like to sample Big Thicket nightlife (and I don't mean the four-legged kind), Honkytonk Road is the place to start. That name was given to the section of Highway 96 on the south side of the Neches River where there was a string of beer joints. For ages, the counties to the north have traditionally voted "dry" in elections to determine whether alcoholic beverages could be sold, and they have kept the roads hot driving "cross the river" into Hardin County to get their liquor. True, Jasper County has always produced some of the finest homemade whiskey (moonshine, white lightning, corn squeezings, shinny—name your poison) one could ask for; but it was more exciting to pile into the Model T Ford with all your friends, go to Frank Arnold's or Edgar Brown's, both large log buildings, or one of the other establishments on Honkytonk Road, where you could dance and drink and kill yourself on one of the S curves on the road home. Many did just that.

It is told that Edgar Brown once got religion and tried to join the Baptist Church. When he responded to the "call," they wouldn't receive him. Not to worry—if he had faith, God would save him, but they couldn't let him in the Baptist Church since he was associated with drinking and dancing. Anyway, Nancy Morgan, longtime Corps of Engineers secretary, Jasper County native, and a prime cognoscenti of the fun places of those days, told me that there was no better person than Edgar Brown, that he managed his place of business like it was his own home, and that, indeed, is just how his respectful patrons felt, so there were no Saturday night fist and knife fights at Edgar Brown's.

Farther up Honkytonk Road where the highway cuts through a red clay bluff, were the Negro honkytonks. This area was called Red Cut and for more reason than the red gash made where the road cut into the red clay bluff, because it was common to stumble across razor-slashed bodies in the hallways any night. 'The "Law" stayed out of Red Cut, which was more or less a law unto itself. These Negro nightclubs were called "barrel houses" in those days and we used to sit outside in our cars and listen to the music. It was places like this where rock-and-roll really got started. It was eight-to-the-bar rhythm on a piano or guitar and was simply called "Barrelhouse music," but during the late 1930s Tommy Dorsey made it famous as "Boogie Woogie" and many of us danced the jitterbug to it. If this music was accompanied by a wailing lament, it was called "Barrelhouse Blues." My aunt Lida Owens at Bessmay learned to play barrelhouse piano from a Negro woman who worked for her. One, "Crazy Blues," I can still hum.

Anyway, Frank Arnold's and Edgar Brown's places are gone, but you can still take your choice of several. They are very much alive and well and most evenings, especially Friday and Saturday, you can swig cold beer and swing a leg to as good music from local bands as you can find on Sixth Street in Austin or Mickey Gilleys (now defunct) in Pasadena. Country/western, rock, Cajun, and sometimes oldtime hillbilly can be heard most nights.

One evening, after my photographer friend and I had spent a hard day stalking and photographing the wildlife of the Big Thicket (biological, that is), we heard that Blackie Roberson, that nonpareil fiddler, was playing at one of the honkytonks. We took off, and, not wanting anyone to know we were stagging it at a low dive, we parked in the back and slunk in. It so happened that Blackie had got mad and left because the band wanted to play rock music and he liked the oldtimers like "Wednesday Night Waltz," "Under the Double

Eagle," "Over the Waves," etc. We sneaked out the way we came and found our front right tire was as flat as a fritter. Here we were—two women, one of them a knock-out, shapely brunette (not me), changing a tire outside a disreputable dive when a passing car slowed and someone hollered, "Geraldine Watson! Who's that with you?" It was Ernest Spell, who couldn't care less what kind of dive you wanted to habituate. It seemed there was no place we could go without running into Ernest. He changed the tire and we all went off in search of Blackie who, we found, had got drunk, gone home, and passed out so we were not fated to hear any fiddle music that night. Blackie is dead now. Nobody ever has or ever will play "The Orange Blossom Special" like Blackie accompanied by his brother George on the guitar. Ah well!

Before the honkytonk era, the musically talented played at home—usually fiddles and guitars. Banjos and mandolins were not common here then. Since there were no radios or television to entertain, we had to entertain ourselves. After the day's work was over, the family gathered on the gallery (front porch) on summer evenings, or around the fireplace in winter, and the oldtimers would repeat the stories of the family's migrations from Scotland, Ireland, or England to the new world, then westward finally to the Neches River, relating stories of tragedies and wars and reaffirming the family's moral values.

I grew up hearing tales of the Civil War and the dread "Northerners." (They weren't called "Yankees" by my people.) We sang the old songs of lost loves, of wars, death, sailing ships, trains, and hard life, many of the songs brought over from the old country, over the mountains of West Virginia, Kentucky, and Missouri. There were also gay songs with nonsense syllables called "old fool songs," and "play party" songs to which the young folks danced. Some called it "square dancing," but since many considered dancing a sin, they just changed the name. Sometimes, family musicians would walk from one neighboring farm to the other, serenading other families sitting out on their porches in the dusk.

Some of my fondest childhood memories are of visits to Aunt Myrt and Uncle Bud Eason who lived out in the country near Pickering, Louisiana, where they had migrated from the Ozarks with the rest of Mother's people. All their children, Jay, Bookey, Buddy, and Lurline, played musical instruments. Uncle Woodrow, who lived nearby, played guitar, fiddle, dobro, dulcimer—you name it, he played it—and did until he died in his eighties. When we went to visit, they all came together and played and sang all the songs now called "folk" or "bluegrass." We just called it hillbilly. And Oh! What food! Aunt Myrt made banana pudding in a huge dishpan to feed us all. What happy times! They are all gone now, but Bookey's daughter Geraldine and her husband, Herbie Stutz, had a band that played for the patrons of the Big Thicket's premier country music emporium, the Starlight Club at Honey Island. It too, is gone and the last time I passed that way, a church occupied the site. I could make a comment here, but will let it pass.

There will always be a place for our music and an audience for it. Rather than dying out, as the music of most changing cultures does, it has become more popular than ever and the very old songs, on which I grew up, are preserved forever in books in libraries and on records by famous people.

I play lots of instruments—not well, but still I play: piano, violin, dulcimer, autoharp, guitar, harmonica, etc. So I sit by myself and play and sing the old songs while my children play hard rock. They will come around eventually and, by the time they are as old as I am, they will be reminiscing and singing the old songs Mama used to sing. My mother always went about her work whistling and singing the old ballads and fool songs. I learned them simply by listening to her—not realizing that I was doing so, and I know them by the hundreds. My favorite was "Take Me Back to Renfro Valley," a rendition of the 1930s based on an earlier "Take Me Back to West Virginia," which was, in turn, based on an old Scottish ballad. The last time I saw my Daddy alive, I was sitting in the swing under a big tree in the back yard playing my guitar when he came and sat down beside me. "Sister," he said. (he had called me sister ever since I was born as the second daughter.) "Sing 'Take Me Back to Renfro Valley' for me." So I sang "Renfro Valley." I would like to give it here for some of the oldtimers who remember and haven't heard it for sixty or seventy years, but couldn't find out if it is copyrighted and can't take the chance of being sued.

When I'd finished, Daddy stood up and said, "I wonder why God let me ever leave the country." He then walked across the yard and went into the house. The next morning, he died of a heart attack while I was at the library at Lamar University. This section is dedicated to my mother, Retha Ellis, who taught me to love wildflowers, poetry, and song.

INDIAN MOUNDS

River Mile 51.2

About one and a half river miles below the railroad bridge, the river turns to the northwest and makes a big bend. At the beginning of the bend is a cutoff

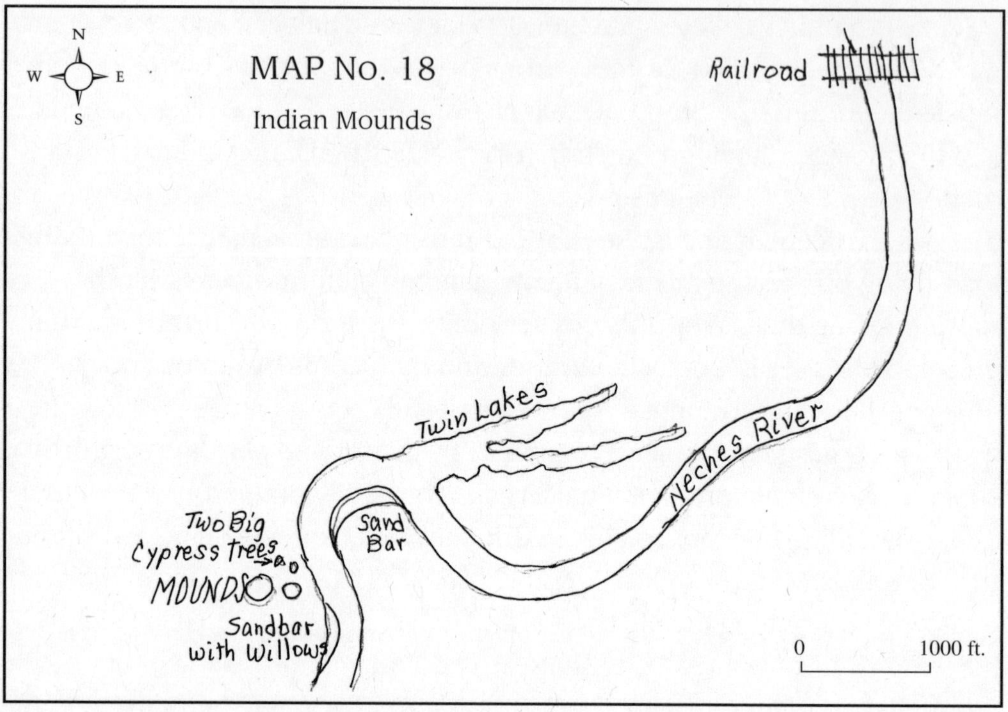

lake with two branches called the Twin Lakes. At the downriver end of the bend, across a sandbar and shallow swale are two mounds which have been known always as the Indian Mounds.

I have always heard of these mounds and wanted to see them for myself, so one day I called Darrel Shine, eminent surveyor, scion of one of the earliest area families, and faithful friend of the Big Thicket cause. Believe me, to say someone local was a friend of the Big Thicket cause, is to say that here is a person with confidence in who and what he is and indomitable courage. Not many people were willing to buck the powers-that-be in the social and economic life of Southeast Texas to aid and abet those involved in that unpopular movement. I have few friends in this world and am proud to list Darrel Shine as one of them. I might add that his company was contracted to survey the Neches River Units of Big Thicket National Preserve and he made certain that the Indian Mounds were within the boundary.

Anyway, Darrel had a special interest in the mounds, was the first to tell me of them, and was happy to put his big boat in the river and take me there. No doubt they were used by the Indians as they had the same advantages that Peach Tree Ridge in the Jack Gore Baygall Unit had: above-flood elevation, access to water, plenty of fuel, good pottery clay, and abundant fish and game, and just the right size for a few family units.

I found evidence of another, more recent use in pieces of broken pottery jugs of the type used by illegal whiskey makers during Prohibition days, and, as is generally the case with unusual natural phenomena, legends have arisen about buried treasure and other tales.

The mounds' location relative to the river, and the fact that the composition of the red clay soil was identical to that of the adjacent terrace bluff across the river, led me to conclude that the mounds were not constructed by Indians, but were the result of the river cutting off and isolating a portion of the upland during some ancient flood. But why ruin a perfectly good story? It is much more intriguing to view the mounds with a sense of mystery and wonder than with cold scientific theory.

BATS

River Mile 50.5

A couple of bends below the Indian Mounds, I noticed ahead a flock of buzzards on a sandbar behaving in a rather strange manner. I pulled over to the far bank and held onto an overhanging branch to watch them at my leisure. With wings outspread, they strutted and pirouetted about with grace and elegance. I still don't know if they were performing some meaningful ritual or just drying their wings after the brief morning rain shower, but it was a lovely sight to see.

After paddling awhile, I decided to pull over to a short sandbar and stretch my legs a bit, and was surprised to find the body of a small, reddish-brown bat. It was certainly the wrong time of the year for bats to be about. They should have been hibernating in some dark, sheltered spot or else have flown south. Bats are to be seen here during warm weather when there are insects to be scooped out of the air. Our most common bat is the little brown bat which roosts in old abandoned buildings, barns, hollow trees, and most anywhere it can find shelter and not be disturbed in the daytime. It does its sleeping hanging upside down by its toes.

Bats as a whole are an extremely interesting and diverse group and are the most widely distributed group of mammals in the world, except for the rodents. There is no part of the world, save for the polar regions, where they are not found. Bats are mammals, feeding their young with milk from the breast, and are the only mammals that have attained true flight. Our bats are insectivorous and about the size of a mouse, but around the world, bats are found to vary from the size of a bumblebee to the size of a house cat, and eating habits vary from fruit to the blood of living creatures. There is even a fishing bat, which skims low over the water, uses the sonar device which all bats have to locate prey, and, when a small fish is located just below the surface, reaches down with long-taloned feet and grasps it.

Being mammals, our bats are covered with real fur. There is also great diversity of coverings on bats throughout the world, from nothing to long, silky hair. Their eyes are small and sometimes hidden by fur, which has caused some to assume they are blind and thus say, "blind as a bat."

Bats rely on echolocation to find prey. That is, they emit high-pitched squeaks which echo back to their sensitive ears, and their brains determine the exact location of things in their path. How they decide which is edible or not, I don't know. Just another mystery to wonder about on the river.

Cypress Swamp

GENTRY LAKE

River Mile 47

I couldn't resist paddling up Gentry Lake a short way, as it was still early in the afternoon and the view into its cypress-mirrored waters was so enticing.

The river at this point cuts into a terrace, so the cutbank side of the lake is above normal flood level. It was a steamboat landing and has always been a favored campsite for fishermen, hunters, and campers.

Gentry Lake was the terminus of an important overland route in the early days. In fact, the route was an extension of the Old Wagon Road, which began at Yellow Bluff, crossed the bottom at the Open Gap, and followed the old Neches bluff line past Jack Gore Baygall, past Silsbee, and dropped into the bottom again at the point where it crossed the new Highway 96 bypass. From there, it followed ridges and hummocks to the river. As with most of the early roads, it was at one time an Indian trail, and I suspect, dugout canoes were kept on both sides of the river for convenience in crossing.

Below Gentry Lake, a wide utility line crosses the river. The Texas Water Board, in another of its schemes to transport East Texas water to the Houston megalopolis, proposed this right-of-way as a route for a water pipeline. Since it crossed Park Service property I, as the Park Service ecologist, wished to do a botanical survey of the site. Huge chunks of broken concrete protected the high bank from erosion, so I tied my boat to a sturdy willow, which had grasped a foothold in the stones, climbed to the rim, checked out the vegetation, and returned to my boat.

The current here was unusually swift and was intent on crashing me and boat onto the rocks while I was equally intent on avoiding them. So engrossed, I was startled to hear a loud snort and splash and realized a buck deer had swum directly into my boat. Dogs were baying in the adjacent woods, and the deer was as intent on evading the dogs as I was in avoiding the rocks, so we met in midstream. Of course, by the time I grabbed my camera, the current had swept me downstream and the buck was just a dot on the water.

WEISS BLUFF

River Mile 41

At river mile 43, there is a sharp bend and a straight stretch where considerable effort was made to prevent the river from washing out a pipeline by building an elaborate system of riprap. This is a niche point, as there are high red bluffs on both the west side of the river where the pipeline crosses and the east side a short distance downriver at Weiss Bluff. The early settlers, as did the Indians, took advantage of these high areas for transportation routes. It is the terminus of the Weiss Bluff/Bevilport Road and the Opelousas Road crossed the river here. Goods brought from the west side of the river to Laurel Lake and Arabian Bluffs were barged down river to the warehouses at Weiss Bluff in the summer, since this was as far upriver as boats could go during times of low water.

Weiss Bluff was an important riverport and in the 1880s the community boasted a population of over 2,000, but with the coming of the railroads, it fell into disuse and decay. It is said that Indians came here in the 1840s to trade, and paid for goods with gold dust that they carried in turkey quills.

At one time, a road connected Weiss Bluff with Colliers Ferry near Beaumont. In the dim past, and nobody remembers why, it was called the Old Military Road, but later it was just the River Road. It followed the river on the stream levee and there were low bridges over the sloughs. When passable in dry weather, it connected Beaumont with Bunn's Bluff where Captain Loving lived, past Ed Stedman's Park Farms (now Four Oaks Ranch), Charles Linn's Lakeview, then on to the Weiss home and cemetery. As with most early homesites and road routes, there is a good spring and an artesian well at Weiss Bluff.

Simon Weiss is buried here. A Polish-Jewish immigrant, he left Poland in 1816, and, traveling the world on the business of the Masonic Lodge, he came to Texas in 1836 where he married one of the Sturrock girls of Tyler County and was made a deputy collector of customs by President Sam Houston. In 1838, he took his family and a load of cotton by keelboat down the Neches River to Sabine Pass. He engaged in merchandizing at Grigsby's Bluff for awhile and then settled at Weiss Bluff where he operated a merchandise business and spent the remainder of his life. Simon Weiss was a man of culture, education, and considerable wealth. He owned several sailing vessels in the England-West Indies trade and did much to develop riverboat traffic on both the Neches and Sabine Rivers. Simon's sons, Mark, Valentine, and William, were active in both the riverboating and lumbering business and Simon, William, and Napoleon were well-known captains. The family is still prominent in Beaumont.

SHINNY LAKE

River Mile 40.7

Just below Weiss Bluff, a large slough known as Shinny Lake enters the river on the west side. It was so named because there was once a whiskey still

Whiskey Still

here. It is a very pleasant place, with a low wooded bluff on the cutbank side, and its poor accessibility from the upland no doubt made it suitable for the activity which gave it the name.

Shinny, white lightning, and moonshine are local terms for illegally-made whiskey. Prohibition, that era when laws prohibited the sale of alcoholic beverages in the United States, occurred during the Great Depression of the early 1930s. With human nature what it is and many men out of work, there was a great demand for and a subsequent supply of the forbidden elixir. The remote waterbodies in the Neches River bottomlands provided ideal sites for whiskey stills since there would be no one around to notice the smoke of the fires nor the distinctive odor of cooking sour mash.

Moonshining is an intriguing subject and I knew my readers would want to know all about it, so I called Bill Brett, the author of that erudite and enlightening tome: "He wanted to know and I knowed so I told him." Bill can tell you just about anything you want to know about Southeast Texas, its people, animals, etc., and a lot you probably don't want to know. He once provided as refreshment at a high-class, formal function that I attended, a fruit jar of what connoisseurs described as "the finest whiskey ever to pass their palate," even though champagne was served by tuxedoed waiters. (Where it originated, we will not inquire.) When I asked for the recipe for corn whiskey, he insisted that what he would tell me (in case the law might happen to read my book), was strictly hearsay and should not be construed as personal experience. Be that as it may, here is Bill Brett's recipe:

First you grind the corn and put it with water and sugar into barrels to ferment. After fermentation, you pour off the liquid from it into a large boiler with a copper tube coming from the top and build a fire under it. The tube is coiled and the lower part is allowed to go through a tub of cold water, condensing the steam into alcohol, which drips from the end of the tube, through a filter of charcoal, and into jugs. The charcoal is important as it refines the alcohol and filters out the "fusel oil." Fusel is a mixture of amyl, butyl, propyl, and isoamyl alcohols and is extremely toxic. It causes, if ingested, a condition called jakeleg, a paralysis of one side of the body which causes one leg to drag. Jakeleg was first diagnosed as a result of persons drinking Jamaican gin and thus it became "Jakeleg."

Thinking such a serious subject deserved a second opinion, I went to Spell's barbershop and approached Ernest Spell, someone else who knew something about everything and everybody and who could and would tell you all about it. Ernest gave me a recipe—not the best recipe, he said, but the one used by the backwoods shinny makers, moonshiners, or bootleggers, whichever term you prefer, during the Depression. His account was confirmed and augmented by Cleo Gore whose father, Lee Gore, made a living in the business, as well as other customers who talked while getting their hair cut.

Before you begin your enterprise, the weather must be right. If the temperature is under 80 degrees, the mash won't ferment. You take a 55-gallon barrel, put into it about 100 pounds of rye and or corn, 165 pounds of sugar, and some yeast, and fill it with water. (The sugar must first be melted.) The mixture takes about fourteen days to ferment in 90-degree weather. The grain will go to the bottom of the barrel and when it has fermented sufficiently, it will rise to the top of the water. That is the time to strain the water from the mixture and put it in a copper boiler. (If the boiler is galvanized metal, the whiskey will "eat your guts out," whatever that means.) You build a fire under it and bring it to a boil. You must be careful not to get the fire too hot nor let the boiler steam dry, as an explosion can result.

The boiler has a mushroom-like attachment on the top which has a circular depression around the steam vent. This attachment is called a puke drum. (Puke is a local word for vomit.) The steam percolates into the puke barrel and the impurities settle into the depression while the purified steam escapes through the copper pipe at the top. The coiled pipe goes through a barrel of cold water, thus reducing the steam to liquid, which drips into another container.

After all the liquid has condensed, the boiler is thoroughly cleaned and the process repeated with the semirefined liquid. This is done several times, each time cleaning the impurities from the bottom of the boiler and the puke drum. The more the liquid is put through the refining process, the higher the alcohol content. Finally, it becomes pure grain alcohol: 190 proof. If it goes as high as 200 proof, it is weakened by adding water. With this method, there is no need to filter it through charcoal, except for "ageing it." Some people add red oak chips to give it color.

The local law usually turned their heads the other way when it came to bootlegging, most of the time because the profits, a well as the product, were shared with them. Federal "Revenuers" were not so understanding, but enforced the law rigorously. Cleo Gore said that the Feds "came in like gangbusters." They were required before making a raid on a still to inform the local sheriff, who informed the still operator. Naturally, the feds were not very popular with the locals and, I am told, there are several of them that never left the area. They are still at the bottom of Franklin Lake, along with a few of the early state game wardens, or so it is said.

Some of the bootleggers also met an untimely end. Walter (Sonny) Burge, said that when his father made shinny on the river, there was an old man who didn't make it, but would transport it to Beaumont in his Model T Ford. The Revenuers learned of his nightly trips down Cook's Lake Road and one night laid in wait for him where the bridge now crosses Village Creek Slough. When he approached, they stopped his car and opened machinegun fire, cutting him to pieces.

Aubrey Cole, the Jasper County sheriff, told me of a popular fellow who was caught making shinny, arrested, and tried. The jury said there was no doubt he was guilty and they had no choice but to find him guilty, which they did. Then they took up a collection among themselves and paid his fine.

The whiskey trade in those days was a dangerous and risky business, both in manufacture and distribution, but the necessity of making a living during a depressed economy and the greed for money drove people to it. Some of the bootleggers were desperate and reckless men. Jim Martindale once told me about riding his horse in the river bottom and suddenly seeing a gun barrel stuck out from behind a tree with a voice saying: "I'd stop right there if I wus you. Jis turn your horse's head back towards whar you wus coming from." He did.

Ernest Spell's older brother, Floyd, decided to go into the moonshining business and Ernest's job consisted of sitting in the top of a tall pine and ringing a cowbell to warn his brother of approaching Revenuers. He was a small boy at the time.

There are many parallels between the bootleg whiskey trade then and the drug trade now. In distributing their wares, the bootlegger would go to a country dance and pass around a free jug of whiskey to whet the appetites and dull the judgment of the revelers. After that, everybody bought a jug and the activities of the evening were considerably enlivened. On one such occasion, Cat Eason, who was assisting Floyd by being his "front man" at a dance, had passed the bottle around to mellow potential customers and, in the process, mellowed himself. It so happened that a Frenchman out of Louisiana was present and began flirting with Cat's girlfriend and the two got into a fight. Two of Cat's cousins, Cooter and Toad Ard, who had never got along with Cat anyhow, joined the Frenchman and when Floyd arrived, the three had Cat down on the ground by the door stoop going after it with their knives. Floyd jumped in to save Cat and was severely cut, but with the help of others, managed to separate the antagonists. Cooter Ard had a deep cut which severed a section of his liver, so the Ard boys were out of it. When Cat saw that his friend Floyd had been injured in his defense, he was incensed. Despite all Floyd could do to dissuade him, Cat reentered the house. Standing at the door, he beckoned to the Frenchman: "C'mere, you s.o.b." But the Frenchman said: "No, you come over here." Cat said: "Meet me half way." The Frenchman did and Cat grabbed his left hand with his, held on, and they slashed away at each other.

After the Frenchman conceded defeat, the injured were taken to Silsbee to be repaired. Doctor Beasley, the Silsbee doctor, sent them on to Hotel Dieu, the hospital in Beaumont, but Cat wouldn't have it. He insisted that the doctor sew him up right then. "I will have to put you to sleep. You won't be able to stand the pain." "Nobody's gonna put me to sleep," yelled Cat. "But I don't have enough anesthetic to kill the pain," the doctor protested. "That som-a-bitch didn't give me nothin when he cut me. I don't need nothin for you to sew me up. Go to it." So Cat lay there without flinching while the medic put almost two hundred stitches in him. Cat got up, walked out, and a few days later was back at the still. He later removed the stitches himself with pliers. The Frenchman was laid up in the hospital for nearly two months.

The authorities told Floyd, out of regard for his mother who was a widow, to discontinue the practice and they wouldn't arrest him. He continued and was arrested and put on five years probation. Many years later, Ernest worked on oil rigs in Saudi Arabia and many other far parts of the world. Alcoholic beverages were forbidden in most of these countries but the Americans wanted their liquor so Ernest installed modernized whiskey stills on oil barges and in cellars of the company compounds. Thus the skills and expertise garnered from the shinny stills of the Neches River bottoms brightened (or darkened according to your viewpoint) the lives of American oil workers throughout the world. If Ernest was ever taken to task for what I revealed, I could only assure the authorities that Ernest Spell was an outrageous liar and not to be held accountable.

JASPER-ORANGE COUNTY LINE

River Mile 40

Here at the confluence of Village Creek and the Neches on the east side of the river is the boundary between Jasper and Orange Counties. Some maps show it to be farther to the south. I have had Jasper County on my left through out this voyage, while Tyler and Hardin on my right were equally divided.

Jasper County was settled in 1824 when John Bevil established a homestead at the present site of Jasper. In 1834, the Bevil settlement became the municipality of Bevil with Bevilport as the seat of government. In 1835, the name was changed to Jasper to honor an American Revolutionary War hero, William Jasper. In 1836, after the war of Texas independence, it became Jasper County with John Bevil's homesite as the county seat. In 1839, it was included in the impresario grant of Lorenzo de Zavala as a part of the municipality of Nacogdoches. At one time, Jasper County extended all the way from the Neches to the Sabine but when the Texas Republic became a state in 1846, it was divided in half on a north to south line and the eastern half became Newton County.

Some early pioneers in upper Jasper County were Hanks, Smythe, Bevil, Holmes, Everett, Blount, Pickle, and Byerly, with Ellis and Primrose in the forks of the river. Coming downstream, one found Scott, Bean, Withers, and Richardson families, to name a few. Each family deserves more detailed treatment, but I've simply run out of time and will have to leave something for the young historians coming along. These families lived in close association with the Neches River and there were many roads through the bottomlands to give river access to those who lived in the adjacent uplands.

In Orange County, as one nears the coast, the low floodplain becomes wider and more marshy, and few families chose to settle near the river. This county spans the low, flat land between the Neches and Sabine Rivers and is bounded on the south by Sabine Lake. Orange was a part of the municipality of Jefferson and the first community was called Cow Bayou from the estuarine body of water by which it was located, but the community was renamed Jefferson in 1835. In 1852, the county was separated from Jefferson County and named Orange County by George Patillo who had an orange grove on the east bank of the Neches. A community called Madison, later renamed Orange, was designated county seat. Other than the Patillos, the only family of note in this area was the mulatto Ashworth family.

VILLAGE CREEK

River Mile 39.4 4:40 pm

From the river, the mouth of Village Creek looks little different from the many sloughs entering the river, for it is more narrow than could be expected for a major creek. So I was especially alert not to miss it. A major clue is the color of the water current joining that of the sand-colored Neches. Due to tannic acid leached from its forested watershed, Village Creek water is the color of tea. Across the river from the creek mouth is an extensive bar of snow-white sand, fed by the tremendous amounts of quartz sand transported from the creek's headwaters in the sand dunes of the second ridge of the Willis Geological Formation. This sand forms the many sandbars and riffled shallows of the creek's streambed.

Village Creek forms when Big Sandy Creek and Kimball Creek meet near the Hardin-Polk County line. Roughly following U.S. Highway 90 between Livingston and the Neches, there is a ridge which divides the watershed. Drainage on the south side of the ridge enters Village Creek watershed while that on the north side enters Wolf Creek and the Neches north of Steinhagen Lake. The principal tributaries of Village Creek are Hickory, Turkey, Beech, and Mill Creeks from the north and Cypress Creek on the south. These creeks are fed by many small spring branches which seep from the sands of the Hockley scarp, a geological feature dividing the Willis from the younger formations to the south. It was thought that this feature divided the Pleistocene and Pliocene epochs, but modern geologists discredit the premise.

This creek was once much larger than at present. Over the past 30 to 50 thousand years, it has changed with the climate and rise and fall of sea level. During low sea level, it cut a deep valley, then, as sea level rose, it filled the valley with alternate layers of sand and thin layers of a cementing silicious silt. As we are in a period of decreased rainfall, the size of the stream and its floodplain have diminished and it is again cutting downward. In its meanderings, Village Creek has moved westward, leaving behind terraces of sand dunes which support surprising xeric (desert-type) ecosystems.

Some sections of the old stream remain as wide, deep pools, connected by recently cut, narrow, shallow channels. Oldtimers from some of the earliest settlers, say the creek was much deeper in the early days and barges were poled and pulled upstream and floated downstream to the trading posts on the river. They say that clearcutting of the virgin forests between the turn of the century and the 1940s removed the protection from the sandy soil and it quickly washed into the streams, filling the beds, and causing floods. Clearcutting of the second growth forests in the Village Creek watershed continues as the forest products industry, which controls about 90 percent of the land, seeks to convert the natural mixed forests into pulp pine plantations. Record floods followed the cutting of the original forests and cultivation of the land a hundred years ago and have been repeated in the past few years. Nobody seems to connect the clearing to bare earth of thousands of acres of forest, drainage projects for real estate developments and rice fields, and channelization of the upper stream, to devastating floods in the lower watershed, but scream for the government to support flood control plans which are mind-boggling from an economic and engineering feasibility point of view. Guess it is in our nature to want to have our cake and eat it too. We want to live in beautiful forested areas near streams and we also want to exploit the land for whatever money we can squeeze from it. In this case, you can't do it unless you want to build houses on 12-foot pilings.

Village Creek was thus named because of the many Indian villages which once were alongside it. Farmers on the adjacent uplands and bluffs have large collections of artifacts found while cultivating their land. County Road 420 was an Indian trail which connected these villages. I have been told that in the 1920s the University of Texas did some excavating of an Indian dwelling site on a bluff just above where Highway 69 crosses the creek, but I've not been able to get any definite information as to their finds.

As it is today, Village Creek is one of the most beautiful streams in the country and is a very popular canoeing stream. One can launch at McNeeley Bridge at the end of County Road 420 at Old Providence, one of the earliest settlements in Texas, at Road 418 between Silsbee and Kountze, Road 327 also between Silsbee and Kountze, or Highway 96 about three miles south of Silsbee. The section between Road 418 and 327 is the most popular as it is a nice, relatively easy day's outing, and it flows through the Nature Conservancy's Larsen Sandyland Sanctuary. This sanctuary is on a deep sand terrace and preserves an amazing diversity of vegetational communities, particularly the xeric vegetation on the bare sand dunes. Many species are endemic to the area—that is, they are found nowhere else in the world. The Larsen sanctuary is open to the public for hiking along its trails or canoeing. Incidentally, it was a gift arranged by Arthur Temple, Jr., an environmentally conscious forest products industry mogul who is respected and honored by even the most rabid conservationists, a very rare thing, indeed.

LAKEVIEW

River Mile 37.5

As I glided over this broad, glassy stretch of river in the early afternoon, it was so quiet that I could hear the rattle of dry leaves falling from the sycamores in the forest. A strange haze suffused the landscape. Trees, banks, and sandbars were colorless in varying shades of grays and whites; and sun, sky, and river had turned to silver. Only the crystal sparkles dancing on the water showed movement.

The presence of a mixture of trashy and classy riverbank camphouses heralded the Lakeview real estate development coming up ahead. Some misguided souls sought to retard the erosion of their property by dumping trash, old stoves and refrigerators, tires, etc., over the bank. One with perhaps a little more imagination, and doubtless a "Trekkie," had pulled an old barge upriver and sunk it along the bank as a water break. Printed in bold letters on its side was its name: U.S.S. ENTERPRISE. I love people with a sense of humor.

A break in this ugly setting is a jewel called the Lakeview Sandbar. It is the last large sand beach on the river and is extremely popular with the water-, sand-, and sun-loving public. The National Park Service maintains it as a day-use recreation area. It is accessible, for the time being, through a real estate development named Lakeview because it surrounds a series of cutoff, or abandoned-channel lakes. Since, too frequently, beer drinking goes with outdoor recreation, every summer claims its victims from drowning and boating accidents at this site.

Aside from being a very attractive spot with its acres of snow-white sand, a wide expanse of cool, clean water (there is no industrial or municipal pollution above this point), and lovely, sweeping willows framing sky and water, the area is a geologically significant niche point. It marks the division between forest and coastal plain. The river is estuarine from Lakeview south. That is, it has reached sea level and is influenced by tides. Since the current slows as it meets incoming tides, it drops its load of sand it has carried down from the upper watershed. As it fills the stream bed, the river, following the line of least resistance, cuts another. For that reason, this estuarine area is laced with abandoned-channel lakes and vast cypress swamps.

Since the land area is only about five feet above sea level, the banks are low and marshy. The closer to the sea it gets, the broader are the marshes and the fewer the cypress trees. Here, coastal, brackish-water vegetation begins to appear. Emergent aquatics such as wild rice, tall reeds, the crinum lily and Louisiana blue iris make a lovely show in the spring.

A sand company has anchored a barge in midriver just below Lakeview to capitalize on this ever-replenishing supply of sand. A large pump sucks up sand and water from the bed of the stream onto the barge. The water runs out holes in the side and the sand settles in the bottom. When the barge is full of sand, a tug boat comes upriver and takes it down to where the sand can be dried, stored, and sold. It doesn't seem to cause much turbulence nor have any visible harmful effects, other than being an eyesore.

I decided to desert the river at Lakeview and take the fresh water canal which is the western boundary of Cypress Island and cuts through the Beaumont Unit of Big Thicket National Preserve. Three reasons: One, I don't want to see any more of these trashy camphouses on the banks; Two, I want to go up into Cook's Lake without paddling up Pine Island Bayou; Three, I'm tired of paddling with no current to help (getting soft in my old age). Guess I covered too much distance this first day, hoping to camp at Lakeview the first night. I hadn't remembered that the current slowed to a stop after Village Creek and, being too hard-headed to change my plans, I fought it a bit hard. The current down the canal will be swift and it does have some natural beauty.

PART THREE, DAY 1, FIRST NIGHT

At the white beach of Lakeview sandbar, I took the sharp turn onto the canal and selected the steep little sandbar on the third short bend from the river, erected my tent and built a small supper fire.

The weather changed as the sun went down, and clouds began to fill the sky in fluffy clumps, but there was no rosy hue as is usual with such conditions. A wind came up. First it was an ominous sound far off in the forest, then, as it moved through the tops of the tall trees, it had the sound of distant rapids and waterfalls. When it hit the exposed point of land where my camp was set up, it had reached a furious intensity which whipped my flimsy tent about and wrenched the pegs from the ground. The possibility of spending the night with a collapsed tent over my head seemed quite likely until I placed my heaviest gear in each corner. The fore and aft lines were securely tied to trees by stout ropes, so my shelter held.

When everyone warned me before departure that the weather man had predicted 40 percent chance of rain and increasing cold, I said, "I have rain gear, tent, and warm clothes. No big deal!" And that morning when the poor showing of clouds produced a brief pattering of raindrops, barely dimpling the water surface, I laughed, "O.K., so it rained!" What I didn't expect was the possibility of a real storm. Rain, cold, or wind, O.K., but bolts of lightning bouncing around when I and my tent were the tallest things on the sandbar—huh-uh! The safe thing to do would be to wrap a poncho around myself and sit out in the woods among the shrubbiest trees there. Surprisingly, there was no thunder or lightning and no rain—just the furious wind and dropping temperature—a blustery, dry norther. Hardly the great storm which would have made such a smashing finale to my epic: "How I survived the worst storm of the year in the wilderness!"

It was dark by 7:00, but I took to my tent. Wearing a heavy sweatsuit, I climbed into my sleeping bag and felt quite cozy and safe from the elements. Two idiots in a motorboat roared past and almost swamped my boat, which was moored at the foot of the sandbar. I got out and pulled it higher on the bar, thinking that heavy rains during the night might cause the water to rise and wash it away.

A small plane passed over real low. Guess the pilot was looking for a landing field. It must have been awfully wild up there. I felt glad to be safe and said a prayer for the pilot.

Taking out my flashlight, I read a few chapters from my Bible and marveled at the transition from the Old Testament's philosophy of "an eye for an eye and a tooth for a tooth" to Christ's philosophy of "Return good for evil, and Love thy neighbor as thyself." As I read, I was overwhelmed by a great sadness. How the simple teaching of Christ has been misused and abused through the ages, as, indeed have the simple teachings of Buddha and Mohammed, by those who wished to use the names for political power and profit! I share Christ's hope for a better world, one where every person treats others as he would have others treat him. Then there would be no more war, no crime, and no hunger or suffering. Sure, I dream! But as George Bernard Shaw expressed it: "You see things and you say 'Why'? But I dream things that never were, and I say 'Why not?'"

Ah well! One thing about the forest and river and these quiet days and long nights without radio, television or anyone to speak with, you do a lot of pondering over things as they were, as they are, as they ought to be, and as they might be. Shakespeare, who had something to say about most everything, described the situation well:

> And this our life, exempt from public haunt,
> finds tongues in trees, books in the running brooks,
> Sermons in stones, and good in everything.
>
> *As You Like It*

Lower Neches Valley Authority Canal

Part Three

Day 2

L.N.V.A. CANAL

River Mile 37.4

The morning after the storm, the canal was smooth and lovely, reflecting the still-green trees and the few maples and Chinese tallows which had begun to turn color. The bends are small compared to those of the Neches, and only the first few have sandbars. The canal was constructed in 1925 and, though it is artificial, it follows a series of sloughs and cypress swamps, so retains a natural configuration. One particular cypress swamp on the right is broad and deep and one can paddle about and explore it to some extent. I wanted to save my paddling arm for Cook's Lake, however, so I passed it by.

One bend is especially wide where a slough from the interior of the island enters the canal and becomes like a lake. Daddy and I once came here fishing, and witnessed a sad sight. A mother with her two teenage children, a boy and a girl, had come to picnic and swim. The young people were splashing about in the shallow water near the shore when the girl slipped off into a deep hole. She couldn't swim, so the brother jumped in to help and was dragged under also. The mother was almost drowned trying to save them, but managed to struggle to shore and go for help. Divers found the bodies while we were there and brought them to shore. Their limbs were frozen in that last moment when the muscles relaxed in unconsciousness and they drifted downward. The air in their lungs, mixed with blood and mucus, oozed out and formed exotic pink foam flowers about their mouths. The mother was a pitiable object. I always feel a chill when passing this point, so I was glad to continue down the canal.

But this was a beautiful day—quite a few degrees cooler than the day before, thanks to the dry norther which had roared through the night before, and everything was fine, but for some unexplainable reason, I felt a sudden necessity to cut my voyage short and leave the water. There was an exit point a short distance ahead and some cabins where one could possibly find a telephone. I chose one where children were playing about the yard, pulled up to the high bank, tied up my boat, and clambered up by roots and toeholds.

My daughter was surprised to get my call and, in the absence of a real reason, I used the excuse that my arthritic shoulder was bothering me, which it was, but not enough to prevent my continuing if I had really wanted to. Since she didn't know where the little road left the blacktopped Cook's Lake Road, I arranged to walk to Cook's Lake Road and meet her there. She misunderstood and waited three hours at a point a mile down the road from where I was standing waiting. She finally went home, I hitched a ride to Burges' store on the Eastex Freeway and called her to pick me up there, which she did.

I used to question these sudden urges to change plans and try to reason them out, but do no longer. There was a reason why I should not continue down thc canal to the bayou and thence back to the river. That night, safe at home with aspirin and Pepto-Bismal handy, I developed stomach pains, nausea, and vomiting and continued quite miserably ill for two or three days. I wasn't sick enough to be totally incapacitated, but that long, hard paddle, most of it against the tide, in such a sorry condition would have been quite an ordeal. I think I would just have put up my tent, crawled into my sleeping bag and waited for the park rangers to make their routine patrols, find me, and haul me home. It's amazing what wonderful, happy times I can have on the river in between these ignominious starts and finishings.

Since I have covered the canal, the bayou, and Cook's Lake so many times, I will continue to describe them and my experiences there to enlighten my readers.

CYPRESS ISLAND

River Mile 30 to 37.5

Cypress Island is the eastern three-fourths of the Beaumont Unit of the Big Thicket National Preserve. It was formed when the Lower Neches Valley Authority dredged a canal from Lakeview on the Neches to Suicide Bend on

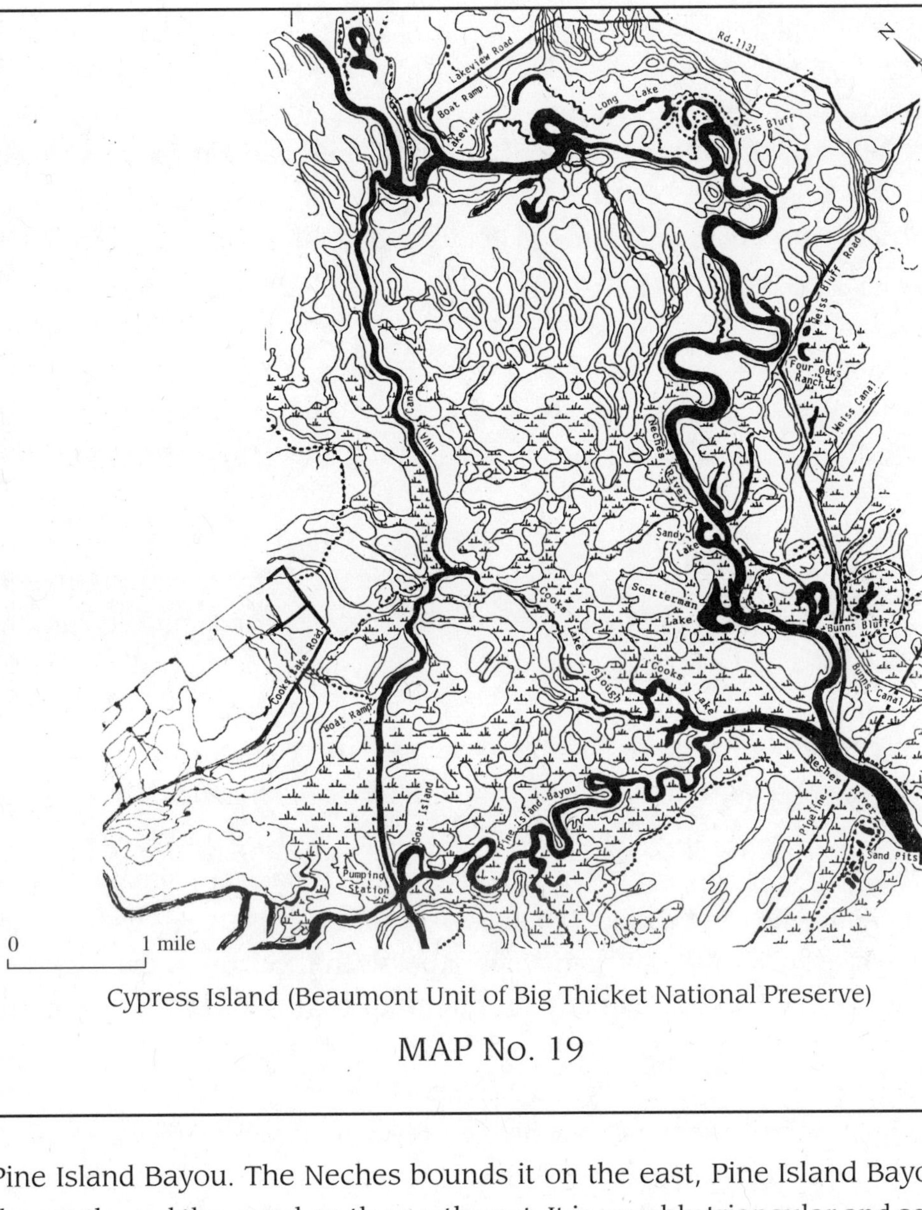

Cypress Island (Beaumont Unit of Big Thicket National Preserve)

MAP No. 19

Pine Island Bayou. The Neches bounds it on the east, Pine Island Bayou on the south, and the canal on the northwest. It is roughly triangular and several thousand acres in size. The upper, or northern, portion reaches ten feet above sea level in elevation and the lower, five feet and less, and the entire island is laced with cypress swamps and sloughs.

I once inadvertently spent a night on this island. The annual Big Thicket Festival was coming up and we were planning routes for the hikes and field trips. We wanted those who were supporting the preservation of the Big Thicket to see some of the inaccessible areas. Everyone had seen the Hyatt Preserve and the Sternenberg Preserve, Kirby Forest, and Rosier Park, so I wanted to offer something new. The only means of access to this large island is by boat and there are no trails. Few would dare strike out into this maze of swamps and deep forests on their own, so I assayed to blaze a trail across the island beginning at the most easily accessible point where a short road off Cook's Lake Road led to the LNVA fresh water canal on the west side of the island. We ferried across the canal in my flatbottom boat and entered the island by an old logging road. After about five minutes' walk along these long overgrown ruts, we came to the point of a narrow peninsula surrounded by a deep slough with a half-rotted log partly spanning it. A jump of two or three feet landed us safely on the opposite side and from that point on there was nothing but several thousand acres of forest, thicket, cypress sloughs, and shallow swamps.

With me were two Lamar University students, Nancy McClintock and her sister's fiancé, Jim. As we wound our way over the narrow ridges, trying to route a dry trail, we flagged our route with surveyors tape so we could find our way back. I had a compass and tried to follow in an easterly direction the route that the topographic map indicated was the highest land. As we entered the center of the island, the forest became more open and parklike and the trees larger. Fragrant lady's tresses orchids were everywhere. We stopped to measure with our binocular straps, one of a grove of the most magnificent basket oak and sweetgum trees I had ever seen. In fact, we spent so much time marveling at the beauty of the forest that we let the time pass until we suddenly realized that the sun had dropped below the horizon. With the closed-canopy forest, it was difficult to be aware of the sun's exact location in the sky. Quickly assessing our situation, we decided that it would take us well after dark to make our way back to the canal and the boat. If we were caught in the middle of the island with no light and could see neither the compass or flags, we would become hopelessly lost. People have been known to be lost on this island for days, some perishing before being found. We decided our best course of action would be to make our way to the river, which surely must be near, flag a passing fisherman and telephone my family from one of the camphouses on the Four Oaks Ranch Road across the river. At first, we took a winding course over the ridges and around the sloughs, but, as time went on, we used the last daylight to compass a straight eastward course to the river.

We plunged into sloughs which I wouldn't have dared to put a foot into in daylight. Poor Nancy, being short, had to be lifted across some of the sloughs.

It's strange how, in emergencies, one loses one's usual sense of fear. As we strode into the yellow, muddy water, cottonmouth moccasins slithered in right alongside us and, in our urgency to reach the river before total darkness, we didn't even care.

We did reach the river just as darkness settled in. There was no moon but some starlight gave a dim outline of objects, trees, and water. I knew we were somewhere above Charlie Schwartz' cabin on the east side of the river and, if we could make our way downstream opposite his cabin, we could yell across and he would come get us. Stumbling over terrain and through brush where I would have been keeping a sharp eye out for cottonmouths normally, we forged ahead until we were stopped by Sandy Lake. Knowing it was useless to try to find our way around it in the dark, we retreated to an open bluff beside the river to wait until morning light to continue.

Mosquitoes

If anyone thinks the mosquitoes of Cypress Island are bad in the daytime, they should try a nocturnal encounter. We had no matches for a fire to smoke them off and wore short sleeves. The little vampires came in waves. One swarm would converge on us, fill up with blood, and leave. Then we could literally hear the next swarm—hum-hum-hum—growing closer and closer until they took their turn at the banqueting tables. Testing the theory that mosquitoes operate only near ground level, Jim climbed into the fork of a tree and secured himself with his belt but the precariousness of his perch wouldn't allow that level of relaxation which invites slumber. Nancy tried to sleep with her face in my lap, her arms beneath her and me fanning mosquitoes off with a leafy branch.

As we had several hours to kill, and we were all three biology majors, we discussed what we knew about mosquitoes. Light will attract mosquitoes for miles, but close up, carbon dioxide and warmth draw them. A warm blooded animal is an essential link in their reproduction cycle. The female mosquito will not mate until she has had a blood meal—the proteins in blood being necessary for the formation of her eggs. So the passionate and eager male goes about frantically searching for a donor. When he finds one, he begins to hum loudly: "Here it is! Come and get it!" The male mosquito has no biological need for blood as he sustains himself by sucking plant juices, so it is the male who hums and the female who bites. She has a long proboscis with six shafts: four are cutting and piercing tools, one for injecting a thinning agent which prevents coagulation (this is what causes the sting) and the other for sucking up the blood. Our presence there that night was no doubt responsible for a considerable population explosion among the mosquitoes of Cypress Island. Once made fertile, the female looks for stagnant water in which to deposit her eggs, and, on Cypress Island there is surely no stint of that. If the water dries up before the eggs hatch into larvae, or "wiggletails," as we kids once called them, they lie dormant until it rains or the river rises. Then, a couple of days afterwards, they rise in billows to harass the countryside.

One can't help thinking how the Indians and early settlers must have suffered from the mosquitoes. No screens on doors or windows, no insect repellent. I can remember country people using canopies made of loosely woven cheesecloth over their beds at night. They also built smudge fires. What a choice! To be bitten and stung all night or choke on smoke! The Indians also used smudge fires and, in addition, slathered themselves with alligator grease. Probably the experience of smelling an Indian with a generous coating of rancid alligator grease discouraged that practice among the more fastidious Europeans. The Indians no doubt accepted mosquitoes along with the cold and the rain. One can become so inured to discomfort or pain that one no longer feels it. One learns to live with the inevitable, as we did that night on Cypress Island.

Apparently, none of the mosquitoes which lunched off us that night carried malaria, encephalitis, or yellow fever, or any of the other disease organisms to which some mosquitoes are an intermediate host, for none of us suffered anything worse than a night of abject misery.

The size and ferociousness of Big Thicket mosquitoes have inspired many yarns and jokes. One of them says that a Southeast Texan took a Yankee cousin camping up on the Neches. When the shades of evening descended, so did hordes of hungry mosquitoes. The Yankee fled to his tent, slapping and scratching. After awhile, he peered out into the night and, seeing the lightning bugs flitting about through the trees, exclaimed, "My God! Now they're out looking for us with lanterns!" Some yarns are even worse than that.

Seriously, I remember once in the early 1940s, after a hurricane had left water two to three feet deep on the streets of Beaumont and Port Arthur for a week, we had a plague of mosquitoes which would rival any plague featured in holy writ. There were clouds of them that literally darkened the skies. Everyone went about in mosquito net hats, long sleeves, and gloves even though it was 100 degrees in the shade. During that time, a coast guardsman, standing watch one of those nights, was killed by the mosquitoes. Actually, it is said that some Arctic mosquitoes can suck a human dry in four hours, and I'll be willing to pit our Big Thicket mosquitoes against Alaskan mosquitoes any day!

If someone feels he really must find something positive to say about mosquitoes, there is the time that Napoleon sent an army to Haiti to subdue a slave rebellion and from there to conquer the Mississippi Valley. In Haiti, the freedom fighters got an assist from an army of mosquitoes. Out of 33,000 French soldiers, 29,000 fell to yellow fever. Napoleon not only pulled out of Haiti, but sold his interests in America to the United States for peanuts. We owe the Louisiana Purchase to mosquitoes! How about that!

Dr. Walter Reed, an army surgeon, mounted an attack on yellow fever by proving that it was caused by mosquitoes. He and his aides exposed themselves to the danger of this almost always fatal disease and some of them died. One of the fatalities had a wife and small children, and when she applied to the army for his pension, was told that she and the children were able to work and therefore, would not be supported by the government. An account of this is given in a book called *The Germ Hunters* that I once read and which is now out of print. Dr. Reed was a great hero who saved millions of lives and I wonder how many people even know his name! At least a hospital was named for him.

Since the mosquitoes rendered sleep impossible that night on Cypress Island, we wiled away the hours of darkness with conversation. I gave my impassioned "save the Big Thicket" speech to the audience of two. Then Jim and I, having the same religious background, which emphasizes individual participation in congregational singing, harmonized on all the hymns we could remember. I, being a history buff, recounted the course of civilization from the beginning (giving both the Creationist and Secular Humanist views), to the discovery of atomic power and on to two possible futures: a golden age when all humans would be educated, profit by the lessons of history, and live in peace and prosperity. Or the alternative: a continued, wasteful exploitation of natural and human resources for the enrichment of a greedy, avaricious few until natural resources are depleted and they turn on each other with all the nuclear weapons at their disposal for control of the last fuels, arable land, and slave labor. With the water, soil, and vegetation contaminated and the protective outer layers of the atmosphere destroyed, the heat of the sun will ignite all combustible matter and the earth will be destroyed, as the Christian Bible predicted millennia ago, by fire.

In between musical and philosophical diversions, we contemplated what thoughts and actions were taking place with our families. Nancy said "no way" was her mother going to stand still while her daughter was lost all night in the Big Thicket. She would have the sheriff's posse, rescue squads of both counties, the Coast Guard, etc., searching for us. I said "no way" would my husband submit me to the humiliation and embarrassment of having a search party rescue me from the woods. Sure enough, my husband calmed Mrs. McClintock by assuring her that we had just let dark catch us and as soon as it was daylight, we would walk out. If we had not reported in by 10:00 AM, they would seek help.

Frequently, we would see a light coming over the open expanse of the river and Nancy would announce, "It's a rescue boat!" But, as it came nearer, the light would veer abruptly up, so apparently it was some gigantic species of lightning bug. When we told our tale back at Lamar U to any and all who would listen, Dr. Mike Warren, entomologist and head of the Biology Department, postulated that it could be a species hitherto unknown to this area of large, tropical lightning bugs which exhibit the behavior we described. We planned how we would respond when the county sheriff, who loved publicity, shined his spotlight on us and announced to the news media, which usually accompanied him on such affairs, that he had saved us. Said I: "As for me, I will walk back into the woods and stay with the mosquitoes and moccasins, and when asked, you will say: 'Geraldine Watson? She is probably home in bed. She is certainly not here with us!' I will not be rescued by Billy Payne!" I later had cause to have more respect for Sheriff Payne when he made a stand and refused to allow someone to illegally dictate policy in a matter concerning one of my sons.

With the first dim light of dawn, we again began to push southward, and, reaching Sandy Lake, walked out on the long, narrow sand spit which almost closed the lake off from the river. The connecting channel was deep and about 30 feet wide. So we sat down on a log on the sand spit like three crows on a telephone wire, and discussed alternatives: Jim could swim the river and walk over to the Four Oaks Ranch Road and hitch a ride to a telephone, or we could swim the channel and work our way downriver and yell at Charlie Schwartz to come get us.

Before we made a decision, we heard the sound of a powerful motor and Behold! Around the bend a large tugboat hoved into view. I had never seen a tugboat this far upriver. We stood up and hailed the crew, who swung the boat over and extended a gang plank down to our perch. "What on earth are ya'll doing way out here?" the person in charge said. We said we had crossed the island and decided we didn't want to go back the way we came. A few minutes later, we were ensconced in the galley eating breakfast and drinking coffee. I'll just bet that we broke some kind of record here—like the first time anyone was "lost" in the Big Thicket and was rescued by a tugboat. The boat serviced the sand barge just below Lakeview and about once a month made the voyage between berth and barge. Luckily for us, this was one of those days. They pulled in and unloaded us at Four Oaks Ranch where the caretaker let us use the telephone at about five minutes before 10:00. In spite of what my husband told Mrs. McClintock, he and David were on the island at daybreak looking for us.

They were not the only ones looking for us. Allene Bachman had telephoned my home on Big Thicket business and was told that I had failed to return from the Beaumont Unit the day before. Since everybody knew I had been receiving threatening calls, it created quite a stir. She immediately started calling everybody telling them that Geraldine Watson was missing, then called her attorney husband, Cleve, and he took the day off. They put their boat into the river and began cruising around the island looking for us. By that time, we were sitting on the tugboat with our feet up and drinking coffee.

A few weeks after our night on the island, Nancy and two student friends and I decided to return to the island and try to find the beautiful grove of large trees we had seen. We went straight to the peninsula but when we reached the narrow neck, our path was blocked by cottonmouth moccasins. There were so many of them, we could not make a way through them to reach the cross log. I took a long stick and began flipping them off the path. They immediately went back to their original position. Finally, Nancy, who was shivering with dread, begged to leave, so I threw down my stick and said "O.K., little brothers, you're trying to tell me something. I read your message." We went home.

Strange things continued to occur on the island. During the following Christmas holidays, a young friend from Austin, Robin Cravey, came over to see some of the Big Thicket. After my telling him about our adventure in the Beaumont Unit and how magnificent the forest was, he just had to see it. Though it was a gray day with no sun and getting along toward afternoon, we threw my boat into the back of my van and, in spite of my sensible husband's remonstrances, we took off to try to find my flagged trail.

We crossed the canal and proceeded down the old rutted road to the peninsula and the cross log, talking excitedly and turning aside to examine mushrooms growing in the forest. Suddenly, we realized that we were back at the canal. There was the boat. We laughed and said that we had somehow turned around, so proceeded once more down the trail eastward. Presently, we passed an old hog pen on our right which I was certain was on our left going in. Cautiously, I kept walking, peering ahead to find out which it would be: the cross log or the boat and canal again. You know the answer! I got really serious then and said, "Robin, we've got to concentrate on where we're going. I'll keep my eye on the ruts and you keep your eyes on the compass. We'll walk straight due east and not veer to right or left." Silently, we strode purposefully ahead. After a bit, Robin said: "Geraldine, we're not walking east, the compass needle is pointing in the opposite direction!" "No! It can't be! The compass is faulty. We haven't turned around." Then there was the pig pen on the wrong side again. Since I'm a hard-headed woman, I wouldn't give up. For a full hour, we tried to make it to that log until Robin finally said, "Geraldine, I don't know what is happening here, but I think we had better give up and go back." That night, the weather turned really bad. It rained and froze. If we had crossed that log, it's a good guess, Robin being a city boy and I with a terrible sense of direction, that we would have gotten lost and died of exposure before morning.

When spring break time came, Dr. Peter Marks and the crew from Cornell University who had been doing research in the Big Thicket for years, arrived. They were particularly interested in flood plain forests so, naturally, I told them about Cypress Island and we planned to explore it the next day. Peter Marks and his colleague, Dr. Paul Harcombe, of Rice University, were excellent woodsmen. Next morning, after crossing the canal, we walked along the old road straight to the log, across the slough on to a beautiful day on the island. After that, I went onto the island alone and collected plant specimens as part of my job with the Park Service with no trouble at all. I did take reasonable precautions like taking a compass and leaving early on good sunshiny days.

Why were we prevented from entering the island on those occasions? I don't know. I have never been superstitious, but a number of inexplicable incidents in my life have led me to conclude, as Hamlet told his friend, "There are more things in Heaven and Earth, Horatio,/ Than are dreamt of in your philosophy."

REGAL FERN BOG

River Mile 34 to 35

On the east side of the Neches between the river and Four Oaks Ranch Road is an unusual area, named Regal Fern Bog by Ned Fritz who has a mania for naming every natural feature he sees, but I guess he had the right here since he saw to it that the Beaumont Unit crossed the river to take in the bog.

Regal Fern Bog is unusual in its diversity of habitat. It occupies an old river channel which cut into a terrace, then changed course. Eroded sand from the terrace filled the abandoned channel and raised the northeast section slightly higher than that nearer the river. Seepage from the upland kept the upper area boggy with seasonal shallow standing water, while the lower was subject to infrequent flooding from the river. The center is raised by a pointbar deposit of sand and the area between the center and the river is typical low terrace habitat and is frequently flooded. These differences in elevation seem minor but the influence on vegetation is dramatic. Because the upper section is not flushed by frequent floods, organic debris has accumulated, rendering the soil and water acidic. The lower section is influenced by seasonal incursions of brackish water from the river which raises the pH of soil and water. Most plants are very selective when it comes to soil pH, so different communities dominate according to the pH factor.

Ferns usually are very sensitive to light, moisture, and pH, but the regal fern, *Osmunda regalis*, is one of the most adaptable. It grows in open savannahs which have alternate wet and dry periods, in full sun or full shade, tolerates a wide pH range, and thrives under frequent fire. Perhaps this adaptability is the reason the species has survived unchanged so long—three hundred million years according to paleobotanists who have found it embedded in coal. It is thus called a "fossil species." Natural food lovers relish the young fronds, so one might say that it has fed both man and dinosaur.

Regal Fern Bog can be reached from the river, but it is best to approach it inland. The Four Oaks Ranch Road follows the east side and you can literally step from your vehicle onto the short slope bordering the bog and view it dryshod. Cypress and tupelo trees cast a green shade over the lush ferns and other emergent aquatics, mosses, and patches of black water. After driving through the clearcuts and real estate developments east of the bog one gets the sensation of suddenly entering a dim, mysterious, magic realm, another world. Rotted logs in the bog are covered with many species of moss and lichens and, sometimes, with cottonmouth moccasins, so watch your step if you wish to venture into the bog. Also watch for broken glass as the community dumped their trash over the edge prior to inclusion in the preserve.

Four Oaks Ranch

FOUR OAKS RANCH

River Mile 34

On this bluff, the Orange County pioneer, George Alexander Patillo, built his home and grew fruit trees and produce and raised cattle. He had come from Georgia in the early 1830s with his bride, the former Sara Allen. He served in various capacities in the government of his new home through Spanish, Mexican, Republic, and state administrations.

The liveoak trees Patillo planted along the drive past his house have survived to this day and are a landmark on the Neches. Their down-sweeping branches are almost as thick as the trunks themselves and still retain a vestige of the Spanish moss which once hung to the ground. The ranch house also survives, though fast falling into ruin from neglect. Built in 1855, it has housed generations of the descendants of Patillo's fifteen children, as well as a succession of owners, among whom were Capt. W. M. Fletcher, a Beaumont pioneer, and Ed Stedman, founder of a wholesale food products company. He had planned to turn the 360-acre place into a truck farm, but the plan failed, probably due to frequent flooding. A Houston family, the Levys, have owned it since 1958, and used it for a weekend retreat, until vandalism made it difficult to manage.

A few years ago, someone had the idea of operating a restaurant there but the venture failed, possibly because of the difficulty of access, but more probably because the area was dry and no alcoholic drinks could be served with the food. It's like serving pizza without beer or Mexican food without margaritas—some things just seem to go together and in this time of easy transportation, diners go where they can get what they want.

The last owner committed what I consider a sacrilege. He had the low-hanging limbs of the big oaks removed, which totally ruined the grace and symmetry of the trees.

What a shame the National Park Service could not have acquired the house and trees along with the Neches corridor and could have operated it as a historic site. While our government can find billions for destructive schemes, it won't spend a dime on preserving the evidence of our heritage of vision, ambition, and hard work on which our country was built, to inspire and encourage all those who come and observe. Every example of pioneer dwellings within the bounds of the Preserve were either excised from the boundary or torn down. Ah well! I suppose I've harangued enough on that subject.

GEORGE BURGE

Before stock roaming at large was prohibited, the George Burge family ran hogs and cattle on Cypress Island. Due to the closed-canopy trees, cattle grazing, and the frequent floods, the woods were open and free of undergrowth, and it was easy to herd the animals on horseback. In the 1940s, all this changed. Rayburn and Steinhagen dams decreased the flooding and the island was seldom under water and the canal was dredged, diverting water which would have flowed through the sloughs of the island. Laws were passed and grazing was discontinued. Also, a contract was given to cut the timber. Bridges were built across the canal and the sloughs and roads following the hummocks were constructed. At this time, Daddy and I went to fish the lakes in the island and it looked like the whole world had changed. The huge loblolly pines on the hummocks were cut as well as the best of the oak and cypress. Fortunately, there was a period of wet weather, the water rose and prevented a complete harvest of the trees before the contract expired.

Walter Burge rode with his father and brother through those forests, tending cattle and hogs and hunting and fishing. They lived off the land in those days, but Prohibition presented an opportunity to make money and George Burge, like most every enterprising man of that time, had his still. His was not one of those penny ante operations, however, for he sold his whiskey wholesale at $1.25 a gallon. The Revenuers were active in the area, but George Burge was canny enough to elude them. Sonny told how they had burst into their home one day and tore it apart looking for liquor. After completely devastating it and finding nothing incriminating, they left the place a shambles for the wife and children to repair. One local moonshiner was not so lucky. He had managed to evade the pursuing officers to deliver his merchandise, but when he returned, they were waiting for him at the old log landing on Cook's Lake Road, and shot him to pieces. We hear a lot about the conflicts between bootleggers and the G-Men in Chicago and New York, but there was just as much action here in Southeast Texas—just nobody talks about it.

I knew Sonny Burge's mother. Years ago, when I wrote newspaper articles, I featured her collection of cypress knee art. It was truly amazing! She would go into the swamps, find just the knees she wanted for the article in mind, saw them off, clean and polish them and, lo, they became a grotto for a virgin and child, or a lamp base, or just an attractive ornament. She had found a way to express her creativity and love of beauty. Some sneer at these cypress knee creations, but they have value as folk art.

SCATTERMAN LAKE

River Mile 31.2

Not too far below Sandy Lake is Scatterman Lake. They are probably the largest of the abandoned channel lakes up to this point on the Neches and, as are all the others, are rimmed with groves of tall cypress trees standing in the shallow water.

These trees, and the big hardwoods in the adjacent woods, were once festooned with Spanish moss and great drapes of it hung down to the water. While some moss can still be seen scattered along in these backwaters, most of it has disappeared, due, they say, to air pollution. Spanish moss is not a moss but a flowering plant belonging to the pineapple family, of all things! If you search, you can find the little yellow flowers in the masses of scale-like gray-green leaves. It is an epiphyte, a plant which receives its sustenance from the air, so while it is absorbing moisture and nutrients from the air, it is also taking in hydrocarbons from automobile exhaust and the hydrogen sulfide, ozone, and all those other goodies which the prevailing south winds funnel up the Neches valley from the downstream petrochemical plants.

As some remind me: "Do we want this apparently useless plant or do we want transportation, electricity, plastics, and all the other amenities of modern life which the oil industry provides?" Thinking people, however, have begun to see such insignificant things as Spanish moss as one in a line of upright dominoes representing all life forms on earth. Someday, one of them is going to go down and set the whole line to falling and nothing can stop it.

One November day, Ranger Ken Tiege and I were at the back part of Scatterman Lake tacking up hunting posters when we saw a lovely sight. There was a cone-shaped islet about 12 feet in diameter with a large cypress tree in the center. Covering the mound were hundreds of lady's tresses orchids in full bloom. They are called the fragrant lady's tresses, because of their pleasant, vanilla-like odor.

At the mouth of Scatterman Lake on the east side of the river is an ocean-going ship about the size of a Navy destroyer escort. It was moored there several years ago and apparently abandoned, for it has now partly sunk. I'm wondering what the Park Service policy is going to be regarding such derelicts now that they have acquired the river corridors. Since its removal would be next to impossible, they probably have no recourse but to leave it there so people like me can be amazed and wonder about its history.

BUNN'S BLUFF

River Mile 30.8

If you don't hit this section of river at the right time of day when the tide is going out and there is a good flow of water, you have a battle on your hands. With the tide coming in and pushing water upstream, you are going with it even though you would prefer and are indeed valiantly paddling to go downstream. I was unlucky one trip and hit it just right to meet the incoming tide. Since I couldn't make much headway downstream, I decided to explore some of the backwater areas.

I think they stretched it a bit when they named this site Bunn's Bluff, for there is not much relief to the topography here in this tidal area, but it is above water except in the worst floods, and this was important in the early days. Bunn's Bluff was named for a young Englishman, Joseph Bunn, who came here in 1842 to make his fortune. Coming up the Neches, he was struck with the beauty of this spot. There were huge trees shading the point which overlooked the river. The river circled around the south and west and a cutoff lake with a majestic cypress grove was on the north side. He decided that this was the place he wanted to settle, so he bought some land and built a cabin of materials obtained at the site—logs, hewn cypress shingles, and mud and moss for a chimney. He later replaced it with a huge log cabin with many rooms and great fireplaces. Joseph Bunn married and had a large family. His daughter married the steamboat captain William O. Loving.

Bunn's Bluff became one of the busiest trading posts along the river with large wharves and spacious warehouses. There was also a store where local people came to buy goods brought upriver which were needed and couldn't be made at home, often paying for them in produce.

Joseph Bunn recorded in cool, meticulous detail in his account book a robbery of his store: "July 31, 1882, at about 30 minutes past 3 o'clock in the afternoon, two men came into the store and wanted to look at some pant cloth. They bought 30 cents worth of merchandize and handed me a $20.bill. When I opened the money drawer to get change, they demanded the money in the drawer and presented pistols. The drawer contained $70. one 2 1/2 dollar gold piece, and, I suppose, about $60. Or $70. in silver. The man that took the money was about 5 feet, six or 7 inches tall and weighed about 175 pounds and was about 30 years of age and of dark complexion, thin face and sharp nose." My source of information did not reveal whether or not the miscreants were caught and punished. More than likely, not.

CHARLIE SCHWARTZ

River Mile 30

Here, where Pine Island Bayou enters the Neches, Charlie Schwartz, river rat extraordinaire, lived most of his life. He died several years ago. The funeral director, a Baptist preacher, and I lowered Charlie into the three-by-six-by-six-foot hole. The preacher said a prayer, and I as the sole mourner, gave a brief eulogy, and we sent Charlie off on his second journey to the "other world."

Charlie had come to this part of the Neches River around the turn of the century (from where, I don't know). He trapped, fished, and lived off the land until World War I and the long arm of the draft board reached into the swamps and brought him out and shipped him off to England. There, he met a winsome schoolteacher named Lillian, married her and brought her back to his home. Any illusions she might have had of America where the streets and everybody's pockets are lined with gold were dispelled when they arrived at Charlie's shanty at the end of Cook's Lake where it branches off into two sloughs.

When Charlie paddled downstream to Beaumont for supplies, Lillian didn't get to go along to see the bright lights and happy people; Charley chained her to a tree so she wouldn't run away while he was gone. One day while he was away on his monthly foraging trip, a terrible storm came up, the bayou rose and the water was up to Lillian's neck when he got back. Unfortunately, they never had any children to brighten her bleak and lonely existence. She told me that she cried day and night for years, but finally accepted her fate. Records in the Park Service files give a different story of Lillian's origin, but this is what she told me herself.

When I met them, he and Lillian lived in an incredibly cluttered two-room cabin built high on pilings on the east bank of the river opposite its confluence with Pine Island Bayou. I was exploring the east bank looking for an easy, quick route into Cypress Island than that which I had been taking. His cabin site was the only place from Lakeview to Beaumont where a boat could be launched, and he gladly gave consent for us to use it. Charlie gave himself wholeheartedly to our cause. He and his assortment of boats were always at our disposal when we needed to show influential visitors the beauties of the island. His knowledge of the island, its intricate maze of waterways, its animal and water life, and general history were invaluable. We became friends and he shared with me his care and concern for the island and its wildlife.

Charlie apparently had legal rights to 640 acres of the island, for in the 1940s when Kirby wanted to log it, the company lawyers talked him into signing papers that gave them title to the land and gave him exclusive lifetime rights to hunting, fishing, and trapping, as well as a homesite on the east bank of the river. In the early 1970s, the company sold a hunting lease to a hunting club there. Charlie was inflamed. He strapped on a big six-shooter (the kind we call a "hog leg") and strode threateningly up and down, cussing a blue streak, the gun slapping against his knee. Word got around that he was "patrolling his territory," so there wasn't much hunting done there that year. He no longer hunted and he didn't want anybody else killing his deer, bear, and panthers (if you can believe him). A story he once told me explains his unusual feeling of responsibility for the island and its denizens.

Years ago, Charlie became ill and was hospitalized. He was declared clinically dead but was revived. During the time he was "dead," Charlie went on a "trip." He was wafted to the ethereal regions where he encountered a vast veil, or curtain. It appeared to be made of faces: old people, young people, babies and children, and felt glutinous to the touch. The curtain parted and Jesus Christ stood there welcoming him into Heaven. Jesus showed him around and what he saw was too beautiful—too wonderful—too incredible for human words to describe. Jesus told him he had a choice: he could stay in Heaven or he could return to his life on earth. "Well, this is certainly fine," said Charlie, "And I want to come here someday, but I have to go back to the Neches River. There is something I have to do there." So Jesus opened the curtain and Charlie woke up back in the hospital. In a short time, he was physically fit and back on the river.

For years, Charlie wondered why he had come back and what this "mission" could be. Then we came along with our scheme to make his island a unit of the Big Thicket National Preserve, forever protected by the National Park Service, and he knew. Maybe we could have saved it without his help, but it would have been hard. Now that the Park Service is going to allow hunting on the island, I often wonder if hunters will be stalked by Charlie's ghost. If you can believe the many tales of such "hauntings" up and down the river, we might have very few applicants for hunting permits in the Beaumont unit.

The inclusion of the island in the National Park System was not a happy conclusion for Charlie. The land he had lived on for over three-quarters of a century was not legally his—he was only a leasee. When he signed the lease, he never dreamed he would not be allowed to live out his life there. If he had had title to the site where his house stood, he and Lillian would have had a lifetime residency, but Kirby had the title and they were tossed out. Charlie had an angel, though, in Bill Jewel who was in charge of land acquisition for the Park service. He was so moved by Charlie's plight that he went to court and fought for Charlie's right to his little place. A compromise gave him another site slightly downriver where a nice, small house was erected. The problem of relocating his electrical service arose and Gulf States Utilities refused to take the line to his house without a substantial sum of money changing hands. Charlie had no money, so Bill Jewel paid for it out of his own pocket. When people mouth off about these "mindless, soulless government bureaucrats," I get angry, for I think of Bill Jewel—a federal employee with a tender heart and a great soul. Upon reading this, Bill insisted on my mentioning that Ned Fritz also contributed to Charlie's relocation. If I erred, it was in not giving Bill Jewel adequate praise.

Lillian died several years before Charlie. Her mind finally snapped one day. She got Charlie's six-shooter and chased him, buck naked, down the road, cussing him, and shooting at him. Fortunately, some men came along in a pickup truck and pacified Lillian, and Charlie escaped to the woods. She was taken to a "rest home" in Vidor where she spent the rest of her days happily. I don't believe for a minute that her mind snapped. She probably got to remembering how she had spent the best years of her life, alone in a swamp, chained to a tree, and decided to get even.

Charlie took in a young man boarder to help him with fishing, which he still did on a small scale. Though in his nineties, he was still a strong, active man. Eventually, he also went to the nursing home where the nurses made much over him and spoiled him totally.

A neighbor of Charlie's, a Mr. Burge, who sort of looked after him during his last days on the river, telephoned me when Charlie died and I drove down the river road to help lay him to rest. I wondered if he had died gladly, eager to return to that wonderful world he had visited so briefly. I also wondered that if the grace of God is so all-inclusive that a mean old cussin', rompin' and stompin' reprobate like Charlie Schwartz made it into Heaven, maybe I have a chance. Perhaps God could see inside, past the blustering and posturing and found that his heart was pure. But chaining Lillian to a tree? He probably repented of that when Lillian was chasing him down that road with that big six-shooter blazing away.

PINE ISLAND BAYOU

River Mile 30

The Neches River that connects Sandy, Scatterman, and Bunn's Bluff Lakes is more narrow than the river above or below them, but when Pine Island Bayou enters, from there downstream it widens to a good half-mile across. The bayou, at its confluence, is wider than the Neches and from Suicide Bend to its mouth was probably a course of the Neches in times past.

Pine Island Bayou

Pine Island Bayou rises in northeast Liberty County, flows southward until it encounters a meander ridge called the China Ridge (named for a community called China) then it flows southeastward until encountering another meander ridge called the Neches Ridge where it turns abruptly northward until joined by Little Pine Island Bayou and Black Creek. It again turns and, cutting through another ridge of resistant clays, meanders eastward to the Neches. The points where the bayou meets these ridges are natural holding basins for floodwaters and it has been a source of amazement to me that some of them have been chosen for very expensive real estate developments. The fact that the houses are up to their eaves in muddy water when we have the floods which invariably follow hurricanes upsets everyone and they scream "flood control," but then when the waters recede, more houses go up.

Possibly in the 1950s, Jefferson County attempted to relieve the situation by clearing a couple hundred feet of the banks of all vegetation and cutting through the bends in order to rush floodwaters downstream. As it was, the mature trees and shrubs along the banks formed a shading canopy that prevented weeds and brush from growing. When they were cut, each trunk sprouted dozens of shoots, sunlight produced a lush growth of weeds, and the result was an extremely dense brush which impeded the flow of water much more effectively than the original natural condition. Then, where the crumbly clay soil was disturbed and laid bare by the channelizing, rain and floodwaters quickly eroded it to be carried away to fill the downstream channel when it reached the dead water of the tidal area, thus reducing the lower bayou's holding capacity. Incidentally, the Hardin County side of the Bayou remained in its natural state, as Hardin County did not have the funds to participate in the drainage project.

Pine Island Bayou is estuarine upstream to its confluence with Black Creek, for tides come in to this point. Since the headwaters flow through calcareous clay prairie soils, the water of the bayou is yellow and turgid. Black Creek flows through acidic forest land, so it is the color of black coffee. The contrast is strongly marked where the two streams join and the bayou is half-light and half-dark a good distance downstream.

Riverboats traveled Pine Island Bayou upstream to the confluence of Boggy Branch. An important port was Concord where a north/south road crossed the bayou a short distance from the present highway bridge. The *Handbook of Texas* gives 1880 as its date of establishment, but I hear and read of references to its presence at a much earlier date.

Just downstream below the present highway bridge is the site of Voth where John Henry Kirby had a sawmill built in 1902. The concrete and brick remains of the mill are still there and are quite impressive to those of us who were there when it was a thriving, populous town. In roaming the site in recent years, I had the eerie feeling that I had died and returned centuries later to the ruins of the civilization which I had known.

In my days as a guide to birdwatchers and nature lovers in the Big Thicket area, I had many experiences on this bayou. One of the most memorable was when David, who was about 12 years old at the time, and I put in at the Highway 105 bridge between Beaumont and Sour Lake and let dark catch us before getting out. We were delayed because we had actually seen a pair of ivory-billed woodpeckers with their family in the area where Little Pine Island Bayou joins Big Pine Island Bayou: at that time, very wild country but now extensively developed and drained. We had been seeing woodpeckers of all sorts all day and when we rounded a bend and David whispered hoarsely: "Mama! Ivorybills!" I looked up expecting to see more pileated woodpeckers and was so startled by what I did see, I dropped the paddle into the boat with a loud clatter. The birds had been picking up acorns on the bank under a grove of water oak trees but flew into the trees at our approach. They flew over the bayou and up Little Pine Island and out of sight.

Trying to gain time, I took a cutoff that led us into the maze of narrow channels where Black Creek joins the bayou, and by the time we reentered the bayou, it was still light but, unfortunately, I was disoriented and, since the tide was pushing the current upstream, I made the mistake of turning upstream. We lost valuable time before I realized I was in dead water and had to turn back.

It was a dark, misty night with no moon or stars and the only light I had to guide by was the reflection from the lights of Beaumont which illuminated the low-hanging mist. This faint glow reflected on the water in the center of the bayou and I kept the prow of the boat in that point of light. We had the little backwater boat which is more unstable than a canoe and, on top of that, it had sprung a leak and had a couple of inches of water in the bottom which had soaked our life preservers. It was cold winter and we were heavily dressed and booted, so I had David put on and fasten one of the wet life preservers and I put the other at my feet. David perched in the prow, straining his eyes for obstacles in the water. I especially feared those just under the surface that would flip us if I hit them. There was a moment of sheer terror when I faced head-on the broad root end of a floating tree, but David yelled and I swerved to just barely miss it. I still have a chill when I see such a floater in the river. I was very calm and kept telling David everything was all right and not to be afraid. When we finally reached the bridge, pulled our boat out of the water, and prepared to load it and leave, I was shaking so hard, I couldn't put the key into the door and David had to open the car.

Actually, Pine Island Bayou is a nice canoeing stream with a lot of diversity. Maxine Johnston and I canoed the stretch between the Old Sour Lake Road and Highway 105 before those forests were so mutilated and it was a pleasant trip. The stretch between Highway 105 and the Beaumont Highway (69/96) can be easily made in a day if the water is right. A good indicator of water level is this: at the 105 bridge, there are stumps in the water. If they are just visible, the level is good; how much of them is exposed indicates how many portages you will have to make around logs and debris. From the Beaumont Highway to the Neches River is a long day's paddle, depending on the tide, but there will be no portages.

Anyone planning to canoe the bayou from the highway to the Neches should contact the National Park Service to inquire if the saltwater barrier at

Suicide Bend is in place. I came upon it once and had to pull a heavy aluminum river boat with an outboard motor up and down a steep, brushy bank to get around the barrier. There is another barrier on the Neches just below Lakeview. They are put in place in late summer when the river level gets low and saltwater intrudes upstream and gets into the canal that provides water for the municipalities of Beaumont and Port Arthur. At one time, they also served to prevent intrusion of the polluted downstream waters. The Neches River was so polluted a few years ago, that it was not only dead, it was toxic. When tides pushed the water upstream, all aquatic life swam ahead of it to remain in safe waters. When the barriers were put in place, everything caught behind them died, except the crabs, that is, for they crawled out of the water to safety. Dr. Richard Harrel, professor of limnology at Lamar University, and his students can be credited largely with forcing the cleanup of the Neches.

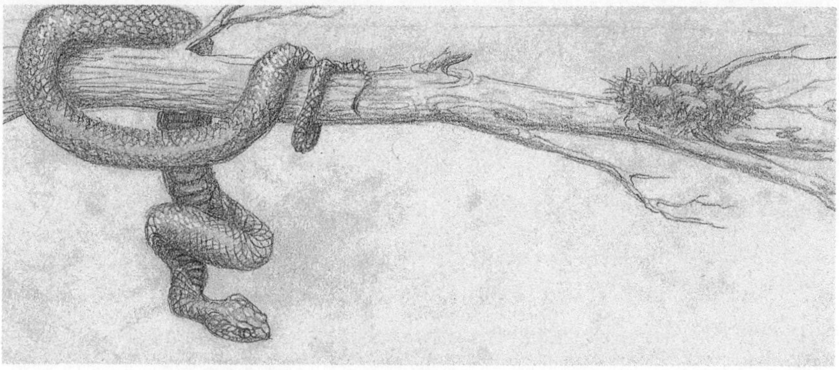

SNAKES

Daddy always said that there were more snakes on Pine Island Bayou than anywhere else and I believe he was right. The king of this herpetological realm is, of course, the cottonmouth moccasin. It is always found at the edge of water as its principle diet is frogs. It can be seen swimming in water, though, and one way to tell whether it is a cottonmouth or a water snake (Natrix spp.)is this: the water snake creates a wake behind it as it swims, the cottonmouth does not. If you want to get close enough, another difference is in the eye. The cottonmouth, as do all pit vipers, has a cat's eye pupil while the water snake's pupil is round.

Cottonmouths in the lower Big Thicket area are a charcoal gray color while those in the upper Thicket in Tyler, Jasper, and Polk Counties are colored much like the copperhead and not quite as large as the southern relatives. The reason for this might be because the extensive lower floodplains of

Pine Island Bayou are composed of sediments from the gray calcareous clays of its upper watershed. Thousands of years of blending into the background gave those snakes with the dark gray coloring an advantage over the more colorful snakes in evading predators, so they survived to breed more dark snakes while their colored brothers did not.

In the upper areas, floodplains are small and there is almost always a layer of leaf litter—all shades of brown—and those snakes with a mottled brown coloring are more likely to be overlooked by hawks, owls, wild hogs, etc. The snake's instinct is: "Don't move and they won't see you. If they trap you with claw or foot, bite and run."

That is my theory about their coloration. Herpetologists say that young cottonmouths have bright colors and get darker as they get older. I won't be offended if you don't like my version.

Cottonmouths, and copperheads as well, when young, have yellow tail tips which they flip back and forth like a squirming worm. This attracts small frogs, lizards, and skinks which get the surprise of their aborted lives when dinner turns out to be the diner. These yellow tips turn brown when the snake reaches fourteen to sixteen inches in length. But the adults still vibrate their tail tips, sounding in dry leaves just like a rattlesnake which might be mimic behavior. It certainly serves the intended purpose of ridding the immediate area of any trespassers. If that fails, the cottonmouth might spray the intruder with a fine jet of foul-smelling musk which it can shoot as far as five feet.

Of the 300 or so hospital cases of snakebite in Texas, only seven percent of them are from cottonmouths. They have a reputation for being mean but they have been kind to me. Having had innumerable opportunities to put the bite on me, they have allowed me to meet my demise in some other, future fashion. I met one once, nose to nose as I was crawling through a thicket too dense to walk in upright. We both froze and I backed ver-r-r-y slowly until I was out of striking distance—then jumped up and screamed. No matter how friendly you feel toward snakes and even though you know most of them are harmless and those who could do you in are too docile to take the trouble, it is instinctive to jump and yell when coming upon one unawares.

Not only do cottonmouth moccasins have a bad reputation among people, but other snakes apparently feel the same way. The king snake, which eats other snakes, has a distinctive odor that warns other snakes of its presence so they run away. The cottonmouth is the only snake which will stand its ground and fight it out with the king snake.

Beside the cottonmouth, other poisonous snakes in the Big Thicket area are the copperhead, pygmy rattler which we call ground rattler, eastern diamondback rattler, the timber rattler, and the canebrake rattler, which is now lumped in with the timber rattlers. These are members of the pit viper group and have a hemotoxic venom. That is, it is a blood (hemo) poison (toxin). This type of venom destroys the erythrocytes (red blood corpuscles) which carry oxygen to the cells. Without oxygen, the cells die and, depending on how much venom is injected, the flesh around the wound rots away. Pit viper venom is slow-acting so that the blood can circulate it throughout the entire system of the victim. This aids in its digestion. Fortunately, pit vipers are shallow biters, which reduces the damage to humans. In the panic of snakebite, some people cut into the wound. This is dangerous as the venom contains an anticoagulant and the victim might bleed to death where he could have survived the snakebite.

One of our most common poisonous snakes, though not often found in floodplains, is the copperhead. Its venom is very mild and I have known quite a few people bitten by copperheads, but none who were seriously affected. One woman died because the doctor who gave her an antivenin shot did not first test her for an allergy to it. Another, a child, lost a foot because the hospital put her foot and leg into a stocking of ice, (a method which was soon discontinued) and she lost circulation in the limb. I would not go to a hospital if bitten by a copperhead, but would put the injured part in a tub of warm water, wash it well and get a tetanus shot at my doctor's office.

Rattlesnakes roam about within 20 minutes' crawling time from a central den where as many as 100 might congregate. The very idea is the stuff of which nightmares are made. Even the scientific name of he timber rattler is dreadfully suggestive: *Crotalus horidus horridus*!

While I give little thought to most snakes, it does give me chills when, on rare occasions, I run across timber rattlers. They are really big! In the Big Sandy Unit, I stepped over a coiled-up timber rattler and the mound of coiled snake could have filled a Number 2 washtub! The wedge-shaped head was flat in the center of the coil. What a shock! I levitated at least several feet! Someone gave me a dead timber rattler once which they claimed was a road kill (after I told them it was a $200 fine to kill one in the preserve). I skinned it and found inside a grown squirrel, swallowed headfirst. The forepart of the squirrel had already been almost digested by the stomach acids while the last part of it seemed untouched. I wondered if the snake would have regurgitated the indigestible parts as a chicken snake does when it eats a hen's egg. It swallows the egg whole so as not to lose the juices, then wraps around something and squeezes, breaking the egg inside. It then compresses the shell and spits it out. A snake can digest the fragile bones of mice and birds, but a squirrel has some pretty big bones. By the way, snakes have a bony plate in the top of their palate in order to protect their brain from large objects that pass through their hinged jaws.

Another poison snake of our area is the coral snake, which possesses a neuro (nerve) toxic venom, as do the cobras. This venom causes a neurolysis (deterioration) of nerve cells and therefore, paralysis of the body. When the infected blood reaches the heart, death is immediate and certain. On the river one need not be concerned with coral snakes for they like leaf mulch, rotted wood, and forest litter to burrow in, and so are more likely to be found in deciduous or mixed slope and upland forests. One is very unlikely to be bitten by a coral snake. They have such a docile nature that you have to pick one up and literally slap it around to make it bite. Then, it will have a hard time getting enough grip to get any venom into you. Unlike the pit vipers, which have long fangs in the upper front jaw and only have to take a slap at you to do the job, the coral snake's hypodermic teeth are very small and in the back of their jaws. They would have to grab the thin skin between the fingers to really get a good hold. For this reason, only 40 percent of coral snake bites result in severe poisoning. A coral snake bite produces numbness and tingling of the face, scalp, and fingers, but then intense anxiety produces the same symptoms, so damage might be much less than anticipated by the bitee.

Probably the most unusual snake we have which is sometimes found in floodplains, is the nonpoisonous hognose snake, sometimes called a puff adder. It is so slow that it depends on sleeping toads for prey, so, unlike other snakes, it hunts by day while toads are asleep. Few predators eat toads, for they have potent poison glands in their skin, but the hognose gets around this by producing more adrenaline to neutralize the toxins.

The hognose has coloring similar to a copperhead, but its nose is shovel shaped for burrowing and its behavior is definitely unique. Having no poison fangs for defense, if threatened, it first plays cobra: hissing and spreading its hood. If this doesn't work and the snake is touched, it discharges fecal matter, regurgitates the contents of its stomach, and emits foul-smelling fluids from its anal glands. If all this fails, it acts out a drama worthy of an academy award, going into convulsions and flopping over belly-up, its tongue hanging out, obviously dead. No amount of pushing around or shaking rouses it. Finally, when it is left alone, it opens an eye to see if all is safe, collects itself, and nonchalantly glides away.

There are many species of nonpoisonous snakes in our area, one of the most common being the rat snake, though they generally prefer dry uplands. I once found a huge rat snake in a nest of baby bunny rabbits. It was in the process of swallowing one of the bunnies while its nest mates, though plenty large enough to jump and run like crazy, merely sat motionless, waiting their turn. The thing to do is let nature take its course, after all the snake needs to eat too, but who can stand still for a big snake to eat a nest of bunnies? I just had to rescue them!

The most common snakes on the river are the nonpoisonous water snakes. They might be six or seven feet long and may be seen sunning themselves on logs or climbing up on overhanging limbs in the hopes of snaring a bird. It is not uncommon to have one drop into your boat when you are paddling along beneath the overhanging limbs tending a trotline. Since they like to eat fish too, you might find one on your trotline where he has tried to snag an easy lunch by robbing your line and found himself a victim. To catch a fish, the water snake swims around in a circle until his side touches a fish. This triggers muscles to strike at the point where the prey is.

Water snakes, when disturbed, will discharge the extremely malodorous contents of their cloaca and musk glands toward you. If that doesn't get rid of you, they will certainly bite, for they are aggressive. While their bite isn't poisonous, it is dangerous, for their fangs have many bacteria and your wound can become severely infected. One should always have a tetanus shot when bitten by any kind of snake.

My photographer friend and I witnessed a once-in-a-lifetime scene on Massey Lake. We were paddling about in our boat when we saw two large water snakes hanging from a dead snag about ten feet above water. There was a hollow in the top of the snag and the stub of a limb. The snakes must have been seven feet long, for about four feet was hanging free. They were doing a stylized dance, much like Balinese dancers, sometimes forming an upside-down heart with their chins touching at the cleft. They would rub chins awhile and then one would go down the entire length of body, gently biting as it moved, repeated by its mate. It was so fascinating that neither of us thought to record it on film—probably something never done before—even though we both had excellent cameras with us. My friend, who is deathly afraid of snakes, was ooing and ohing and groaning and begging me not to get any closer.

Somehow, people who are afraid of snakes, see them everywhere they go. I never see snakes, that is unless I am with someone else. My photographer friend and I were once walking down a trail when she stepped right on top of a copperhead. She just stood there screaming. "Well, get off the poor thing," I said. Which she did—both feet at the same time—and fell right on top of the unfortunate snake ,which just managed to escape with its life.

If a person thinks he has been snake bit, the mind can duplicate expected symptoms. There was a park ranger in Big Bend National Park who had a large rattlesnake strike his leg. He made it to his vehicle and decided he wouldn't waste time going to headquarters, but would go straight to the hospital at Alpine. As he drove, the classic symptoms of rattlesnake bite began to appear: icy sweat, dizziness, nausea, and shaking. His leg even began to swell. He made it to the hospital just in time and collapsed in the emergency room, gasping "Snakebite!" and passed out. When he came to himself, his leg was no longer swollen and he was told that the snake had missed his leg entirely. There are even cases of people dying of heart attacks when being snake bitten. Actually, with a real bite, there is immediate sharp, burning pain, swelling and discoloration of the affected limb, and violent nausea and vomiting.

There are more snakebites in Texas than any other state, but actually they are very rare. Throughout the entire United States, only an average of one person per year dies of snakebite. More people die from reaction to the treatment than from the bite itself and some actually die from fright. There is really no need to commend your soul to God and prepare to die if bitten. Just stay calm and quiet and try not to get excited. You can survive even if you don't get help. The Indians treated snakebite by pressing a freshly-killed animal over the wound to absorb the poison. My mother tells how her mother was bitten by a snake once and her mother grabbed up a chicken from the yard, cut it open and slapped it over the bite. The flesh of the chicken turned bright green and the child suffered no ill effects from the snakebite.

And now, if you are still interested in snakes, I have more for you. Snakes are reptiles. Reptiles dominated the earth about 70 million years ago until the beginning of the Cenozoic era when cataclysmic environmental changes on the earth eliminated many creatures. On land, no animal over 50 pounds survived, and only about one-third of the reptiles. Scientists believe that a giant asteroid struck the earth, causing dense clouds of dust to envelop the planet for several years. The sun was so dimmed that plant life, which depends on sunlight, was almost exterminated. Animals able to burrow and stay underground and eat insects and worms, seeds, lichens and algae had an advantage over those which had to withstand the severe competition for food and water on the surface.

Snakes came into their own at this time, but they were not snakes as we know them today. Strangely, this is one point on which science and the Bible agree: snakes had legs! Many snakelike lizards today have a tendency to lose their legs, some have only vestigial legs and others, like our glass snake have none at all. Snakes began to lose their legs in recent times (geologically,) and only during the mid-Miocene time did they develop poison glands. Also newly developed are the thermal pits, a sensory devise which helps locate prey by body heat and are also used to find warm winter quarters.

Without locomotive appendages like legs, snakes move about by contracting muscles on alternate sides and using belly scales for traction. They can move pretty fast. The coachwhip, a grassland snake, can get along at six miles per hour. The flexibility necessary for such maneuvering is possible as its entire body is made up of vertebrate, as many as 435!

The study of reptiles, herpetology, is a fascinating hobby for many people, though one must really know what one is doing to successfully keep snakes in captivity. When my oldest son was in his herpetology phase, we had a six-foot indigo, a rat snake, and a hognose snake in residence at one time. He made an error in judgment in taking his rat snake, a fine, five-foot specimen, to school for show-and-tell. Another child just had to see what was in the box and he was thrown off the school bus. His snakes were always given their freedom after a brief exposure to civilized life.

Snakes perform a very useful function in the balance of things. Just as birds control insects, snakes control rodents. If it were not for them, the world would be overrun with mice, rats, rabbits, and other little things which eat greenery and the world would be a barren wasteland. On the other end, snakes also are eaten by hawks, owls, and other snakes. Pineywoods rooter hogs once kept the snake population under control. It is said that the heavy layers of fat on their jowls prevent snake venom from reaching blood vessels. Even people eat snakes, and those who have tried it say rattlesnake meat tastes a lot like chicken.

Some people say: "I'm not afraid of snakes, but I respect them." Balderdash! We are all terrified by those little wiggly bits of skin and bone. Why are we so afraid of snakes? Is it really something instilled in us by cautious parents, or has it been passed down in our genes from Eve who lost Paradise through her association with a snake? Or perhaps we look down there and see the power of Death in that little creature and realize the ease and suddenness with which he could put an end to our existence and that is what shakes us up.

Some behaviorists say that children under three years of age have no fear of snakes. It is instilled in them by adults, and that this antipathy is restricted to those of the Judeo-Christian tradition. Since the devil in the form of a snake caused Adam and Eve to introduce crime and punishment into a hitherto perfect world, the reptile we have today is still blamed. I know certain religious folk in my area who truly believe that any snake they come across is the devil himself and must be killed. (Try explaining THAT to a Park Ranger who is writing out a ticket over a snake carcass!) It is O.K. to kill a deer or squirrel in season, but never a snake! (Try explaining THAT to a backwoodsman!) Snakes are protected by the rules and regulations of the National Park Service.

Other cultures in the world take the opposite approach from ours. For instance, the rattlesnake enjoys semideity status with the Hopi Indians of the Southwest who incorporate them in their religious rites, giving them messages for the gods, and turning them loose into the desert. In Central America, the venom of the rattlesnake is drunk as an aphrodisiac.

The python is worshipped in Africa, and in India and Burma, the king cobra is deity. I have seen movies showing women kissing the nose of a rearing king cobra. In Mexico, Quetzalcoatl, the god of civilization who invented agriculture, metallurgy, and was a patron of the arts, is represented by a feathered serpent. The Loa, chief god of Voodooism, quietly strong in the southeastern United States, especially Louisiana, is a snake.

The Greeks, Romans, and Egyptians also had their snake gods, and the Greek god of medicine, Aesculapius, carried a staff with a snake twined around it. This staff, or caduceus, is still used as a symbol of the medical profession today. Each Greek home had a household snake that lived in the house, spied on the inhabitants, and reported to the gods. The householder was careful to supply it with food and tell it good things about the household to relate to its masters.

I can't understand man's proclivity for bowing down and worshipping most any and everything. I myself, as I often say, have a very stiff knee. My ancestors came to this country to avoid having to bow and scrape before degenerate kings and religious demagogues and I guess it is just bred in the bone.

COOK'S LAKE

River Mile 30

Pine Island Bayou is extremely broad where it enters the Neches, but after about a half mile, it abruptly turns to the left in a channel so narrow one almost overlooks it. The broad portion continues as Cook's Lake. If water level is high or the tide is out, the swiftness of the current is enough to distinguish it from the placid waters of Cook's Lake.

Cook's Lake continues broad, more or less paralleling the bayou, and then begins to branch into smaller channels and cypress swamps. There are few places as beautiful as this. You can wind around among the tall cypress trees for hours in a canoe, or park your boat and walk through parklike forests of giant oaks. My favorite time of day here is late afternoon and evening. The afternoon winds die, the air is still and the water becomes a mirror, reflecting trees, sky, and water birds gracefully floating over the surface of the water to their rookeries in the interior of the island.

Cook's Lake was named for a family of German immigrants, Koche, later changed to Cook, who with some other families, came to Texas with the hope of settling on rich farm lands. Something went wrong and the man with his wife and children were left at Sabine Pass. They made their way to Pine Island Bayou where they stopped and made a crop and where the father died. The mother and sons constructed rafts, placed their possessions on them and poled and pulled them up Village Creek to a site called Cook's Bluff, a high bluff on the creek directly in front of and about a quarter of a mile from my present home. A previous settler was at the location, but the Cooks paid him $25 and he vacated in their favor. The settlers used a trail which crossed the creek at this point so it became known as Cook's Road and the family ran a ferry across the creek. Later, the German families legalized their claim with a Lorenzo de Zavala grant. At one time, Cook land extended north and south all the way from Cook's Road to Pine Island Bayou and, east to west, from Village Creek to the Neches River. A lawyer friend told me how the Cooks were cheated out of much of their land by Kirby, and I don't doubt it for I have heard many similar stories. This area by Village Creek, where I also reside, was known as Cook settlement and most of the people who live here are descendants of the original settlers. A great-great-great grandson of the first Cook, Bert Rutherford, lives on the site of the first Cook cabin.

This section of Pine Island Bayou and Cook's Lake is within the Beaumont Unit of Big Thicket National Preserve. I have had so many experiences in this area, it is impossible to chronicle them all: some good, bad, foolish, dangerous, etc. Most people are afraid to enter the island. It is so easy to get lost, both by boat in the cypress swamps or afoot on land, that they avoid it. Someday, the National Park service will provide hiking trails and marked canoe routes so everyone can experience it also, hopefully, at no risk.

SAGA OF THE *BAYOU QUEEN*

This area always brings to my mind the brief, ill-fated reign of the *Bayou Queen*. The *Queen* was a fifteen-passenger pontoon pleasure barge with bright blue astro-turf carpet, a horseshoe of red leather cushioned seats around the railings and a gaily fringed canopy over all. The pilot sat at a console in back center within easy reach of the refrigerator-bar and guided the stately craft through the cypress trees like a swan gliding in and out of lotuses.

My brother-in-law owned the barge, trailer, and motor, used it briefly and decided to sell. I saw that barge. I fell in love. Having no money, I began to plot a scheme by which it could become my own.

The beautiful cypress swamps of the Beaumont Unit are inaccessible to the public except those with boats and a knowledge of the area and there is a dearth of things to do in the Beaumont area for entertainment and recreation. Anyone should be happy to pay a reasonable fee to sit in luxury, enjoy the scenery, sip a drink and eat snacks served by my lovely daughter-in-law, June, in a cute sailor suit. Since David was between jobs, he would make an ideal pilot and tour guide. My husband would take care of maintenance and I would be publicist and business agent. The barge was just the right size for small parties, Sunday school classes, birdwatchers, etc., and dawn and dusk birdwatching expeditions would be very popular. It would also make this beautiful area available even to the very aged and the wheelchair-bound.

The potential was brilliant. My banker, knowing my sense of honor if not the tour business, put up the $3,500. I prepared and distributed a flyer and went about to properly legalize my venture, which meant applying for an operator's permit and liability insurance.

The insurance matter was disposed of post haste. Since I was carrying passengers and operating in navigable waters, the same rates applied to me as an oceangoing passenger liner and only Big Oil or Aristotle Onassis could afford that insurance. So my log book, which each passenger signed upon boarding, stated: "I am aware that the operator of the *Bayou Queen* has no insurance and that I am here at my own risk. The owner shall in no way be responsible for anything which might happen to me on this barge."

The operating permit was something else again. The U.S. Coast Guard had jurisdiction and applied rules and regulations for oceangoing passenger vessels to my little barge. They simply had no experience with a small operation such as mine, and the young officer in charge took gleeful delight in asserting his authority. "There are no barriers in the Neches river to prevent you going out to sea," he stated. "So we must see that you are fitted to do so." "Nothing," I countered, "but my little 25 horse power motor and the open, fragile nature of my craft, not to mention my sanity!" To begin with, he explained, I would have to go to pilot's school, which would take six months, and get my pilot's license. I would have to know how to navigate by radar, magnetic compass, and the stars, and how to compute arrival times based on speed of vessel, speed and direction of currents, tides, winds, etc. "But," I argued, "I won't be a hundred feet away from the bank at any time and will operate only in the daytime. I have no radar nor magnetic compass and can't see the pole star because of overhanging trees. Why should I spend all that time and money for something I don't now or will ever need?"

Then there was the matter of "equal facilities for men and women." He suggested that I rent two "Johnny-on-the-spots" and place them on the four by twelve-foot bow deck. "I can see it now," I intoned: "Off we go for a scenic tour of the National Park's beautiful cypress swamps, and what do we see? Majestic cypress trees towering to the sky and reflected in the mirrored waters, with water birds rising gracefully before us? No! We see two toilets looming up on the bow obscuring everything else, including the pilot's view of snags, floating logs and sandbars. Besides, if someone can't 'hold it' for the two-hour cruise, he needs to be home—he's sick!" I placed a chemical toilet beneath one of the lift-up seats and improvised a circular curtain (fire-proofed, of course) which could be raised and hung from the canopy frame in the event of an emergency, and they accepted it.

Life preservers! I had just bought all-new USGS-approved life jackets, but would they do? Nooo! They had to be Type I (or was it Type II?) which would hold up an unconscious body in midocean for two weeks. Then they had to test its stability when fully loaded on the river, so I invited friends and relations in order to have a full load, the inspector came aboard and off we went. I had just assured them that there were no boats on this section of river larger than mine, when around the bend chugged this enormous tugboat—the same tug that serviced the sand barge up the river monthly and that picked us up off the sand spit that morning. I swore it was the first I had ever seen on the Neches, but I don't think he believed me.

At this time, my husband was found to have cancer and underwent radical surgery with radiation and chemotherapy. I had lost my maintenance department! (The smallest of my concerns at this time, I might add.) While David and I were with my husband at the hospital, someone stole the motor, batteries, gas tanks, and everything else except the toilet, which was hidden by the cover. All in spite of the fact that it was berthed at an expensive marina right in front of the caretakers' cabin. The only other owner whose boat was burgled was a doctor who was also in the hospital. (I suspect this was dirty work by the caretaker.) There was nothing to do but replace them. Since I knew little about such things, I made the mistake of buying a different brand of motor, which required a complete change of controls and other fittings, which necessitated the hiring of a marine mechanic to install them and make alterations.

David got a job in Denver and took off, and I was the Watson Tour and Guide Service. Giving up on going "legit," I began operating on a word-of-mouth, contributions-only basis. (I couldn't advertise.) No passengers had an inkling of how terrified I was when things would go wrong but I acted like I knew exactly what I was doing. Surprisingly, I was able to cope with all emergencies.

What a shame! It was a simply beautiful two-hour tour. We passed the remains of the fleet of riverboats which had plied the Neches before trains, highways, and bridges put them out of business, past coastal marshes of wild rice and tall reeds alive with water birds, through areas where legend says Jim Bowie, of Alamo fame, smuggled in slaves after the law forbade their importation, and where the pirate, Jean LaFitte, reputedly buried treasure. Entering broad Pine Island Bayou from the Neches and then up the equally expansive Cook's Lake, we wound through the cypress trees of the sloughs and deep swamps which lace the unit. Finally, we arrived at the Madonna Tree and admired the bonsai-shaped cypress, which looks as if it belongs in a classical Chinese painting, the hollowed inside of which forms a grotto where cypress knees form realistic images of the holy family. There we had drinks

Madonna Tree

and snacks and talked about the natural and human history of the island and its environs.

After operating a few months on a low-key level, I made enough to recoup my expenditures and, finding a buyer with cash in hand, I gladly turned over barge, keys, boat club membership card, etc., and had the first good night's sleep since I bought the thing. I have since heard former boat owners say that the two happiest days of their lives were when they bought their boat and when they sold it. True! True! Well! So much for private enterprise and small business in America! But it was a beautiful dream.

GEORGE BUSH

My daughter was digging through my files the other day and came across a picture of me and George H. W. Bush walking down a trail together. It reminded me of an event which should rank among my most memorable, as the man who I took into Cypress Island that day became president of the United States.

Richard Nixon was running for reelection and George Bush was stumping East Texas for votes for the Republican candidate, and we hoped while he was here to show him enough of the Big Thicket to impress him and gain his support for a bill creating the Big Thicket National Preserve. Allene Bachman was an ardent conservationist and a member of an old, wealthy, and prestigious family. She was a supporter of the Big Thicket cause and, since she was the Republican campaign fund chairman for East Texas she persuaded George Bush to include the Big Thicket in his itinerary.

I was to be Mr. Bush's hostess and the plan was for me to join him and a busload of media people at Woodville, stop at the Hyatt Longleaf Pine Preserve to view orchids and carnivorous plants, on to the beautiful slope forest of the Sternenberg Preserve along Village Creek, circle around through the traditional Thicket around Saratoga, then to the Beaumont Country Club docks where Allene would be waiting with her famous bandana picnic lunches and we would cruise through the cypress swamps of the proposed Beaumont Unit in her spacious boat.

A few days before the tour, an aide called shortening the time allowed for us, so I had to drop the traditional Thicket from the itinerary. The next day, more time was lopped off and the day before the tour, the aide called to say that Mr. B. was scheduled to meet with some ladies' groups in Woodville and would be unable to make any stops in Big Thicket, but I would be welcome to come to Woodville and ride on the bus to Beaumont with him. I told him how I felt about riding a bus with a bunch of media people and Republicans and, if Mr. B. wasn't that interested in the Big Thicket he and his whole party could go to hell, and hung up. About an hour later, the aide called back and said that Mr. Bush did want to see some of the Big Thicket and that the schedule had been rearranged; so we saw the orchids and carnivorous plants at Hyatt, walked the trail at the Sternenberg Preserve (now the Kirby Trail in the Turkey Creek Unit) and proceeded to the country club docks. By the time the media people crowded in, the boat was packed. As we proceeded up the Neches toward Cypress Island, I explained the ecological and historical significance of the area, pointing out blooming irises, southern wild rice, etc. At least I tried to do so, but was drowned out and interrupted by the media people asking Mr. B. about the party's position on Viet Nam. I kept saying, "Please, let's don't talk about the war. We are here to see the Big Thicket."

They ignored me. Finally, I raised my voice and said, "O.K.! You all want to talk about Viet Nam? Let's talk about Viet Nam!" Having one son a paramedic in the Air Force and another son who was war age, I was a rabid anti-war activist, and proceeded to bring out some points and facts about the war which Mr. Bush hadn't covered in his answers. Then, in the ensuing silence, I said, "Oh look! There is a flock of roseate spoonbills!" So the tour was finished without further interruptions.

Allene Bachman was furious with me. She said, "Geraldine Watson will never lead another field trip in the Big Thicket! She was rude and, furthermore, she didn't smile the whole day!" All of which, I suppose, was true. Nobody was happy about that day. Some were angry because the traditional Thicket was ignored—all my fault, naturally.

A short time after, George sent his wife, Barbara, for a more in-depth look at the Big Thicket and Ned Fritz was assigned to come down from Dallas and be host. He got her and party lost in a titi thicket where they got scratched up, clothes torn, and hair disheveled. Still later, the secretary of the interior, Walter Hickle himself, wanted to come view the Big Thicket and personally asked that Geraldine Watson be his hostess, which I was and was most charming and gracious to the great man. Guess it shows how really small you are when you can gloat over such petty triumphs, but I must confess to secretly chortling over the affair. Later, Allene forgave me. She lost a teenaged daughter, Sally, in a tragic automobile accident. One of twins, Sally was beautiful, intelligent, and caring about the world and its people! What a loss! She could have contributed so much good in a lifetime. Having daughters of my own the same age, I empathized with Allene and felt the loss personally. Guess when we're hit by real tragedies, little things like screwing up a field trip fall into their proper perspective.

Allene was "born to the purple." From one of Beaumont's leading families, her father, brother, and husband were prominent attorneys. She could have spent her resources on pleasures but devoted them to her home, family, and the environment. Allene was a birdwatcher and an active member of the Texas Ornithological Society and the Audubon Society where she met Texas' premier environmentalist, Ned Fritz, another lawyer, and was hijacked into his Texas Committee on Natural Resources.

Unlike Allene, I was "born to the cotton." My Daddy always told me: "Sister, don't ever forget. The Democrats are for the poor and the worker, and the Republicans are for the rich and powerful." My husband was a Republican, though poor and a worker. The oil company for which he worked convinced him that what was good for the Company was good for the worker and he tried to explain this and the "trickle down" theory to me. What "trickled down" to him was cancer and an early death from the toxic, carcinogenic chemicals he handled in the lab where he worked. In the days of obscene profits after the oil industry was deregulated, his company didn't care enough about the workers to spend a few hundred dollars for a ventilator over the lab tables where they cooked up the chemicals being tested. Ah well! That's in the irretrievable past, but being the unambitious dilettante that I am, it is safe to assume that I will always be among the poor workers.

And what does all this have to do with the Neches River? The Neches River is part of the Big Thicket National Preserve and Allene and her Republican friends had no small influence in putting the legislation through congress. We are fortunate that Allene chose to use her position of privilege and influence to soften what might have otherwise been a very hard anti-environment stand by the Republicans in power. George Bush afterwards was known as an "environmental president," and I want the world to know that it was due largely to Allene Bachman. I am not forgetting that it was a Republican President who signed the bill creating a Big Thicket National Preserve.

Allene, a heavy smoker, died of cancer a few years ago, and, though we were of two different worlds, socially and economically, we were of the same heart and I still feel her loss keenly. I will always see her as she appeared once at a Big Thicket hearing dominated by hysterical, threatening rednecks who were whipped to a frenzy by lumber company propaganda. Representing the Big Thicket Association, she stood in perfect composure and in a firm voice, gave her statement supporting a National Preserve. She just exuded class.

The Big Thicket cause was fortunate in having a few really high class supporters, chief among whom is Maxine (Mickey) Johnston, retired head librarian at Lamar University. There are about a half dozen people without any one of whom there would be no Big Thicket National Preserve. Mickey was a key element and the fact that I have not mentioned her prominently in this chronicle does not lessen her importance to the cause, or to me. Her contribution would be a book in itself. Her major area of concern was the traditional Thicket in the triangle between Sour Lake, Batson, and Kountze, as she lived in Batson and knew that area best. My experience and knowledge was chiefly in the eastern portion of Big Thicket country and so my attention was concentrated there.

While I'm naming names of those without whom the Big Thicket would not have been saved, I might as well add a few more. It was Lance Rosier who kept the idea alive for forty years and never gave up. Without Dempsie Henley, of Liberty, we well-meaning but inexperienced nature lovers would never have got the cause off the ground. Ralph Yarborough championed the cause in the Senate and Bob Eckhart in the House. Orrin and Lorraine Bonney got the backing of the powerful Sierra Club and Ned Fritz gave it his legal and legislative expertise. The problem with naming names is you always forget a few and wind up hurting feelings. Too bad.

BEAUMONT

River Mile 27

I did not include the river from Pine Island Bayou to Beaumont in this adventure. No particular reason. Guess I had made that trip so many times that I had lost interest, or perhaps I was just tired. It is certainly worth one's while, however, for it is completely different from the upper river. It is very broad and lakelike with almost no banks. Cypress swamps are at every turn and much of the surrounding terrain is in coastal marsh with tall reeds, sedges, and wild rice. The water level fluctuates with the tides and if the north wind blows and the tide is out, the adjoining cypress swamps are almost dry. Actually, this is the best time to paddle down the river with the current going out with the tide and the north wind at your back. Incoming tidal currents and the south wind in your face make for hard work. (Probably the reason I didn't take it on.)

There is much history in this stretch of the river, most of it in the realm of legend. Rather concrete testimony, however, to the days of riverboat travel can be seen in the long line of wooden hulls where the riverboats were tied up for the last time and just left to rot. When the tide is low, there they all are, row on row.

Legend has it that the pirate, Jean LaFitte, who ruled the Gulf of Mexico from his stronghold on Galveston Island, buried treasure along the Neches where the coastal marshes meet the forests. Asked about it in later years, the ex-pirate said, "Stories have been circulated that I have hidden silver and gold all along the Gulf Coast. It is true. There are things hidden here and there, but I haven't the slightest idea of the exact spots nor would I wish to waste time trying to recover lost valuables or buried treasure." Incidentally, when Jean LaFitte disbanded his colony on Galveston Island, some of the former (we assume) pirates went to New Orleans, some inland, and some to the Sabine-Neches area where they no doubt became the progenitors of our leading families.

LaFitte's comment was enough to fire the brains of gold bugs from all over the country, but a small taste of our swamps, marshes, snakes, mosquitoes, and dense thickets discouraged all but the most rabid. Years ago, when I wrote a weekly article entitled "The Big Thicket—Past, Present, and Future" in a local paper, I did a series on lost treasures of the Big Thicket. I had no idea it would be taken so seriously, but gold nuts descended upon me like locusts on a wheat field, all thinking I had some inside information. One of the most sensible, and the most interesting, was Andrew Carnley, a Silsbee postman who had some tales to tell. Andrew is a member of an old area family who lived along the old road which went by Massey Lake to Laurel Lake bluff on the river, so he spent his lifetime in the area. It seems Andrew's grandmother's youngest brother, Allan Lewis, in the fall of 1885, found a small barrel of gold east of Silsbee near the river. He dug it up and reburied it closer to home. It was American gold: five, ten, and 20-dollar pieces and buried only eight to ten inches deep. He moved two saddlebags of the gold to his sister's house and buried another two saddlebags just north of Weiss Bluff. When he needed money, he would go to his cache in the dead of night and return with a hat full of gold pieces. A few months after reburying the gold, Allan died of pneumonia. On his death bed, he called Andrew and his brother to him and told where the gold was hidden, but apparently his mind wasn't too clear for Carnley, who had actually seen gold the old man had brought home and held it in his hand, said that he had "dug up half of Hardin County and never found it." Carnley's passion for lost treasure led him to locate all the old Indian trails, French and Spanish trade routes, and early settler roads through Hardin and Tyler County. He is probably the foremost authority on this subject and I learned a great deal from him.

Carnley also figured in a tale retold in J. Frank Dobie's book *Coronado's Children*, called, "The Brass Hand." The early Spaniards carried a supply of brass spikes with one end sharpened and the other shaped like a clenched fist with the index finger extended. These were driven into trees to point the direction of a trail, and it seems Carnley had found three of them near the Neches River pointing to each other and forming a triangle. Of course, this indicated where treasure was buried. None was found so it was assumed that someone had beaten them to it. I don't know how many times I've heard that story. Just as the treasure seekers followed the map to the hidden treasure, someone had been there before them and dug it up. The Old Spanish Trail goes through Southeast Texas and Louisiana, and the Old Mexican Road goes eastward through Tyler County to Nacogdoches. I grew up listening to tales of Spanish gold and buried treasure, many of them involving ghosts and the supernatural.

Another legend of the Neches concerns the French explorer, LaSalle, who in 1687 was killed by a group of his men and buried somewhere in this part of Texas. Members of the Beaumont Country Club, which occupies the oak-crowned hill overlooking Collier's Ferry site, say that LaSalle was buried on that hill. I've never inquired what evidence exists to support the claim. If it makes them happy to tell an interesting story about their beautiful club grounds, let them. After all, who is to say it isn't true.

Another type of treasure—black treasure—was brought up the Sabine and Neches Rivers in the form of Africans to be sold to landowners in Texas and Louisiana. After Mexico forbade any more importation of slaves in its territory of Texas, there was a brisk slave smuggling business along the Gulf Coast. Jean LaFitte brought the slaves he captured from the Spaniards up the Neches and Sabine, took them inland and sold them to the Bowie brothers, Rezin, John, and James of Texas hero and Alamo fame.

Local history concerning the first settlers in Beaumont, Noah and Nancy Tevis, can be verified in the hundreds of their descendants, many of them still in the area. In 1825, Noah and Nancy Tevis, with seven children, came to this bluff where the Opelousas Trail crossed the river. They farmed about twenty acres and raised corn, sweet potatoes, figs, peaches, cattle, and children. In 1834, he applied to the Lorenzo de Zavala land office in Nacogdoches for formal ownership and received a half league (2,214 acres) on the western margin of the Neches River.

Before the Tevises, there was a trading post for Indians, trappers, and explorers on the bluff. According to records of the American Fur Company, it was an important fur center in the 1700s. French trappers and traders dealt in beaver and mink pelts and, no doubt, bear and deer hides also. Horses, metal objects, cloth, and trinkets were traded to the Indians for hides and furs. When the first white men came to the Beaumont area, they reported two semipermanent Indian villages on opposite sides of the Neches, and in 1806, it was reported that they were raising crops. These were probably Attakapas, who lived mostly by hunting and gathering. It has been said that the Attakapas were cannibalistic. However, Cabeza de Vaca's journal recorded only their horror when starving Spaniards ate their own dead fellows, so some historians believe the Indians learned the practice from the Spaniards. Be that as it may, the Indians of the lower Neches must have had a good life. They roamed the coastal marshes and upstream into the forests in dugout canoes; in fact "Attakapa" means "children of the water." They migrated along the river seasonally from the coast to upland, hunting game, fish, and alligators with spears, nets, and bow and arrow. They gathered oysters, crabs, birds' eggs, plants, nuts, and berries. Alligator oil was used, not only as mosquito repellent, but to burn in lamps of shell and dried moss. From the plentiful tall reeds of the marshes, they wove beautiful baskets, mats, wall hangings, and all sorts of useful and decorative things. The Attakapas hunted the southern edge of the forested area in the first quarter of the 1800s and were then seen no more, no doubt exterminated by the white man's diseases as were many other entire tribes.

Another leading pioneer family of the Beaumont area on the east side of the Neches in the 1830s was the Ashworth family: Aaron, Abner, William, and Jesse. They were wealthy ranchers and reputed to be mulatto because of their dark complexion. After the Republic of Texas was established, the Texas Congress passed a law prohibiting free "persons of color" from living in Texas, but the Ashworths were permitted to stay because they were there at the signing of the Declaration of Independence, but more probably because they had the means to buy influence. The family was forced to leave the area, however, in 1856, when an Ashworth cousin, Jack Bunch, killed a deputy sheriff. According to my source, he was "lynched, executed, and hanged." Whether separately or simultaneously, it seems any of the three would have accomplished the purpose. The entire family fled. I suspect it was the white settlers' envy and greed to take over the Ashworth land and property rather than outrage over the law officer's death that provoked the expulsion of the swarthy Ashworths.

The site on the Neches was called Tevis Bluff until Tevis sold fifty acres to Henry Millard, agent of the Huling Company, who laid out a town site and named it Beaumont, either for his relative, Jefferson Beaumont, or for a slight hill southeast of the site which the French called "beau mont" which means "beautiful hill." (Probably Spindletop Dome, a salt dome.) It grew steadily and became county seat of Jefferson County in 1838. In 1840, lumber mills came in to process the virgin cypress and longleaf pine floated down the Neches and Pine Island Bayou, and in 1901, discovery of oil at Spindletop ushered in the Oil Age, after which Beaumont became a petrochemical center.

Perhaps the real reason why I didn't want to end my epic journey in Beaumont is that I didn't want to suffer the shock of leaving a world of forests, clean water, and birdsong for one where the acrid stench of sulfur dioxide in the air from the refineries and chemical plants chokes your lungs, where shacks and junk piles cascade down the river banks, and the noise of traffic and industry deafens you. When I get angry and impatient with the Park Service's myriad of rules and regulations, all I have to do is compare what I have experienced going down the Neches River through the Big Thicket National Preserve with civilization down here on this end and I raise my eyes to Heaven and say, "Thank you God. At least we will always have a good part of the Neches River."

CONCLUSION, PART 3

These days on the river have been times of pleasure in the present, and times of introspection and reflection. The scenes before which I passed brought to my remembrance events and people from the past who had given me joy and inspiration, and snatches of songs and poetry I had heard or read somewhere sometime. Being a lover of poetry from childhood, I memorized much of what I read; and, since the various aspects of nature have always been favorite subjects of poets, my entire trip was a running poem. Wordsworth, who said so many things so well, summed up my feelings about my voyage down the river:

> I have learned
>   to look on Nature, not as in the hour
> Of thoughtless youth; but hearing often-times
>   The still, sad music of humanity,
> Nor harsh nor grating, though of ample power
>   To chasten and subdue. And I have felt
> A Presence that disturbs me with the joy
>   Of elevated thoughts; a sense sublime
> Of Something far more deeply interfused,
>   Whose dwelling is the light of setting sun,
> And the round ocean and the living air,
>   And the blue sky, and in the mind of man.
>
>   "Lines composed a few miles above Tintern Abbey"

Index

C

D

E

S

T